TWO KOREAS IN TRANSITION

Implications for U.S. Policy

Edited by Ilpyong J. Kim

IN DEPTH
BOOKS

Rockville, MD

Published in the United States by Paragon House Publishers

INDEPTH BOOKS
One Metro Square
51 Monroe Street, Suite 1201
Rockville, MD 20850

First printing: October 1998

Printed in the United States of America

Cover design and typesetting by Larry Orman

Library of Congress Cataloguing-in-Publication Data

Two Koreas in transition : implications for U.S. policy / edited by Ilpyong J. Kim.
    p.   cm.
   ISBN 0-88702-067-4 (pbk.) : $16.95
   1. Korea—Politics and government—1988- 2. Korea (North)—Politics and government. 3. Korean reunification question (1945-) 4. United States—Foreign relations—Korea (North) 5. Korea (North)—Foreign relations—United States. I. Kim, Ilpyong J., 1931-
   DS922.4635.T86   1998
   951.904—dc21   98-43364
                                          CIP

Contents

Maps

Acknowledgments

A symposium, "Two Koreas in Transition: New Challenges and U.S. Policy," was held on the campus of the University of Bridgeport (Connecticut) on April 15, 1995, under the auspices of the Professors World Peace Academy. Some of the papers presented at the symposium were later published in *INDEPTH: A Journal of Values and Public Policy.* In addition to the efforts of those writers, the symposium benefited from the contributions of Selig Harrison, who gave a timely and thoughtful luncheon speech on North Korean policy toward the United States; Fred Turner, professor of political science at the University of Connecticut, who chaired a panel and provided commentary on the papers presented at the symposium; and Chung Gi Kim, minister of economic affairs at the Embassy of the Republic of Korea, who delivered a dinner speech, "Korea-United States Economic and Trade Relations," on behalf of Ambassador Sung Soo Han.

I would like to express my appreciation to the symposium paper writers who revised their work for inclusion in this volume. Three additional papers—by Hakjoon Kim, Kongdan Oh, and Mark Barry—were solicited to strengthen the balance of book, and for these the editor is also grateful. I would like to thank Rebecca Salonen, managing editor of *INDEPTH,* for the time and energy she has devoted to copyediting all the papers for publication. Had it not been for her judicious editing, this book would not have been as readable as it is. However, any omissions or faults in the book are solely the responsibility of the editor.

Introduction

Two Koreas in Transition

Ilpyong J. Kim

I n the concluding years of the twentieth century, North and South Korean politics, economy, and society are in transition. The Kim Il Sung era of North Korean history ended with his death in July 1994, and the Kim Jong Il era began on October 8, 1997, when he was appointed general secretary of the Korean Workers Party (KWP), ending the mourning period of three years and three months. The junior Kim will be elected by the National Supreme Assembly, the North Korean legislative body, as president of the Democratic People's Republic of Korea (DPRK) when the country celebrates the fiftieth anniversary of its founding on September 9, 1998.

In South Korea a presidential election was held on December 18, 1997, and a new president of the Republic of Korea (ROK), Kim Dae Jung, will be inaugurated on February 25, 1998. The DPRK in the north and the ROK in the south have coexisted for the past fifty years, since the founding of their republics in 1948, though conflicts between the two systems have persisted. Whether the newly elected president of South Korea and the newly appointed leader of North Korea can get along well and maintain stability and peace on the Korean peninsula is still uncertain. They have yet to resolve the question of reunification in the remaining few years of the twentieth century and in the early twenty-first century.

North Korea in Transition

The DPRK was founded on September 9, 1948, under the auspices of

Ilpyong J. Kim recently retired as professor of political science at the University of Connecticut and will serve as distinguished visiting professor at Pohang University of Science and Technology in Korea in 1998–99.

the military government of the Soviet Union, while the ROK was established on August 15, 1948, during the United States military occupation of South Korea (1945–48). Kim Il Sung was installed to head the North Korean government, and Syngman Rhee was elected by the National Assembly to be the first president of the Republic of Korea, in the South. The North Korean political system followed the Soviet model. The general secretary of the Korean Workers Party was more powerful than the government leaders and exercised full control over the politics, economy, and society, just as party leaders exercised power in the Soviet Union and East European countries.

Kim Il Sung became the protege of the Soviet Union after he was chased out of Manchuria by the Japanese military forces and joined the anti-Japanese partisan movement in the Soviet territory of Siberia in the 1940s. Kim was known among overseas Koreans as the leader of the anti-Japanese guerrilla movement in Manchuria and Siberia, but he did not have a political base in North Korea that would have permitted him to be elected to head the KWP or the new government in 1945, when Japanese colonial rule ended. Therefore, it was Soviet assistance which brought Kim to the leadership of the party and government, thus establishing the party-state system in North Korea.

The nature of the North Korean state, as Hakjoon Kim has stressed, was totalitarian, based on communist ideology. Kim Il Sung founded the KWP in 1945 and controlled it for a half-century, until he died in July 1994. The structure of the KWP was patterned after the Communist Party of the Soviet Union (CPSU), and its reins of power were in the hands of Kim Il Sung. Thus only a dozen or so members of the Standing Committee of the KWP Central Committee's Politburo controlled the North Korean government. The rules of the party call for a party congress every four years, but none has been held for the past seventeen years, the last one being the Sixth Party Congress of October 1980.

The original structure of the government of the DPRK also followed the pattern of the Soviet system but gradually evolved into an institutional structure with Korean characteristics. Kim Il Sung headed the government for five decades, as prime minister in the 1950s and 1960s and then as president of the DPRK, after constitutional changes in 1972 which created the new post. Kim also served as chairman of the Administrative Council, which performed cabinet functions with a premier, nine deputy premiers, and forty-some cabinet members. Kim was also chairman of the Central People's Committee, a super-cabinet including sixteen members of the KWP Politburo. The cabinet posts in the DPRK government were interlocking positions with the members of the KWP Politburo (ten full members and eight alternate members) and the secretariat. The party has full control of the government organizations, and the bureaucracy is also subject to party control.

Although the North Korean political system was based on the Soviet model, it has evolved to resemble the political institutions of the Choson dynasty (1392–1910). Kim Il Sung ruled North Korea like the kings of the Choson dynasty. The ideology of *Juche* (self-reliance) was the functional equivalent of Confucianism, the official ideology of the Choson dynasty. A high-ranking member of the KWP and professor of *Juche* ideology at Kim Il Sung University, Hwang Jang Yop, who defected to South Korea in January 1997 via Beijing, asserts that North Korea is no longer a Marxist or communist state. It abandoned its original ideology of Marxism when it officially adopted *Juche* during the height of the ideological conflict between the Soviet Union and China in the 1960s.

Some analysts have compared Kim Il Sung with the Korean historical figure Taewongun, the father of King Kojong (1852–1919). When Kojong was enthroned at the age of twelve, Taewongun ruled Korea as regent. From 1864 to 1873 he carried out a staunch isolationist policy, bringing about the isolation of Korea, which became characterized as the Hermit Kingdom. Eventually, however, Queen Min influenced the Confucian officials to oust Taewongun. The succession of King Kojong to his father's rule opened Korea once again to the outside world and initiated the long overdue reforms that launched the modernization lifting Korea from a feudal society to a modern state. If the analogy of Kim's regime to Taewongun's is correct, the isolationist policy of Kim Il Sung may be replaced by the open door and reform policy of Kim Jong Il after the dynastic succession in 1997.

The main characteristics of Kim Il Sung's economic policy have evolved from the Soviet model of autarchy and planned economy. North Korea carried out a series of economic development plans in the 1950s, but the strategy shifted to a more ideologically oriented economic development based on *Juche* in the 1960s, when the Sino-Soviet conflict erupted. Therefore, the first two decades of North Korea's development were similar to the development model of the Soviet Union, giving priority to heavy industry with secondary emphasis on light industry and agriculture. However, due largely to the Sino-Soviet conflict, the economic policy shifted in the 1960s from its dependency on economic assistance from the Soviet Union and other communist countries to a policy of self-reliance.

However, due to the structural problems of the North Korean economy, economic growth in the 1960s slowed down to no growth in the 1980s, leading to a disastrous famine and shortage of fuel and consumer goods, exacerbated by flood and drought in the 1990s. The decline of economic output in the 1970s and 1980s was caused by structural problems and the mismanagement of the bureaucracy. To alleviate the economic crisis, in the 1980s North Korea attempted a piecemeal reform and opening of its economy to foreign investment. Kim Jong Il, who was designated heir to his father at the Sixth Party Congress in October 1980, took a trip to China in June 1983 to learn more about the Chinese model of structural reform and open door policy.

Upon his return from China, the junior Kim experimented with the joint venture law in 1984, soliciting foreign investment and improvement of relations with capitalist countries like the United States and Japan. However, Kim's attempts to reform his country's economic system did not yield good results, due largely to the opposition of internal conservative forces who resisted any change, and more specifically because of the hostile international environment, which blocked any effort by the capitalist countries to launch joint venture enterprises in North Korea. Despite a huge effort by the Korean residents in Japan, only a meager investment from the West European countries occurred, insufficient to enable a North Korean economic take-off.

Kim Jong Il has been portrayed to the outside world as a reckless and unpredictable leader. Because of this image, Kim was perceived as someone who might start a war any time, and against whom the United States and the allies of the ROK should maintain vigilance. Kim Jong Il and North Korea are painted in such dark terms that the true nature of Kim as a leader and the facts and realities of North Korea are rarely assessed. The self-imposed isolation of North Korea has created a mystery wrapped in a riddle. Is Kim Jong Il reckless and unpredictable? No foreigner has ever interviewed him in depth, nor has any foreign leader met him—except for those Chinese leaders who hosted him during his visit to China in June 1983 and, more recently, Oleg Shenin, chairman of Russia's Council of the Union of Communists Parties, who met him on September 2, 1997, in Pyongyang. Shenin was the first foreigner Kim had met since 1983, when he visited the PRC. Shenin reported that Kim was ready to invite foreign guests to celebrate his formal ascension to power.

"I saw that Pyongyang is ready for contacts with the world and during the celebrations Kim Jong Il will, naturally, meet many foreigners," Shenin said. He said that Kim was expected to become supreme leader of the DPRK's ruling KWP around October 10, the anniversary of the party's founding. Shenin also reported that Kim would become the president of the DPRK, the other top post, when the DPRK celebrates its fiftieth anniversary in September 1998. Thus Kim is moving into the positions of power and leadership that his father held for a half-century and appears to be breaking the country out of its isolation and insulation.

Kim Jong Il began to consolidate his power when he was appointed first deputy chairman of the National Defense Committee in May 1990. He was elevated to the position of supreme commander of the Korean People's Army in December 1991, became marshal of the republic in April 1992, and was appointed chairman of the National Defense Committee in the same month. These positions prepared the younger Kim to take full control of the military. He was able to replace more than a thousand generals and senior officers in the military with a younger generation of officers who are loyal to him. Though Kim never had any military training or combat experience, he is able to control the military purely by administering titles and positions.

Kim Jong Il was reportedly born in Siberia on February 16, 1942, and came to Pyongyang in 1945. He completed elementary school in 1954 and high school in 1960. In 1964 he was graduated from Kim Il Sung University with a major in political economy. His graduation thesis, "The Role of the County System in Administrative and Economic Development," was praised as a major contribution to the political economy of North Korea. He started his political career in the organization and guidance department of the KWP the same year. After a decade in party organizational work, through which he was being groomed for succession to leadership, in 1974 Kim was elected to the Central Committee of the KWP. Thus Kim has had more than a quarter-century of leadership and management training in the party-state system.

After his apprenticeship under his father, Kim Jong Il has now succeeded in taking over the top leadership position of North Korea, first assuming control of the military, which could easily challenge his legitimacy and leadership, and then the KWP organizations, which control the government bureaucracy. Is he likely to continue his father's policy of isolation and self-reliance, or open North Korea to foreign investment and trade? Some observers and analysts assert that the younger Kim will persist in his father's isolationist policy, eventually leading North Korea to collapse—the same fate of the East European countries in the aftermath of the cold war. However, some experts in the United States argue for the possibility of North Korea's opening to the outside world and gradual reform of its outdated economic system in order to avoid collapse.

The new North Korean leader traveled extensively in China and observed the reform and the open door policy in practice. He expressed a desire to learn more about the Special Economic Zone in Shenzhen. Kim was unable to adopt the Chinese model and implement his own reform and open door policy in North Korea during the mid-1980s, due largely to stiff resistance from his father's generation of conservatives, revolutionaries, and hard-liners, and also because of the hostile international environment. Kim appears ready to accept the inevitability of reforms because of North Korea's economic crisis. The question remains how soon and at what speed such economic changes can be implemented, in view of the deteriorating economic situation in North Korea.

After the collapse of the communist system and the end of the cold war, in December 1991 North Korea introduced a reform program, following adoption by the Administrative Committee (cabinet) of Reform Bill 74 establishing the Najin-Sonbong Free Trade Zone. Chongjin was made a free trade port, after the pattern of what China attempted in 1978 as a prelude to the implementation of the economic reform and open door policy. To facilitate such a reform program, North Korea adopted more than thirty new laws, including the foreign investment law, in 1992. In March 1993 the Comprehensive Plan for National Construction was proclaimed, to support the economic reform and open door policy.

For the development of the Najin-Sonbong Free Trade Zone and for the solicitation of foreign investment, the North Korean government created a new Committee for External Economic Relations and the Committee for the Promotion of External Economic Cooperation under the Department of the External Economic Committee. To invite foreign investment, North Korean authorities dispatched government officials abroad to explain and publicize the new policies. Foreign businessmen were permitted to visit North Korea without entry visas. After all these efforts, by 1996 North Korea had succeeded in reaching $840 million worth of foreign investment agreements for Najin-Sonbong.

The Najin-Sonbong Zone International Investment and Business Forum was held in Sonbong September 13 to 15, 1996. During the meeting, the DPRK government concluded contracts and agreements with foreign businessmen and investors. Contracts for six projects were concluded, ranging from a hospital to a motorcycle factory, worth $270 million, and agreements were made on ten projects, including a concrete block factory, worth $570 million. The forum was reportedly the largest investment promotion program undertaken in the Tumen River Economic Development Area (TREDA) in 1996. It was co-sponsored by the Committee for the Promotion of External Economic Cooperation (CPEEC), the United Nations Development Program (UNDP), and the United Nations Industrial Development Organization (UNIDO). As a member of the United Nations since 1991, North Korea has participated actively in United Nations development projects in the 1990s.

The DPRK External Economic Cooperation Committee revealed the long-term vision for the three port cities of Wonsan, Nampo, and Najin-Sonbong during an international forum on Najin-Sonbong investment held in Tokyo in October 1997. "The Najin-Sonbong area, as a free trade zone equipped with financial service functions, will specialize in intermediary trade," a DPRK official announced during the forum. On the future of Wonsan and Nampo, the DPRK official said, "On the basis of their existing infrastructures, the two ports will serve as bonded-processing export zones focusing on consumer products." During the recent World Economic Forum meeting in Hong Kong, other DPRK officials confirmed plans to turn Wonsan and Nampo into bonded-processing export zones instead of making them free trade zones like Najin-Sonbong. In a bonded-processing zone, enterprises are allowed to freely import raw materials from abroad before processing them for re-export, without paying customs duties or local taxes. In a free trade zone, financial services are offered to enterprises operating there, allowing them to engage in intermediary trade.[1]

Thus, there has already occurred a clear indication of changes in North Korean economic policy during the three-year mourning period after Kim Il Sung's death. If there is no reform, there will be economic collapse in North Korea. Therefore, economic reform and opening to the outside world was the most urgent task of the new leadership. A number of foreign investment laws have been adopted, establishing the legal framework for foreign firms operating in North Korea. Initial investments from foreign countries have remained small, on the order of $150 million, and more delegations for the promotion of foreign trade have been dispatched abroad. About 90 percent of the total foreign investment has been made by the pro-North Korean Chochongryun (Federation of Korean Residents in Japan). Most of these investments were concentrated in light manufacturing and re-tailing areas.

However, following the announcement of Kim Jong Il's appoint-ment to the post of KWP general secretary on October 8, 1997, North Korea moved to establish private enterprises for the sake of inviting foreign investment, introduced an independent accounting system in public enterprises, and expanded the Najin-Sonbong Free Trade Zone. These measures are along the same policy lines that the Chinese gov-ernment implemented in the 1980s. However, the debate in the top North Korean policymaking circles has not ended on the question of continuing Kim Il Sung's isolationism based on *Juche* or moving gradu-ally to adopt an open door policy, increasing foreign investment and trade, and introducing structural economic reform following the Chi-nese model of development.

The conservative hard-line position remains that the party and the government must persist in Kim Il Sung's policies. If this view pre-vails, therefore, foreigners should not expect any change from Pyong-yang.[2] The moderate pragmatists in the government bureaucracy, on the other hand, seem to hold the position that North Korea can over-come the present economic crisis by introducing structural economic reform and foreign investment. The DPRK held a month-long series of investor seminars in eight Japanese cities in September 1997. Ho Maeng Chol, a section chief of the DPRK Committee for the Promo-tion of External Economic Cooperation, told an audience of about fifty Japanese businessmen that "the Najin-Sonbong zone will be treated differently, and we will guarantee free economic activities there." According to the report presented by DPRK officials, the Najin-Sonbong trade zone attracted sixty-five investment contracts totaling $370 mil-lion in 1997, with the companies being mainly from the PRC, Hong Kong, the United States, and Japan. Poor infrastructure in the zone has been a major concern, the DPRK said, though investment flows from Hong Kong and Southeast Asian nations should resolve the prob-lem. "But we can't deny that most of the foreign investment has been put only in the service sector," not in industrial projects, Ho said.[3]

On October 12, 1997, Japanese Foreign Minister Obuchi Keizo noted a change in the attitudes of North Korean leadership when North Korea responded positively to the Japanese offer to provide food aid.

However, the debate continues as to whether North Korea will maintain Kim Il Sung's policies or launch economic reform policies as Kim Jong Il assesses his position after assuming his new titles. Observers speculate that the younger Kim may serve as the Deng Xiaoping of North Korea and introduce the economic reform and open door policies since he represents a new generation and also recognizes the changing environment on the Korean peninsula. He cannot continue his father's policy of *Juche* because he has neither the legitimacy nor the charisma to lead the 23 million people in North Korea. Kim Jong Il is seen as likely to follow the political style of Deng Xiaoping since Kim favors the leadership style of bureaucratic management rather than the charismatic leadership of his father or Mao Zedong.

It is likely that Kim will take gradual steps to introduce economic reform at home but open the door more rapidly to foreign investors and trade in order to avoid the collapse of the party-state system in North Korea. But the rhetoric of upholding *Juche* and the policies of Kim Il Sung will be expressed in the editorial pages of the party newspaper by the ideologues and hard-line conservatives as a form of protest. Kim cannot afford to stamp out his father's ideological legacy in North Korean society and alienate the conservative hard core of his father's generation and the 23 million people who respect and revere his father's memory.

South Korea in Transition

The Republic of Korea will be celebrating its fiftieth anniversary on August 15, 1998. When it was founded in 1948, the government structure was based on the American-style presidential system because Syngman Rhee, the first president of the republic, opposed any attempt by the Constituent Assembly to introduce the parliamentary cabinet system. He ruled the republic for twelve years with an iron hand and was finally ousted by a student uprising in April 1960. The Second Republic, under the leadership of Chang Myon (John M. Chang), began in August 1960 and was based on a cabinet system, but it did not last more than a year. A military coup staged by then-Major General Park Chung Hee on May 16, 1961, introduced a short-lived military regime (1961–63) which launched political, economic, and social reforms. The presidential system was restored under Park Chung Hee, who ruled eighteen years, until he was assassinated by his own security director in 1979.

During the Park regime a series of economic development plans produced a high rate of economic growth. In the post-Korean War competition between North and South Korea, as they raced to build their economies, societies, and military power, in the 1950s North Korea seemed to be winning. However, the competition turned in favor of South Korea in the 1960s, when the military coup ushered in Park Chung Hee. Under his leadership a series of the five-year economic development plans were completed in the 1960s and 1970s. While the North Korean economy suffered from structural problems and diminishing economic assistance from the Soviet Union and China at the height of the Sino-Soviet conflict, the South Korean economy began to take off.

For nearly four decades South Korea maintained an 8 to 9 percent economic growth rate. By 1995 South Korea had achieved a per capita income of $10,000 and joined the OECD (Organization of Economic Cooperation and Development), elevating the country to the status of an advanced industrial country. However, the growth rate dropped to 7.1 percent in 1996, and was expected to be less than 6 percent in 1997. The declining growth in 1996 was accompanied by a rapid deterioration in the balance of payments. The current account deficit, somewhat more than $8.9 billion in 1995, ballooned to $23.7 billion in 1996, which was about 5 percent of South Korea's GDP. Because of the accumulation of balance of payments South Korea's overseas borrowing requirements have also risen.

The economic downturn in South Korea brought serious economic troubles. Many Korean business firms have experienced great financial difficulties since the beginning of 1997. In January 1997 the Hanbo group, a major business conglomerate, defaulted on its $6 billion worth of obligations to banks and other financial institutions. The bankruptcies of other business groups—such as Sammi, Jinro, and Dainong—followed. The near-bankruptcy of Kia, the third-largest auto-maker and the eighth-largest conglomerate in South Korea, brought about a political crisis in the Kim Young Sam government. Some critics charged that these conglomerates had financed the presidential election of 1992 and the legislative elections of 1996, at the expense of business investment. Contributions to the election campaigns ultimately brought down the large business firms because their survival largely depended on government intervention in securing aid from financial institutions or influence in bankruptcy bail-outs.

The Korean government intervened extensively in the operations of the financial market, especially in the 1970s, when the nation's banking system was forced to provide cheap loans to accelerate the development of heavy and chemical industries, considered to be of strategic importance. As long as government intervention persisted it was difficult for South Korea's financial industry to develop in pace with other sectors of the economy. As a result, the financial industry remains highly inefficient. Moreover, the banking industry continues to be obligated to make political contributions to various election campaigns. Financial industry reform based on market principles and political campaign reform based on a clean election system will eventually separate politics from economics in South Korea, but their interconnection has been a major source of corruption and irregularity in the electoral system.

When the Kim Young Sam government came into office in 1993, it targeted for either elimination or relaxation some 2,200 regulations restricting economic activities. By May 1997 more than 90 percent of these regulations had been eliminated or substantially modified, but many so-called "core" regulations have remained intact. Thus, a great many business firms in South Korea have felt that deregulation has not gone far enough, and reforms have failed to reduce the cost of doing business in South Korea. Therefore, many foreign as well as domestic business firms have left South Korea for China and Southeast Asian countries, where they find cheap labor and lower business costs.

Thus, the economy of South Korea faces an unstable financial market, an uncertain future for its stock market, an increased number of bankruptcies, and at the same time foreign pressures to open its markets to the outside world. The South Korean economy is in crisis as a recession begins, and it is being forced into structural reform. Therefore, candidates in the presidential election held on December 18, 1997, all advocated reform of the Korean economy to solve the current economic crisis. All the presidential candidates stood for democracy, deregulation, and introduction of market principles. Government intervention during the Park Chung Hee regime brought about rapid economic growth but retarded the development of a market economy.

The presidential election of 1997 will also determine the outcome of the governmental structure. The ruling party, the New Korea Party (NKP), advocates the continuation of the presidential system, while the opposition parties, the National Congress for New Politics (NCNP) and the United Liberal Democrats (ULD), advocate a constitutional amendment to change the current presidential system to a parliamentary cabinet system. There were five presidential candidates: Lee Hoi-chang of the New Korea Party, Kim Dae-jung of the National Congress for New Politics, Cho Soon of the Democratic Party, and Rhee In Je, representing a splinter group of the NKP, the People's New Party (PNP). A new alignment among the political parties has also taken place: Kim Jong Pil's ULD made a deal with Kim Dae Jung's NCNP to join in supporting a single presidential candidate, Kim Dae Jung of NCNP, in order to create a cabinet system of government. If Kim Dae Jung won the election, he promised to appoint Kim Jong Pil to the post of prime minister, and after two and a half years, in the year 2000, they agreed that Korea's constitution would be amended (requiring a two-thirds majority of the National Assembly) to introduce a cabinet system of government. Then Kim Jong Pil would serve the remaining two and a half years as prime minister, the chief executive under the cabinet system.

South Korea's transition to democracy has been progressing since 1987, but it has been thwarted by the existing political culture of South Korea, which is basically authoritarian and bureaucratic due to the influence of Confucianism, practiced in Korea for the more than five hundred years of the Choson dynasty.[4] To implement the lofty ideals of democracy, South Korea needs to establish separation of powers among the executive, legislative, and judicial branches and also to introduce laws honoring human rights and civil liberties, which are still lacking because of the influence of three decades of military dictatorship. Moreover, the government should suspend its economic intervention and introduce measures promoting business competition in a market economy.

Implications for United States Policy

The two-Koreas problem was created by the cold war, but it must be solved in the post-cold war context. The United States policy since the end of the Korean War has been to prevent recurrence of the war and to maintain peace and stability on the Korean peninsula. However, the United States changed its policy when it decided to negotiate with the DPRK regarding nuclear issues in the 1990s. When North Korea announced in 1993 it was withdrawing from the Nuclear Non-Proliferation Treaty it had signed in 1985, the United States dispatched former President Jimmy Carter to persuade North Korea to return to the NPT and halt its development of nuclear weapons—not only a direct threat to the security of South Korea but also a danger to the nonproliferation efforts of the United States.

After three years of negotiations, the DPRK and the United States reached an agreement at Geneva in October 21, 1994, which was known as "Geneva Agreed Framework between the United States of America and the Democratic People's Republic of Korea." The Agreed Framework has been invariably interpreted, by both critics and supporters, as a vague document, the terms of which are neither well defined nor legally binding. However, supporters of this agreement, including the policymakers of the Clinton administration, see the possibility of supporting gradual reform of the regime in Pyongyang through its efforts to implement the Agreed Framework.

Thus the containment policy of the cold war era has now shifted to a policy of engagement with the DPRK. Under the new policy the Bush administration started a dialogue with North Korea in January 1992, when an under secretary of state met in New York with Kim Yong Soon, a North Korean official in charge of the international relations department of the KWP. Subsequent dialogue and negotiations between United States representatives and DPRK officials regarding nuclear issues in 1992 and 1994 seemed to indicate changes in United States policy rather than maintaining the politics of confrontation.

North Korea expected to establish diplomatic relations with the United States after the Gorbachev government of the Soviet Union opened diplomatic relations with South Korea in 1991. When China entered into diplomatic relations with South Korea in 1992, the cross-recognition idea was implemented, and North Korea anticipated that the United States and Japan, allies of the ROK, would also recognize North Korea since North Korea's allies, the Soviet Union and China, had recognized the government in the South. However, the end of the cold war and the collapse of the communist system in the Soviet Union and East European countries left North Korea the sole Stalinist regime, without the support of any ally except China. Its diplomatic isolation, coupled with economic crisis, and the famine caused by flood and drought in 1995 and 1996, forced North Korea to turn toward engagement with the United States.

In order to halt the nuclear development program in the North and urge acceptance of the inspections of the International Atomic Energy Agency (IAEA), the United States took the initiative in 1991 to announce that no nuclear weapons existed in South Korea. However, the North resisted opening its two plutonium processing sites in

Yongbyon to the IAEA, causing a great uproar in the South as well as throughout the Western world. The prime ministers of North and South Korea negotiated the so-called Basic Agreement (Agreement on Reconciliation Non-Aggression Exchanges and Cooperation between the South and the North) and signed it in December 1991. This agreement pledged the signatories to non-aggression and called for a cessation of interference in each other's domestic affairs. The two parties also promised to "recognize and respect" each other. Moreover, the Basic Agreement set up the Joint Military Committee, a military hotline, and the North-South Liaison Office. The Basic Agreement represented a diplomatic breakthrough based on the changes in American policy toward the Korean peninsula after the cold war.

North Korea also agreed to accept inspections by the IAEA beginning in May 1992. Six inspections took place before Pyongyang halted them in early 1993 as a result of controversy over the history and transparency of the nuclear development in Yongbyon. In late 1992 North Korea demanded access to all United States military installations in South Korea to confirm that nuclear weapons had in fact been removed. In the latter part of 1992 evidence of reprocessing plutonium sites in North Korea surfaced, and the IAEA requested special inspection of two suspected sites, which was turned down by North Korea. Thus the efforts of IAEA to inspect the suspected sites were rebuffed, and the Pyongyang government threatened to again withdraw from the NPT in March 1993.

During the controversy surrounding IAEA inspections, the Clinton administration attempted to defuse tensions and bring North Korea back to the NPT. The Bush administration's approach to North Korea, using trade sanctions and threats of military action at the height of the nuclear deadlock, was abandoned by the new administration in Washington. Scheduling of joint United States-DPRK talks helped North Korea to save face and reverse its intention to withdraw from the NPT. The United States-DPRK talks began in July 1993. Washington representative Robert Gallucci proposed to North Korean officials that the United States secure modern light water nuclear reactors (LWR) to replace Pyongyang's out-of-date graphite reactors in exchange for the DPRK's acceptance of regular IAEA inspections and resumption of North-South talks. This offer ultimately became the core of the United States package which the DPRK accepted a year later.

The Agreed Framework of 1994 calls for the following steps: North Korea would freeze its existing nuclear program under enhanced IAEA safeguards. Both sides agreed to cooperate in replacing the DPRK's graphite-moderated reactors with LWR power plants. The two sides agreed to move toward full normalization of political and economic relations, to work together for peace and security on a nuclear-free Korean peninsula, and to strengthen the international non-proliferation regime.

In accordance with the terms of the 1994 framework, the United States government in January 1995 responded to North Korea's decision to freeze its nuclear program and cooperate with United States and IAEA verification efforts by easing economic sanctions against North Korea in four areas. The United States would authorize transactions related to telecommunications connections, credit card use for personal or travel-related transactions, and the opening of journalists' offices. The DPRK would be authorized to use the United States banking system to clear transactions not originating or terminating in the United States and to unblock frozen assets where there is no DPRK government interest. Further, the United States would allow imports of magnesite, a refractory material used in the U.S. steel industry for which North Korea and China are the world's primary sources. Finally, transactions would be facilitated by the United States related to future establishment of liaison offices, case-by-case participation of United States companies in the light water reactor project, supply of alternative energy, and disposition of spent fuel as provided for by the Agreed Framework, would be facilitated by the United States in a manner consistent with applicable laws.

North Korea agreed to accept the decision of the Korean Energy Development Organization (KEDO) with respect to the model for the LWRs after first refusing to accept South Korean-designed LWR model reactors. North Korea also agreed that KEDO would select a prime contractor to carry out the LWR project. KEDO subsequently announced that it had selected the South Korean-designed Ulchin 3-4 LWR as the reference model for the project and that a South Korean firm would be the prime contractor responsible for all aspects of the LWR project, including design, manufacture, construction, and management. Thereafter, North Korea negotiated directly with KEDO on outstanding issues related to the LWR project.

On December 15, 1995, KEDO and the DPRK signed the Light Water Reactor Supply Agreement. KEDO teams made a number of trips to North Korea to survey the proposed reactor site, and in the spring of 1996 KEDO and the DPRK began negotiations on implementing protocols to the supply agreement. North Korea and the United States held a series of meetings in Kuala Lumpur, Malaysia, during May and June 1996 concerning the LWR project. The seven-member North Korean delegation was headed by Vice Foreign Minister Kim Kye-gwan, and the eight-member United States delegation was led by Deputy Assistant Secretary of State for East Asian and Pacific Affairs, Thomas Hubbard.

The two sides agreed on the South Korean LWR model and that the Seoul government would play a major role in the LWR project. However, North Korea's chief delegate told reporters, "We don't care where the reactors are manufactured.… Our persistent assertion has been understood by our dialogue partner, based on which an agreement has been reached." However, North Korea indicated its intention to deal only with the United States in matters involving the reactor project. Thus Kim asserted, "The United States will assume full responsibility throughout the process of selecting the type of reactors.… The United States alone will make the final settlement of the project." Since North Korea is not able to pay the cost of the construction, which is estimated at $5 to $6 billion, the United States, Japan, and South Korea will underwrite the project.

However, on the reimbursement of the cost of the LWR project, North Korea demanded that investments in their graphite-moderated reactor, frozen under the Agreed Framework, be written off, and that the costs be reimbursed over thirty years, in installments after a ten-year grace period. Both sides compromised, and agreement was reached on reimbursement over a seventeen-year period, in installments following a three-year grace period for each of the two LWR reactors. Thus, the North Korean nuclear development program has been frozen, and the United States policy of engagement with North Korea has been effective. The engagement policy is likely to enhance cultural, trade, and personnel exchanges with North Korea and eventually lead to the recognition of the DPRK as an independent state.

Notes

1. "Wonsan, Nampo to Be Bonded-Processing Export Zones," *Korea Herald*, November 3, 1997.
2. *Nodong Shinmun*, October 28, 1997.
3. AP-Dow Jones News Service, October 6, 1997.
4. See Ilpyong J. Kim, "South Korea's Transition to Democracy," *Encyclopedia of Democracy* (Washington, DC: Congressional Quarterly Press, 1995).

Chapter 2

The Nature of the North Korean State

Hakjoon Kim

M ore than two years have passed since Kim Il Sung, state chairman of the Democratic People's Republic of Korea (DPRK) and general secretary of the Korean Workers' Party, died. Although Kim Jong Il, Kim Il Sung's eldest son, groomed since 1973 as his successor, immediately took over the country under the title of the Great Leader (which had previously been conferred upon the senior Kim alone), the junior Kim has not yet assumed either of the two official posts vacated by the death of his father.

This has raised a good number of questions on the nature of North Korea as a state. How can the presidency of the state be vacant for such a long period? How can the post of general secretary of the ruling party be vacant for so long, particularly in the totalitarian party-state system? Implicit in these questions is the serious debate about whether North Korea is a normal or abnormal state.

The official posts that Kim Jong Il holds at present are as the supreme commander of the Korean People's Army, with the rank of marshal, and as chairman of the State Defense Committee of the DPRK. He has held the first post since April 1992 and the second since April 1993, fifteen months before his father's death. Does Kim Jong Il gov-

Hakjoon Kim was senior press secretary to and spokesperson for the President of the Republic of Korea. At present he is chairman of the Board of Trustees of Dankook University, Seoul. This essay was originally presented at the International Conference on Northeast Asia and Korea in the 21st Century, sponsored by Choong-Ang Ilbo, May 30–31, 1995, at the International Hotel, Moscow. An early version was printed in Korea and World Affairs.

ern North Korea in his capacity as the Supreme Leader of the People's Armed Forces of the DPRK? Is North Korea under de facto martial law, without its official declaration?

Although these questions are important, a more serious one is concerned with the hereditary succession of power. In the world today there are only a few nations who have hereditary rulers. Only in Japan, the United Kingdom, a few more Western democratic countries where there is a constitutional monarchy, and in Saudi Arabia and other feudal monarchies does this system still exist. In light of this fact, North Korea, which is not a constitutional monarchy and which has in the past criticized feudal monarchies, has, in its hereditary leadership, an extremely unusual system.

Therefore, a fundamental question arises: What exactly is the nature of North Korea as a state? In fact, a couple of responses have already been offered. One is that North Korea is the first Marxist dynasty in the history of mankind.[1] The other is that "North Korea is the last bastion of pure Orwellian Marxist totalitarianism left in the world."[2] However, those answers are not sufficient to fully explicate the nature of the North Korean state.

This essay is an attempt to provide an explanation of how North Korea can be viewed, according to the grammar of Western political science.

The Traditionalist School

The earliest analyses of the nature of the North Korean state came from the right-wing, conservative sector. In academic terms, these views came to be known as the "traditionalist school."

According to the analyses of this school, one should view the DPRK, established on September 9, 1948, with Kim Il Sung as Central Committee chairman of the Korean Workers' Party and prime minister, as created by and in essence a satellite country of the former Soviet Union. As all are well aware, immediately after the defeat of the Japanese on August 15, 1945, the Korean peninsula was divided into two parts along the 38th parallel. The northern part was occupied by the Soviet army while the southern part was occupied by American troops. After three years of occupation by the Soviet army, North Korea had been thoroughly molded to the form of a Stalinist party-state system.[3]

What was Kim Il Sung's role in this process? According to the traditionalists' interpretation, Kim was someone that could never have become the supreme authority figure in North Korea without the absolute support of the Soviet army.

In the 1930s, Kim began his communist career as a member of a Manchurian branch of the Chinese Communist Party. He soon joined the Northeast Anti-Japanese Allied Army, which had been organized by the Chinese Communist Party in Manchuria and participated in anti-Japanese activities mainly in the Chinese-Korean border areas. He was forced to flee to the Russian Far East in 1941 after a defeat by Japan's Chinese invasion army (Kwandonggun). There he was active at an intelligence camp run by the Soviet army.[4] The Soviets' high evaluation of Kim as a potential leader led to his fateful selection as the supreme leader of North Korea. In addition, it was through the support of the Soviet army that Kim was able to maintain his position in the early development of the North. Since that time, as summarized by the traditionalists, the DPRK has trodden the path of a model totalitarian dictatorship with Kim Il Sung an integral part of that framework.

According to Carl Friedrich and Zbigniew Brzezinski, a totalitarian dictatorship has eight distinguishing traits or trait clusters. These are (1) a single official ideology, (2) a single mass party led by one man, the "dictator," (3) a secret police which controls through terror and violence, (4) a monopoly on the media, (5) a monopoly on the effective use of all weapons of armed combat, (6) a centrally planned command economy, (7) the control of law and justice by the powers that be, and (8) a tendency towards expansionism.[5]

The DPRK embodies all of the above characteristics. The country is ruled by a single official ideology known as the *Juche* (self-reliance, autonomy, independence) ideology. Despite the fact that *Juche* has a theoretical facade, it is little more than a pseudo-religion. *Juche* does not emphasize either the autonomy of the state or the autonomy of the party, nor does it stress the self-reliance of the nation or the self-reliance of the individual. This ideology places complete emphasis on the *Juche* of the leader alone.

In North Korea the powers have declared *Juche* to be "the sole ideological system." No other system or way of thinking is deemed acceptable. All other ideological systems are heresy, and their espousal is severely punished. It is not an exaggeration to state that because of this rigidity in thinking, *Juche* is already nothing more than ossified dogma. In this sense, North Korea may be termed a unitary ideological system. In fact, North Korea actually calls its system "a unitary system."

Second, North Korea is a country controlled by a single person known as its Leader (*suryong*). Up to July 1994, the Leader of North Korea was Kim Il Sung, and currently it is Kim Jong Il. North Korea's theory of the Leader is such a strange one that today in civilized countries it is hard to find a similar example. According to North Korea's official explanation, a human being receives his natural life from his biological parents and his life as a social being from a parent-type figure known as the Leader. This parental Leader in turn deserves the devotion of his "children," or the people of the state.[6]

The fidelity pledged to the Leader does not end with his generation. As a Leader of a new generation comes on the scene, the people's fidelity is to be transferred to the new Leader. In the case of North Korea, this means explicitly that the devotion shown to Kim Il Sung is to be transferred to Kim Jong Il. In actuality, after the death of Kim Il Sung, North Korea officially adopted the slogan, "Kim Il Sung is Kim Jong Il, and Kim Jong Il is Kim Il Sung."

This analysis reveals that North Korea is, in reality, to be led by the members of the Kim Il Sung family or clan. In other words, the country exists for Kim Il Sung and his family, not the other way around. The inevitable conclusion is that North Korea is controlled by a feudal-style clan system. That is the reason that the traditionalists call North Korea the personal territory or the private land of the Kim Il Sung/Kim Jong Il family.[7]

This point alone is reason enough to define North Korea as a feudal nation. North Korea-watchers in the West who belong to the traditionalist school propose that North Korea did make its original departure as a Stalinist party-state, but that with the application of a theory supporting feudal-type leadership after 1967 the country degenerated into a feudal party-state.

In North Korea, the Leader heads and controls a single mass party, which rules the country. The party established for the purpose of executing the *Juche* ideology is called the Chosun Rodongdang, the Korean Workers' Party. In a country of twenty-two million, this totalitarian party comprises approximately 9 percent of the total population, or two million members.

The Chosun Rodongdang exemplifies fidelity to Stalinist-style one-party system theory. In North Korea it is the one organ in which all power is centered. The Chosun Rodongdang leads the state, and thus leads the government. Further, because of its control of the military, the party effectively commands the actual armed forces.[8] In this sense,

North Korea represents the prototype of Wiatr's "monoparty system" or Sartori's "totalitarian unipartism," in that the Chosun Rodongdang is the only party legally permitted to exist, and it controls the political process.[9]

In North Korean society there are three major pivots upon which everything turns: the party, the military, and the government. Yet it is the two million members of the Chosun Rodongdang who occupy the most influential positions; they are indeed a privileged class. Among the two million party members, approximately half can be described as being "red aristocrats" who enjoy a high standard of living, including social privilege and material comforts. Considering this factor alone, North Korea certainly cannot be described as being a classless society, when in fact it is obviously quite hierarchical. Rather than a society composed of equals, it is a society of inequality. In this sense, North Korea also epitomizes Orwell's dictum that "all animals are equal but some are more equal than others."

Third, North Korea is a country where a secret-police force, monopolized by the Leader and high-level officials of the Chosun Rodongdang, systematically uses terror and violence to control the country. There are several politically motivated police-type organizations, beginning with the State Security Ministry and the Social Security Ministry, which target the populace for public acts of violence. The most extreme example of this is the curtailment of human rights in the twelve camps containing the country's 200,000 political prisoners.[10]

North Korea, through this type of model terror politics on a national level, has become a repressive regime. The idea of human rights, as found in civilized countries in the West, is unknown in North Korea.

Fourth, the media as controlled by the Chosun Rodongdang is part of a system which continuously subjects the North Korean people to brainwashing. Where authentic journalism and private publication are blocked from the outset and newspapers and broadcasting are from beginning to end all party propaganda, ultimately the media is merely a reflection of the will of the Leader and the party. Further, its purpose becomes nothing more than a tool to infuse into the minds of the people the party dogma.

The vehicles of the Chosun Rodongdang are a daily newspaper called the *Rodong Shinmun* (Workers' Newspaper), and a theoretical monthly called *Kulloja* (Workers). The official government organ is the daily *Minju Chosun* (Democratic Korea). The North Korean people are required to endlessly study these organs.

The content of these publications is also directly related to the drive to turn Kim Il Sung and his family into objects of worship. In this process of personality cult development, or idolization, the family history of Kim Il Sung is presented as one and the same with the flow of North Korea's modern history. According to North Korea's official version, Kim Il Sung's great-grandfather was an initiator of an anti-American movement, his grandfather was an organizer of an anti-Japanese movement, and his parents were great anti-Japanese fighters who deserve to be called "the parents of all Koreans."

In this sense, study (*haksup*) is a very important feature of the North Korean polity and society. Officially, the North Korean people are required to devote eight hours a day to the study of messages sent by the authorities. A second eight hours are to be used for labor, and the remaining eight hours may be spent in the ordinary pursuits of human life, including sleeping. Against this backdrop, one may call North Korea a huge study organization.

Fifth, North Korea's economy operates through a system of central planning and command. Following the orders and under the control of the Leader and the party, both of which stress the importance of autonomy and self-reliance in economics, the North Korean economy is planned and operated. Therefore, the creation and distribution of all property is according to the exclusive discretion and monopoly of the Leader, the party, and those otherwise in power. In this vein, some scholars term the North Korean economy as part of "the distorted world of Soviet-type economies," and "one of the most closed and rigid command economies."[11]

A related phenomenon is the recent strengthening of the Chongmuwon, or cabinet, composed of leaders of the organizations in charge of the economy under the control of the party. When the Chongmuwon was granted the right to speak for its ministries regarding economic planning and execution, its breadth of influence increased tremendously. Following this, it can be inferred that a group of economic-managerial bureaucrats has come into being. In other words, we have seen the emergence of technocrats in the North Korean power structure.

In the late period of the former Soviet Union, the growth of administrative-economic-managerial bureaucracy showed a tendency towards "group conflict and political change." In other words, as H. Gordon Skilling has argued, on the specific issues, these officials suggested their respective opinions and recommendations, and in this process informal groupings even occurred. Slowly, the Soviet totalitarian dictatorship changed into "quasi-pluralistic authoritarianism," according to Skilling.[12]

Then, does the appearance of technocrats in North Korea imply that the Soviet case will be repeated in North Korea? The answer is negative. Technocrats in the North are under the strong control of the party. In this sense, application of a bureaucratic model to North Korea is premature. Alfred Meyer, a noted Sovietologist, argued that "the Soviet Union is a bureaucracy writ large."[13] His thesis was that the Soviet Union was ruled or governed by the powerful officials of the party and the government, not by the totalitarian oligarchs. However, the control of the party in North Korea is so pervasive and strong that the technocrats, albeit influential, have not built their respective castles of influence.

Sixth, the Chosun Rodongdang completely controls the military. The Military Committee of the party is in full charge of the armed forces. The People's Armed Forces Ministry belongs not to the cabinet but to the party secretariat. The Leader is "the Supreme Leader of the Party, the Military, and the Government." In this sense, North Korea is a "garrison state." According to Harold Lasswell, a garrison state is "a world in which the specialists on violence are the most powerful group in society."[14] In such a state, military values are dominant, and all activities are subordinated to war and the preparation for war. The garrison state is therefore a political order that considers military power its highest goal and value.[15] Originally, this theory was applied to Nazi Germany and Fascist Italy, militaristic Japan and Bolshevik Russia. However, it can also be applied to some third world countries, including North Korea.

Even more than North Korea's power structure, its political system owes its very existence to the military. Out of North Korea's population, almost 23 percent, or five million people, are members of what is known as the "people's armed forces," including the regular army and a type of reserve force known as the Workers-Peasants Red Militia. Even junior high and high school students, including girls, are organized into the Loyal Militia of Red Youth. Not only does the military have clear superiority over other institutions in terms of coercive power, its organizational strength also places it in potential competition with the Chosun Rodongdang. This fact in itself provides ample evidence of the position of the military in North Korean society.[16]

The people of North Korea are in various ways subject to the strong influence of the military. They are in fact at all times prepared to fight a war and are conscious that they are living in a quasi-state of war. In short, the people feel that they too are members of the garrison. It is because of this that it is difficult for the residents of North Korea to have a civil society or a consciousness of themselves as being simply citizens.

Seventh, in North Korea law and justice are under the control of the political authorities. North Korea has never accepted the principle of the separation of the three powers of government, the independence of the judicial branch, or constitutionalism. Naturally, the courts follow faithfully the orders of the party and/or any figures of authority. It is not strange to see that the state chairman appoints and dismisses the chief of the Supreme Court under the constitution. As has been pointed out above, in circumstances such as this, the protection, much less the extension of human rights, is not to be expected. The North has a system which allows for gruesome public executions. Even a case of burning at the stake was reported in June 1994 by the Western press. Obviously, law and human rights in North Korea stand at the opposite pole from what is common practice in the West.

Eighth, the North has adopted an expansionist theory which insists that South Korea needs to be "liberated" by the North. According to North Korea's official explanation of this policy of expansionism, South Korea is a colony of the United States and therefore needs to be liberated by the North. In order to support this view, North Korea has developed a theory of people's revolution, including a scenario in which the people of the South rise up and drive the United States Army out of the country. After the South Korean government is subsequently overthrown, then a new people's government will need to be established. North Korea's concept of a federal-type reunification finds its origins in this scenario. Following the people's revolution in the South and the foundation of a new communist-style people's government, then a federation with the North can be formed and a communized united country can be established.

Under North Korea's totalitarian dictatorship, what quality of life do its people enjoy? Frequently, a totalitarian dictatorship defends itself by claiming that its emphasis is on "government for the people" rather than on "government by the people" and that, while it may not be able to provide freedom for its people, it does provide bread and butter. If North Korea cannot allow its people to exercise freedom, then at least is it giving them an abundance of material goods?

The traditionalist school has a rather negative response to this question. To begin with the conclusion, North Korea's totalitarian dictatorship has failed to provide its people with material goods in their lives.

Immediately after two separate countries were established on the Korean peninsula in 1948, the South was supposed to become the peninsula's major agricultural production region while the North would be its industrial heartland. The expectation was that the two sides would have a complementary economic relationship.

This assumption also carried the implication that North Korea had the greater potential for economic development. Not only did the North have more factories, which had been operated by the Japanese (and abandoned when their occupation ended), it also had greater mineral and water-power resources. In fact, after the Korean War the North did surpass the South in speed of reconstruction, and on that foundation until the mid-1960s it maintained an aggressive stance towards the South.

In light of this, 1962 proved to be an important year for both the North and the South. In that year, the South implemented its first five-year economic development plan, solidifying its commitment to industrial development. In North Korea, in his New Year's address to the nation, Kim Il Sung promised that year that the people of the North would "eat white rice with meat, wear silk clothes and live in well-heated tile-roofed homes." However, in economic competition with the South, the North has been left far behind. Exactly thirty years from the date of his promise, in his 1992 New Year's address, Kim Il Sung reiterated that he would make North Korea a place where people "eat white rice with meat, wear silk clothes and live in well-heated tile-roofed homes."

There is no doubt that North Korea's economic situation is seriously difficult. While it is not easy to obtain exact statistics regarding the North Korean economy, in looking at the information that is available as a whole, North Korea's GNP is only 1/16 that of the South. As of 1990, the per person annual income was $600 to $900, while in the South it ranged from $6,000 to $6,500. Especially after 1990, annual economic growth has been in the minus column, leading North Korea experts to compare the North Korean economy to a sinking boat.[17]

In these circumstances, the lifestyle of the average North Korean is approaching a poverty level. As the official campaign to "eat [only] two meals a day" shows, the country is facing a serious food shortage. In addition, the North has not been able to raise the level of clothing and housing it can provide to its people. In economic terms, North Korea is a poor, backward, socialist country.

What is the level of social equality in the North? Poverty is equally distributed throughout all of North Korean society. However, there exists a privileged class of "red aristocrats" numbering approximately one million. The children of this class are able to attend special schools and even special universities, and they end up employed in privileged posts. Their promotions are faster than others'. Being able to live in Pyongyang itself is a privilege, and those who reside in the country-side will pay bribes to be granted permission to move to the capital city. On the other hand, if someone is unlucky enough to have the wrong background or is branded an unreliable element, then he will find himself forever discriminated against in entrance to schools, in choice of profession, and finally in the material benefits he may obtain socially.

Borrowing from the expressions used by North Korea itself, out of the total population, 30 percent or so receive "preferential" treatment and 50 percent "average" treatment. The remaining 20 percent, as suspected unreliable elements, are subject to oppression and surveillance.[18]

The Revisionist School

Up to this point, we have approached our examination of North Korea from the point of view of the traditionalist school. However, after the 1960s in the West, a leftist interpretation spread. It was this milieu that led to the rise of the revisionist school. Let us now examine how North Korea is viewed by the revisionists.

The revisionists maintain that while North Korea was occupied by the Soviet army, Kim Il Sung had comparatively a greater degree of autonomy. According to this interpretation, one may not compare the occupation of North Korea with the occupation of Eastern Europe. In Eastern Europe, the Soviets transported their system and personnel to the region and exercised complete control over the situation. Those countries became Soviet satellites. However, North Korea under the Soviet occupation enjoyed a relatively greater amount of independence.[19]

According to the revisionists, Kim Il Sung was not merely a puppet of the Soviets. As an anti-Japanese resistance fighter, Kim was supported by the people of North Korea, and while he did receive support from the Soviets, with his anti-Japanese credentials he was able to purge the pro-Japanese faction and implement the reforms of socialism, symbolized by the revolutionary land reform and the nationalization of all industries. Finally Kim, mobilizing the support of the people, was able to create the organization which propelled him to the post of supreme leader in North Korea.

With this background, the DPRK was in fact a more legitimate state than South Korea. In the words of Bruce Cumings, "North Korea evolved an indigenous political system in the late 1940s; its basic structure has not changed substantially, so that in the fundamentals what you see in 1949 is what you get in 1989."[20]

How, then, does one evaluate the path the DPRK has followed since? The revisionists state that North Korea has made an effort to become an autonomous and self-reliant country. Without having to resort to dependence on outside powers, the country has been able to increase national pride and become an economically self-reliant nation. The revisionists point out that North Korea maintained autonomy in the midst of disputes and confrontation between the People's Republic of China and the former Soviet Union. In addition, they argue that recent history also shows that the North has made efforts to achieve independent development.

On this front the revisionists claim that the *Juche* ideology has special significance. It is the only theory that can steer North Korea onto the path of reunification as it provides for national autonomy and is oriented in the masses.

Some pro-North Korean revisionists evaluate North Korea's one-man rule, supported by the theory of one Leader, as being tolerable. Although they do allow that the worship of Kim Il Sung as an individual is excessive, until the point that United States-occupied South Korea accepts the *Juche* ideology and is liberated, Kim Il Sung's one-man dictatorship, which is nationally orthodox, is inevitable.

If one accepts the rationalization of Kim Il Sung's dictatorship, then the inferior standard of living that North Koreans have endured may be explained. The revisionists argue that while the North Koreans are attempting to establish a self-reliant economy without the help of foreign powers, a little poverty is to be expected.

At this juncture, for the sale of objectivity, we should consider Western observers who have rated North Korea's economic achievement quite positively. Joan Robinson, a Cambridge economist, wrote after her visit in 1964 that "all the economic miracles of the postwar world are put in the shade by these [North Korean] achievements." The French agronomist Rene Dumont argued that "in agriculture and probably industry, too, North Korea leads the socialist block." And Harrison Salisbury, a leading American journalist in East Asian affairs who visited North Korea in 1972, wrote of "a tremendous technical and industrial achievement." He said, "On a per capita basis it is the most intensively industrialized country in Asia, with the exception of Japan."[21] However, these observations generally refer to the period of the mid-1960s and early 1970s, when the North Korean economy seemed to have outpaced that of the South.

Finally, according to the revisionists, the criticism by the traditionalist school that North Korea has expansionist tendencies has no merit, in light of the fact that the North is conducting a morally acceptable effort to liberate the South. They claim that it is only natural that a divided country would want to reunite. Further, the pro-North Korea revisionist scholars contend, the North's efforts through a people's revolution to liberate the South from its subjugation to foreign powers cannot be criticized on moral grounds. In an extension of this line of reasoning, the revisionists claim that in comparison to the South, which wants to maintain the status quo, the North is much more oriented towards reunification.[22]

Other Theories

It is difficult to find points of contact between the traditionalists and the revisionists on the true nature of North Korea. The traditionalists criticize the revisionists as presenting a view which is ideologically skewed, as well as being a Marxist interpretation far from the reality of the situation in the North. On the other hand, the revisionists criticize the traditionalists for reflecting a point of view that belongs to the cold war era—in other words, a type of reactionary conservatism which disregards the actual situation in North Korea.

In the debates between these positions, certain themes emerge. North Korea is viewed as being either "one of the third world's developing countries" or "one of the communist countries in the process of modernization." This position is a reflection of an effort to analyze North Korea without leaning to either the left or the right and instead maintaining a neutral position. As part of this effort, theoretical models for explaining North Korea have been presented.

One theoretical model is that of the "mobilization system." In his research mostly on third world African models, David Apter has found examples of a type of solitary political leader with a record of anti-imperialist activities who forms a system of government which is able to maintain his authority for a long period of time. This "heroic" figure sets modernization and development as the country's goal, and in an effort to pursue this even goes to the extreme of depending on the forced labor of the country's people.[23] Apter sees that these regimes have to some extent accomplished modernization. A good number of North Korea-watchers feel that the situation in the North fits the basic description of the mobilization system.[24]

Another related theory is that of the theocratic system. Once again, we find in the work of David Apter the point that in third world developing countries there is a great tendency to rely on one "heroic" national leader. When this tendency becomes exaggerated, then the supreme power figure gathers so much charisma that he is mysteriously transformed into a living god.[25]

From the perspective of Apter's work, North Korea is a typical theocracy. In North Korea, Kim Il Sung is a living god, or a "half god, half human" figure. The *Juche* ideology has become the scripture of the "church of Kim Il Sung," and the people of North Korea have become the "true believers." After the death of Kim Il Sung, the North Korean authorities began to stress "the trinity of *Juche*": Kim Il Sung is portrayed as the Holy Father, Kim Jong Il is portrayed as the Holy Son, and the Chosun Rodongdang is portrayed as the Holy Spirit.

In countries such as North Korea, the theocracy carries with it the dogma that the Leader is infallible. Though the pope in the Roman Catholic church is considered infallible only in matters of faith and doctrine, North Korea's Leader cannot commit any errors and is a creature completely without fault. Further, no one is allowed to challenge the perfection of the Leader, and any activity which questions the perfection or infallibility of the Leader is a serious crime which is considered to have violated the sanctity of his position.

The third theory is that of the "guerrilla state" model. Haruki Wada, whose work tends towards "objective" revisionism, suggested this idea. According to him, since the late 1960s, North Korea has become a guerrilla state characterized by a siege mentality. In the mental framework which holds North Korea as encircled by the strong and hostile military forces of the United States and South Korea, the North Korean people have been "indoctrinated" into seeing themselves as guerrillas and the Leader as the commander of the guerrilla forces.[26]

Fourth, there is the theory of the "revolutionary mass-movement regime." Robert C. Tucker, an American Sovietologist, described this model, which is for brevity called "the movement regime."[27]

This regime is an outgrowth of the revolutionary movement to displace the pre-existing system of order and to achieve national renovation. The revolution is to be accomplished with the active participation of masses of the people under the leadership of a single party. This party is a militant, centralized, revolutionary party which takes power in the name of the movement and the nation and then assumes the new function of governing the country single-handedly. According to the traditionalist school, North Korea does not fit this concept because it was created by the Soviet occupation forces. However, the revisionist school argues that many elements in the mass-movement regime can be found in the establishment and evolution of the DPRK.

The fifth theory is known as the corporatism model. Bruce Cumings has suggested the revolutionary socialist corporatism theory to explain North Korea. According to him,

> the application of the universal truth of Marxism-Leninism to the concrete realities of Korea has resulted in a peculiar and fascinating form of socialist corporatism (in North Korea), mingling together classic corporatist verbiage and images, but growing out of the Korean political culture, with the progressive rhetoric and practices of Marxism-Leninism.[28]

A New Totalitarianism

The new source materials revealed after the collapse of the Soviet Union, and testimonies by increasing numbers of defectors from the North, support the conclusion that North Korea is a totalitarian state. In this context, the "new totalitarianism" suggested by Gavan McCormack should receive serious attention, partly because he was a leading revisionist, regarded as even a pro-North Korea Marxist.

In a controversial article published in 1993, however, McCormack severely criticized the North Korean state and Kim Il Sung. His conclusion was that "any simple model will be inadequate to map the complexities of North Korea's regime and society as a whole." He stressed that the "new totalitarian" model is "a form of rule characterized by (1) an extreme focusing of surveillance penetrating the day-to-day activities of most of its subject population; (2) moral totalism; (3) terror; and (4) the prominence of a leader figure with mass support." In a nutshell, according to McCormack, "No society in the world since the death of Stalin so closely fits the model of totalitarian rule as North Korea."[29]

Is there any possibility that the totalitarian dictatorship will be changed in North Korea under Kim Jong Il? Some North Korea-watchers predict that in the process of inevitable reform and future openness, the technocrats and their influence will become more salient. Implicit in this argument is that North Korea may move first towards "quasi-totalitarianism," and then towards "consultative authoritarianism."[30] If so, the Kim Jong Il regime will retreat from totalitarian dictatorship, and North Korea is living through the twilight of totalitarianism.

Others argue, on the contrary, for the durability of North Korean totalitarian rule. However, at a time when every other socialist country in the world is changing, North Korea cannot remain the only nation to adhere to the ways of the past. Fortunately for North Korea, the opportunity for reform and openness came with the death of Kim Il Sung. We may hope that Kim Jong Il will lead his people in establishing a democratic polity.[31]

Notes

1. Anthony Paul, "Inside North Korea, Marxism's First 'Monarchy,'" *Reader's Digest*, February 1982, pp. 73-77.
2. U.S. Senator John McCain's remarks, cited by Chae-Jin Lee, "U.S. Policy toward North Korea in the 1990s," *Korean Studies* 16 (1992), p. 16.
3. U.S. Department of State, *North Korea: A Case Study in the Technique of Takeover* (Washington, D.C.: USGPO, 1961); J. W. Washburn, "Russia Looks at Northern Korea," *Pacific Affairs* 20, 2 (June 1947), pp. 152-60; Glenn D. Paige, *The Korean People's Democratic Republic* (Stanford: Hoover Institution, 1966).
4. Dae-sook Suh, *The Korean Communist Movement, 1918-1948* (Princeton: Princeton University Press, 1967), pp. 220-93; Chong-sik Lee, "Kim Il-sung of North Korea," *Asian Survey* 7, 6 (June 1967), p. 377.
5. Carl J. Friedrich and Zbigniew Brzezinski, *Totalitarian Dictatorship and Autocracy*, 2d rev. ed. (New York: Frederick A. Praeger, 1965), pp. 15-27.
6. Kim Jong Il , "On a Couple of Questions Which Are Raised in the Study of the *Juche* Thought" [in Korean], *Selected Materials on North Korea: Selected Writings of Kim Jong Il* [in Korean] (Seoul: Far Eastern Studies Institute, Kyungnam University, 1991), p. 320.
7. Young Whan Kihl, *Politics and Policies in Divided Korea: Regimes in Contest* (Boulder: Westview Press, 1984).
8. For an excellent analysis of North Korean party-military relations, see Suck Ho Lee, *Party-Military Relations in North Korea: A Comparative Analysis* (Seoul: Research Center for Peace and Unification of Korea, 1989).
9. J. Wiatr, "The Hegemonic Party System in Poland," in S. Rokhan and E. Allardt, eds., *Mass Politics: Studies in Political Sociology* (New York: Free Press, 1970), pp. 281-91, and Giovanni Sartori, *Parties and Party Systems: A Framework for*

Analysis (Cambridge: Cambridge University Press, 1979), p. 227. Cited by Sung Chul Yang, *The North and South Korean Political Systems: A Comparative Analysis* (Boulder: Westview Press, 1994), pp. 223, 261.

10. *The Human Rights Situation in North Korea: The Reality of Self-Styled Paradise* (Seoul: The Institute for South-North Korea Studies, 1992); Sung-chul Choi, ed., *Human Rights in North Korea* (Seoul: Center for the Advancement of North Korean Human Rights, 1995).

11. Jan Winiecki, *The Distorted World of Soviet-Type Economies* (Pittsburgh, PA: University of Pittsburgh Press, 1988), and Suk Bum Yoon, "A Preliminary Estimation of an Econometric Model for North Korea," *Korean Studies* 15 (1991), pp. 15-30.

12. H. Gordon Skilling, "Group Conflict and Political Change," in Chalmers Johnson, ed., *Change in Communist Systems* (Stanford: Stanford University Press, 1968), pp. 222-29.

13. Alfred Meyer, *The Soviet Political System: An Interpretation* (New York: Random House, 1965), ch. 8.

14. Harold Lasswell, "The Garrison-State Hypothesis Today," in Samuel Huntington, ed., *Changing Patterns of Military Politics* (New York: Free Press, 1962), pp. 51-59. See also Harold Lasswell, "The Garrison State," *American Journal of Sociology* 46 (January 1941), pp. 455-68.

15. Lee, *Party-Military Relations*, p. 13.

16. Ibid., p. 241.

17. For a more elaborate analysis, see Eui-Gak Hwang, *The Korean Economies: A Comparison of North and South* (Oxford: Oxford University Press, 1993), chs. 3, 4.

18. *North Korea: George Orwell's Nineteen Eighty-Four* (Seoul: Tower Press, 1984).

19. Bruce Cumings, *The Origins of the Korean War* (Princeton: Princeton University Press, 1981 and 1990), vol. 2, ch. 9.

20. Ibid., p. 293.

21. Cited by Hwang, *Korean Economies*, p. 98.

22. Gavan McCormack and Mark Selden, eds., *Korea North and South: The Deepening Crisis* (New York: Monthly Review Press, 1978).

23. David E. Apter, *The Politics of Modernization* (Chicago: University of Chicago Press, 1965), ch. 10.

24. Ilpyong Kim, "The Mobilization System in North Korean Politics," *Journal of Korean Affairs* 2, 1 (April 1972), pp. 3-15.

25. Apter, *Politics of Modernization*, pp. 283-87.

26. Haruki Wada, "The Establishment and Evolution of the Guerrilla State" [in Japanese], *Sekai*, October 1993, cited by Chong-suk Lee, *Understanding North Korea* [in Korean] (Seoul: Yoksapipyongsa, 1995), pp. 160-77.

27. Robert Tucker, *The Soviet Political Mind: Studies in Stalinism and Post-Stalin Change*, rev. ed. (New York: W. W. Norton, 1971), ch. 1. See also Robert Tucker, "Communist Revolutions, National Cultures, and Divided Nations," *Studies in Comparative Communism* 7, 3 (Autumn 1974), pp. 235-45.

28. Bruce Cumings, "Corporatism in North Korea," *Journal of Korean Studies* 4 (1982-83), pp. 241-68.

29. Gavan McCormack, "Kim Country: Hard Times in North Korea," *New Left Review* 198 (March-April 1993), pp. 21-48.

30. The quoted terms are from Skilling, "Group Conflict," pp. 227-29.

31. Dae-Sook Suh, "North Korea in the 1990s," *Korean Studies* 16 (1992), p. 41.

Chapter 3

The Nature and Evolution of *Juche*

Han S. Park

N orth Korea's nuclear weapons program has become a focal issue in recent discussions of world peace, and the world itself
is puzzled by the mysterious and unpredictable nature of
Pyongyang's behavior. In order to understand political behavior, one
must find the locus of gravity in the network of symbolic interactions
which compose the society itself. Some systems evolve around the
way in which economic forces underlie the interactive network of
political life; others are founded on the structure of power which al-
locates values and opportunities; still others are centered on what is
termed "political culture," distinguishing the legitimate from the illegitimate. North Korea, in this sense, might be defined as a system in
which the idea of *Juche* functions as the locus of the entire system.
Thus, without a proper and comprehensive knowledge of the premises
and constraints of the ideology of *Juche*, one may not be able to understand North Korea in terms of its behavioral orientations and value
preferences.

The purpose of this chapter is to explore the nature of *Juche* and
examine the process of its evolution. *Juche* is not a ready-made static
doctrine; rather, it is a lucid and flexible idea that accommodates historical events. Therefore, the ideology can be expected to undergo
transformation as the North Korean political system faces new challenges in the ever-changing historical context in which it must operate.

Tracing the origin of *Juche* is difficult because it has gone through
various stages of ideological evolution from its beginning as a slogan.
The Korean word "*juche*" is common and has been in use as long as

Han S. Park is professor of political science at the University of Georgia, Athens.

the language itself. It simply means "self-reliance" or "self-support" and can be applied to individuals and groups. The term was in fact casually used during the Japanese occupation by all those people who lamented the lack of national capability which was felt to have invited colonization. It is not surprising that Kim Il Sung reputedly used the concept as early as the 1920s since he was involved at various times in anti-Japanese activities.[1] However, the use of the term *Juche* does not coincide with the birth of the ideology. In any case, one may discern five distinct stages in the evolution of the ideology.

Juche As Anti-Japanism (Mid-1920s to Early 1950s)

As the reputed creator of *Juche* ideology, Kim Il Sung used the concept extensively to express his deeply felt sentiment against Japanese colonial power, and especially against those Korean political leaders who had been incapable of preserving political sovereignty. The notion was that Koreans must fight and win back their nation through developing combat capability and spiritual solidarity against the militarily stronger colonial power. In fact, the formation of Kim Il Sung's charisma was rooted in the legend that he had sacrificed his personal ambitions to fight against Japanese occupation of Korea. Even as a little boy of twelve, he was said to have been preoccupied with the imperative of national independence. Liberation from Japanese control was the single most important goal for the country, which naturally advanced the theme of anti-colonialism as implied by the term *Juche*. At this stage, the term meant little more than antagonism toward a specific target. In this sense, *Juche* was not yet even a rudimentary form of ideology.

Juche As Anti-Hegemonism (Mid-1950s to Mid-1960s)

In the Korean War (1950-1953), North Korea met a new enemy, who helped South Korea and destroyed much of the northern half of the country with massive air strikes. That new enemy was the United States of America. The city of Pyongyang was practically levelled, leaving millions of people dead or wounded. Ever since the war, there has been a genuine fear among North Koreans that American forces might renew hostilities. The fact that United States military forces have remained in the South, conducting routine military exercises, has always made North Korea uneasy.

Also, the Sino-Soviet dispute of the 1960s, which drove the two communist giants to the brink of war, coupled with Soviet involvement in Eastern Europe and Vietnam, stimulated the birth of anti-hegemonism in the North Korean political and diplomatic stance. Pyongyang was put in a precarious position between the two superpowers of the communist bloc; North Korea did not wish to antagonize either of them by maintaining close relations with one at the expense of the other. This led North Korea to declare a policy of equidistance, and thus, "self-reliance." The Soviet Union became the more convenient target to criticize because of Moscow's expansionist policy, while China, on the other hand, provided a role model of sorts by plunging into the massive indigenization of Marxism-Leninism during the fanatic phase of the Great Proletarian Cultural Revolution in the late 1960s. While North Korea did not express great enthusiasm for the Cultural Revolution, it also did not publicly denounce the Chinese campaign or its creation of a personality cult surrounding Mao Zedong. In fact, North Korea began its own concerted efforts to develop an indigenous ideology and the charismatic leadership of Kim Il Sung. Just as Mao had criticized the Soviets for Moscow's hegemonistic policies, Kim expressed displeasure with Soviet expansionism. At the same time, this doctrine of anti-hegemonism was consistent with Pyongyang's interest in denouncing the American influence in South Korea. In short, the ideological support for political sovereignty under *Juche* became reinforced by the political reality surrounding the peninsula.

Juche As Nationalism (1960s to 1970s)

By the end of the 1960s, North Korea had become a stable regime devoid of any immediate opposition to the government. The leadership of Kim Il Sung could not be challenged and was steadily gaining charismatic power. All political enemies had been eliminated from the leadership circles by the end of 1950s. Furthermore, the North Korean economy was almost fully recovered from the Korean War. At this time, what Pyongyang needed was a persuasive ideology with which to legitimize Kim's charismatic leadership and to demonstrate ideological superiority over the South. These circumstances prompted the accentuation of nationalism as the cornerstone of *Juche*. South Korea was at that time led by Syngman Rhee, who had been educated and had lived a long time in the United States. The Rhee regime was under strong American influence, and this provided Kim Il Sung with the necessary ammunition to condemn the South as miserably un-nationalistic and pathetically subject to foreign domination. In comparison, the North was in a position to declare a policy of equidistance from its communist allies and to join the non-aligned movement. This political climate also proved to be an ideal situation for Pyongyang to adopt nationalism as the foundation of *Juche* ideology.

In the mid-1960s nationalism was still primarily anti-foreignism, without a coherent philosophical structure. But as the ideology grew more advanced in the late 1960s and 1970s, it came to identify a set of goals and strategies to express nationalism. Specifically, *Juche* was defined in terms of three analytically distinct objectives: political sovereignty, economic self-sufficiency, and military self-defense. Political sovereignty forced the regime to limit its political and diplomatic ties to only those countries with which Pyongyang was ideologically compatible, a handful of socialist countries. In this period North Korea campaigned against the South in terms of its legitimacy. Isolated and empowered by its nationalist sentiment, Pyongyang believed that the Seoul regime could be overthrown by its own masses on the grounds that it lacked nationalist solidarity and, thus, political legitimacy. The North Korean government believed that people in South Korea could be induced to participate in an anti-regime mass movement, but only if a "trigger" disturbed its precarious stability. The infiltration of the Blue House, the presidential residence in Seoul, by a North Korean combat unit in 1968 could be interpreted as the expression of Pyongyang's determination to disrupt political stability in the South in the hope of inciting mass uprisings against the regime.

The policies of economic self-reliance have certainly deterred economic growth, forcing North Korea to fall further behind its neighbors, especially South Korea. This period (1960s and 1970s) happened to coincide with the high growth years for the Newly Industrializing Countries (NICs) in East Asia. All of the East Asian "tigers" employed an export-led strategy toward economic growth. Instead of promoting a balanced growth, as was the case in North Korea, all the NICs concentrated their efforts on the production of export goods that would be competitive on the international market. North Korea alienated itself from world economic activities in order to establish a *Juche* economy.

What has been most detrimental economically is the principle of military self-reliance. Kim Il Sung's opinion of the importance of military power was unambiguously demonstrated in his early career, when he was involved in campaigns for national independence. In Manchuria, his group was known for its militancy and its ability to secure weapons. He criticized Kim Koo, a patriot who had a broad base of support and proven nationalist leadership, for his non-violent strategy. According to Kim Il Sung, non-violent revolution would not be effective against colonialism and expansionism.[2] In fact, military self-reliance was viewed as a necessary condition for political sovereignty. From this point of view, no amount of resources devoted to the building of military strength can be too large. North Korea has consistently invested an inordinate proportion of its national product in the weapons industry.

It is no secret that North Korea's primary source of foreign currency earnings is the export of a wide range of armaments, from conventional weapons to sophisticated missiles. There seems to be no shortage of demand for North Korean weapons in the international market, especially in the Arab world. The controversy surrounding North Korea's nuclear weapons production needs to be enlightened by the greater view of North Korea's ideological doctrine of military self-reliance.

In short, the policies designed to adhere to the principles of political, economic, and military self-reliance may not be designed to attain maximal material payoff. In fact, they have been largely counterproductive for development and often detrimental to the welfare of society. However, these principles were intended to promote nationalism among the masses and to demonstrate North Korea's superior regime legitimacy over that of its southern counterpart.

Juche As Paternalist Socialism (1980s)

As the ideology became intimately tied to the regime, a new theoretical dimension was articulated in which the leadership itself was "sanctified." This process coincides with a quantum leap in the charismatization of the Great Leader. It also coincides with the need of the regime for the official promotion of Kim Jong Il's leadership qualities, beginning with the Sixth Party Congress in 1980.

The process of a leader's charisma formation evolves, to use Robert Tucker's theory, from the formative stage of "charismatic aspirant" through the progressive stage of "charismatic luminary," and eventually to the stage of "charismatic giant."[3] By the late 1980s, Kim's charisma was developed to the level of "charismatic giant," whereby his leadership was believed to be predestined. He came to be seen as a natural leader, like the father in a family. At this point, his leadership slipped out of the realm of the "social contract." For a leader who has solidified his leadership on the grounds of paternalism, his position is not subject to impeachment of any kind because such leadership is perceived as being a matter of the natural order. In the context of Confucianism, respecting one's father is an obligation, and fulfilling the son's duty constitutes the utmost virtue. The fact that this is the case regardless of the father's conduct or contribution to the wellbeing of the family bears profound implications. Most of all, the leadership of the father is not to be judged by what it does but by what it is. To this extent, the basis of regime legitimacy no longer fits in the theory of the social contract, but Kim Il Sung is given the natural right to rule.

Another significant implication of paternalism is that it implies that not only the father but his entire family is destined to rule. This of course will naturally justify the hereditary succession of power by the son. It is interesting to note that the young Kim's ascent to power was initially promoted on the basis of his qualifications and ability, rather than on the grounds of the hereditary relationship. In fact, one scholar at the Kim Il Sung University unequivocally stated to this author in the summer of 1981 that the legitimization of Kim Jong Il's leadership would have been easier if he had not been the son of Kim Il Sung; he explained that the junior Kim's ability and achievement tend to be discredited because of his hereditary relationship with the Great Leader. His superb qualifications, according to this scholar, stand on their own merit.[4] However, as the charismatization process picked up its pace, the young Kim benefited from the family relationship. When the father attains charisma as the paternalist leader, the son is naturally expected to be included in the charisma of the family. At Mankyungdae, the birthplace of Kim Il Sung, in the early 1980s a family museum was erected in which the Kim clan are recognized as the leaders of the Korean independence movement. The historical documentation ends with the young Kim, who has demonstrated unusual leadership qualities and unparalleled patriotism.

Juche As *Weltanschauung* (Late 1980s to 1990s)

Juche has now evolved into a full-scale world view with a philosophical foundation. As discussed earlier, the articulation of the structure of human nature and the theory of the "socio-political body" is a relatively recent development. This is not to suggest that *Juche* represents a unique or complete world view but that it now presents a world view with some coherent structure as opposed to being a mere political slogan.

Juche's idea that man is the center of the universe is by no means a new perspective; nor is the doctrine of political sovereignty or self-determination. Furthermore, nothing is new about *Juche*'s emphasis on human consciousness as the determinant of human behavior. What is original, however, is the theory of human functions.

Chajusong, the first of the three components of human nature, takes a basic value position, that man is the center of the universe. Man's relationship with nature and society is clearly prescribed. Nature exists for the sake of human beings; therefore, man is entitled to exploit natural resources. Yet, man also has the obligation to manage and control the global physical environment. According to *Juche*, science is a tool designed to utilize as well as rehabilitate nature for the advancement of human wellbeing, not just for the present time but into the eternal future. No person should be subject to another person's capricious control, nor should he submit to institutional manipulation. Institutions, as in the case of science, are designed to serve human beings rather than being served by them. Even ideologies themselves are regarded as institutional means to human wellbeing.

Consciousness, or *uisiksong*, refers to the human faculty with which to make value judgments for specific behavioral choices. While *chajusong* is given, in that all persons are endowed with the right to be their own masters, *uisiksong* must be cultivated and developed through education. It is for this reason that ideological education becomes an integral part of human development, and such education should be continuous throughout one's life. The practice of "education through work" in the form of "Factory College," where college-level courses are offered to workers at their factories, needs to be seen in this context. North Korea introduced an eleven-year public education system in conjunction with the expansion of *Juche*, for the regime felt it necessary to provide ideological education. The eleven years of compulsory education are followed by "education through work" in all walks of life. Practically all workplaces and schools in North Korea are required to set aside at least one full day each week for "conferences" in which every citizen participates in political education designed to promote *uisiksong*.

As *uisiksong* becomes the engineering force of human behavior, one must create specific means and programs to realize what *uisiksong* dictates. Here comes *changuisong*, creativeness, to seek ways of implementing desirable ideas in concrete historical situations. This aspect of human nature might be perceived as the cognitive attribute. At this juncture, a rational and scientific assessment takes place in terms of the validity and effectiveness of specific approaches and concrete programs.

Furthermore, *Juche* prescribes a proper relationship among the nation states of the world. International division of labor is regarded as counterproductive as it perpetuates the dependence of nations with raw materials and labor upon nations with capital. The ideology basically adheres to the claims of the dependency theory, which views the world system as essentially exploitive so long as nations are unable to sustain self-sufficiency in basic needs and military self-defense.[5] Here, *Juche* is faced with the formidable task of discounting the achievements of the Newly Industrializing Countries, especially South Korea, because the NICs have shown that the international division of labor and export-led economic strategies could produce prosperity, challenging the very premises of the dependency school. Furthermore, the epidemic breakdown of socialist systems in eastern Europe and the Soviet Union itself, as well as the successes of reform-oriented Chinese development, forced North Korea to dissociate from them. This very need for dissociation from other socialist manifestations has been instrumental in the rapid transition of *Juche* itself as a unique ideological system.

Juche As Theology: The Ultimate Challenge

With the development of the concept of the "socio-political body" in 1986 and the ensuing establishment of the Academy of *Juche* Science, the ideology of *Juche* has been rapidly transformed into a religious doctrine or theology. From the point of view of the "socio-political body," society is viewed as a living organism whose component parts perform coordinated functions. An obvious question in this context is whether the "socio-political body" can be maintained when the leader, in this case Kim Il Sung himself, passes away. Although his son Kim Jong Il will succeed him as the "brain" of the "body," no matter who the occupant might be the life span of the "body" must coincide with the physical existence of the leader. Thus, the "religionization" of *Juche* is inevitable as the leader, the brain of the body, is sublimated into the realm of immortality. Hwang Jang Yop, widely regarded as the architect of the ideology and its most profound theoretician, commented to this author that "*Juche* will not be perfected as a philosophical system without being 'religionized,'" a point that was never made until late 1992. Indeed, without acquiring a religious character of sorts, the theory of the socio-political body will self-destruct when the leader disappears from the scene.

In this context, one can understand why the Pyongyang leadership has allowed Christian churches as well as many *Juche* theoreticians to become deeply involved in studying the possible linkages between the ideology and Christian theology. One should not be surprised that *Juche* theoreticians have even advanced the theology of an eternal life and the concept of a supernatural being or God, of sorts. The eternal life proclaimed here is attained when a biological (isolated) individual acquires a social life by overcoming innate human desires and egoistic lifestyle and integrating himself thoroughly into the life system of the national community, thus becoming part of the immortal social life. An example of this is found in people who have sacrificed their lives for national and social causes and are remembered throughout history. In this way, martyrdom is sanctified as a path toward the eternal life.

As to the nature of the supernatural entity, *Juche* theoreticians envision that such a being is embodied in a symbolic construct that can be inferred from perfected personhood, which cannot be realized but only imagined. Li Chi-soo, another leading *Juche* theoretician and the director of the Academy of *Juche* Science, conceives that the spiritual and moral qualities of man have made steady improvement over the course of history, as evidenced by the fact that the killing of fellow human beings is no longer institutionalized, as was the case for the medieval knight. If, as expected, human moral quality develops continuously despite inevitable short-term fluctuations, we can envision a situation in the remote future where human nature can be perfected. It is this imagined state of perfected humanhood that helps us imagine the characteristics of "God." According to Li, man should strive to expedite the process through which human nature is perfected. It is the *uisiksong* that enables man to extend his mind beyond existential constraints and be able to envision God. In this sense, one might infer that in this ideological system human development or the quality of man must be assessed in terms of proximity to the perfected state of human nature. This human development is thus induced and represented by *chajusong.*

The difference between political doctrine and theology is that the latter addresses itself to the question of human mortality. A doctrine that has an organized theory concerning the afterworld distinguishes itself as a religious doctrine not a political ideology. In this sense North Korea's *Juche* has indeed acquired a theological quality.

"Eternal truth" has long been used to refer to the *Juche* ideology, but the notion of "eternal life" is relatively new. However, it has become the cornerstone of the theological aspect of the belief system. According to *Juche* theoreticians, a biologically mortal human being will acquire an immortal life when his/her existence is integrated into the society itself. The society, unlike the individual, does not perish after a finite life span. It endures and outlives individual members of the society. Thus, individual achievement, whether intellectual, material, or political, will evaporate "just like the morning fog" with little meaning or value unless the achievement is integrated into the life of the society itself.

Then how does one become immortal, and where does eternal life exist? Immortality is gained when one's individual life is felt by the society and history. In other words, when one makes a lasting contribution to the society, one's presence will not disappear just because his/her biological existence is terminated. Thus, eternal life is essentially in the minds of members of the society, not only at the present time but into eternity. In this sense, national heroes, martyrs, artists, intellectuals, workers, and even peasants who have made concrete and enduring contributions to social life itself can attain eternal life.

In this perception of eternal life, there are several important questions: Are there varying degrees of eternal life depending on the magnitude and significance of the contribution? If one's contribution is not acknowledged by other members of the society at the time but is recognized in the future, will such a contribution acquire immortality at the time of rediscovery or at the time of the work itself? What if a potential contribution is never recognized due to accidental disappearance of the pertinent record or because of the insensitivity or ignorance of people? These questions have not yet been addressed.

Nevertheless, the notion of eternal life is apparently concrete and realistic to at least the mass public of North Korea. North Koreans are told that the state of human nature is imperfect but that one can improve by cultivating qualities that the image of "God" calls for. The

God of *Juche* is inseparable from human beings. In fact, God is the extension of man, in that a perfected human being is the real form of the ultimate embodiment of the transcendental being. According to *Juche*, God is caring, compassionate, and above all loving rather than commanding or controlling; nor does He have a grand blueprint for a predestined human history. Although there have been short-term fluctuations, human beings have made steady improvement over the long course of history in terms of developing compassion and perceiving as admirable the ability to love. In ancient and medieval times, physical coercive capability was the sole determinant of leadership; but as history progressed, humans found virtue in living together with love and compassion. What ties society together is no longer sheer force but persuasion and legitimacy, with certain respectful values such as liberty and equality.

The scientific mind of mankind has made even more dramatic progress toward perfection. Here, perfection may never be attained but always pursued and approximated. The imagined perfected stage, however, represents the quality of God; thus He is and grows within and by mankind itself. When I attempted to convey to a leading *Juche* theoretician that the Christian God supersedes human achievement in the society, he inquired how one could maintain an unwavering faith in such a God, when the concept is so vague and cannot be explained scientifically. The God of *Juche* in this sense is experiential because He is inferred from the existential nature of the human being. This view of God is also practical and functional because He leads people to improve the quality of their lives. To the extent that an individual becomes perfected, as he/she attains "social life" through becoming an integral part of the community, human development is the process of acquiring eternal life.

While there may be logical inconsistencies and philosophical inadequacies in this "theology," the issue is not its objective persuasiveness but whether or not the masses in North Korea believe in the doctrine. If so, who are the true believers, and how many are there?

Considering the rigorous requirement of ideological preparedness for members of the Korean Workers Party (KWP), it is reasonable to conclude that most party members are true believers, which accounts for 15 percent of the population. Additionally, young people who have gone through the complete process of ideological education, including membership in the League of Young Socialist Workers, could well be true believers. Even a conservative estimate suggests that 20 to 30 percent of the 22 million people in North Korea may have developed firm faith in *Juche*. They are the fanatical supporters of the Kim leadership and the hereditary succession of power.

In short, *Juche* is more than a simple slogan. Through its course of development, this system of beliefs and values has evolved into a grand ideological structure. To characterize the ideology only as a convenient device with which to justify Kim's power and leadership is the result of an incomplete and inadequate understanding.

Notes

Material for this paper is drawn heavily from the author's notes taken during his trip to Pyongyang at the invitation of the Academy of *Juche* Science in 1993. The scholars at the academy provided factual information and helped produce the present analysis. The author, not the academy, is solely responsible for its content.

1. North Korea claims that the idea of *Juche* was officially proclaimed in 1930 in President Kim's report titled "The Path of the Korean Revolution" at the Meeting of Leading Personnel of the Young Communist League and Anti-Imperialist Youth League held at Kalun in June 1930. See *Kim Il Sung Encyclopedia* (New Delhi: Compilation Committee of Kim Il Sung Encyclopedia, 1992).
2. Kim Il Sung's opposition to non-violence is documented unambiguously in his autobiography, *Segiwa doburo* [With the century] (Pyongyang: Korea Labor Publishers, 1992), especially pp. 229-302. Kim criticized Ahn Chang Ho, a renowned nationalist leader, for advocating a non-violent resistance movement.
3. Robert Tucker, *Stalin As Revolutionary: 1879-1929* (New York: W. W. Norton & Company, 1973).
4. Refer to Han Shik Park, "*Chuch'e*: North Korean Ideology," in Eugene Kim and B. C. Koh, eds., *Journey to North Korea* (Berkeley: Institute of East Asian Studies, 1983).
5. For a typical dependency theory argument, see Andre Gunder Frank, *Latin America: Underdevelopment or Revolution?* (New York: Monthly Review Press, 1970).

Chapter 4

A New Perspective on Economic Reforms in North Korea

Taekwon Kim and Hyunwook Koh

There is a fast-growing body of literature on issues related to the North Korean economy and reform efforts.[1] Though previous studies have made a great contribution to our understanding of the issues, our knowledge and understanding of North Korea remains very limited. The great number of studies on North Korea have been either too descriptive or too general. The lack of scientific and rigorous empirical analyses may be attributed to (1) the paucity of data on North Korea and (2) the lack of an analytical framework for theoretical and comparative studies.

The uniqueness and peculiarity of North Korea may be the reason for the lack of an analytical framework for comparative economic analysis. However, this lack limits fruitful future research in two respects. First, at the cost of oversimplification, theoretical development yields critical insights sometimes blurred by the sheer complexity of real phenomena. Second, lack of an analytical framework further hinders the development of a comparative framework, a common ground on which we can base our assessment of the experiences of other economies in transition, such as China, Vietnam, and the former Soviet bloc. Since multicountry studies from a comparative perspective can yield important implications as to what part of the experience of

Taekwon Kim is assistant professor in the Graduate School of International Relations and Pacific Studies (IR/PS), University of California, San Diego (UCSD). Hyunwook Koh is professor of economics at Kyungnam University, Masan, Korea. This paper is based on work done while he was visiting IR/PS, UCSD.

a specific country can be transferred or learned by others with fewer difficulties (or with minimum learning costs), a comparative approach would enable us to ask what aspects of other countries' experiences in economic reform can be duplicated by North Korea.

This essay attempts to provide a new perspective to serve as an analytical basis for understanding the economic reform efforts of socialist countries. Within that framework, we reexamine past (economic) reform efforts and discuss some implications for future reform in North Korea. We hope that our intellectual exercise here will be useful for building a comprehensive comparative framework for studying the North Korean economy.

An increasing number of studies are appearing on the issues related to economic reforms in countries like China and Vietnam, the eastern European countries, and Russia from a comparative perspective.[2] Some studies particularly try to provide a framework within which the experiences of different countries can be compared.[3] We hope that our work will contribute toward building a comprehensive analytical framework within which experiences from various countries can be compared.

In this research, the economic system is the main window through which we look at the economic reform efforts of North Korea. Some caveats are in order. First, the economic system is not the only window that could be used to look at social phenomena. Other windows are as useful as the economic system—the political, cultural, and social systems, for example. Second, in our study we focus our attention on economic reform efforts in particular rather than on economic policies in general.

Although specific economic reform measures and their consequences can be better understood by looking at the totality of all related economic information, for simplicity and clarity of analysis we confine our attention to economic reform efforts seen through the window of the economic system. However, this does not mean that other factors are unimportant. At the risk of oversimplification and possible omission of important variables, we will attempt to (1) shed new light on the issues related to the economic reform of North Korea; (2) help identify (economic) variables critical to the performance of economic reform; and (3) refine and expand our framework so that other important variables can be also considered, and also in order that the framework can be utilized for international comparative studies of economic reform and economic policies in general.

This paper proceeds as follows: In the first section, we examine the concept of the economic reform and operationalize it within our framework. In the next section, we select several economic reform measures applied by North Korea and interpret them within the framework developed earlier. Finally, the third section concludes with implications and prospects for future economic reform in North Korea.

Economic Reform in Theory: Targets and Measures

Targets of Economic Reform

We define economic reform as a part of economic policy applied to gain long-range sustained productivity growth. In particular, economic reform may be regarded as a set of policy measures and actions intended to realign the structure of an economic system for higher efficiency. Three characteristics of our view on economic reform should be emphasized. The first is that economic reform measures are of a long-term orientation and of a dynamic nature. Second, economic reform measures are also concerned with the adjustment process. In other words, we are interested in more than a static comparison of cause-and-effect relationships. We are specifically interested in the dynamics of the adjustment process of an economic system. Lastly, we do not equate economic reform efforts with those designed to transform an economic system, such as converting a centralized planned economy into a market-oriented one. Our approach bears some similarity to that of G.H. Jefferson and T.G. Rawski,[4] but with a significant difference.[5] Even though they state that the objective of reform is long-run productivity growth, Jefferson and Rawski implicitly assume that the productivity increase comes from the transition to the market economy, so that adjustment cost is equivalent to the cost of transition to a market-oriented economy. By contrast, we view economic reform as structural adjustment efforts undertaken for the purpose of enhancing the productivity of an economic system. Attempts to adjust the structure of an economic system can be either reactive (efforts to adjust to the internal and external changes after they materialize) or proactive (efforts to prepare for the possible problems caused by internal or external changes).

The structural adjustment of an economy does not necessarily mandate reducing the direct command and control of government in economic activities. Empirically, it seems that all the socialist planned economies except North Korea's, including those of the former Soviet bloc, are now geared toward transition to market economies. Thus, economic reform in the case of those countries is almost equivalent to transition to a market economy, and the main question is how to minimize the transition costs. However, it is not clear whether economic reform is also equivalent to the transition to the market economy in the case of North Korea.[6] By disassociating economic reform from the transition to a market economy, we will be able to make a more balanced and scientific assessment with less ideological bias. This approach is warranted for a better understanding of North Korea, a society that does not view a market-based economy as desirable.

We argue that increasing productivity is indeed the goal of an economic system. Thus, identification of specific types and sources of productivity increase is necessary to understand the mechanism through which the specific reform measures affect the productivity of an economic system. According to Jefferson and Rawski, there are three types of productivity change. The first is due to change in allocative efficiency.[7] This kind of efficiency is achieved when allocation of production inputs is changed between two different production activities. The second type of change is due to increased X-efficiency, which is affected by the managerial efficiency of the system. The last type is due to technological changes caused by the use of new inputs, new production technology, or new organization. The last one, in principle, is the only source that sustains the long-run improvement of productivity. However, the first two kinds of efficiency serve as an important source of productivity increase during the early stages of economic reform.[8] The graphs in figure 1 depict the different sources of productivity change.

Fig. 1. Three Sources of Productivity Change

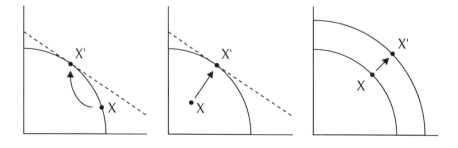

Numerous factors affect productivity. Among them are methods, capital, technology, and management. For example, capital investment helps to improve labor productivity without other major changes. Improved methods of operation are mostly related to labor productivity since improved or new skills contribute to the methods improvement. The incentive scheme determines the speed of methods and management improvements. In particular, it should be noted that technology alone will not give productivity gains. In fact, adding technology can actually reduce productivity, especially if it leads to inflexibility, high costs, or unsuitable operations. These factors all accompany the change in the organization of the participants engaged in the production activities.

Economic Reform Measures

Given that the organization and structure of an economic system affect the technical relationship, productivity as a performance indicator highlights the importance of the organization and structure of an economic system, particularly the relationships among the participants. Therefore, it is necessary to understand the relationships among the participants in order to identify the basic characteristics of factors to affect productivity. For this purpose, we will rely on the work of Paul Gregory and R.C. Stuart to identify the four dimensions that describe the relationship among the participants: (1) organization of decision-making arrangements, (2) mechanisms for the provision of information and for coordination, (3) property rights, and (4) incentive mechanisms.[9] The first two dimensions stipulate the order and rules of action during production activities while the last two dimensions characterize the distribution of rewards or income and the distribution of the outcome of production activities. These four characteristics help us to identify the possible instruments of economic reform.

The organization of decisionmaking arrangements characterizes the distribution of authority (that is, who possesses decisional power) and the organizational structure of an economic system. The most common topology of organizational structures is a binary classification: centralized versus decentralized. The second dimension is related to the mechanism of providing information and for coordinating decisions in an economic system. Two possible mechanisms serve this purpose: the market mechanism and the command (planning) mechanism. This dimension is also related to the first dimension since the market mechanism connects different organizations, and planning and command is a major control mode within an organization. Furthermore, a decisionmaker needs information in order to make a decision. Therefore, effective distribution of decisional power is affected by the mechanism through which information is collected and transmitted. Neither a pure market-oriented economic system nor an economic system exclusively planned and controlled exists in reality. In this sense, the first and second dimensions above provide the basic description of the hierarchical structure of an organization.

The third dimension stipulates the controllability of assets by the participants engaged in the production activities. According to J. M. Montias, "The word ownership refers to an amalgam of rights that individuals may have over objects or claims on objects or services.... These rights may affect an object's disposition or utilization."[10] There are three types of property rights: *the right to dispose* of the object in question, including transferring it; *the right to utilize* the object in question; and *the right to use the product or service rendered* by the object in question.[11] These three types of property rights may be assigned to an individual, to a group of people, or to an organization. The fourth dimension characterizes the means of motivating the participants. An incentive mechanism (material or moral) should induce participants at lower levels to fulfill the directives of participants at higher levels.[12] The incentive mechanism is also costly to manage, but a good incentive mechanism contributes to the productivity of the system. Since property rights affect the behavior of a participant in dealing with an object, the structure of property rights is closely related to the incentive mechanism.

Figure 2 depicts the relationship between reform measures and productivity change. Next, we turn to the identification of reform measures affecting each of three different sources of productivity change: allocative, managerial, and dynamic efficiency.

Allocative efficiency is determined by the resource allocation decision. In particular, allocative efficiency increases when resources are deployed to yield the maximum contribution. For this purpose, information is needed on the potential contributions of resources to different activities. In other words, the allocative efficiency is determined by (1) who makes the decision and (2) how the decisionmaker collects the information necessary for the decision. Therefore, to improve the allocative efficiency, the policymaker must consider the reform measures related to the arrangement of decisionmaking and its orga-

Fig. 2. Reform Measures and Productivity

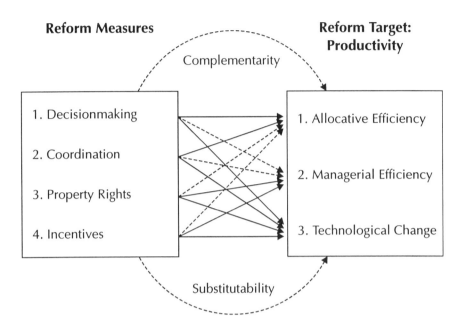

Reform Measures

Reform Target: Productivity

Complementarity

1. Decisionmaking

2. Coordination

3. Property Rights

4. Incentives

1. Allocative Efficiency

2. Managerial Efficiency

3. Technological Change

Substitutability

nizational structure and to the information transmission mechanism to improve the allocative efficiency.

X-efficiency, or managerial efficiency, is mainly determined by the motivations of the participants. In general, managerial efficiency improves as an organization reduces its (organizational) slack—that is, makes better use of resources. In order to reduce organizational slack, one can rely either on close monitoring with coercive control and command, or on a self-participating incentive. In general, as the system becomes more complex, it becomes more difficult to monitor and control the activities of the participants. In other words, direct monitoring and control becomes more costly as the complexity of organizational activities and the ensuing information requirement grow. This implies that the need for a properly designed incentive mechanism increases as an economic system grows, or as a government faces the need for increased information in policy formulation and implementation.[13] The proper incentive system has been shown to be critical to the performance of economic reform in China.[14] At the micro-level, managerial efficiency is related to the incentive mechanism and the arrangement of property rights. At the macro-level, efficiency is also affected by the internal structure of the organization.

The last source of productivity change is of a dynamic nature. As we argued above, this kind of efficiency is the only source of continuing productivity improvement over time. Technological change is the root of this kind of dynamic efficiency. In other words, upgraded technological capability can produce an improvement in dynamic efficiency. All four dimensions of reform measures affect the dynamic efficiency of an economic system: an outward shift of the production frontier is made possible by changes in the structure of organization, by improvement in information transmission mechanisms, by improvement in coordinating various production activities, or by use of proper incentive mechanisms to encourage innovations.

Effectiveness of Reform Measures

As we see in figure 2, different reform measures can affect the same target, i.e, a specific source of productivity change. This implies the existence of a relationship between different reform measures in terms of their effectiveness relative to a specific target. Two different types of such relationships exist. The first is a substitutable relationship, meaning that two different reform measures may serve the same purpose or goal. The second type is a complementary relationship, which means that the total contribution by different reform measures will be greater when they are used together than the sum of the contributions made by each measure applied separately. In other words, a complementary relationship implies the existence of a synergistic effect from the combination of different reform measures.[15]

We can identify complementary or substitutable relationships between reform measures. First, the institutional arrangements of decisionmaking and for the provision of information and coordination cannot be separated. This is because a decisionmaker needs information in order to make a decision. Thus, a reform planner must *simultaneously* consider the economic reform measures related to the decisionmaking arrangement and the mechanisms for the provision of information and coordination. We have already identified the close relationship between incentive mechanisms and property rights. Thus, we expect to find a strong complementary relationship between the privatization of some types of property rights and material incentive mechanisms.

There are also other types of complementarities between micro instruments of incentive mechanisms.[16] For example, Susan Gates and her colleagues identified the following pairs of reform measures as complementary: (1) privatization and price rationalization, (2) privatization and promotion of competition, and (3) privatization policy for this year and the next.[17]

We can identify a desirable package of reform measures with respect to a specific target by examining the characteristics of the relatedness among the reform tools.[18] The complementary reform measures must be implemented together for best results, but substitutable reform measures should not be used together because substitutability implies redundancy in their effectiveness as instruments. This relationship determines which reform measures should be combined in a package and which measures should be implemented in a mutually exclusive way. It should be noted that a corollary of the complementary reform package is the complementarity of omitted reform measures.[19]

The relationships among reform measures and the concept of an appropriate package of reform measures shed light on *the possible sequences* of actual reform policy implementation. In other words, complementarity means constraint on the current choice of a reform measure once a specific choice of reform measure is made. Of course, the complementarity cannot spell out the exact ordering of reform policy measures over time, but the concept of complementarity suggests possible candidates for the next stage of implementation given the history of specific reform measures chosen. This idea is somewhat similar to the notion of "induced institutional innovation" discussed by Justin Lin and Douglas North.[20] Lin and his colleagues attributed the success of Chinese reforms to the fact that economic reform measures have been induced (that is, under the current structure of an economic system, a reform measure was selected to enhance the effects of the previous reform measures).[21] They further suggest that even though reform measures in China were not designed as a package at the outset, Chinese experience provides a useful lesson for designing reform policies in other economies.

So far, we have confined our analysis to the level of the economic system. However, there are certainly other variables affecting the relationship between reform measures and productivity, such as social norms, culture, political systems, and so on. A system view helps us to recognize and identify the relationships among various reform measures. This is possible because our analytical framework provides a structure of relationship between reform measures and productivity change via the window of an economic system. We can certainly extend our framework to include economic, political, and cultural systems as subsystems of a grand system. The logic of interrelatedness can be applied to the grand system framework.

However, we do not attempt to build a larger framework for two reasons. First, incorporating the political system requires knowledge of how the political system works. Since we have a very limited knowledge of the North Korean political system, the task is beyond our capability. Second, the main purpose of this essay is to extract and highlight the relationships among the economic variables. In the analysis of North Korean economic reform, we hope to contribute more by narrowing our focus, rather than by considering everything that bears upon the North Korean case, such as *Juche* ideology, the political system, the social structure, and international relations.

Reappraisal of the North Korean Experience

In this section, several cases of North Korean economic reform efforts are examined to illustrate the application of our framework. The North Korean economy may be characterized by four main features: (1) development of heavy industry, (2) inward-oriented policy, (3) simultaneous development of the defense sector and the economy, and (4) massive labor mobilization.[22] These features have been major factors constraining and shaping the overall economic structure. Given this big picture, the economic reform measures may be reinterpreted in the agricultural, industrial, service, and foreign sectors, respectively.

Reform Measures in the Agricultural Sector

The agricultural sector of North Korea is characterized by the dominance of the collective farm system. It is well known that through a series of land reform measures North Korea had totally eliminated private ownership of land by 1958.

In order to boost productivity in the agricultural sector, North Korea introduced in 1965 the Chongsan-Ri Method, a "collective management system" in which a number of "lower work-unit contracts" become the primary production unit. By reducing the work-unit size, this system contributed to enhancing workers' sense of responsibility and to providing more opportunities for their active participation in farm management. This measure changed the structure of decision-making arrangements. At the same time, privately owned "kitchen plots" were permitted and agricultural product markets were set up to sell farmers' surplus products. However, the share of production from the kitchen plots is estimated to be less than one percent of the total agricultural production in North Korea. In this sense, introduction of kitchen plots is mostly symbolic.

Recent rumors suggest that North Korea is considering a policy of abolishing all private ownership of land (including kitchen plots) and peasant markets in the near future. On the other hand, a free market continues to expand in urban areas in the form of a black market. This may be the reason that North Korea is reviewing its policies. As this issue illustrates, reform measures in the agricultural sector have been constrained by the structure of property rights—that is, not allowing private ownership—which is also connected to the emphasis on the collective management system. Thus, all reform measures have been incomplete or ineffective since the prevalence of the ownership issue has hindered the development of a set of effective reform measures.

Two elements characterize the reform measures in the agricultural sector. The first is the emphasis on incentive schemes, particularly moral incentives. North Korea has consistently mobilized the population relying on moral incentives such as mass movements, moral exhortations, and political campaigns as substitutes for pecuniary incentives. For example, the government provides live band music, one holiday for every ten working days, and so on. Second, and more importantly, the structure of property rights has governed the provisions of the incentive scheme. Incentives are usually given not to individuals but to their work-units. In this regard, North Korea has maintained socialistic features even with material incentives. According to our framework, these reform measures are incongruent, and the real effect of this system is very limited.

Reform Measures in the Industrial Sector

Reform efforts in the industrial sector can be represented by two major measures: the Taean Work Team System and the Independent Accounting System (IAS). First, the Taean Work Team System was introduced by Kim Il Sung himself as the solution to management problems in industrial plants. It has enhanced communication between workers and the managerial staff by requiring the mobilization of administrative personnel in "on-the-spot" guidance, a variant of the Chongsan-Ri Method which was introduced in the agricultural sector. Two main features of the Taean system are collective management and the use of material incentives. The collective management system was intended to incorporate the technician and managerial staff in the decision-making process, which had been completely dominated by Communist Party officials. The Taean system combined ideological indoctrination and material incentives to stimulate the workers and boost productivity. The material incentives included prizes, paid vacations, and honorific titles for the work team that surpassed production quotas. Thus, according to our framework the Taean system has two elements: a change in the structure of decisionmaking arrangements and a change in the incentive scheme.

However, material incentives alone have not been enough to induce people to work harder. The Three Revolution Team Movement was launched in 1973 to address this matter, and the state sent groups of upper-level party cadres, technicians, and students to factories all over the country to attack conservatism, bureaucratism, and other ills. However, moral and ideological motivations are still primary. Overtime work is not compensated, and use is made of intensive labor mobilization programs that include the army, students, and even prisoners. This again illustrates the incongruence of the set of reform measures, particularly between utilization of material incentives and the emphasis on collective management, which limits the actual distribution of rewards to the group and not to individuals. This is the reason the measures have been ineffective.

Continuing problems in the industrial sector have forced North Korea to introduce into state enterprises the Independent Accounting System (IAS), which can be characterized as a decentralization of decisionmaking processes. Compared with the Taean system, IAS focuses on the operational details of enterprises, with an emphasis on responsibility, accountability, and incentives to make decisions and retain the profits locally. North Korea defines IAS as a transitional socialist system combining central management by the state with autonomous management by the enterprise.

However, decentralization and increased autonomy did not solve the problem of low productivity. The government was so strict in applying this system to enterprises that the anticipated effects did not take place. In order to guarantee effective decentralization, accompanying mechanisms of information transmission and coordination of transactions among enterprises should be aligned, as demonstrated by the experience of China.[23] In the case of North Korea, even though official guidelines stipulate that the enterprise may also set the price of its products, the enterprise did not seem to enjoy such autonomy.[24] In short, North Korea was trying to increase productivity of state enterprises by providing them with autonomy and material incentives. However, these reform measures were ineffective because the material incentive scheme did not support the autonomy given to the state enterprises since there was the excessive emphasis on collective ownership, and it gave no explicit recognition to individuals in the distribution of compensation.

August 3 People's Consumer Goods Program

The August 3 People's Consumer Goods Program is part of a set of economic reform measures in the industrial sector. Designed to solve the imbalance between consumer goods and producer goods, the program is characterized by (1) the production of consumer goods, (2) products based only on waste materials, industrial by-products, locally obtainable materials, and unutilized labor, (3) production locally organized by administrative districts at home and workplace for local consumption, and (4) products sold directly to district consumers through "direct sale stores."[25]

As shown in many studies, the performance of the August 3 People's Consumer Goods Program is remarkable. For example, the share of production under this program amounts to about 10 percent of the total production of consumer goods. The number of commodities covered by this program now ranges around 6,000 items, in the Pyongyang area alone. The success of this program can be explained according to our framework by the subtle combination of property rights and material incentives.

Despite the remarkable success of this program, North Korea still experiences an overall shortage of consumer goods. Two causes may be responsible. First is the misallocation of resources between consumer and producer goods sectors. Second is the X-inefficiency—that is, managerial inefficiency originating either from poor monitoring and control or from low incentives. In order to cure the problem, North Korea needs an appropriate incentive mechanism and improvement of resource allocation, which can be achieved by rationalizing input prices in both consumer and producer goods markets.

However, the fundamental limitation of the August 3 People's Consumer Goods Program is that it considers only the material incentive side, ignoring the importance of the allocative efficiency at the macro-level. Contrary to North Korea's own view that the success of this program is an aspect of victorious socialism in the *Jiche* tradition, outsiders tend to see it as just another move to squeeze a little more production out of overworked people and depleted resources, rather than representing a real reform.[26]

"Revolution" in the Service Sector

Two main features characterize the reform measures of the service sector imposed since 1991. First, North Korea has emphasized the quality of service by promoting a self-sacrificing attitude on the part of workers and understanding of consumers' preferences and basic needs as being as important as an increase in the quantity supplied. Second, "cooperative restaurants" were introduced. These restaurants are organized and managed mainly by housewives; they are funded by cooperative members and by bank loans. Profits are distributed to the members, and all the equipment and raw materials used are purchased from the commercial network. Although we do not have statistics reliable enough to make an assessment, it is interesting that North Korea is emphasizing consumer interests, which is more typical of capitalist economies. However, the reform measures in this sector do not indicate that North Korea has abandoned its old principles. Rather, it seems more appropriate to interpret these measures simply as efforts to compensate for the shortage of consumer goods.

Reform and Open-Door Policies in the Foreign Economic Sector

The area of economic reform where North Korea has been most flexible and lenient is in the foreign economic sector. Beginning with an emphasis on foreign trade with advanced capitalist countries in the early seventies, the total imports from these countries by North Korea reached 53.7 percent of its total imports in 1971. However, the foreign trade sector did not function well.

North Korea also has introduced a series of joint venture programs to facilitate foreign direct investment. As the first step in a series, the Joint Venture Law was enacted in 1984. Then North Korea formed the Chosun International Joint Venture General Company in 1986. In 1992, three additional laws were enacted related to foreigners' investments. The Free Economic and Trade Zone was established in the Najin-Sonbong area, and direct trade with South Korea was begun in 1988.

However, all these measures have been just as ineffective as the other reform measures in domestic sectors. Again, these measures were isolated from and misaligned with other reforms. In particular, very restrictive clauses in the joint venture laws made foreign direct investment unattractive. Foreign investment can be seen as a part of resource allocation to the economy. However, inconsistent economic measures and unfavorable domestic conditions in North Korea distorted the process of efficient resource allocation, thereby resulting in the failure to attract foreign investments.

Meanwhile, North Korea has displayed a more lenient attitude toward foreign investments and enterprises in the Free Economic and Trade Zone. For example, it was agreed to allow foreign enterprises to partially control the employment of workers in their enterprises and also to share management and administration with foreign partners. However, only a set of consistent and congruent reform measures will help North Korea acquire the foreign capital and technology which is desperately needed. In this sense, careful observation of development of the economic reform measures in this sector is warranted.

Implications and Future Prospects

The economic reform measures in various sectors can be characterized by (1) changes in the organization of decisionmaking arrangements and (2) introduction of material incentives. Material incentives can be effective with an appropriate arrangement of private ownership, but in the case of North Korea, the emphasis on collective ownership has limited the effectiveness of material incentive schemes. Note that a proper arrangement of property rights does not necessarily imply disposition rights, the concept of private ownership in capitalistic economies. As the experience of China illustrates, acknowledgement of the right to utilize products and the right to use of property, however, is necessary for material incentives to be effective.

At the macro-level, a fundamental problem in North Korea is the misallocation of resources. Traditionally, labor has been the major input for production in all sectors in North Korea. Mobilization of the general population was successful in the early stages of economic development, where economic efficiency and productivity can be achieved through effective utilization of idle resources. However, that approach is only initially successful and has limitations in the long run. Continued substitution of labor for capital will eventually reach a negligible or near-zero point of marginal productivity, so that the economy faces a slow-down of productivity and efficiency in later stages. For continued growth of productivity and the economy, expansion of labor must be accomplished by an increased supply of capital and advanced technologies.

This fundamental problem is well illustrated by Kim Il Sung's 1994 New Year's message. In the Communist Party's official report on the performance of the Third Seven-Year Economic Plan, North Korea admitted for the first time that it had failed to achieve the target growth in the overall industrial sector, particularly in energy, steel, and synthetic fiber industries. These industries require heavier capital investment and more advanced technologies for sustained growth.

In sum, North Korea failed to appropriately adjust its economic structure to the stages of development and external environment. Our analysis indicates that North Korea unsuccessfully deployed the reform measures as structural adjustment instruments. Rather, the reforms have been at best myopic in nature, patchwork in character, and simply reactive to the problems.

Now, let us turn to the prospects of the economic reform efforts in North Korea. Some argue that economic reform in North Korea began in the 1980s.[27] These scholars tend to interpret the introduction of material incentives or partial property rights as an effort to move the economy toward being more market-oriented. This view of economic reform assumes that any reform measures without market elements will eventually fail. This conclusion prescribes uniform policy measures for all countries regardless of differences in the level of GNP and personal income, resource endowments, institutional arrangements, and so on. However, as experience in former socialist countries tells us, "the variations in market forms that occur across regions and across time, and the new forms that are evolving in the reforming formerly planned economies, show that there exists no uniquely optimal market system."[28] In particular, the choice facing a reform planner is not whether to choose a free market system but how to design the institutional arrangements that best suit that specific country. The institutional arrangements should provide a congruent set of economic measures at the industry and macro-economy level.

The above discussion suggests many ways to boost economic growth via productivity increase. Multiple options provide a certain degree of freedom and offer a real challenge to North Korea. In order to be successful, reform measures must be designed carefully, giving special attention to reform processes and the congruency among the reform measures chosen.

However, this is not to suggest simply following the Chinese model's piecemeal approach. North Korea certainly has not followed either Russia's "Big Bang" or the gradual reforms of China. It is also not clear whether North Korea will turn to either one of them in future, given North Korea's emphasis on self-reliance under *Juche* ideology. However, in order to solve economic problems, North Korea should design and implement a set of congruent economic policies and reform measures, some of which may conflict with the supreme doctrine of *Juche*. It is premature to be either totally optimistic or pessimistic about the future prospects of the North Korean economy. If North Korea manages to survive this crisis, it will be the only case where a socialist approach has proved viable. If North Korea fails to overcome, it will be forced to choose between giving up "self-reliance" and accepting total collapse.

We close with a final remark on the recent attempt by North Korea to expand foreign economic relations. Many observers regard North Korea's declaration of the Free Trade Zone (FTZ) as the most significant change, considering her long adherence to the "self-reliance" line. Although we can acknowledge North Korea's flexibility in applying concrete economic policies, the basic line of the socialistic, self-reliant, planned economy has never changed. Flexibility in some specifics does not represent an effort to transform the economy toward a market-oriented one. Kim Jung-woo, vice minister of foreign economic relations of North Korea, has made this clear.

> This [FTZ] is not a change in our line of self-reliant national economy. Our line of self-reliant economy does not exclude all of cooperative relations while it opposes any economic subordination. This [FTZ] serves to complement our line in our own way.... Since the area (FTZ) is for opening, you can say we reform or open in this particular area. However, it is wrong to say that all of our area in the northern part of the Republic is going for reform or opening. We never use the expression of "reform" or "opening." Since we have modified anything if necessary from the past and have never shut down our doors, the words of reform and opening are not relevant to us.[29]

Notes

Hyunwook Koh wishes to express his gratitude for the financial support of the Korean Ministry of Education, which enabled him to write this paper while at the University of California, San Diego.

1. See, for example, Sungwoo Kim, "Recent Economic Policies of North Korea: Analysis and Recommendation," *Asian Survey* 33, 9, pp. 864-78; and Doowon Lee, "Assessing North Korean Economic Reform: Historical Trajectory, Opportunities, and Constraints," *Pacific Focus* 8, 2, pp. 5-29.
2. For example, Justin Y. Lin, Fang Lai, and Zhou Li, "Why China's Economic Reforms Have Been Successful: Its Implications for Other Reforming Economies," mimeographed paper, Peking University and Chinese Academy of Social Sciences, 1994. For this kind of study, see the papers presented at the conference titled "The Evolution of Market Institutions in Transition Economies," held at the University of California, San Diego, May 14-15, 1993 (hereafter, UCSD Conference).
3. See, for example, Susan Gates, P. Milgrom, and J. Roberts, "Complementarities in Economic Reform: A Firm-Level Analysis," paper presented at UCSD Conference; G. H. Jefferson and T. G. Rawski, "Economic System Reform and the Firm's Investment Decision As Analogous Theories of Economic Transition," paper presented at UCSD Conference.
4. Jefferson and Rawski, "Economic System Reform."
5. There is also another difference between our study and that of Jefferson and Rawski. In "Economic System Reform," Jefferson and Rawski compare the economic reform to investment decisions by firms. In their model, they directly relate the reform measures to the output of reform or targets of reform via the analogy of production function. In our model, we explicitly consider the production relationship with reform measures as parameters to affect the technical relationship.
6. See, for example, Wankyu Choi, ed., *Socialism of North Korea in the Transition Period* [in Korean] (Seoul: Daewang Publishers, 1992).
7. Jefferson and Rawski, "Economic System Reform."
8. Ibid.
9. Paul R. Gregory and R. C. Stuart, *Comparative Economic Systems*, 4th ed. (Boston: Houghton Mifflin Co., 1992).
10. J. M. Montias, *The Structure of Economic Systems* (New Haven: Yale University Press, 1976), p. 116.
11. Gregory and Stuart, *Comparative Economic Systems*, pp. 20-21.
12. Ibid., p. 22.
13. Agency theory provides an excellent framework for this kind of question. Agency theory starts by recognizing that the interests of principal and agent do not always coincide. Rather, there is ample room for conflict. Both have asymmetric sources of power: authority given to the principal versus informational advantage given to agents.
14. For example, see T. Groves, Y. M. Hong, J. McMillan, and B. Naughton, "Autonomy and Incentives in Chinese State Enterprises," mimeo, University of California, San Diego, 1991.

15. Gates, et al., "Complementarities in Economic Reform," and Jefferson and Rawski, "Economic System Reform."

16. Techniques for analyzing complementarities among incentive instruments have been developed by Milgrom and Roberts, and Holmstrom and Milgrom. See Paul Milgrom and J. Roberts, "Rationalizability, Learning, and Equilibrium in Games with Strategic Complementarities," *Econometrica* 58, pp. 1255-77; and B. Holmstrom and Paul Milgrom, "Measurement Costs and Organization Theory: The Firm as a Cluster of Attributes," mimeographed paper, Stanford University, 1993.

17. Gates, et al., "Complementarities in Economic Reform."

18. Based on notions of the economies of scope and substitutability in reform instruments, Jefferson and Rawski delineate the package of reform measures, which they call "comprehensiveness." See their "Economic System Reform."

19. Jefferson and Rawski, "Economic System Reform."

20. Justin Y. Lin, "An Economic Theory of Institutional Change: Induced and Imposed Change," *Cato Journal* 9, 1 (Spring/Summer 1989), pp. 1-33; and D. C. North, *Institutions, Institutional Change, and Economic Performance* (Cambridge: Cambridge University Press, 1990).

21. Lin, Lai, and Li, "Why China's Economic Reforms Have Been Successful."

22. Soo Young Choi, "Economic Policy and Development Strategy in North Korea," *North Korea Studies* 3, 4 (Winter 1992), pp. 28-47.

23. Lin, Lai, and Li, "Why China's Economic Reforms Have Been Successful."

24. We can infer this fact from the following statement quoted from the book, *Theory of Social Economy Construction*. "It is imperative that all products be exchanged and allocated according to the need of society. However, there is a danger that the profit-seeking transactions distort the production such that products and their transactions are profit-oriented." Cited by Chi Hae-Yung, *Organization and Incentive Structure of State Enterprises and Collective Farms in North Korea* [in Korean] (Seoul: Korea Development Institute, 1993), p. 23.

25. Hy-Sang Lee, "Inter-Korean Economic Cooperation: Realities and Possibilities," in S. Mosher, ed., *Korea in the 1990s: Prospects for Unification* (New Brunswick, NJ: Transaction Publishers, 1992), p. 19.

26. Ibid.

27. See, for example, Sungwoo Kim, "Recent Economic Policies of North Korea"; Doowon Lee, "Assessing North Korean Economic Reform."

28. John McMillan, "Getting Incentives Right," in P. Gourevitch and P. Guerrieri, eds., *New Challenges to International Cooperation: Adjustment of Firms, Policies, and Organizations to Global Competition* (La Jolla, CA: University of California, San Diego, International Relations and Pacific Studies, 1993), p. 102.

29. Quoted in *Sisa Journal*, 153, October 1, 1992.

Korean Peninsula

- ⊗ National Capital
- ⊙ Provincial Capital
- ● City
- ▬ International Boundary
- ─ Provincial Boundary
- ─ Demarcation Line
- ▬ Demilitarized Zone

0 25 50 75 km
0 25 50 mi

CHINA

RUSSIA

Tumen

Unggi
(Sunbong)

Hoeryong

Musan

Najin

Ch'ongjin

Linjiang

Hyesan

Hamgyong-
bukdo

Yanggang-do

Kanggye ⊙

Chagang-do

Kimch'aek

Hamgyong-
namdo

Tanch'on

Dandong

Pukch'ong

Sinch'ang

Douggou

Sinuiju

P'yongan-bukdo

Hamhung

Hongwon

**NORTH
KOREA**

Hungnam

*Korea
Bay*

Sunch'on

P'yongan-
namdo

⊙ Sain-ni

Wonsan

⊗ P'yongyang

*Sea of Japan
(Eastern Sea)*

Namp'o-si

⊙ Namp'o

Hwanghae-
bukdo

Kangwon-do

130°50'

37°30'

Ullung-do
(South Korea)

Sariwon

Hwanghae-
namdo

⊙ Haeju

Kaesong-si

Kaesong ⊙

Kyonggi-do

Ch'unch'on

Sokch'o

Uijongbu

Kangnung

Inch'on-
Jikhalsi

Soul-t'ukpyolsi

Kangwon-do

Samch'ok

⊗ Inch'on

Seoul

Wonju

*Yellow Sea
(Western Sea)*

Suwon

P'yongt'aek

Chungju

Chech'on

Ch'ungch'ong-
bukdo

Yongju

Ch'ungch'ong-
namdo

⊙ Ch'ongju

Andong

Kongju

Sangju

Taejon

Kimch'on

Kyongsang-
bukdo

P'ohang

Kunsan

Chonju

⊙ Taegu

Kyongju

**SOUTH
KOREA**

Cholla-bukdo

Ulsan

Kyongsang-namdo

Chinhae

⊙ Kwangju

Chinju

Masan

Pusan

Sunch'on

Samch'onp'a

Ch'ungmu

Koje-do

Cholla-namdo

Mokp'o

Yosu

Western Channel

Tsushima
(Japan)

Chin-do

Korea *Strait*

Eastern Channel

Iki

⊙ Cheju

Cheju-do Cheju

JAPAN

Administrative Notes

- The North Korea capital of P'yongyang is located in the province of P'yongyang-si.
- The South Korea province of Kyonggi-do is administered from Seoul.
- The South Korean province of Kyongsang-bukdo is administered from Taegu.
- The South Korean province of Kyongsang-namdo is administered from Pusan.
- The South Korean province of Kwangju is an individual province, and the administrative capital of Cholla-namdo province.

©1992 Magellan Geographix℠ Santa Barbara, CA

Chapter 5

Prospects for Political and Administrative Development in North Korea

Pan Suk Kim

The Democratic People's Republic of Korea (DPRK or North Korea), about the size of Mississippi, with a population of approximately 22.2 million and a workforce estimated at 11.1 million in 1992, has an economy similar to those of east and central Europe.[1] North Korea's gross national product (GNP) per capita income was estimated at $1,260 in 1988, versus South Korea's estimated $3,850.[2] Until the mid-1970s, however, North Korea's GNP per capita was believed to be higher than South Korea's.[3] Since 1990, North Korea has recorded a negative economic growth rate every year (-3.7 percent in 1990, -5.2 percent in 1991, and -7.5 percent in 1992).[4]

North Korea has been under the one-party rule of the Korean Workers Party (KWP) since 1948, and Kim Il Sung remained the party head until his death on July 8, 1994.[5] North Korea's development strategy relies on a highly centralized, state-planned system. Expansion of heavy industry is seen as the catalyst to development of the entire economy and is an essential aspect of *Juche*, the ideology which controls life in North Korea, and which the KWP applies in developing national programs and policies.[6] In 1987, party membership was claimed to be "over three million" (about 14.8 percent of the total population).[7]

Pan S. Kim is assistant professor in the Department of Public Administration, University of Inchon, Korea.

Political Reform in a Comparative Prespective

Study of worldwide political development has been extensive since the early 1960s, but there has been no agreement on a single view.[8] Although the concept of political development is beyond the scope of this chapter, it has been generally associated with increasing democratization and institutionalization, growing bureaucratization and professionalization of politics, formalization of politics, decline of ascription, rise of achievement in political roles, and increasing clarification and resolution of political jurisdictions (the gradual disappearance of parallel or overlapping functions).[9] In socialist countries, however, political development is doomed unless major leadership changes are possible. The term "reform" (*kaehyuk*) has not been used in North Korea. Instead, "revolution" (*hyungmyung*), "movement" (*undong*), and "battle" (*jun* or *juntoo*) have signified North Korea's mobilization and policy change strategies.

With respect to reform, Ilpyong Kim and Jane Zacek have identified two major themes in communist systems: one dealing with internal and external conditions conducive to reform, and another concerned with economic reform and its strategies.[10] Parris Chang defines political reform in China as political efforts "designed primarily to enhance efficiency and economic modernization, not to promote democracy as we understand it in the West because Chinese leaders do not believe in the consent of the governed and their own accountability to the people."[11] In fact, economic policy is made by incumbent politicians in the context of political institutions, and the choice of alternative policies is subjected to economic analysis influenced by the agendas of political parties and interests.

The practical challenge of reforming a communist country is management of the politics of redistribution of resources and power in the transition from central planning to competition. Reform-minded leaders need simultaneously to mobilize groups that will benefit from reforms into an effective coalition of support, and to win over the groups who will lose as a result. Otherwise, reform policies will be blocked by the groups most threatened by them. The classic form in which this issue confronts reformist leaders in communist states is the question of how to create an effective political counterweight to the center, the central communist party and government bureaucracies.

Generally speaking, reform implies an apolitical form of meritocratic pluralism, meaning that the political system is divided into various subsystems based on some notion of functional specialization: specialized competence in the various scientific, professional, and cultural subsystems. In North Korea, however, such capacity is limited. Political power in North Korea is highly concentrated in Kim Il Sung and Kim Jong Il in a monolithic political system. The *Juche* ideology has only limited room for a political rider to change horses in the course of socialist nation-building. As a result, it is almost impossible to see a dark horse advocating different policy preferences, and there is no general policy of opening nationwide. This implies that there is no direct encouragement of open-mindedness, pragmatism and flexibility, or opposition to dogmatism and superstition in North Korea.

North Korea differs from the Soviet Union and China in institutional strategies designed to tackle this issue.[12] In the Soviet Union, Mikhail Gorbachev decided that the only way to create a counterweight was to open up the political arena to mass participation and political competition. Changing the political rules of the game was a high-risk gamble (one that eventually led to the dismantling of Communist Party rule), but he believed he had no other choice: "Restructuring will only spin its wheels unless the main actor (the people) is included in it in a thoroughgoing way.... There is only one way to accomplish these tasks—through the broad democratization of Soviet society."[13] According to Rolf Theen, *perestroika* has a number of dimensions, including the growing critique of the Stalinist system, the new information policy (*glasnost*), legal reform, the attack on the *nomenklatura*, and a radical change in party-state relations.[14]

In China, Deng Xiaoping's actions show a very different calculation. He opted to retain the traditional communist bureaucratic policy, making only minor modifications. He apparently believed that he could use local officials as an effective counterweight to the center without changing the political rules. As a consequence, the Chinese based economic reforms on the old hierarchy. A formula for Chinese reform is summarized as follows: agricultural decollectivization, a dual-track system combining market and plan, decentralization to local governments, particularistic contracting, stimulation of the nonstate sector, special economic zones for foreign investment, opening to the outside world, and gradual depoliticization (not liberalization) of society.[15] In essence, all these changes imply that the Chinese Communist Party's leaders decided to shift the base of party legitimacy from politics to competence, and to do that they had to demonstrate that they could deliver the goods.

In North Korea, Kim Jong Il and his political supporters seem to have decided to stick with their authoritarian system because the maintenance of political status quo is less risky than a process of political change that might go out of control and subvert communism. Kim Il Sung and Kim Jong Il have feared most the overthrow of Communist Party rule, which they saw in Eastern European countries and the Soviet Union. Thus, although the regime searches for low-risk ways to improve the standard of living, its dependence on the military will continue undiminished as long as Kim Jong Il feels insecure in the near term.[16] Although experts expect that North Korea may follow the Chinese model down the road, there are significant differences between China and North Korea.

For example, contests for leadership succession after Mao's death in 1976 (during the period 1978–80, between Deng Xiaoping and Hua Guofeng; in 1980–87, between Hu Yaobang and Zhao Ziyang; and in 1987–89, between Zhao Ziyang and Li Peng) motivated contenders to propose innovative solutions to China's problems. Deng acted as political entrepreneur, using innovations in the economic policy to discredit Hua Guofeng and attract support among groups in the CCP Central Committee and Politburo. Zhao Ziyang advocated a tax-for-profit policy, while Hu Yaobang promoted the profit contracting approach.[17] Although some factions, such as the *Yanan* and the *Kapsan*, were observed until the 1960s, there is no such factional group or competition for top leadership today in North Korea.[18] Also, strict centralized management of the economy by directive as under the pure Soviet model has never existed in China.[19] The decentralizing movement took place in 1958, and thus China retained a somewhat flexible system, while in North Korea a rigid Stalinist-style system remained.

Political Succession and Charismatic Leadership

Throughout 1993, the North Korean media was bent on promulgating the legitimacy of Kim Jong Il's leadership. Particularly after mid-October 1993, North Korea staged various events praising Kim Jong Il through various government and mass organizations, and suggested the consideration of the junior Kim as president or general secretary. However, the party plenary session in December of 1993 ended up nominating Kim Young Ju as vice president.

Indications of an abnormal atmosphere regarding the power succession in North Korea attracted wide attention even before Kim Il

Sung's death. According to an interview with Stephen Linton, Columbia University professor and aide to the Reverend Billy Graham, on his recent visit to North Korea he came away with the impression that Kim Il Sung himself was leading all state affairs.[20] In view of the characteristics of the power structure within the North Korean system, delay of the final schedule of power succession was not meant to weaken the structure of succession and power organization, but to make Kim Il Sung appear as occupying the seat of power, able to handle all state affairs for the time being.[21] Nonetheless, apparently Kim Il Sung effectively turned over daily operation of the party, the government, and the military to his son. It is, therefore, fair to say that Kim Jong Il is viewed by North Koreans as a god or the center of the nation's "brain" (*noesoo*) who does supervise daily governmental affairs.

In the meantime, Kim Jong Il's stepbrother, Kim Pyung Il, a colonel in the (North) Korean People's Army and ambassador to Bulgaria, was ordered home in December 1993. On March 18, 1994, the Finnish Foreign Ministry officially announced that Kim Pyung Il (then forty-one years old), second son of Kim Il Sung, had become North Korean Ambassador to Finland.[22] These moves were seen by North Korea-watchers as indications that the Kim clan members were reaffirming their determination to install Kim Jong Il on the throne of his father.[23] Recently, however, Kim Pyung Il was recalled again to Pyongyang, and there is speculation that the recall reflected a power struggle.[24]

Interestingly, a change in the leadership structure in Pyongyang was highlighted by the election of Kim Il Sung's younger brother, Kim Yong Ju, as vice president. His appointment came two days after he was reinstalled in the all-powerful Workers' Party politburo. Kim Pyung Sik, a former leader of pro-Pyongyang Koreans in Japan, will share the vice presidency, with others. As long as Kim Jong Il continued to receive the strong support of Kim Il Sung, there was no power struggle. And given the possibility that the aim of his uncle Kim Young Ju's vice presidency was to help bridge the gap between the older and younger members of Pyongyang's aging leadership, indications of Kim Young Ju's future role need to be carefully watched.[25]

In other words, the reinstatement of Kim Young Ju was prompted by the view that it would not be a stumbling block in Kim Jong Il's power inheritance scheme. This observation is reinforced by the fact that Kim Sung Ae, Kim Jong Il's stepmother, known to be in discord with Kim Jong Il, appeared in the plenary meeting of the North Korean Women's Union and highly praised Kim Jong Il. Perhaps uniting behind Kim Jong Il is the only option for all of them to survive the grave uncertainty down the road.[26]

Changes in individual political fortunes in North Korea do not absolutely forecast their future. There are instances in which someone once dropped from the power structure was not completely eliminated from the system. Some have been reinstated after a certain period, although others vanished once and for all. These political events were carried out by the party political establishment to sustain the Kim Jong Il succession and confirm that the nucleus of the party's power consisted of the partisan veterans (anti-Japanese guerrillas who fought for national independence), leading military personnel (marshals and generals of partisan origin), and the second generation of partisans. The order of North Korea's political structure is revealed primarily in the official reports listing the names, in order of importance, of those seated on the speaker's platform during a party congress, at major national celebrations such as anniversaries of the regime and the party, and also attending the funerals of high-ranking cadres. As of 1993's forty-fourth anniversary of the North Korean regime, the party Political Bureau had twelve full members who made up the nucleus of political power, reduced from thirteen due to the death of So Chol. Among them, three Political Bureau Standing Committee members, Kim Il Sung, Kim Jong Il, and O Chin U, made up the core within the nucleus of political power.

There have been some ups and downs.[27] The twentieth session of the Sixth Plenum of the Party Central Committee held in December 1992 saw the discharge of Yon Hyong Muk from his position as premier of the Administration Council and the promotion of Kang Song Son, who was the responsible secretary of the party and chairman of the People's Committee for North Hamgyong Province, as his successor. The choice of Kang to be promoted indicates that Kim Jong Il is concerned about economic reforms and North-South relations. A year later, Kim Dal Hyon was released from his position as vice premier and chairman of the State Planning Commission, and Pak Nam Gi and Yun Ki Bok were released from party secretary positions. John Merrill asserts that the party plenum had endorsed economic policies Kim Dal Hyon had long advocated, although he was moved to an unspecified post.[28]

O Guk Yol was discharged from the position of chief of the Armed Forces General Staff in February of 1988, became director of the KWP Operations Department, and now commands the troops of the department. According to Kim Jong Il's instructions on maintaining the capability of riot control, O Guk Yol's department combatants have shifted from the past unconventional type of training designed for operations against the South to maintenance of the system and the capability for waging conventional warfare. In the meantime, the North Korean government, to comply with Kim Jong Il's directive, increased the salary and special treatment of the combatants.[29]

Generational change in the power structure could affect national policy in the near future. North Korea observers say that a covert struggle between Kim Jong Il's supporters and Kim Il Sung's aged honor guard has been taking place since the death of Kim Il Sung. These observers believe that when Kim Jong Il becomes president and general secretary of the KWP, Kim Il Sung's old supporters will be ousted.[30] The party's traditional political structure revolves around a one-man core. Kim Il Sung was the core of the first generation of leadership, and Kim Jong Il is the core of the second. The notion of a one-man core is closely related to the articulation of a line that defines the policy direction preferred by the core leader, and the existence of a core leader suggests the degree to which North Korean politics is personalized rather than institutionalized. Personal relationships (*ingan gwankye* in Korea, similar to *gwanxi* in China) within the power nucleus and loyalty to the senior and junior Kims are critical factors for survival and success in North Korean political life. The political line connects policy to power. In other words, policy and power are indivisible, so criticism of policy preferences and initiatives associated with the core leader are inevitably political assaults on the power of the leader. In terms of the power structure, there are many leading figures, but they are mere "common people," without real authority in North Korea. At present, no evidence of significant policy change has been observed since Kim Il Sung's death. Morever, it will take time for the Kim Jong Il regime to establish a new equilibrium, including a balance between the country's economic problems and the succession question.

In the months before Kim Il Sung's death, the North Korean press intensified its campaign of lionization of Kim Jong Il, even surpassing its treatment of Kim Il Sung. At the same time, 1994 broadcasts of Kim Il Sung's doings dwindled, and intelligence organizations noted that the propaganda emphasizing Kim Jong Il's greatness, and events inspiring admiration for and loyalty to Kim Jong Il, increased. De jure succession will be eased because Kim Jong Il has been set up as de facto ruler next to Kim Il Sung. North Korea's new constitution, revised in April 1993, stipulates that the Supreme People's Assembly is endowed with the right to dismiss the president, implying that the junior Kim can be elected president at any time if North Korea needs to expedite the power succession plan.[31] The real question about power succession is whether he shares the senior Kim's charisma, or can inspire the same unquestioning faith in his followers.[32] It does not seem possible now to distinguish between Kim Il Sung and Kim Jong Il. Kim Jong Il has apparently secured status as a *suryung* (great leader), and the transfer of power in North Korea seems to be the handing over of the mantle of leadership as *suryung*. In this connection, North Korea, especially the Juche Academy of Science, is transforming the ideology of *Juche* into a religious doctrine, establishing Kim Jong Il as a natural "great leader" (*suryung*) and the brain (*noesoo*) of the socio-political body.[33]

Kim Jong Il's essential task is securing this invisible authority as *suryung*, rather than simply possessing visible and tangible authority as president or general secretary of the party. There is no office called "suryung" in the North Korean political system, but the conclusion of *Juche* thought, the basic ideology guiding North Korea, is the "theory of suryung." Because it is not through being president or general secretary that Kim Il Sung will rule, but through his authority as *suryung*, the key to a smooth succession is for Kim Jong Il to accede to this authority. Thus, the junior Kim has worked hard to highlight his image as "a great leader" (*widaehan suryung*). In a recent symposium held in North Korea, Kim Jong Il was described as "a great ideologist and theorist, statesman, and military strategist who claims both literary and military accomplishments and is the people's leader, infinitely faithful to the fatherland and the people."[34] Lenin, Stalin, Mao Zedong, and Kim Il Sung all touted themselves as great thinkers, and North Korean authorities assert that Kim Jong Il has published many lofty discourses, implying that he is intellectually well endowed and therefore fit to be a great leader.

Weber's concept of charismatic authority is helpful here. For Weber, charisma is personal, in a way that is "specifically foreign to everyday routine structures."[35] This, indeed, is why it can be a revolutionary force. But once the old order has been toppled, charismatic authority itself has to be "routinized" if the new movement is to be successful, and this process involves a fundamental transformation. In its pure form charismatic authority may be said to exist only in the process of origination. It cannot remain stable, but becomes either traditionalized or rationalized, or a combination of both.[36] That it is transitory implies that charismatic authority is a phenomenon that contains the seeds of its self-destruction. This is clear as a charismatic leader attempts to consolidate his position, but it is nowhere more obvious than when leaders retire, die, or disappear and the disciples are confronted with the problem of succession.

Weber argued that political succession could take a variety of forms but that the most viable were where the successor was designated, either by the original leader or by his followers, and where hereditary charisma was the basis of change. But we should not become side-tracked here. Charisma can serve only as a transitory basis for power, by challengers to the established order. Once the old order is displaced, the challengers have to routinize their own authority. That goal is more easily attained when the leader is a charismatic figure who can provide a personal framework within which his operatives can work, but this only masks the temporary nature of charismatic authority.[37]

And the concern with the problem of succession is evident in the attempts of analysts to evaluate the prospects of success for new institutional orders. For example, will the North Korean state exist in its current form after Kim Il Sung? What are the long-term prospects for the current regime in North Korea after Kim Il Sung? On a more general level, Weber's discussion of charismatic authority redirects our attention to timing of the development. The common property shared by his concepts of traditional and rational-legal authority is that they require considerable time to create.

No Way Out Except Reform?

According to *Yonhap*, an eleven-man North Korean delegation led by Hwang Jang Yup, a secretary of the KWP Central Committee and chairman of the SPA Foreign Affairs Committee, has visited the special economic zone in Zhuhai, Guangdong Province, collecting information on Chinese economic reforms.[38] They toured an industrial complex, and upon meeting Zhuhai Party Committee leaders Hwang expressed deep interest in industrial development in the area.

North Korea has in general taken a new attitude toward economic reform and opening up and in 1984 formulated the Joint Venture Law in an attempt to attract foreign capital.[39] Recently, North Korea began to show interest in Chinese-style opening up through special economic zones. Earlier, North Korea had believed that Chinese-style economic opening up would ultimately destroy the socialist political system, and therefore tried to distance itself. However, having noted the successes in the special zones in China and the fact that the political system had remained intact, North Korea apparently reevaluated the circumstances. President Kim Il Sung and then-Premier Yon Hyong Muk made tours of the special economic zones in China in October of 1991. In December of 1991, North Korea officially designated Najin and Sonbong in North Hamgyong Province "free economic trade zones" as mandated by the Administrative Council. President Kim Il Sung openly expressed interest in and support for China's economic reform during the events marking the September 9 holiday (anniversary of DPRK's founding) in 1993.

North Korea by that time was reported to be suffering from economic difficulties, including negative growth. Thus it appears inevitable that North Korea will take steps toward economic revitalization, even if only for the sake of maintaining its political system. President Kim uncharacteristically admitted failure in the Third Seven-Year Plan (1987–1993) during the Twenty-First Plenary Session of the Sixth Party Central Committee in 1993.

As mentioned earlier, North Korea dispatched Hwang Jang Yup, one of the real power-holders (*silse*) within the government, to Beijing with the intent of improving relations with China and grasping the true mechanics of Chinese-style reform. During his stay in China in January 1994, Hwang Jang Yup intensively toured the local special economic district, an agricultural science research institute, various plants and enterprises, and major industrial facilities. The government-operated Beijing broadcast network reported that in a meeting with Hwang Jang Yup, Chinese President Jiang Zemin explained Chinese reform and opening up and the resulting successes in the socialist market economy, and that Hwang praised the achievements of China in building socialism with characteristics typical to China. It was also learned that before and after Hwang's visit, North Korea had sent a team of experts to Chinese special economic districts. Changes appear to be taking place in North Korea, at least in economics.[40]

North Korea opened the Najin-Sunbong area on December 28, 1991, according to Decree No. 74 of the State Administrative Council. Since then, three North Korean ports along the Eastern Sea coast, including Chongjin, have been opened. In addition, the opening of Sinuiju would inaugurate North Korea's opening up of areas near the

Western Sea. Though the development of the economic zone around the Tumen River, which empties into the Eastern Sea, is still merely an idea without clear prospect for investments which has been promoted by the United Nations Development Programme (UNDP) Project, the Sinuiju development plan is likely to be realized because this area is contiguous with China's Western Sea economic zone, now under full-scale development. People are interested, in particular, in the possibility that North Korea will introduce a Chinese-style opening policy, especially since the opening of Sinuiju could be promoted in connection with China's policy.[41]

When Sinuiju and Nampo open, in the next stage, North Korea will have economically open areas on both the Eastern and Western Sea coasts. Though North Korea has been skeptical of China's attempt to open up while maintaining a socialist market economy, North Korea has no choice but to find a new way through the economic vortex created by the collapse of the Soviet Union and East Europe and China's economic reforms. North Korea worked out a "region-lock-out opening policy" (*kukchi pyeswoehyong kaebangchaek*) as a means to protect its system from the shock of the opening up as well as to break the economic deadlock. This policy was experimentally applied to the Najin-Sonbong area and was aimed at preventing the wind from an open area blowing into other areas, by banning people's contacts with open areas and by evacuating "unpatriotic" residents and those in the neighboring regions. Some residents of the Najin and Sonbong areas have been replaced, and now residents of northern Sinuiju are reportedly being moved out.

North Korea has developed this opening-up policy internally while it has been enduring difficulties externally because of its nuclear policy. Although it assumes a nuclear confrontational policy, North Korea is well aware that it has no choice but to take a line of peaceful coexistence based on economic exchanges. Sonbong, Najin, and other "open" cities now conducting border trade with China are actually precursors to the second-stage open cities of Sinuiju and Nampo. Sinuiju is vital to North Korea. This border city competes with China's Dandong and Donggou and can play a prominent role in bolstering North Korea's development. It has abundant hydroelectric power through the Supung power station, an abundant water supply and railway connections, and is convenient to river and maritime navigation. Dandong International Airport just across the border is directly linked to Hong Kong, Shanghai, and Beijing; and in the port of Donggou, four 40,000-ton boats can berth simultaneously. However, at present it is far from certain that North Korea will open up further.[42]

The Direction of Reforms

Kim Il Sung admitted some degree of economic stagnation in his New Year's address in December 1993, and North Korea's launching of reform stems from dissatisfaction with the policy of great economic expansion, where available funds were concentrated on growth, preventing significant personal gains. However, there is no clear indication of a political rejection of the extremes of "leftism" in North Korea, while Deng Xiaoping clearly abandoned extreme leftism in China. Reform measures have zigzagged through three stages: (1) isolation and a hardline policy from the 1970s to 1983, (2) an open door policy from 1984 (the Joint Venture Law of 1984) to 1989, and (3) a screened open door policy from 1989 (limited and conservative, perhaps due to China's Tiananmen Square massacre and the fall of Eastern European socialist regimes in 1989).

In his New Year's address on December 31, 1993, and at the Twenty-First Plenary Meeting of the Sixth Party Central Committee, however, Kim Il Sung designated the next three years as a "period for adjustment in the sector of socialist economic construction."[43] The Seoul-based daily *Hankuk Ilbo* summarized Kim Il Sung's address as follows: (1) the Third Seven-Year Plan was a failure; (2) the North Korean Worker's Party plenary meeting designated the next three years as a readjustment period in which North Korea will emphasize "agriculture, light industry, and external trade," a shift in priorities of a national development policy; (3) the civilian-led South Korean government was strongly denounced; (4) provocative remarks were made regarding the nuclear issue on the Korean peninsula, aimed implicitly at the United States; and (5) the reunification policy was mentioned. Many newspapers commented on Kim Il Sung's address.[44] Though in his address Kim Il Sung admitted to "difficulties and obstacles in economic construction," he said that "during the Third Seven-Year Plan [North Korea] made long strides in all fields of socialist economic construction in spite of... unexpected international events and tensions." Also, Kim Il Sung described the new economic strategy in his address, emphasizing the development of agriculture, light industry, and foreign trade.[45]

Generally, risk must be taken to achieve reform, and consideration must be given to the consequences. The whole macroscopic environ-

Table 1
Path of Reform in North Korea

Step 1 (Independence to 1960s):	Political and social consolidation Collectivization of land and all industries Mass mobilization and moral incentive policies
Step 2 (1970s):	Three (ideological, cultural, and technological) Revolution Team Movement Technology and capital transfer (heavy and defense industries) Isolation policy based on self-reliance (*Juche*)
Step 3 (1980s):	Establishment of rules and regulations for foreign investment and joint ventures: the Joint Venture Law of 1984 Economic and technological exchanges with other countries Emphasis on the development of science and technology Cautious step toward open-door policy
Step 4 (1990s):	Economic development as an urgent task Development of special economic zones Industrial restructuring: light industry over heavy industry Agricultural reform Trade promotion

ment must create the climate for reform in North Korea, including the establishment of Kim Jong Il's leadership in building socialism with North Korean characteristics, macroscopic economic development, opening-up, establishment of the new system of economic reform, and support of the overall framework of reform. However, no clear movement in this direction by the top North Korean leadership has been observed. North Korean leaders seem to anticipate serious economic problems ahead, but apparently they do not yet agree on solutions and directions.

Reform is the driving force of development, development is the goal of reform; and stability is both the prerequisite for and the guarantee of reform and fulfillment of the goal. The relationship of the three variables—development, reform, and stability—will determine the path of construction of the national economy or its opening-up.

Kim Il Sung seemed to believe that changes in the North Korean system should take place in an orderly manner, under firm party control, and with doctrinal unity and adulation of the top leader. In other words, he regarded politics as central to socialist development and to the guidance and shaping of economics. Does Kim Jong Il have a dif-

Figure 1
Relationship among Development, Reform, and Stability

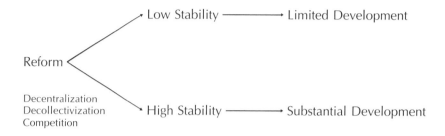

ferent view from his father's? No matter what he may think personally, until now he has only quoted and affirmed his father's statements.

In the long run, however, Kim Jong Il would be wise to take a different initiative from Kim Il Sung's. Kim Jong Il may need to study historical lessons which can be learned from other countries' experiences. For example, Hua Guofeng and his supporters in China were nicknamed the "whatever faction" because they used the slogan of the "two whatevers": "Whatever decision Chairman Mao made, we resolutely support; and whatever instructions Chairman Mao made, we will steadfastly abide by."[46] But Hua's faction did not succeed, while Deng's did. Deng Xiaoping and his allies concluded that China would have to join the world because no country had ever achieved modernization in a closed system. It would not be wise for Kim Jong Il to follow the path of the "whatever faction" of Kim-Il-Sungism.

In the past, North Korean reform has been sporadic at best. Instead of swift and comprehensive radical transformation of the entire system, which might have threatened the vested interests of many groups, Kim Il Sung and Kim Jong Il were extremely cautious. Party leaders did not impose a radical and rapid change but instead incorporated bureaucratic groups into the design of reforms, thereby slowing the transition. To minimize the threat to central economic agencies, North Korean leaders apparently have decided not to expand the market sector radically while implementing the plan. Nevertheless a series of debates has taken place in policymaking circles in Pyongyang over whether or not to adopt the open-door policy and economic reform (see table 2).

Ilpyong Kim asserts that "the conservatives seemed to be arguing that the country should continue to carry out its policy of self-reliance and preserve the ideological, cultural, and technological revolutions without outside help, while the reformers argued that North Korea should learn more about the Chinese and the Soviet experiences with

---

Table 2
Policy Positions on Recent Reform

Issue Areas	Conservatives	Reformers	Adjustment
Central Planning	Pro	Anti	Pro
Industrial Restructuring	Pro-heavy	Pro-light	Pro-light
Decentralization	Later	Sooner	Later
Foreign Trade	Reactive	Proactive	Proactive
Means of Economic Regulation	Administrative	Economic	Administrative
Incentives	Moral	Material	Moral & Material

---

economic reform and should also open its door to the outside world."[47] The policy allowing enterprises to dispose of their above-quota output at market prices creates economic incentive for managers and ministry officials to press for more market opportunities, while allowing central planners to save their functions and their faces. According to *North Korea News* in Seoul, an article by Kim Jong Il in the March issue of the party theoretical journal *Kulloja* reaffirmed the need for central planning to enforce the party's control over the economy, but disavowed a Stalinist-style "command administrative system" as a remnant of an unstable society.[48]

Legal Framework

Recently law become an expression of economic reform in North Korea. The North Korean government seems to recognize the need for a legal framework to support the development of the national economy, and several other laws are either in the drafting stage or are pending approval by the Administrative Council and the Supreme People's Assembly. North Korea has already announced new laws on banking and leasing of land by foreigners—the latest in a series of measures over the past two years to put in place a legal framework for economic opening.[49] The revised constitution, a land lease law, a foreign investment bank law, and a revised customs law are among those newly promulgated. For the first time in its history, in August of 1990 North Korea began to allow foreign direct investment.[50] It is interesting to note that the joint venture law was formulated after Premier Kang Sung San made an official trip to China (August 5 to August 10, 1984), and it was revised under his premiership in 1994.[51]

Following the Leninist interpretation of law and the state, North Korean communists have taken an instrumentalist approach to law. Lenin did not see law and the state as anything but the coercive expression of the economic power enjoyed by the ruling class. Law has thus been crudely viewed in North Korea as pure political machinery determined by the economic infrastructure.[52] Instrumentalists consider that class struggle replaced bourgeois law with socialist law. Legal instrumentalism has been particularly evident in the political ideologies and practices of Kim Il Sungism in North Korea. Party control of both

---

Table 3
Legal Reform

Establishment of rules and regulations for foreign investment and joint ventures in the 1980s: The Joint Venture Act of 1984 and passage of several new laws regarding economic and social affairs in North Korea. The most recent laws are:

- The Family Law (October 1990)
- The Foreigners' Investment Law, the Joint Venture Project Law, and the Foreigners' Enterprises Law (October 1992)
- The Foreign Exchange Control Law, the Foreigners' Investment Enterprise and Foreigners' Tax Law, the Free Economic Trade Zone Law (January 1993)
- The revised constitution (April 1993)
- The Construction Law, the Land Lease Law, and the Foreign Bank Law (December 1993)
- The revised Joint Venture Law of 1984 and the Law on Lawyers (January 1994)

administrative and judicial decisionmaking functions ultimately determines outcomes. A powerful decisionmaker in its own right, the party has immunized itself to legal challenges. Law functions instrumentally in the sense that it upholds party rule in very immediate forms.

In recent history, North Korea advocated rebuilding its legal system and renewing rules for the party to replace the idea that laws are what issue from the mouths of political leaders. In 1993, the state constitution was renewed and many new laws, particularly concerning economics, were passed. Since the 1970s, the North Korean leadership has shown interest in foreign trade and economic cooperation with the West in addition to ties with other socialist countries. New forms of economic cooperation among collective, public, and overseas enterprises have been legalized, and the very system of ownership and operation has been challenged. The present leadership appears to understand that the North Korean legal system must be strengthened to provide orderly development of the national modernization program. To keep its house in order, it will be necessary for North Korea to establish social order and operate the state enterprise under the law.

However, one must recognize certain important impediments to establishment of a modern legal system in North Korea. First, a modern legal system, with a separation of powers among the police (public security), procurators, and courts, is lacking and should be established. Second, North Korean society has been a strict class society since the mid-1940s. Higher rank in the party, government, or military provides better access to the amenities of life and greater privileges and immunities, which cannot otherwise be bought. Third, a modern legal system cannot function without lawyers who have reasonable levels of education and experience in law. North Korea does not seem to be responding to the problem of supervising the implementation of the constitution: there is no recourse available to individuals to challenge unconstitutional legislation, illegal administrative rules, and interference by party committees. Fourth, North Korean leaders continue to pay only scant attention to legal procedures in carrying out their wishes. They appear to believe that the ends justify the means. In carrying out anticrime or anticorruption campaigns, North Korean leaders circumvent the law at will. Finally, the rule of law will be difficult to implement. Law enforcement officials make clear that class is the determinant of judicial results. No principle in the constitution or law is permitted to conflict with the desires of the Communist Party leaders.

Administrative Reform

After the fall of socialist regimes in central and eastern Europe common areas for administrative reform in those countries became (1) transition from systems of one-party rule to pluralist systems with democratically elected and accountable governments, (2) abandonment of the principle of democratic centralism in favor of far-reaching deconcentration and decentralization of political power under the rule of law, (3) rejection of the principle of unity between politics and economics, and (4) denationalization of a large share of the previously state-controlled productive capital and deregulation of the national economy.[53] In post-socialist countries, the underlying purpose of administrative reform is to replace a nationalized, centralized, and planned economic system with a market economy and a pluralistic political structure. In socialist countries such as North Korea, however, such ambitious administrative reforms are not likely to take place in the near future unless a new political order emerges.

In a practical sense, administrative reform attempts to merge the real with the ideal.[54] It deals with very practical matters of everyday public business, with petty details at one end and assessment of government performance and expectations of government at the other.[55] In North Korea, a limited range of issues is considered for improving government performance.

State Management

In order to make reforms compatible with its socialist economy and to be less interventionist in public management, including state enterprises, the North Korean government must recognize the need to pursue restructuring. Of course, this would not be easy and government intervention would continue to be pervasive. Nevertheless, it would be wise to separate the administrative and economic functions from the political functions. The chief functions of the government should be the conduct of macroeconomic policy, the preparation of sectoral and regional developments plans, and the provision of social services. Governmental reform must endeavor to strengthen macroeconomic management and administrative functions while revising the role of line ministries and bureaus. The second possible objective would be to improve the administrative efficiency of the government and to clarify responsibility to reduce functional overlaps.

North Korea's Finance Minister Yun Ki Chong emphasized managerial improvement in the Seventh Session of the Ninth Supreme People's Assembly, on April 7, 1994: "[North Koreans] should properly implement the independent economic accounting system [*tonglip chesanje*] in conformity with the demand of the Taean work system, intensify the local budgetary system [*chibang yesanje*], and further improve and intensify the financial management work."[56] The independent economic accounting system is a planned operation of the socialist state-run enterprises in which the plants and enterprises make both ends meet and contribute to the state while enjoying relative managerial independence under the state's central guidance.[57] Unlike the system of the former Soviet Union but similar to that operating in Cuba, under the independent cost accounting system North Korean enterprises are allowed to buy and sell goods among themselves at centrally approved prices.[58]

The local budgetary system is socialist, managing the overall economic life of both the local area and the state by enhancing the local area's responsibility while ensuring the state's central guidance.[59] According to the system, the basic budgetary unit is the county (that is, the base of the local area's economic and cultural development). Overall, the North Korean government emphasizes unitary management, planned agreement, conformity with regulations, and "revolutionary spirit" (moral incentives).

The *Taean* work system, embodying the *Juche* idea and the mass-oriented line, is a managerial and guidance system applied to state-run enterprises. The *Taean* management system was established by Kim Il Sung after he visited the Taean Electrical Appliance Plant (heavy engineering works) in December of 1961, and it has become the management method of North Korea, adapted to industry as the *Chongsan-ri* Method.[60] It presents basic principles of socialist economic management, facilitating coordination of political, economic, and technological guidance; the state's guidance and each unit's creativity; unitary control; and political and moral stimulation.[61] It is a three-stage process: (1) the government sets goals for production as part of a seven-year plan, (2) enterprise management makes proposals based on available capacity, and (3) agreement is reached on target production figures after collective discussions with the workers, the party secretary, the factory manager, and a series of committees. A process of consultation ensues between the State Planning Commission and individual enterprises, resulting in a finally agreed-upon production plan. Enterprises are allocated resources on the basis of the final plan. Also, there are fewer enterprises than provincial planning bodies, which have a degree of autonomy. Other larger, provincially based enterprises report directly to a commission or ministry. Increased productivity, full capacity utilization, and efficient use of resources in various areas is now being stressed. The solution to economic stagnation is, however, not slogans but technological and scientific improvements and management innovations. One consequence of the earlier inward-looking growth period has been the lack of infusion of modern management techniques into the light industry and service sectors. Since the mid-1980s, North Korea has made only limited attempts to reform enterprises and management, such as imposing financial accountability, offering material incentives for labor, and increasing relative autonomy of state enterprises.[62]

Furthermore, institutional obstacles to reform or opening-up should be lifted, or at least diminished. First, the dominance of the state enterprise system reduces the possibilities for, and the scope of, flexible decisionmaking by joint venture enterprises. Second, clear regulations and procedures are absent with respect to foreign exchange transactions, labor management relations, import-export operations, financial arrangements, management of joint ventures, and infrastructure. Third, there are insufficient skills, information, and management know-how within the responsible government agencies. Finally, top leaders should be aware of the requirements of the situation, including the eventual need to change rather than just improve the management system. Bureaucrats, especially at the national level, however, are seen as among the major losers from reform. To some extent, the use of decentralization and the promotion of nonstate industry are generating a reorientation of key ministries of the central government away from central planning toward general supervision of economic development.

Fiscal Decentralization

Fiscal decentralization is a potentially viable response to the political challenge of administrative reform in North Korea, given the nature of its political institutions. Including expansion of financial autonomy for provincial governments in the reform package could give provincial officials an interest in promoting and sustaining the reform drive. Such a policy package is one of several possible options for creating a political counterweight to the central party bureaucracy and achieving market reform while preserving North Korea's communist institutions. An example would be revenue-sharing contracts between the central government and provincial governments. In China, for example, "eating in separate kitchens," where localities are allowed to keep part of the revenues collected, was introduced in Jiangsu and Sichuan provinces in 1977 and was extended to all provinces beginning in 1980.[63] Fiscal decentralization policies, namely particularistic contracts negotiated by the center with each provincial government, may give central politicians the opportunity to win the gratitude and political support of officials from the provinces. Although this fiscal reform formula will not make all the local governments better off, the central government could shift many of its fiscal responsibilities to them.

Since the 1970s, an appreciable number of reform measures have been introduced in North Korea. In October 1973 Kim Il Sung set forth the novel policy of a local budgetary system under which localities managed their own economic life. According to reports, the total income of the local budgetary system has increased by a factor of 2.6 in all provinces, cities, and counties over the past twenty years.[64] Over 170 cities and counties managed their economies with subsidies from the state in 1973, but since 1977 many cities and counties appropriated their expenditures from their own resources and still returned a large amount of money to the state.[65]

With the establishment of the local budgetary system, North Korea has tried to prop up its rapidly deteriorating economy. At a mass rally in Pyongyang on October 27, 1993, marking the twentieth anniversary of President Kim Il Sung's local budget system directive, Finance Minister Yun Ki Chong declared that the local budget system must be developed and strengthened to stimulate North Korea's sagging provincial, county, and city economies. He then called for the development of commerce and service industries locally, national savings, and increased revenue for development of the local budget system.

To help counties and cities develop their own budget systems, North Korea recently began conferring the title of "exemplary" on counties and cities that develop a workable budget. Kumya County of Northern Hamgyong Province was the first to win the title of "model county of the local budgetary system," and forty other counties followed. The policy of the local budgetary system put forward by Kim Il Sung on October 31, 1973, is known as a socialist budgetary system, giving local units responsibility for management and use of their own creativity under the guidance of the state. The local budgetary system applies the collectivist principle to budgetary management so as to combine local interests with those of the state and make the local and central bodies work in harmony.

However, the local budget system actually slows development of local economies rather than stimulating them as claimed by North Korean propaganda. In North Korea's planned economy, the local budget system restricts the central government's subsidies to local economic development projects and holds local governments responsible for them. In North Korean propaganda, the local budget system calls on local governments to spend within the limits of their revenue and produce a surplus for contribution to the central government. Under this system, small enterprises in cities and counties are not covered by the central government's budget, and local budgets are supposed to support the central budget. Under the circumstances, it is out of the question for a small local enterprise to make money, though it is supposed to do so under the local budget system. North Korea's local economy is based on cottage factories, of which there are 4,000 across the country, according to North Korean media. With no subsidies from the central government, however, it is impossible for these small factories to develop and contribute to the development of the local economy.[66]

Reorganization

Recently, North Korea reorganized some key agencies. In November 1993, the State Auditing Committee, which had been under the control of the cabinet since 1990, was placed under the Central People's Committee (the supreme administrative organization), thus elevating the auditing function in government over the cabinet level. Also, North Korea upgraded the function of its security police by renaming the State Security Ministry, the State Safety and Security Ministry. The Central Election Guidance Committee was retitled the Central Election Committee, implying a more neutral political function by omitting the word "Guidance."[67] In 1994, North Korea also reestablished the Ministry of Trade.

Since the Sixth Party Central Committee meeting on December 8, 1993, it has been predicted that North Korea would reorganize its economic structure as well. Early in 1994, a considerable number of ministers were reshuffled in economy-related ministries, and enterprise agencies were reorganized. Gong Jin Tae was appointed mining industry minister, Lee Choon Suk forestry minister, Kim Kil Yun director of the State Academy of Sciences, Choi Hui Jung chairman of the State Science and Technology Committee, and Cho Yun Hui construction minister.[68] According to the (South Korean) National Unification Board, North Korea has reorganized agencies in both light and heavy industries. The General Bureau of the Shoe Industry, representing a light industry, has been upgraded and renamed the Joint General Bureau of the Shoe Industry; the Korea Silk Company has been upgraded and retitled the Joint Korea Silk Company; and the General Bureau of Unha Trade became the Joint General Bureau of Unha Trade, consisting of several subsidiaries such as the Sariwon Textile Plant, the Kaesung Textile Plant, the Hwangju Fiber Plant, and the Sungjin Fiber Plant. On the other hand, the Kangso District Coal Mining Complex was downgraded to be called the Kangso District Coal Mining General Enterprise, the Kim Jung Tae Electric Locomotive Complex became the Kim Jung Tae Electric Locomotive General Enterprise, the Kumsung Tractor Complex is now the Kumsung Tractor General Plant, and the April Third Machinery Complex was renamed the April Third Machinery Plant. "General enterprises" are combinations of enterprises that deal with similar materials, whereas a "complex" is a group of general enterprises that are technologically related based on a large-scale production unit. Industrial restructuring seems to be the result of the North Korean policy giving new priority to light industry.[69]

Another noteworthy event in North Korea's reshuffle was Kim Il Sung's extraordinary promotion and appointment of Hong Suk Hyong as chairman of the State Planning Committee (December 7, 1993).[70] Hong, who had been chief secretary of the Kim Chaek Steel Mill's party committee, was promoted from candidate member of the party Central Committee (ranking 131 in the party hierarchy) to candidate member of the Political Bureau. The appointment of Hong as chairman of the State Planning Commission is said to reflect North Korea's intention to take advantage of his field/practical experience in mapping out economic plans.[71] Again, a high degree of resistance to such reforms is anticipated. Certain specialists and technocrats could be labeled the "heavy-industry faction" in North Korea, similar to the "petroleum faction" who ran the Chinese economy under the late Premier Zhou Enlai.[72] The "heavy-industry faction" could be credited with the development of North Korea's heavy industry and is strongly represented in economic ministries. (Former premiers such as Li Gun Mo and Yon Hyong Muk as well as current Premier Kang Sung San are Soviet-trained technocrats specializing in heavy industry.)

Conclusion

The reform experiences of the Soviet Union, China, and North Korea differ. In the Soviet Union, Gorbachev introduced democratic political reforms to create the political framework for economic reform. Because the central communist party-state was strong, institutionalized, and wedded to the command economy, Gorbachev expanded the political arena to enfranchise citizens more likely to support market reforms. In China, Deng took the more cautious approach of introducing economic reforms without political reforms. Every reform policy thus had to be channeled through existing communist authoritarian bureaucratic institutions. Yet the Chinese version of communism proved to be surprisingly flexible. The central bureaucracy had been weakened by the Cultural Revolution, and previous waves of decentralization had allowed provincial officials to develop as political counterweights to the conservative center. Over the decade 1979–89, bureaucratic support for reforms broadened, and the momentum of reform was sustained in China despite periodic retrenchments.

As long as cryptopolitics prevails in North Korea, selective liberalization (the so-called "mosquito-net style") will take place slowly. Most factional alignments were eliminated by Kim Il Sung after the Korean War, so a pluralistic power struggle is apparently unlikely. Because of fears of coups and general revolution during their tenure, dictators generally control the power elite by arranging for them to thoroughly hold each other in check, while they are all watched through organs of surveillance. A dictator tends not to cultivate a number-two man while in office because he fears conspiracies. Kim Il Sung designated his son as his successor long ago as a way to ensure a firm power base for Kim Jong Il in the party, government, and military. Thus, it has been said that the present power elite structure currently stands behind Kim Jong Il. For the sake of political stability, the North Korean elite may have no choice but to maintain Kim Jong Il's leadership for the time being. However, his future is still foggy. Kim Il Sung held three top posts (president of the country, KWP general secretary, and chairman of the party's Central Military Committee) until his death on July 8, 1994. The empty posts constitute a vacuum of political power until they are filled by Kim Jong Il, but there has been no announcement he is assuming those positions.

The most desirable outcome of the leadership succession would be the launching of reform measures. Kim Il Sung and his followers attempted to enhance communication between workers and farmers on the one hand and the managers and leaders on the other through the *Taean* Work System for the solution of management problems in the state-run enterprises and the *Chongsan-ri* method for the solution of organizational problems in the agricultural cooperatives. However, there is little to identify the junior Kim's own initiative in political/administrative reform or major policy changes. Kim Il Sung put socialism first and development second, as did Mao in China. Kim Jong Il's policies seem not to differ from his father's, at least for the time being. In the last years of the Kim Il Sung regime, as one analyst put it, "the lessons of history are unequivocal: to reform or to die."[73] So far, there is no indication of major political or administrative reform efforts, such as separation of party and government (*dangjung-boonli*), or changes in the state bureaucracy or the establishment of the civil service. Dissidence is not tolerated, and the political situation permits only one philosophy, one system, and one line, without any pluralistic components. The Kim-Il-Sungists' emphasis on class struggle and permanent revolution compelled the KWP to continue to base its recruitment on politics rather than functional competency. Given the degree of cohesion among the power elite, overt expression of dissatisfaction with reform and liberalization appears less probable. Even if they were to understand that opening up to the outside world is inevitable as a response to changes in their environment, they would pursue a very careful path.[74] Although its political system and power structure are rigid, technological and economic changes could eventually stimulate reform in the North Korean political system regardless of Kim Jong Il's political calculation in the future. In other words, economic and technological reforms can be separated from social and political reforms in the long run.

North Korea's reform can be measured by Pyongyang's "good faith" involvement in international confidence-building. Simple expression of shifts in policy priorities does not necessarily mean that Pyongyang would seriously intend to carry out new policies such as agriculture-first, light-industry first, or trade-first. Economic transparency, a tangible shift in resource allocation in favor of nonmilitary and light industrial sectors, and substantial investment in science and technology, government reorganization, and public management innovations should be made to promote initiatives (i.e., policy, political, and administrative capacities). Reform in socialist countries generally may have solved some problems, but it has created new ones in the process.

Notes

1. World Bank, *Historically Planned Economies: A Guide to the Data* (Washington, DC: World Bank, 1993), p. 145.
2. It must be noted that North Korean statistics vary widely. South Korea's current GNP per capita income is estimated at over $7,000. Byoung-Lo Philo Kim, *Two Koreas in Development* (New Brunswick, NJ: Transaction Publishers, 1992), p. 67.
3. Ibid.
4. Young Ock Yoo, "A Symbolistic Study of the Possibility of De-Kimilsungization of Juche Ideology," *East Asian Review* 6 (Spring 1994), p. 54; and Korea Bank, *Estimated Value of North Korean GNP* (Seoul: Korea Bank), 1992.
5. For the Korean Workers Party and Kim Il Sung, see Chong-sik Lee, *The Korean Workers' Party: A Short History* (Stanford: Hoover Institution Press, 1978); and Dae-Sook Suh, *Kim Il Sung: The North Korean Leader* (New York: Columbia University Press, 1988).
6. Paul Collins and Frederick Nixson, "Public Sector Management and the Transition to a More Open Economy: Cautious Reform in the Democratic People's Republic of Korea (DPRK)," *Public Administration and Development* 13 (October 1993), p. 378.
7. Nicholas Eberstadt and Judith Banister, *The Population of North Korea* (Berkeley: Institute of East Asian Studies, University of California, 1992), p. 39; Hwan Ju Pang, *Korean Review* (Pyongyang: Foreign Languages Publishing House, 1987), p. 82.
8. The study of political development was rare until the 1950s. In 1960, Gabriel Almond and James Coleman published a famous collection of essays on the subject. See Gabriel A. Almond and James S. Coleman, eds., *The Politics of the Developing Areas* (Princeton, NJ: Princeton University Press, 1960); Harry Eckstein, "The Idea of Political Development: From Dignity to Efficiency," *World Politics* 34 (July 1982), pp. 451-86; Myron Weiner and Samuel P. Huntington, eds., *Understanding Political Development* (Boston: Little, Brown and Company, 1987); and Vernon W. Ruttan, "What Happened to Political Development?" *Economic Development and Cultural Change* 39 (January 1991), pp. 265-92.
9. Eckstein, "Idea of Political Development," p. 454.
10. Ilpyong Kim and Jane Zacek, "Introduction," in Ilpyong J. Kim and Jane Shapiro Zacek, eds., *Reform and Transformation in Communist Systems: Comparative Perspectives* (New York: Paragon House, 1991), p. 137.
11. Parris H. Chang, "Political Reform in China," in Kim and Zacek, eds., *Reform and Transformation*, p. 137.
12. Susan Shirk argues that the difference in the strategies of the Chinese and Soviet leaders may derive from their different generational perspectives: Deng's cohort of leaders are first-generation founders of the communist revolution in China, whereas Gorbachev belonged to the fourth generation of communist leaders in the Soviet Union. Susan L. Shirk, *The Political Logic of Economic Reform in China* (Berkeley: University of California Press, 1993).
13. Ibid., p. 11.
14. Rolf H. W. Theen, "Political Reform in the Soviet Union," in Kim and Zacek, eds., *Reform and Transformation*, p. 25.

15. Shirk, *Political Logic*, pp. 12, 16; Joseph Fewsmith, *Dilemmas of Reform in China: Political Conflict and Economic Debate* (New York: M. E. Sharpe, 1994), p. 9.

16. Rinn-Sup Shinn, *CRS Report for Congress: North Korea: Policy Determinants, Alternative Outcomes, U.S. Policy Approaches* (Washington, DC: Congressional Research Service, Library of Congress, 1993), p. 15.

17. Shirk, *Political Logic*, pp. 37, 247.

18. Kim Il Sung has had to deal with three groups since independence: (1) the domestic group that operated underground in Korea and Japan; (2) the *Yanan* group that returned from China and formed the New Democratic party (*sinmindang*); and (3) the Soviet-Koreans that returned to Korea with the Soviet army. Suh, *Kim Il Sung*, pp. 72-73, and Byoung-Lo Philo Kim, *Two Koreas*, pp. 110-11.

19. Shirk, *Political Logic*, p. 29.

20. *Choson Ilbo*, February 8, 1994, p. 5; and FBIS, *Daily Report*, February 8, 1994, pp. 26, 28-29.

21. A foreign news report noted that Kim Yong Ju—who at one time, it was learned, had been nominated as successor to Kim Il Sung but disappeared from the power structure for seventeen years before returning to the Political Bureau last year—said in a conversation with diplomats from the third world that Kim Jong Il would retain the posts of secretary of the Workers Party and supreme commander of the People's Army until Kim Il Sung died. Kim Il Sung arranged a grand banquet at the Kimsusan Assembly Hall on July 27, 1993, in celebration of the fortieth anniversary of the so-called liberation war. Kim Il Sung's younger brother, Kim Young Ju, was there listed as former vice premier of the Administrative Council. Kim Yong Ju, who returned as a Political Bureau member, said that the succession to power would not take place until Kim Il Sung's death.

22. FBIS, *Daily Report*, March 21, 1994, p. 50; and *Choson Ilbo*, March 19, 1994, p. 2.

23. Ro Kwan Chung, "An Analysis of Kim Il Sung's New Year Message," *East Asian Review* 6 (Spring 1994), p. 85.

24. *Hankuk Ilbo*, May 9, 1994, p. 8.

25. *Korea Times* (in English), December 13, 1993, p. 6.

26. FBIS, *Daily Report*, December 9, 1993, p. 28; and *Chungang Ilbo*, December 9, 1993, p. 4.

27. B. C. Koh reported that a high turnover rate in leadership positions in the KWP was observed. In view of the fact, particularly, that Kye Ung Tae, Chon Pyong Ho, and Han Song Yong, all of whom are considered core personnel of the Kim Jong Il order, are dual-hatted as party secretaries in addition to being Political Bureau members, it seems the political power structure is being firmed up for the Kim Jong Il succession. B. C. Koh, "Political Change in North Korea," in Chong-Sik Lee and Se-Hee Yoo, eds., *North Korea in Transition* (Berkeley: Institute of East Asian Studies, University of California, 1991), p. 8.

28. John Merrill, "North Korea in 1993: In the Eye of the Storm," *Asian Survey* 34 (January 1994), p. 13.

29. A combatant senior lieutenant receives a salary of 155 won per month, considerably more than other senior lieutenants' 100 won per month. Special treatment of combatants includes a triple allowance of rice and double food allowances over those of other military officers, rank by rank, and nearly equals the allowance levels accorded to members of the Second Security Guard division of the General

Guard Bureau, which is in charge of Kim Jong Il's personal protection. *Naewoe Tongsin*, November 18, 1993, pp. f1-f2; and FBIS, *Daily Report*, March 3, 1994, p. 28.

30. *Hankuk Ilbo*, June 30, 1993, p. 3; and FBIS, *Daily Report*, June 30, 1993, p. 24.

31. Moon Young Huh, "Prospects in 1994 for Changes in North Korean System and Policies," *East Asian Review* 6 (Spring 1994), p. 26.

32. Shinn, *CRS Report for Congress*, p. 7.

33. For more details on *Juche* as theology, see Han S. Park's chapter in this volume.

34. Hyun Joon Chun, "Specialist Analyzes Kim Jong Il Power Base," *Mal* (Seoul, in Korean), November 1993, p. 34; and FBIS, *Daily Report*, December 21, 1993, p. 22.

35. Max Weber, "Politics As a Vocation," in H. H. Gerth and C. Wright Mills, eds., *From Max Weber: Essays in Sociology* (New York: Oxford University Press, 1946), pp. 77-128; Max Weber, *The Theory of Social and Economic Organization*, trans. A. M. Henderson and Talcott Parsons (Glencoe, IL: Free Press, 1947), p. 363; and Robert W. Jackman, *Power without Force: The Political Capacity of Nation-States* (Ann Arbor, MI: University of Michigan Press, 1993), pp. 87-92.

36. Weber, *Theory of Social and Economic Organization*, p. 364.

37. Jackman, *Power without Force*.

38. *Yonhap*, January 21, 1994; and FBIS, *Daily Report*, January 21, 1994, p. 29.

39. Yun Kuk-han, "North Korea's Moves to Introduce 'Chinese-Style' Opening," *Hangyore Sinmun* (Seoul, in Korean), February 8, 1994, p. 8, and February 14, 1994, pp. 52-63.

40. A North Korean government delegation for "science and technology cooperation" headed by Kim Ung Ho, vice chairman of the State Commission of Science and Technology, visited China and returned by train on December 2, 1993. A delegation from Kim Il Sung University led by its first vice president, O Kil Pang, visited China on December 6, 1993. FBIS, *Daily Report*, December 6, 1993, p. 21.

41. *Chungang Ilbo* (in Korean), February 14, 1994, p. 5.

42. China seems to believe that linking its three northeastern provinces (Jilin, Liaoning, and Heilongjiang), where Shenyang is a central city and Dandong, Dalian, and Danggou are also located, to Sinuiju, will contribute to development of the Yellow Sea sphere, unlock North Korea's economic potential, stimulate regional economic cooperation with South Korea, and thus promote stability on the Korean peninsula. *Chungang Ilbo*, February 14, 1994, p. 5.

43. FBIS, *Daily Report*, January 3, 1994, p. 22.

44. *Hankuk Ilbo*, January 4, 1994, p. 3; and FBIS, *Daily Report*, January 5, 1994, pp. 10-12.

45. FBIS, *Daily Report*, January 3, 1994, p. 22.

46. Shirk, *Political Logic*, p. 35; and Fewsmith, *Dilemmas of Reform*, p. 11.

47. Ilpyong J. Kim, "Reform in North Korea," in Kim and Zacek, eds., *Reform and Transformation*, p. 301.

48. Merrill, "North Korea in 1993," p. 14.

49. Ibid., p. 16.

50. *Choson Ilbo*, August 24, 1990.

51. Chin Kim, "North Korean Joint Venture Laws," *California Western School of Law Journal* 19, 2 (1989).

52. Pitman B. Potter, ed., *Domestic Law Reforms in Post-Mao China* (New York: M. E. Sharpe, 1994), p. 23; and V. I. Lenin, *The State* (Peking: Foreign Language Press, 1975), p. 14.

53. Joachim Jens Hesse, "Introduction [of Administrative Transformation in Central and Eastern Europe]," *Public Administration* 71 (Spring/Summer 1993), p. 1.

54. L. Wingo, "Introduction: The Ideal and the Real in the Reform of Metropolitan Governance," in *Reform As Reorganization* (Washington, DC: Resources for the Future, 1974), p. 2.

55. Gerald E. Caiden, *Administrative Reform Comes of Age* (New York: Walter de Gruyter, 1991), p. 31.

56. FBIS, *Daily Report*, April 11, 1994, p. 31.

57. Ibid.

58. Collins and Nixson, "Public Sector Management," p. 380.

59. Ibid.

60. The *Chongsan-ri* method is an on-the-sport management method developed by Kim Il Sung in February 1960 during a visit to the Chongsan-ri Cooperative Farm in South Pyungan Province. Byoung-Lo Philo Kim, *Two Koreas*, pp. 229-31.

61. FBIS, *Daily Report*, June 27, 1993.

62. Collins and Nixson, "Public Sector Management," p. 380.

63. Shirk, *Political Logic*, p. 149.

64. FBIS, *Daily Report*, October 30, 1993.

65. Ibid.

66. FBIS, *Daily Report*, November 6, 1993; and *Yonhap*, November 6, 1993.

67. Moon Yong Huh, "Prospects in 1994," p. 21.

68. FBIS, *Daily Report*, January 10, 1994, p. 13, and May 6, 1994, p. 18.

69. Je Kyoon Park, "Some Changes in the North Korean Economic Structure," *Dong-A Ilbo*, March 15, 1994, p. 3; and FBIS, *Daily Report*, March 15, 1994, p. 36.

70. FBIS, *Daily Report*, December 8, 1993, pp. 22-23.

71. *Chungang Ilbo*, December 9, 1993, p. 4; and FBIS, *Daily Report*, December 9, 1993, p. 28.

72. Chang, "Political Reform in China," p. 121.

73. Nicholas Eberstadt, "Can the Two Koreas Be One?" *Foreign Affairs*, Winter 1992/93, p. 154.

74. Hyun Joon Chun, "Kim Jong Il's Power Base," *Mal* (Seoul, in Korean) 89 (November 1993), pp. 68-75.

NORTH KOREA

- ✪ National Capital
- ◎ Provincial Capital
- • City
- ▬ International Boundary
- — Provincial Boundary
- — Demarcation Line
- ▬ Demilitarized Zone
- ⬇ Primary Ports

0   25   50   75 km
0   25   50 mi

CHINA

Tumen
Namyang
Chongsong
Unggi (Sunbong)
Hoeryong
Musan
Najin
Linjiang
Samjiyon
Ch'ongjin
Chasong
Hamgyong-bukdo
Orang
Sinp'a
Hyesan
Hapsu
Manp'o
Nangnim
Yanggang-do
Kanggye
Kilchu
P'ungsan
Chagang-do
Kojang
Yongnim
Hamgyong-namdo
Pyoktong
Kimch'aek
Dandong
Taegwan
Changjin-up
Iwon
Tanch'on
Sinuiju
P'yongan-bukdo
Unsan
Huich'on
Oro
Sinch'ang
Hongwon
Kusong
Taehung
Chongju
Pakch'on
Kujang-up
Hamhung
Kaech'on
Pukch'ang
Hungnam
Sunch'on
Yodok
Yonghung
Hwajin-ni
Sain-ni
Yankdok
Wonsan
Onch'on
P'yongyang
Majon-ni
Namp'o-si
Namp'o
P'yongyang-si
Yonsan
Kosan
T'ongch'on
Sinch'on
Hwanghae-bukdo
Kangwon-do
Kosong
Changyon-up
Hwanghae-namdo
Sariwon
Sep'o
Ich'on
P'yonggang
Ongjin
Haeju
P'yongsan
Kaesong-si
Kaesong

Sea of Japan
(Eastern Sea)

Korea Bay

Yellow Sea
(Western Sea)

✪ Seoul

SOUTH KOREA

42°
40°
38°
36°
128°
126°
130°

Yalu
Tumen
Sodu-su
Puktae-ch'on
Changjin-gang
Songch'on-gang
Taedong-gang
Nam-gang
Imjin-gang
Bukhan-gang

Chapter 6

An Assessment of United States-DPRK Relations: Lessons for the Future

Mark P. Barry

United States relations with the Democratic People's Republic of Korea (DPRK) over the past decade have seen gradual but important changes that reflect an adjustment to the realities of the post-cold war era.[1] These changes would have been less likely without the dramatic transformations in the global strategic environment brought about by Soviet reforms and the demise of the Soviet state. Moreover, the DPRK has made extraordinary use of the nuclear issue as a means of attracting the attention of top American policymakers and engaging the United States diplomatically. From 1987 to 1994, the issue of North Korea in U.S. foreign policy rose from near invisibility (other than as the perennial enemy across the DMZ) to a major crisis that at times seemed headed for war. Because of the rising prominence of the nuclear issue, North Korea was propelled onto the world stage as a long-neglected problem with which the world, led by the United States and its allies, had to finally come to terms.

The Emergence of Two Schools of Thought

Contemporary United States-DPRK relations are shaped by a complex array of interactive factors; however, two essential schools of thought

Mark P. Barry is a legislative research analyst in the Arizona House of Representatives, Phoenix, and serves as a consultant to the Summit Council for World Peace in Washington.

regarding recent U.S. policy toward the North have been evident. These schools favored engagement or isolation of (even confrontation) with the North. As U.S. ambassador to South Korea (ROK), James T. Laney, recently observed, "American policy [toward North Korea] is shaped out of a collage of various sectors of opinions and some are more impatient than others."[2] There are multiple inputs into this process, from within and from outside the U.S. administration, and from the regional actors in East Asia. Moreover, for most of this period, no uniform consensus emerged as to either the precise nature of the North Korean nuclear program or whether to put emphasis more on carrot than stick. But from these multiple influences and forces shaping U.S. policy toward the DPRK, what clearly emerged, intensified but not precipitated by the nuclear issue, were distinctive softer- and harder-line schools urging the contrasting approaches of engagement or isolation of the North (though these schools themselves shift and evolve over time).

On the surface, from the American viewpoint, the global U.S. concern of nonproliferation appeared to be the dominant factor driving recent United States-DPRK relations. Moreover, an overlay was the impact of the forty-year-old Mutual Security Treaty between the United States and the ROK, a consequence of which is the presence of 37,000 American troops in South Korea. Both of these are fundamental U.S. security interests. Related as well were the influence of institutional ties between the ROK and the United States, and the influences of bureaucratic politics and institutional political cultures within each government. Communication of intent and the prevailing tone of interaction in a given period were factors as well. And of course, in the background, are the historical misfortunes of the division of Korea after the Japanese occupation and the Korean War. What also bears examination is the role played by deeply felt and deeply buried historical antagonisms, resentments, grievances, and fears harbored over the years by the United States and the DPRK. This residual hostility is what appears to be more fundamentally driving the development of United States-DPRK relations than most of the above factors. While national interests themselves played their ever-present roles, this relationship, frozen in cold war antagonism, has been also greatly influenced by emotional, attitudinal, and perceptual factors.

What distinguishes the emotional/perceptual factor is that it has significantly influenced many of the other factors, such as bureaucratic politics, institutional political cultures, and certainly the prevailing interactive tone; it was usually not visible but helped shape the more visible causative factors.

Up through the mid- to late 1980s, the cold war perspective or school predominated in discussions of U.S. policy toward North Korea. A notable exception was Edward Olsen of the Naval Postgraduate School, whose writings in the early 1980s urged the United States to begin some process of reconciliation with the North.[3] In some ways Olsen's works forecasted a trend that would emerge in the post-Seoul Olympics environment, which coincided with the era of Soviet reform under Gorbachev. Immediately before 1987, and then again in late 1988, most analysts did not consider modification of long-established U.S. policy toward North Korea because of the close Soviet-DPRK military relationship as well as two incidents of North Korean state terrorism (in 1983 and 1987). Beginning with Assistant Secretary of State for East Asian and Pacific Affairs Gaston Sigur's landmark speech in July 1987, in which the United States moderated its tone toward the DPRK, and then resuming with the December 1988 start of United States-DPRK dialogue in Beijing at the political counselor level, the environment permitted in 1989–90 a more outspoken school in favor of increased contact and improved communication and relations with North Korea. This was partly a reflection of the regional success of the ROK's *Nordpolitik* as well as the effect of steady improvement in U.S.-Soviet relations upon the global political scene. By July 1990, Sigur himself, then a private citizen who had recently visited the North, suggested before the House Subcommittee on Asian and Pacific Affairs that the United States take specific steps to demonstrate sincere interest in improving relations, including amending the U.S. trade embargo to allow telecommunications with the DPRK and inviting higher-ranking DPRK leaders to the United States for informal discussions.[4] While the nuclear issue then only played a small part in that congressional hearing, the committee print was nonetheless later titled *Korea: North-South Nuclear Issues*. That symbolized a turning point, for even in the midst of the rapid changes then involving the two Koreas and their neighbors, the nuclear issue from 1990 on only gained ground in policy-making attention. The two schools, characterized by a softer versus a tougher approach, became identified less by their relative suspicion or trust of North Korea's willingness to open up or freeze its nuclear program than by their broader disposition on the appropriateness of improving the overall United States-DPRK relationship, indeed of engagement versus isolation. Much was said in the press and journals about how dangerous the North's nuclear program was, but seldom were the underlying political problems and issues of building trust between the two countries candidly addressed.

The cold war posture of the contemporary hardline school is characterized by an overall view of North Korea as ominous and a tendency to see it in worst-case scenario terms. The past ten years have also been a time of dwindling U.S. defense budgets as the cold war wound down. Hardline views can in some ways be explained not only by the difficulties of transitioning from the cold war perspective, but also by the desire to protect defense budgets from further cuts and to demonstrate a perceived need to shore up the defense capabilities of South Korea. This school sometimes conveyed a crisis situation, particularly as exemplified in the first six months of 1994. However, it should be noted that although conservatives in the United States and the ROK tended to have similar interests, there were occasions when the two countries themselves stood at odds. At times, there was across-the-board resentment in the South that the United States was dictating policy to Seoul, involving it in issues not corresponding directly to the national interest, and undermining ROK sovereignty. Conversely, the United States would be taken aback by occasional wholesale South Korean shifts to the right, such as occurred at the November 1993 United States-ROK summit, after the July 1994 death of Kim Il Sung, and on the occasions when Seoul has used undemocratic means to crack down on protests against its northern policy.

Because of lack of progress on inter-Korean nuclear inspections and increasing International Atomic Energy Administration (IAEA) suspicions about the North's nuclear program, the isolation/confrontation school was largely ascendant from late 1992 until the DPRK announced its intention to withdraw from the NPT in March 1993. This was a crucial opening for the engagement school, which urged decisive U.S. action to negotiate directly with the North to keep it in the NPT system. This trend reached a high point in June and July 1993 when the first two rounds of United States-DPRK dialogue were held. But again, as virtually no progress came from these two rounds, and as the North evidenced enormous difficulty in dealing and complying with the IAEA (and as the United States played little effective mediating role between the two), a tense atmosphere built up that peaked in early June 1994, just prior to former President Jimmy Carter's visit to Pyongyang. The Carter visit was another opportunity for moderates in the United States to step in, but in South Korea, hardliners mounted a counteroffensive upon Kim Il Sung's death just three weeks later. However, U.S. agreements with the DPRK in August and October aligned the Clinton administration with moderates to forge an accord despite Seoul's serious misgivings and apprehensions.

Defining who represented each school both within and outside the administration was not always a cut and dried matter; what was clearest was only that there were consistently two distinctive schools of thought, but their boundaries were often diffuse. While in a larger sense, the State Department represented more moderate views compared to Defense, tougher views also emerged from senior State officials compared to working level ones; moreover, as one security analyst pointed out, much of the Clinton administration approach toward North Korea had its origins in early 1993 in the Office of the Secretary of Defense (OSD) under the late Secretary Les Aspin.[5] Certain key figures advocating a softer line toward the North, like Rep. Stephen Solarz or Dr. William J. Taylor, Jr., shifted later to the hardline camp (in late 1991 and mid-1994, respectively) due to the course of the nuclear issue. Other figures like Selig Harrison among moderates and Paul Wolfowitz among conservatives maintained consistent positions (although, even here, Wolfowitz is considered the author of President Bush's 1991 program to withdraw tactical nuclear weapons worldwide —including from the ROK—which was a major U.S. contribution to peninsular developments). The Heritage Foundation seemed more on the right on the North Korean nuclear issue and the Carnegie Endowment more on the left, but interesting shifts occurred: Heritage's Richard V. Allen, one of the North's toughest critics, by 1994 came to advocate a variation of a package deal with the DPRK, while Carnegie's resident nuclear expert, Leonard Spector, often sounded very skeptical and conservative. Of anyone, journalists were most consistent in their positions, particularly on the right, such as Lally Weymouth, Charles Krauthammer and William Safire. But in the day-to-day unfolding of events on United States-DPRK policy and the nuclear issue, there was never a doubt that definitive moderate and hardline schools were in earnest competition, both within the administration and in the public arena.

What best characterized the opposing views of the engagement and isolation schools were their respective attitudes about the uses of coercive measures against the DPRK, up to and including military force. If even economic sanctions against the North were understood to increase the chances of war, then clearly one side saw the avoidance of war as the paramount U.S. interest, while the other saw it as a potentially necessary and valid means of preventing even more frightening scenarios through the global proliferation of nuclear weapons and materials. What was surprising, however, was the ease with which the harder-line school favored sanctions (acknowledged as the beginning of the road to ever more coercive measures) and did not rule out the devastating consequences if in response the North were to attack Seoul.[6] The engagement school saw a second Korean War as tantamount to the general conflagration that the hardliners were trying to avoid by maintaining the sanctity of the NPT system; as the former U.S. ambassador to the ROK, Donald Gregg, observed, fighting a war to preserve the NPT is like burning a village in Vietnam to save it. Former President Jimmy Carter expressed this succinctly when he said upon his return from Pyongyang in June 1994, "The administration has said that there was no crisis. I thought there was an impending crisis, and now the crisis is over."[7] There was an enormous gap at the time in perception between hard- and soft-liners as to whether the United States might have come close to war with North Korea. One view was that the problem was all the North's making and if it needed pressure to respond properly then so be it; the other view was that because of a fundamental animus against the North, the administration was avoiding direct talks at the highest level with the DPRK to solve the nuclear issue, and no alternatives were available to prevent escalation toward war.[8]

U.S. policy toward the DPRK is a complex issue, with many inputs from allies and neighboring nations concerned with Korea, divergent views within the administration on how to handle it (especially with its intricate relationship with nonproliferation policy); and it was made no easier by nearly fifty years of a near total absence of relations. Yet, over the past ten years, if anything, the two clearly defined schools of thought were always evident.[9] The simplicity of this division stood in sharp relief to its complexity. This held to the signing of the Agreed Framework in October 1994, at which time the fundamental issues on engagement with the DPRK and halting the North's nuclear program were settled in principle.

Part of the complexity of U.S. policy toward the DPRK was that, rightly or wrongly, it became the domain within the administration of nonproliferation experts rather than the Asian regional bureau. In the end, this worked out successfully in the Agreed Framework, but it was cause for concern up until the Carter visit to North Korea in 1994, and it was sometimes referred to as a hijacking of America's Korea policy by nonproliferation people. Moreover, a common complaint by Asia specialists both in and out of government was that policymakers and the media tended to discount (or even put down) the specialists' views and listen only to the views of policy generalists whose knowledge of Korea was extremely thin. The import of this complaint is that a solution to the nuclear issue not altogether different from that in the Agreed Framework could have been arrived at much earlier and without the 1993 NPT withdrawal crisis and 1994 Yongbyon reactor refueling crisis by paying greater attention to the views of Korea experts.

One final distinction, as Ambassador Laney noted, is that the isolationist school often had better access to the press and networked very effectively among those with shared interests to get its point across.[10] Because of the tremendous media emphasis on North Korea as a threat, it was an easier task to gain a hearing for views that urged getting tough than for views that urged restraint and patience. Also, the two schools did not simply cut vertical divisions, such as between institutions or scholarly communities, but cut horizontal divisions between generations, particularly in the U.S. government. This division posed bureaucratic problems in the carrying out of policy toward the DPRK in the Bush and Clinton administrations, especially in the State Department.

Problems in the United States-DPRK Relationship

Historically, North Korea has been one of the United States' most irreconcilable foes. Relations began frigid in 1945 when it became apparent the Soviets had no intention of allowing an independent, unified Korea. The Korean War turned the United States and the DPRK into utterly hostile, implacable enemies, a state of affairs which did not significantly change during the cold war years. Indeed, the shifts in United States-DPRK relations in the late 1980s were only made possible by the fundamental changes in Soviet foreign policy and the character of the Soviet regime.

Yet, full reconciliation and normalization will require eradicating the legacy of hatred, animosity, and fear which was the permanent feature of the cold war period. While a difficult process for both countries, coming to terms with the resentments and grievances of each is the fundamental starting point. Outwardly, positive, substantive steps can be taken (such as enunciated in the Agreed Framework on freezing the DPRK nuclear program and outlining a course toward normalization), but even that effort can come to naught without a deliberate and fundamental national decision to forgive (or at least forget) the past.[11] The process of the recent establishment of U.S. diplomatic relations with Vietnam indicates that a great deal of soul-searching had been done to bring that about.

The fundamental American interest in Northeast Asia is the maintenance of peace and stability—in a region of crucial economic, political, and military importance, containing three world powers (Russia, China, and Japan) and two rivals for legitimacy in Korea. The United States has long-maintained mutual security treaties with both Japan and the Republic of Korea, with several tens of thousands of troops stationed in each. In the case of the ROK, since 1954 the U.S. aim has been to deter aggression by the North through the American commitment to militarily aid the South in the event of attack, not precluding the use of tactical or strategic nuclear weapons. Given North Korean behavior even in the 1980s, notably acts of state terrorism against the ROK and the particularly close DPRK-USSR military ties in that decade, a sudden North Korean attack upon the South was never hard to imagine. Periods of slight warming in North-South relations, such as in 1985, would be instantly undermined by an outburst of terrorism from the North, leading to the understandably pervasive feeling of long standing: pure distrust of Pyongyang's motives, whether its acts are seen as calculated or "unpredictable" (they are in fact quite rational if not always competent). In this sense, North Korea is the ultimate pariah state—not only an outcast, excluded by the international community, but a society whose leadership thinking and decisionmaking are almost impregnable to Western understanding and whose sources of behavior are apparently derived from an utterly antithetical value system.

North Koreans can be unfathomable as to their intentions and what makes them tick, but our image of the North has long been that as the world's "last Stalinist state," the pinnacle of twentieth-century totalitarianism, the incarnation of Orwell's *1984*. North Korea appears an anachronism on the post-cold war landscape, and U.S. policy toward the DPRK has reflected long-held dispositions and assumptions that look equally as odd today. The United States first and foremost regards North Korea as the foe it could not defeat in the Korean War, in which over 50,000 Americans died, and with whom it technically remains in a state of war. Americans recall the seizure of the *U.S.S. Pueblo* in 1968 and the ax-murder of American soldiers in Panmunjom in 1976. They remember the Rangoon bombing of the ROK cabinet in 1983 and the blowing up of the Korean Airlines jet in 1987—state terrorism directed at the ROK. Americans' first reaction is that the North Koreans are fundamentally belligerent, easily capable of being vicious killers, who can be trusted under no circumstances. Moreover, North Korean rhetoric, especially since the Korean War, has been extremely hostile and vitriolic toward the United States; the United States could not help but reflect back some of the hostility it received, and certainly it justified the constant high state of alert of U.S. troops in the ROK. Given the consistently acrimonious history of relations, it is little wonder that the United States would come to harbor deep resentment, distrust, and fear toward the North. Visitors to Pyongyang have sensed an underlying (although not necessarily overt) animosity and contempt in North Koreans towards Americans that for many justifies one's worst-case assumptions.

The main long-standing U.S. grievance toward North Korea remains its history of unremitting hostility toward Washington. While this has abated over recent years (much DPRK invective has been reserved for Seoul), it is a forty-year legacy not easily forgotten. The Korean War—in contrast to the more recent Vietnam War—remains a very bitter memory to older Americans. One reason is that it was the first American war which achieved only limited objectives despite three years of bloody warfare. The war remains unresolved in that, although an armistice has kept the peace for over forty years, a peace treaty has yet to be signed formally ending the conflict.

Americans' image of North Korea is of both a hostile pariah state and, as Secretary of State Warren Christopher put it, a society "caught in kind of a time warp. It is the most isolated country in the world, unmoved by the winds of change that have swept the region."[12] It is hard to find a modern-day comparison, a point of reference or model to explain the character of the North Korean state and its society. U.S. negotiators with the DPRK readily admit that they indeed know very little about decisionmaking in North Korea and can only presume what its interests and values are. This vacuum of knowledge does not prevent successful diplomacy, but it certainly is an inhibiting factor. While North Korean diplomats attempt to engage Western diplomats in terms more or less according with standard diplomatic practice, this does not mitigate their "time warp" image. North Korea's isolation obviously means it is trying to preserve something, and we seldom see that as anything more than an oppressive totalitarianism—that the North Korean elite is simply trying to preserve its power and survive, nothing more. This corresponds to the priorities within other authoritarian or totalitarian states but may insufficiently describe the North. Even more than the riddle, mystery, and enigma that Churchill saw in the former Soviet Union, North Korea epitomizes the unfathomable. We feel it is so alien to our culture and values that it is hard to find a common base from which to develop a relationship. Fortunately, it has not proven impossible.

A consequence of our image and perceptions of North Korea is both the disposition and assumption that it ought not to exist, that the solution to the problems presented by North Korea's policies (and existence) is simply the collapse or dissolution of the state, followed by its absorption by South Korea. These notions are driven less by logic than by our underlying outlook. The DPRK is so despised and so antithetical to our culture and values that its reform is presupposed (tacitly if not openly) impossible; therefore, for a society already in economic distress with almost no friends, and small enough to be of lesser geopolitical consequence, the best solution seems in fact for North Korea to no longer exist. While this has not been the *de jure* policy of the United States, the ROK, or any other country, it has been much more a latent, if not always conscious *de facto* policy practiced by both. Hatred and contempt for North Korea run so high in South Korea, for example, that upon the death of Kim Il Sung, despite an historic agreement days prior for a North-South summit meeting with him, the ROK (unlike the United States and the United Nations) refused to offer condolences, put its military on high alert, publicized Soviet documents blaming Kim for starting the Korean War, and punished publishers, professors, and students for any expressions of condolence or sympathy for the North. Under the circumstances this was not a logical or beneficial policy for the ROK if improvement in inter-Korean relations were its utmost objective. It was, however, a gut reaction, at least of entrenched conservative forces in the South, who saw this unexpected time of leadership transition as a ripe opportunity to promote DPRK instability; in effect, these forces were powerful enough to tie the hands of the Kim Young Sam administration.[13] Yet, such strongly negative reactions towards the North have been plainly evident in the United States and among elements of the Clinton administration as well.

North Korea has many long-held enemies: historically Japan, certainly South Korea, but in its 47-year history, it has harbored a special animosity toward the United States. First of all, North Korea inherited from the Soviet occupation forces the cold war hostility that Stalin held for the Americans after 1945. During Stalin's lifetime, Kim Il Sung shared the views of Stalin and Mao toward the United States, but the 1950–53 Korean War was a special experience for North Korea that neither elder communist leader could share. North Korea's losses in physical devastation exceeded those of South Korea. The difference was that North Korea was the target of a million bombing sorties over the vast majority of its land surface, and no North Korean needed an explanation for who was responsible. In that era, South Koreans were especially seen as mere American surrogates, propped up by U.S. military and economic power. Thus, the concept of America as utterly villainous and barbarous was not based on propaganda alone (although certainly that has been exploited to the maximum) but on the evidence and consequences of the U.S. war effort to destroy North Korea. Even with the massive influx of Chinese forces to assist the North, the United States nearly succeeded. Middle-aged North Koreans, who were but children during the war, cannot forget what devastation America wrought (whether or not they realize that their country unleashed the war to begin with).

As convenient as it is for an isolated society like North Korea to have an ever-present enemy, for forty years it took little convincing that the United States was enemy number one; and an enemy, in the communist and *Juche* dialectic tradition, should be hated. Since the Korean War, the United States, by the presence of its troops in the ROK, has been characterized as an occupying force with a will to remain permanently in order to maintain its hegemony in Korea and Japan (although today, with uncertainties about Japanese and Chinese power, the United States is more likely seen by the DPRK as a regional stabilizing force, albeit one to be reduced in size). Thus, on the foundation of Stalinist-instilled communist-solidarity hatred for the American "imperialists," the Korean War permanently etched the perceived villainy of the United States into the minds of the North Korean populace—with no small help from the DPRK regime itself.

The enormity of the resentment and hatred toward America cannot be easily grasped. It has been instilled in North Korean young even of pre-school age, who are given toy rifles and bayonets in class and taught to stab cardboard cut-outs of American soldiers. Even North Korean postage stamps have depicted Korean People's Army soldiers killing GIs with fitting slogans. Manipulation of this hatred certainly has had its utility in maintaining a tightly controlled and highly mobilized state. But this indoctrination, along with general North Korean xenophobia and distrust, make it extraordinarily difficult for the DPRK to attempt to develop a qualitatively better relationship with the United States. While the relatively younger generation of technocrats said to be the mainstay of new North Korean leader Kim Jong Il may be more flexible and creative in its attitudes toward the United States than the founding generation, they are by no means liberals. They have little fondness for the United States, but changed geopolitical realities in the region since 1990, as well as the North's worsening economic situation, have led to dramatic DPRK efforts to gain U.S. attention, respect, and political and economic benefits through manipulation of the nuclear issue. The North likely realizes that even to do nothing is to do something; it cannot make time stand still but must act.

Thus, today, the DPRK indeed wrestles with its own image and grievances against the United States in the hope that eventually the United States, which it sees as key to an overall improvement of its diplomatic and external economic relations, will accord it due legitimacy and knock down the international barriers preventing the DPRK from receiving the trade, aid, and investment it needs to survive and develop. It exhorts the United States, in the meantime, not to impose its own values on the North.

The Role Played by the Nuclear Issue

Public awareness of North Korea in the last few years has focused almost exclusively on the controversies over its nuclear program. In the public mind, North Korea has been equated with the nuclear issue. But this has led to the perception that the United States-DPRK relationship is only about the nuclear issue, a narrow way to look at a very multifaceted problem. Unfortunately, the guiding motivation of recent U.S. policy toward the DPRK has largely been the sanctity of the non-proliferation system and not setting a precedent that would undermine it or begin the end of it. Thus, U.S. policy *has* treated North Korea mainly as a non-proliferation problem. It certainly is, but it is also much more, and to the extent U.S. policy has been aloof from the larger implications, it has been "handcuffed."[14] More than the sanctity of the non-proliferation system is tied into this relationship and its outcomes. Larger questions inevitably are part of the picture: peace and stability in Northeast Asia; the implications of another, more devastating Korean War; the link between immediate U.S. policy and longer-range policy facilitating Korean unification; the overall U.S. relationships with China, Russia, and Japan; and not least of all, the matter of normalizing a highly abnormal fifty-year relationship with the North. The legalistic prism of non-proliferation is too narrow to encompass this scope.

Much more has been going on in the case of North Korea's handling of the nuclear issue than simply a threat to the NPT. A lesson the North Korean nuclear problem may hold for nonproliferation policy was well expressed by security analyst Michael Mazarr.

> [T]o the extent that anything profound can be said or done in the effort to restrain proliferation, it will be based overwhelmingly on the details of the specific case, and depend only to a minor degree on broad insights about nonproliferation as an international enterprise…. To the greatest extent possible, nonproliferation should not be considered to be a discipline of its own, but should be tied closely to regional expertise.[15]

Mazarr's point was that "any strategy to avoid proliferation must be specifically tailored to individual countries and situations…. The balance between…incentives, and what they consist of, must be determined on a case-by-case basis."[16] Among the proliferation challenges the United States faces, each case is largely unique. Specific tactics more often than not cannot be transferred from one case to the other. Initiatives that work in one context might be counterproductive in another. Thus, the case of the North Korean nuclear issue best supports the argument that nonproliferation is a specific not general enterprise. Mazarr noted that a technical U.S. approach toward nonproliferation, of control and denial, combined with what even South Koreans perceive as American "hegemonism and arrogance," is inadequate.[17] The United States must recognize that the proliferator has legitimate security concerns and, thus, elements of reassurance must be appropriately combined with those of deterrence and compellence.

Mazarr concurred that U.S. policy toward the North indeed became the "literal hostage of nonproliferation directorates within the U.S. government."[18] Yet, he made a case that an unconventional approach, based more on Korean politics, might have stood a better chance in the long run of causing the North to give up its nuclear program. However, this was precluded by a demand- and sanction-oriented nonproliferation strategy which de-emphasized the regional particulars of the North Korean case. It became a symbol rather than a distinctive case. Mazarr specified that the U.S. nonproliferation approach toward the North violated several general principles applicable to the North understood by those familiar with North Korean political culture: rather than develop personal relationships and build trust (which should precede a legal agreement) the United States withheld personal contacts until substantive issues could be resolved; it threatened North Korea's existence and declared its regime was eventually doomed, thus publicly humiliating the North; it used multilateral institutions like the IAEA and the UN Security Council to pressure (and thus embarrass) the North; and the United States "almost gratuitously" condemned or condescended to North Korea in official statements.[19] This pattern was particularly true through late 1993 and in effect only dramatically changed after the Carter visit to Pyongyang.

What have received widespread public attention, especially since late 1992, are the often articulated American concerns about the implications of not stopping the North Korea nuclear program. Interestingly, administration statements have tended to be cautious and legalistic, while real U.S. fears tended to be voiced by columnists, media personalities, and retired U.S. officials.

A typical example of official expression of administration concern over North Korea was then-CIA Director R. James Woolsey's testimony before the Senate Select Committee on Intelligence in early 1994. He cited three critical challenges that North Korea presents: (1) its effort to develop a nuclear capability (he estimated that the North could have already produced enough plutonium for at least one nuclear weapon); (2) North Korea's war preparations program, including improvements in military capabilities and efforts to bring its society and economy to a heightened state of military readiness; and (3) North Korea's export to the Middle East of missiles which can be made nuclear-, chemical-, or biological-capable.[20] While Woolsey's presentation was broad and inclusive, he was typical of administration officials in usually limiting official concern to North Korean nuclear activities and the issue of its compliance with the NPT and IAEA safeguards, and did not publicly dwell on U.S. fears of the consequences if Pyongyang were not stopped.

However, one of the best expositions of U.S. interests regarding the North Korean nuclear issue was written by Arnold Kanter, former undersecretary of state for political affairs under President Bush, and the highest-ranking American official ever to meet a North Korean official. He designated two kinds of American interests at stake. First, North Korean acquisition of nuclear weapons "would transform the current political and security landscape in Asia beyond recognition."[21] Obviously, DPRK nuclear weapons would dramatically increase the threat to the ROK and the U.S. forces stationed there and vastly complicate the task of defending them. Moreover, the ROK and Japan would most likely succumb to pressure to obtain nuclear weapons for themselves. China and other regional actors would also respond in ways that exacerbated the danger, and the overall result would be a vastly more unstable Asia-Pacific region. Kanter noted that North Korea is not Pakistan and recommended that our policy toward Pakistan "should be taken as little guidance and less precedent" for our policy toward the North.[22]

Although Kanter did not say so, it is implicit that the DPRK was aware of how its threat was perceived. As long as it only threatened to "go nuclear," raising the above dire possibilities, it retained tremendous leverage. But once it *actually* went nuclear, it would touch off a regional arms race that indeed *would go against its interest*. Pyongyang apparently is keenly aware of the distinction between threat and actualized threat.

Second, Kanter explained that, whatever progress the North might or might not have been making in its nuclear capability, its defiance was doing serious damage to U.S. interests. The United States could not allow the DPRK to continue to violate its nonproliferation obligations because it would set a terrible precedent. Kanter worried that, regardless of what North Korea's neighbors decided to do, the global nonproliferation regime could unravel if nations from Ukraine to Iran concluded that the international community would not stand in the way of North Korea's pursuit of nuclear weapons. He stated that "these risks and costs alone are sufficient to argue against a strategy of open-ended negotiations."[23]

Stephen Solarz—who until 1993 chaired the House Subcommittee on Asian and Pacific Affairs and whose stance on the North markedly changed after Desert Storm, as the DPRK nuclear issue arose—wrote that any analysis "must begin with a recognition that the North Korean nuclear project constitutes the most serious threat to the preservation of regional peace and global nonproliferation in the world today."[24] He cited as evidence: (1) an unconstrained North Korean nuclear program would give it the ability to stockpile dozens and eventually hundreds of nuclear weapons; (2) it would increase the risk of another conventional war in Korea, and a nuclear-capable Pyongyang would have enormous leverage to end the fighting on its terms; (3) it would make more likely a nuclear arms race in Northeast Asia; (4) it increases the chances that the ROK and Japan could become victims of a nuclear attack; and (5) it would give North Korea the capacity to earn needed foreign exchange by selling fissile material or completed nuclear weapons to other states or terrorist groups. Solarz adamantly insisted that Pyongyang's real objective was to sell nuclear weapons (and missiles) rather than use them. No better method could be found to completely devastate the global nonproliferation regime and fundamentally undermine U.S. interests.

New York Times columnist William Safire agreed with Solarz' assessment.

> What is the North's strategy? Anyone who still thinks Kim Il Sung is not trying to become a nuclear power is a fool. He is building atomic weapons to sell them to rich rogue states like Iran and Libya, thereby bolstering his shrinking economy, and to use them in forcing the South into unification on his terms.[25]

Both Solarz and Safire openly called for preparing to use the military option to take out the nuclear sites at Yongbyon. Kanter, along with his associate, former Bush national security adviser Brent Scowcroft, also called for a military option during the height of the June 1994 crisis, a surgical strike against the Yongbyon reprocessing facility. They wrote, "Pyongyang must be made to understand that if war is unavoidable, we would rather fight it sooner than later, when North Korea might have a sizable nuclear arsenal."[26]

One of the most outspoken former U.S. officials was Lawrence Eagleburger, Secretary of State in the last months of the Bush administration. He told television audiences in June,

> [I]f you look at what the world will be like five or six years from now, if we do not stop this process in North Korea, it ought to scare the pants off everybody. This is the beginning of the end of controlling the proliferation of weapons of mass destruction.... We are in the beginnings of a nuclear arms race in the Pacific.... They will be selling these things to the Iraqis and the Iranians and the Libyans, and boy, are we going to be in trouble.... It is the kind of foreign policy problem that if you don't deal with the tough situation now, you will have a much worse one some years down the road.... They're out to build a nuclear arsenal so that they can do whatever they like with it and use it to blackmail the

neighborhood.... [T]his is one [where] if in the end it is necessary to use force, we ought to use force because we simply cannot tolerate this process to continue.[27]

Eagleburger complained, as have many other critics, that the Clinton administration has been inconsistent in dealing with North Korea, sometimes threatening action and at other times being conciliatory.

One of the least discussed fears of a North Korean nuclear program, but important to consider, was voiced by the undersecretary of state for political affairs under President Johnson, Eugene Rostow. Writing on post-cold war U.S. foreign policy, he noted that if Saddam Hussein had had a deployable nuclear weapon, the United States would not have put at risk over half a million U.S. troops to force Iraq out of Kuwait in 1991; it would have been politically impossible. Rostow entertained the same fear about North Korean nuclear weapons, that despite the U.S. nuclear umbrella over the ROK and the presence of 37,000 U.S. troops, a U.S. president would not likely find the domestic support to commit U.S. soldiers into a conflict that could involve a nuclear-capable adversary.[28] This ties into Rostow's overall perspective of nonproliferation in the post-cold war world. For him, nuclear proliferation "is an urgent short-term problem that the nations must resolve together if order is to be achieved and maintained"; the future of the global balance of power will be profoundly influenced by how the state system deals with nuclear proliferation.[29] For the sake of overall global security and the maintenance of the balance of power, non-nuclear countries suspected of secretly developing nuclear weapons cannot be treated as full equals in the state system, he argued. UN Security Council Resolution 687, the basis for the 1991 cease-fire in Operation Desert Storm in the Gulf, embodies this principle; and it implies that cases of proliferation, especially by rogue states, cannot be dealt with by only peaceful diplomacy. "Military occupation, perhaps United Nations trusteeship, may well be needed in some cases to enforce the emerging rule," he added.[30] In many ways, Rostow gave legal and theoretical grounding to Secretary Eagleburger's comments above.

The Bush administration probably harbored a more skeptical attitude toward the likelihood of North Korean compliance and resolution of outstanding nuclear issues, but it in fact set the stage for the Clinton administration's successes by announcing the worldwide withdrawal of land- and sea-based U.S. tactical nuclear weapons in September 1991. This decision, not directed toward Korea *per se,* paved the way for the two inter-Korean agreements of December that year, which are dormant and unimplemented but not dead. It also took the unprecedented step of holding the first-ever high-level dialogue with the North in January 1992, albeit on a one-time basis only, as well as canceling Team Spirit exercises that year in support of North-South dialogue. When President Clinton took office a year later, he had little choice but to maintain Bush policy toward North Korea, although unfortunately this included the Bush decision to conduct Team Spirit (a decision fundamentally driven by the ROK). It was not until the North's decision to withdraw from the NPT on March 12, 1993, partially in reaction to Team Spirit, that the United States was challenged to find an appropriate and workable response to what had become a crisis in the nonproliferation system.

At this point emerged Robert Gallucci, then assistant secretary of state for political-military affairs under Bush and Clinton (later appointed ambassador-at-large), as the key official charged with negotiating a resolution of the North Korean nuclear issue. Gallucci has since characterized the U.S. approach that evolved after March 1993 as based on a principle of compartmentalization of the problems represented. While the overall goal has been a nuclear-free Korean peninsula, he said in discussing the Agreed Framework, "the subtext to that was to deal with problems which we can roughly characterize as problems that relate to the past activity of the North Koreans, the current nuclear program, and the direction that the program was headed in the future."[31] While apparently a technical approach, it was also a rational one which succeeded in avoiding a wholesale and counterproductive negative reaction and response to North Korea's seeming intransigence. The accord, fashioned after nearly a month of protracted negotiations, has been appraised on the whole as comprehensive and effective, although by no means an ideal solution to the nuclear issue. The foremost aim of the American approach was to address the future: to block North Korea's acquisition of dozens or even hundreds of nuclear weapons, that is, the North's strategic nuclear program. Second, and of nearly equal importance, was to freeze the entire DPRK program, most especially to insure that spent fuel rods in cooling ponds since June 1994 were not reprocessed and that the operational 5 mw(e) reactor was not reloaded with fresh fuel rods. The last, and certainly the most contentious issue, was transparency of the past, submitting to unprecedented IAEA special inspections of suspected waste sites.

While many, including the IAEA, are less than fully pleased with this last aspect of the agreement, it has been generally acknowledged that any DPRK agreement to submit to special inspections, even if several years off, is still far better than North Korean refusal.

Acceptance of the agreement has not been simply along partisan lines; Arnold Kanter essentially considered the October accord a good agreement, given the administration's strategic decision to use the approach it did and assuming the North complied.[32] Gallucci himself repeatedly has emphasized that North Korea has agreed to do more than is required by the NPT. Nothing in the NPT or the safeguards accord requires the DPRK to freeze its nuclear program and ultimately dismantle nuclear facilities it has been constructing over the past twenty years.[33] Moreover, the DPRK had requested an American negative security guarantee, which the United States has agreed to provide in the accord. What needs to be understood is that North Korea was never exempt from the threat of U.S. first-use of nuclear weapons; a 1978 American declaration pledging not to use nuclear weapons against any non-nuclear state party to the NPT was not meant to apply to the DPRK because of its defense alliances with the USSR/Russia and China.[34] Thus, North Korea has always stood under the threat of American first-use of nuclear weapons, well before its nuclear program achieved notoriety. This unusual circumstance, in which the North felt singled out, from a security standpoint makes understandable its long-standing demands for a non-use pledge from the United States; American acknowledgment of the request was recognition that Pyongyang had a valid security concern that could now be addressed as part of the bargain.

The seven chief criticisms of the agreement, emanating primarily from Republicans in Congress and elements in the press, are generally as follows: First, for the IAEA to wait in effect five years before the North will relent on special inspections damages the nonproliferation regime. Legally, a signatory is required to comply on demand according to the safeguards accord. Second, the nature of this agreement will encourage other states with nuclear programs in development to follow the DPRK's lead and withdraw from the NPT in search of greater benefits. The United States continues to block the sale to Iran by third countries of a light-water reactor (LWR), and Iran has already complained that it has received too little reward for its complete cooperation with the IAEA.[35] Third, North Korea is destined for collapse in the next few years, critics allege, yet the United States needlessly provides life-support through oil, LWRs, and reduced trade restrictions, not to mention the extension of unprecedented political legitimacy (which will eventually rehabilitate the DPRK as a candidate for assistance from international financial institutions). This perception is particularly strong in South Korea, despite the accord. Fourth, the United States has consistently shifted its policy, from declaring the North will not be allowed to possess nuclear weapons (e.g., November 1993) to settling for capping its program, with no assurance it will ever know if the North has produced one, two, or more devices. If it does possess even one or two low-yield devices, some observers contend that is sufficient to deter effective action by the United States and its allies in case of North Korean aggression against the South. In any case, in the end, it is alleged, the DPRK suffers no penalties from its defiance but rather reaps rewards. Fifth, the agreement leaves the DPRK nuclear program infrastructure intact for several years, allowing it later to renege on the agreement and, if possible, proceed with its program. Sixth, the agreement does not address North Korea's export of ballistic missiles, a U.S. concern almost on a par with nuclear proliferation. Finally, the agreement, critics charge, also sets the precedent of inducements—in effect, bribes—as means for maintaining the nonproliferation regime; yet this ignores how the United States has already handled the cases of *South* Korea and Ukraine.[36]

The overwhelming response to these criticisms has been that the agreement, with its imperfections, is preferable to war.[37] While this does not speak to the intrinsic strengths of the agreement—which are the reasons the president, his key advisers and his cabinet endorsed it—the warning of the possibility of a second Korean War ought not to appear rhetorical. To consider as an empty threat North Korea's assertion that imposition of sanctions was equivalent to a declaration of war would have been foolhardy. Secretary of Defense William Perry said in Senate testimony,

> ...[T]he North Koreans had clearly stated that the imposition of sanctions would be considered by them to be equivalent to a declaration of war. Many people wrote that off as rhetoric. I thought it was imprudent to consider it as pure rhetoric and that we had to take it at face value. At the same time, their rhetoric included statements like "turning Seoul into a sea of flames."[38]

As editorials in two leading newspapers pointed out, economic sanctions and military strikes would work "only at the risk of war,"[39] and the United States could not impose its will on North Korea as it could a defeated Iraq, but had to negotiate.[40] Here one must also reject the notion of "compensatory toughness": that the Clinton administration had been weak in Bosnia, Somalia, and elsewhere, and Korea was the one place to get tough.

Other analysts assert the United States conceded remarkably little, while the DPRK gave up a great deal.[41] Despite its right under the NPT, the North agreed to forgo reprocessing (which it also did in the 1991 inter-Korean denuclearization agreement, but arrangements for implementation and verification were never concluded). With U.S. technical assistance, North Korea will store its spent fuel rods, ultimately to ship them to a third country. It has agreed not to refuel or restart its 5 mw(e) reactor, to immediately cease construction of its 50 mw(e) and 200 mw(e) reactors, and to shut down and seal its huge reprocessing facility. All of the above must be done under continuous IAEA supervision. And before significant nuclear components of LWRs are delivered (in at least five years), the North must finally submit to special inspections. (It may alternatively decide to change its inventory declaration, admitting to having reprocessed more plutonium than previously declared, and perhaps avoid special inspections.) These analysts agree that the Clinton administration had originally been mistaken in insisting that transparency of the past be the first step for the North; it was later correct to insist—albeit after the Carter agreement with Kim Il Sung—that ending the DPRK strategic nuclear program, potentially capable of producing hundreds of weapons, was the far greater priority. In short, it was not only more realistic but correct for the United States to deal with the present and future first. Moreover, these analysts assert, as does the administration, that the agreement is not based on trust: if the United States detects any violation of the agreement, it will simply cut off oil deliveries, stop LWR construction, and revert to the point where it was early in 1994.

North Korea receives a supply of heavy fuel oil, amounting to 500,000 barrels annually over five years, to cover the presumed 255 mw(e) total energy production lost to freezing its nuclear program. Within ten years, it gains two LWRs capable of 2,000 mw(e) total output. However, its less tangible benefits are potentially more important, including eventual normalization of relations with the United States at the ambassadorial level, reduction (and presumed eventual termination) of economic and financial restrictions that prohibited international trade and investment, including renewed international lending to the DPRK, and a negative security assurance likely coupled with annual, and eventually permanent, cancellation of Team Spirit. In sum, what these measures potentially can do, as the United States openly acknowledges, is draw the North out of isolation and help integrate it into the political and economic mainstream of East Asia.[42] Some press reports have alleged that the administration's view, like that of South Korea, is that the DPRK will not outlast the duration of the Geneva accord and that all investment in the North will eventually come under the ROK. However, the evidence is to the contrary: the United States concluded that the DPRK regime is likely to survive over the longer term, and therefore it would be necessary to conclude a framework agreement with it. This accord does not prop up a crippled regime, but allows the DPRK to evolve at its own pace and manner into a more integrated and peaceful member of the international community.

The foremost lesson of the North Korean nuclear crisis is that DPRK motives and needs had to be discerned—and directly by U.S. diplomats, not unduly relying on Seoul's "vast experience" in dealing with the North. What the United States learned is that it could legitimately attempt to meet some of those needs and satisfactorily resolve the crisis, but it took many months of contact, both in Geneva and New York, for these realizations to prevail and manifest in concrete U.S. policy. The corollary of this lesson is that direct contact, dialogue, and negotiation on a basis of mutual respect with the DPRK had to ensue, despite the lack of diplomatic relations and the dearth of past contact. As a result, both nations are better for it, and this enhances security in the peninsula and in Northeast Asia. As U.S. Ambassador to the ROK James T. Laney said regarding North Korea in May 1995,

> Our ability to thread our way through problems that occur, and to prevent them from becoming real crises, lies in our ability to communicate with North Korea. By "communicate" I mean to understand and to make ourselves understood. The knowledge we really need to deal effectively with North Korea does not come from spies or satellites; it comes from face-to-face engagement in the diplomatic arena.[43]

Rather than the DPRK's using its nuclear program and the uncertainties behind it solely as a bargaining chip, what is far more convincing, based on a knowledge of North Korean political culture, is that it has earnestly (if not always in a subdued and reassuring manner) sought legitimacy as a nation-state. As Asian affairs analyst K. A. Namkung said,

> What the North Koreans have been asking the U.S. to do is to treat them as equals and respect their sovereignty...as a legitimate country. [Kim Il Sung] knew he was on his last leg [in June 1994] and this helps explain why his talks with President Carter went as well as they did.... There's no question in my mind but that [Kim] was trying to place his imprimatur on a negotiated solution to this not as an exchange between nuclear weapons, on the one hand, and economic benefits from the West on the other, but...a recognition of North Korean legitimacy.[44]

While not minimizing the political and economic benefits eventually to accrue to North Korea in the accord, respect and dignity mean more to the North Korean leadership than material benefit. They have sought recognition of their legitimacy and achievements as a society since 1948, in effect acknowledgment that Kim Il Sung and his *Juche* ideology are no less valuable than any other nation's founding father or guiding principles. From the North's perspective, the accord brings it a new-found legitimacy and acceptance that has eluded it over four decades, especially as Kim Jong Il commences his formal leadership; for the North, it is international acknowledgment by great powers of the achievements of its founder.

Namkung's conclusion is certainly what Jimmy Carter perceived when he visited Pyongyang in June:

> The North Koreans are not on their knees begging for economic aid from the United States, and they're not begging that the United States have diplomatic relations. They look upon themselves as a proud and respected and sovereign nation who would like to have this relationship on a mutually respectful basis because they think it would be better for the United States to have normal relations with North Korea and it would be better for North Korea to have normal relations with the United States. But they don't look upon those things as rewards or bribes to be given to them if they yield on something.... They would like to work it out...[45]

The greatest value of the Carter trip for the DPRK was indeed the legitimacy bestowed upon Kim Il Sung and his nation through the unprecedented visit of a former president of the United States. Out of that profound satisfaction, as well as the knowledge that he did not have long to live, Kim likely chose to be conciliatory to the United States through Carter. Despite the arduous months of hard bargaining over the nuclear issue with the DPRK after June 1993, the United States found a method to meet its criteria for nonproliferation and the security of Northeast Asia, as well as a means to draw the North out of isolation, while satisfying the DPRK's yearning for acknowledgment of legitimacy and respect accorded by the world's greatest power. It is a highly artful diplomatic achievement, and for it to succeed, both sides need to continue to pour their energies into negotiations for its detailed implementation, while the ROK, despite its apprehensions, needs to respect the process and find its own way to come to genuine reconciliation with the North. The June 1995 Kuala Lumpur agreement, clarifying the South Korean role in the LWR supply, is an example of continuing although hard-earned accomplishment, so are the successful activities of the Korean Peninsula Energy Development Organization (KEDO) to implement the Agreed Framework.

North Korea used the nuclear issue not merely as a bargaining chip but indeed to gain U.S. attention and to *demand* that the United States face up to its reality and give it its due. North Korea's yelling alone would not have done it, but its use of the mystery of whether it possessed nuclear weapons, the certainty that it would soon be able to produce considerably more plutonium, and its impossible-to-ignore ultimatum of NPT withdrawal forced the United States to pay attention when otherwise it would never have done so. Unmistakably, for the United States this has been an issue of nuclear proliferation, but as many Asian specialists see it, for the DPRK it has primarily been an issue of obtaining Western respect and legitimacy without compromising its sovereignty and identity. This is not to say that North Korea has had no interest in the utility of nuclear weapons—strategically, politically, and even economically. But to emphasize, as have so many writers, that North Korea developed nuclear weapons mainly to insure its survival misses a key point underscored by Namkung and Carter.[46]

The Influence and Interplay of the Republic of Korea

The DPRK cannot be considered without the ROK; however seemingly irreconcilable, they are two halves of a whole. Each is resolute, stubborn, and adamant in insisting that its way is best. Each has tried to prove it is superior to the other, but by the late 1980s Seoul had become supremely confident that it had won the competition through its *Nordpolitik* policy and economic achievements. Certainly by September 1990 these successes were a chief reason Pyongyang began its prime ministerial dialogue with Seoul, which led to the inter-Korean accords of December 1991; the North could no longer permit the South to pry away its allies and deepen its isolation. No one knows where inter-Korean relations would have gone if the nuclear issue had not arisen and put on hold potential economic exchange and a summit meeting. It was the United States which initially placed so much prominence on the nuclear issue, but eventually nonproliferation policy took on a life of its own in Seoul, not for its own sake, but as a lever that could be used against the North. The irony is that Seoul, which once wanted to delink the nuclear issue from improvement of North-South relations, was now critical and skeptical of the Agreed Framework as an only minimally acceptable agreement from a nonproliferation standpoint that did nothing to improve inter-Korean relations. This was an about-face from Seoul's outlook before early 1993, which was that nonproliferation should take a back seat to improved inter-Korean relations.

With the unexpected death of Kim Il Sung in July 1994, Seoul exploded with deep-seated emotions and hostility that had been previously submerged. The ROK government refused, and still refuses, to offer even *pro forma* condolences to the DPRK for Kim's death, yet this action along with at least modification if not abrogation of its National Security Law (which defines the North as an enemy) are the keys to meaningful progress in the North-South dialogue stipulated in the Geneva accord.[47] At the time of Kim's death, Seoul seemed to thirst for a sense of victory over the North, and that yearning outweighed the wisdom—and its public utterances—that unification by absorption was to be avoided and was an inherently disastrous proposition. Seoul has maintained until very recently that the Kim Jong Il succession was unsettled and incomplete, that his regime would not last long, and that the North after Kim's death had lost any staying power; more recently, the South alleges that the North Korean military has taken control of the DPRK and seeks to threaten the ROK as it deals with its own political turbulence. President Kim Young Sam in some ways was a prisoner of hardliners in his party, and was also ill advised; but he nonetheless quickly aligned himself with those forces which also hampered relations with the United States as it was engaged in dialogue with the North.

While it publicly denies it can be an "honest broker" in this situation, the United States clearly must play a facilitating role between the two Koreas, and at times it must be one of intercession as well. The Agreed Framework insures a U.S. role with the North while the forty-year-old United States-ROK Mutual Security Treaty insures U.S. responsibility for the South. By virtue of a ten-year commitment through KEDO toward delivering LWRs to North Korea, as well as reducing trade barriers and proceeding toward diplomatic normalization, the United States has in effect modified its long-standing policy toward Korea by taking the entire peninsula into account; the United States can no longer focus on the ROK alone. While this should not reflect on America's oft-stated "unshakable alliance" with the ROK, it does mean that the direction and pace of U.S. relations with Pyongyang must be set according to U.S. interests, not simply by deferring to Seoul; during this new period, Seoul may attempt to apply pressure on U.S. policy—as did President Kim Young Sam through interviews with U.S. media just prior to the signing of the Agreed Framework—by pleading that U.S. policy weakens its bargaining position with Pyongyang. Considering the multiple issues the United States must address with the DPRK, aside from the nuclear program—from missile exports and MIAs, to state terrorism and human rights, not to mention its conventional military build-up—it would be easy to stretch out the process of normalization. Seoul clearly does not want the United States to get ahead of it diplomatically with the North. Others argue that the United States should do the opposite—speed up that process as a means of strengthening the Geneva accord and bolstering Kim Jong Il against pro-nuclear hawks.[48]

South Korean speculation over the past two years that the North was undergoing a power struggle and/or was on the verge of collapse is analytically far off the mark and a sign of the ROK's difficulties in coming to terms with dealing with Kim Jong Il. The best evidence indicates that Kim Jong Il is firmly in control. Statements from President Kim Young Sam indicated his willingness to reschedule the postponed North-South summit meeting whenever Kim Jong Il assumed formal power. Western visitors to the DPRK indicated the pervasive feeling that the DPRK population was being very carefully prepared for Kim Jong Il's formal succession, the military perhaps playing a more overt role in social mobilization. They say the one consistent theme of North Korean media is Kim Jong Il's overwhelming presence and leadership in society, yielding the unmistakable message that Kim (often shown in footage or stills with his father) is fully in charge.

Over the long term, indisputably, the United States must be willing to midwife a process of Korean reconciliation. Scholar Manwoo Lee's observations are worth considering.

> Washington must persuade Seoul that the past American policy of doing what is best for South Korea and what is worst for North Korea is inappropriate in today's circumstances. It must make an effort to resocialize South Korea's leaders into thinking that America's new even-handed approach, building good relations with both Koreas, is the surest way to make the peninsula stable and prosperous.... The United States has helped protect South Korea for 50 years; now it is time for South Korea to pay back the debt.[49]

Russia and China are better positioned than previously to support that process by virtue of their new-found ties with Seoul as well as long-standing ties with Pyongyang. Japan is likely to establish full diplomatic relations with the North before the United States does. Complete regional cross-recognition could be finally accomplished by 1996–97. But the U.S. role is as leader of this process; witness the central American role in creating KEDO. And the United States must find ways to lead Seoul in the desired direction, if necessary offering assurances to avoid straining the alliance, while simultaneously reeling in the DPRK in a manner that steadily builds trust and confidence.

Long-Range U.S. Policy toward the Koreas

The Agreed Framework between the United States and the DPRK provides a general roadmap of how relations will develop between the two countries. In November 1994, a delegation led by an Arms Control and Disarmament Agency official traveled to the DPRK as the first Americans to inspect the Yongbyon nuclear complex, including the spent fuel rods in the cooling pond. Since that time, through successive visits, the United States has assessed the condition of the fuel rods and is assisting North Korea in their permanent storage. In December 1994, delegations from each side met in Washington to discuss opening of liaison offices (the United States reciprocated with a visit to Pyongyang in February); a few technical issues remain to date, but the opening of offices may occur in 1997. In spring 1995, the United States, the ROK, and Japan became the founding members of the KEDO consortium, which according to the Agreed Framework and Kuala Lumpur agreement will arrange the supply contract with the

DPRK for the two LWRs. In January 1995, the first shipment of 50,000 tons of heavy oil was delivered by the United States to the North, although a small amount was improperly diverted to industrial rather than energy uses; it also had to be paid for out of a Pentagon emergency fund. On January 21, the United States lifted a few trade restrictions against the North, allowing direct telecommunications (restored in April) and U.S. news bureaus to be set up in Pyongyang, and American steel manufacturers to import from the DPRK the critical mineral magnesite. However, the major restrictions of the Trading with the Enemy Act, Export Administration Act, and other laws remain in effect. According to an unclassified State Department internal memo:

> While many of the current U.S. restrictions in the DPRK may as a legal matter be terminated or relaxed by the executive branch in the exercise of its own discretion without legislation or the need to consult Congress (e.g., the establishment of diplomatic relations, lifting of the 25-mile limit on travel by DPRK representatives to the U.N., the trade embargo), the administration's freedom of movement is circumscribed by a complex web of potentially applicable legislation. Moreover, any such effort would receive the closest scrutiny—and possible resistance—from Congress.[50]

Full diplomatic relations will likely take considerably longer and depend on Pyongyang's degree of cooperation with the IAEA, the ROK, and the United States. Other vital issues of concern to the United States will be raised, including DPRK missile sales to the Middle East, military confidence-building measures, and recovery of Korean War American MIAs; for the North, the primary issues will be ending the Team Spirit and other joint United States-ROK military exercises, negotiating a peace treaty to replace the armistice (or at least a new peace mechanism), and a partial (not necessarily complete) withdrawal of U.S. forces from South Korea. The ROK does not want United States-DPRK relations to go ahead of North-South relations, and in truth would prefer they lag far behind. On the other hand, observers like Selig Harrison urge the United States to quickly move toward full normalization of relations as the best means of reinforcing the agreement.[51] The issue of replacing the Military Armistice Commission (MAC) with a formal peace treaty or "peace guarantee mechanism" is highly contentious: the United States insists it is a matter between North and South, while Pyongyang says it concerns the United States and the DPRK because Seoul refused to sign the 1953 armistice. In reality, the

United States and China, both signatories, if not Russia and Japan as well, will have to get involved as guarantors. Such is the principle behind the joint United States-ROK offer on April 16, 1996, of four-power peace talks involving the DPRK and China. To date, the North has neither accepted nor rejected the offer—a telling sign of how long talks could drag on once begun.

Of course, all of the above is predicated on continued DPRK co-operation and compliance, but the evidence to date is largely reassuring. Even the December 1994 incident of returning a downed U.S. Army helicopter pilot who strayed across the DMZ worked out well. Only in the area of North-South dialogue has the North balked, saying it sensed insincerity in Seoul's November 1994 offer of formal government-to-government economic cooperation and because Pyongyang remains offended by the South's refusal to offer condolences and its earlier taunts that the U.N. Security Council would impose sanctions upon it. "We have a lot of accounts to settle with Kim Young Sam," declared a Korean Central News Agency report, which called Seoul's economic overture a "treacherous confrontation policy."[52] Of course, North Korean objections are also partly delaying tactics and a stalling maneuver, aimed at putting off dialogue until political conditions are deemed more propitious; but there is a genuine lack of trust by Pyongyang that ROK behavior has thus far not assuaged. Nonetheless, in June and July 1995, North and South did hold formal senior-level contacts on ROK provision of rice to ease what the North has now publicly admitted is a serious food shortage; some substantial rice deliveries were made but then suspended. The rice dialogue ended and Seoul now refused to send rice unless Pyongyang meets its conditions. Meanwhile, North Korea has been wracked with two successive summers (1995 and 1996) of severe floods, which caused considerable destruction and sharply reduced its crop output. In a first, Pyongyang asked the United Nations for humanitarian aid, and the U. N. World Food Program responded, led by U.S. donations, with food aid to help stem what is increasingly seen as a severe nationwide food shortage bordering on famine.

North Korea's strategy, as explained by K. A. Namkung, is to protect itself against the ROK by drawing in the United States and Japan until it feels ready to substantively engage with the South. Thus, Pyongyang's policy is to emphasize the United States first, then Japan, and only later South Korea. Its priority is maintaining domestic stability at a time of regime transition. The North still notes the South's characterizing either the DPRK leadership picture as unsettled or North Korean military and economic strength as weak, suggesting the country does not have much time left.[53] These are regarded as taunts and indications of insincerity, not as a basis for serious dialogue.

The return of Republican control to both houses of the U.S. Congress in 1994 did not dangerously threaten the Agreed Framework. There remain a strong anti-DPRK bias in Congress and considerable misgivings about the agreement among most Republicans and some Democrats. However, in 1995, Republicans passed only a few nonbinding resolutions meant to toughen the president's policy. No one in Congress has seen fit to overturn the Agreed Framework itself or to propose renegotiating it (despite campaign rhetoric from candidate Robert Dole). At worst, Congress has threatened to reduce funding of U.S. assistance to permanent storage of the North's spent fuel rods and the United States' contribution to KEDO (which is to supply continuing oil shipments). The purse is the only area where Congress can effectively slow down United States-DPRK ties. Because the Agreed Framework is not a treaty but was achieved through executive discretion, the Senate is not required by law to approve it.

One of the most important things President Clinton can do is to instruct the American directors serving on the boards of the World Bank, the Asian Development Bank, and other international financial institutions not to object to commencing a relationship with the DPRK; rather than interfering, the United States should now encourage such ties.[54] At some point, North Korea will apply for new credit despite its massive defaulted debt. Specifically, the North should be permitted to engage in a debt buyback program whereby it can repurchase its obligations at a fraction of face value.[55] By so doing, the DPRK can tap the extensive financing necessary to rebuild its economy; moreover, it will enable any future projects to develop at a faster rate by being freed of numerous legal problems from creditors who witness new inflows of capital to the North. However, the largest sources of economic and financial support would be bilateral: Japan and Taiwan are prime prospects; South Korea indeed may be last in line if current trends continue.

Further relaxation of U.S. trade restrictions (which the North complains is now long overdue since the signing of the Agreed Framework) is not merely a gesture but can serve the important purpose of promoting the building up of the DPRK economy so that unification can be stable, peaceful, and with the least economic and human cost.

The actual U.S. contribution may be minuscule, but the worldwide effect of the termination or relaxation of the numerous U.S. restrictions against the DPRK would send a go-ahead signal to other nations, such as Japan, Germany, and France, who are more likely to make substantial investments in the North over time. This is not to say U.S. businesses are uninterested: on the contrary, the American Chamber of Commerce in Seoul is ready to send a delegation to Pyongyang as soon as federal regulations are modified, and already representatives of General Motors, MCI, and other major businesses and foundations have made pilot visits to the North. Moreover, some U.S. scholars recommend an international coalition of non-governmental organizations (NGOs) and foundations under American leadership, to facilitate North Korea's entry into the world community. NGO involvement could be a means of leading the way for their respective governments.

Most important for the United States is to maintain a policy of engagement with the DPRK, not one of isolation. Isolation is a poor policy, which fails to build trust, risks constant peninsular crises, and could produce an unwanted, sudden unification enormously costly in human and financial terms. The worst the United States can do, as it has too often in the past, is to drop Korea from its radar screen once it is off the front pages. Korea remains a potentially explosive region that ought not be managed only by the State Department mid-level bureaucracy and KEDO. Yet, the absence of a true coordinator for Korea policy (exemplified by Ambassador-at-Large Robert Gallucci's shift of responsibility in mid-1995 to Bosnia and subsequent retirement, with no one of his rank appointed to fill his shoes for Korea) is alarming, given the evident continuing need for a key U.S. official to bring coherence to inter-agency deliberations on Korea and authoritatively negotiate with the DPRK.

If the United States has determined that the DPRK is likely to survive for the foreseeable future, despite the leadership change and severe economic difficulties—as it appears to have, by concluding the Agreed Framework—then it is in the interests of the United States, the ROK, Japan, and other American allies to assist the DPRK in economic development and modernization as stepping-stones toward unification. The DPRK must be allowed to evolve into a more benign state that can greatly reduce its threat to Northeast Asia. There is no better way to assist it in doing so than by allowing it to engage in Chinese-style economic reforms, *carried out in its own manner and at its own pace.* (After all, North Korea is not China.) Reunification itself must be gradual, taking into account the particular needs of North Korea—which for years to come may not wish to abandon the respect for, pride in, and even worship of its founder, Kim Il Sung, yet may become flexible enough to accede to a rudimentary form of confederation and coexistence with the ROK for a substantial period of time. With Western and ROK patience and support, the DPRK can be equitably reunified with the South; the problem is that genuine unification in contrast to notions of DPRK absorption and collapse still needs to gain greater acceptance in Seoul, Tokyo, and Washington.

The United States has seen its "Modest Initiative" toward the DPRK, begun under the Reagan administration in 1987 by Secretary of State George Shultz and Assistant Secretary Gaston Sigur, reach fruition in the Agreed Framework signed by the Clinton administration in October 1994. The United States followed a prescient course advised in 1992 by Asia scholar Mel Gurtov.

> A marginalized and isolated regime with a nuclear capability can be treated in one of two basic ways: by tightening the screws on it, threatening it with retaliation should it act aggressively, and seeking ways to undermine and overthrow it; or by proposing creative options for ending its isolation and allowing it, with a sense of security, to break out of its rigid policies and world outlook. In a new world order, the latter is greatly to be preferred.[56]

The past decade has seen tremendous winds of change sweep the world, greatly altering the previous patterns of international relations. North Korea and the United States have made historic strides in that time, though not without passing through periods of trial and danger. It appears the worst is past, and although implementation of the Geneva accord will not be smooth, the future of United States-DPRK relations looks definitely brighter and the possibility of peaceful Korean reunification may be closer at hand. By successfully supporting, assisting, and facilitating these processes—improved United States-DPRK ties and North-South relations—the United States will conclude a historical responsibility toward the Korean peninsula begun at the end of World War II. In the post-cold war era, it is vital for the United States to play a central role in putting to rest conflicts and circumstances that arose after 1945.

Notes

1. This article is adapted from my 1996 doctoral dissertation, "Contemporary American Relations with North Korea: 1987-1994," defended at the University of Virginia. The author wishes to thank the following for their comments: Dr. Kenneth W. Thompson, Dr. Shao Chuan Leng, Hon. David D. Newsom, Dr. Ronald Dimberg, Dr. Brantly Womack, Dr. John Redick, Dr. John Merrill, Mr. Selig Harrison, Mr. Paul Chamberlin, Dr. William J. Taylor, Jr., Mr. Scott Snyder, Mr. Young Ho Kim, Mr. Sang In Shin, and Mr. Antonio Betancourt.

2. Steve Glain, "U.S. Envoy to Seoul Aims to Meet Needs of Security without Provoking the North," *Wall Street Journal*, August 9, 1994.

3. For example, cf. Edward A. Olsen, "Modifying the United States' Korea Policy: Offering Pyongyang an Economic Carrot," in T. H. Kwak, Chonghan Kim, and Hong Nack Kim, eds., *Korean Reunification: New Perspectives and Approaches* (Seoul: Institute for Far Eastern Studies, Kyungnam University, 1984), pp. 153-69.

4. Subcommittee on Asian and Pacific Affairs, Committee on Foreign Affairs, U.S. House of Representatives, *Korea: North-South Nuclear Issues*, July 25, 1990, p. 37.

5. Michael J. Mazarr, *North Korea and the Bomb: A Case Study in Nonproliferation* (New York: St. Martin's Press, 1995), pp. 102-3.

6. Former Secretary of State Lawrence Eagleburger is the chief example.

7. "Text of Carter Interview on North Korea Progress," CNN [via Nexis], June 22, 1994, p. 3.

8. In the same June 22 interview (ibid.), Carter said, "I think the most important lesson is that we should not ever avoid direct talks, direct conversations, direct discussions and negotiations with the main person in a despised or misunderstood or condemned society who could actually resolve the issue." The moderate school took most seriously the North's threat that if economic sanctions were imposed on it, that would be regarded as an act of war. However, Ambassador Robert Gallucci cautiously expressed confidence that if the administration had imposed sanctions upon the North, they would have been successful without provoking a military response.

9. Notable dissidents in each camp emerged by spring 1994. Specialists affiliated with the conservative Heritage Foundation, like Richard Allen and Daryl Plunk, began calling for dialogue with the North as a final effort before implementing sanctions. Democratic senators like Charles Robb and Sam Nunn tended to espouse a harder line on North Korea than did the Clinton administration itself.

10. Glain, "U.S. Envoy to Seoul."

11. For an excellent article on this subject, see Patrick Glynn, "Towards a Politics of Forgiveness," *American Enterprise*, September/October 1994.

12. Warren Christopher, "America's Pacific Future," *U.S. Department of State Dispatch*, November 29, 1993, p. 820.

13. Cf. "Seoul's Show-Stoppers in Seoul" [editorial], *New York Times*, September 23, 1994.

14. Selig S. Harrison, "Carnegie Endowment for International Peace News Conference," Federal News Service [via Nexis], June 16, 1994.

15. Michael J. Mazarr, "Nonproliferation: Lessons of the Korean Case," in C.H. Pak, S. W. Nam, and E. Craig Campbell, eds., *A New World Order and the Security of the*

Asia-Pacific Region (Seoul: Korea Institute for Defense Analyses, 1993), p. 241.

16. Ibid., p. 240.

17. Cf. Taewoo Kim, "South Korea's Nuclear Dilemmas," *Korea and World Affairs*, Summer 1992, pp. 267-71.

18. Mazarr, *North Korea and the Bomb*, p. 207.

19. Ibid., pp. 207-8. These points were originally outlined by Professor Stephen W. Linton.

20. R. James Woolsey, "Threats to the U.S. and Its Interests Abroad: Intelligence and Security" [from congressional testimony given on January 25, 1994], *Vital Speeches of the Day*, March 1, 1994, p. 291.

21. Arnold Kanter, "Carrots and Sticks: Resolving the North Korean Nuclear Problem," unpublished manuscript, November 16, 1993, pp. 2-3.

22. Ibid., p. 3.

23. Ibid.

24. Stephen J. Solarz, "Next of Kim: How to Stop the North Korean Bomb," *New Republic*, August 8, 1994, p. 23.

25. William Safire, "Korean Conflict II?" *New York Times*, June 9, 1994, p. A25.

26. Brent Scowcroft and Arnold Kanter, "Korea: Time for Action," *Washington Post*, June 15, 1994.

27. Lawrence Eagleburger, "The MacNeil-Lehrer NewsHour," Public Broadcasting Service [via Nexis], June 2, 1994.

28. Eugene V. Rostow, "United States Foreign Policy after the Soviet Collapse," *SAIS Review*, Summer-Fall 1992, p. 12.

29. Ibid., p. 7.

30. Ibid., p. 13.

31. Robert Gallucci interview, "The MacNeil-Lehrer NewsHour," Public Broadcasting Service [via Nexis], October 18, 1994.

32. R. Jeffrey Smith, "N. Korea Accord: A Troubling Precedent?" *Washington Post*, October 20, 1994.

33. "Remarks by Robert Gallucci at White House Press Conference, " U.S. Newswire [via Nexis], October 18, 1994.

34. According to Charles Maynes, editor of *Foreign Policy* and a former Carter administration official, "Those assurances... were very carefully designed to exclude North Korea." (Carnegie Endowment conference, June 16, 1994, ibid.)

35. Smith, "N. Korea Accord." Hans Blix has noted that "one should be cautious with saying that now the door is open for any nation to delay... verification of their [nuclear] inventories because no two cases are actually the same."

36. The Unitrd States pressured the ROK in the late 1970s into aborting a nuclear weapons program by bolstering military aid to it; Ukraine recently received not only U.S. economic incentives but apparently security assurances.

37. Three of the most important formal defenses of the Agreed Framework by administration officials have been testimony of Ambassador Robert L. Gallucci in *Implications of the U.S.-North Korea Nuclear Agreement*, Senate Subcommittee on East Asian and pacific Affairs, Washington, DC, December 1, 1994; and testimonies of Secretary of State Warren Christopher and Secretary of Defense William Perry in *Hearing of the Senate Foreign Relations Committee on North Korea*, Wash-

ington, DC, Federal News Service [via Nexis], January 24, 1995.

38. William Perry in ibid.

39. "Nuclear Breakthrough in Korea" [editorial], *New York Times*, October 19, 1994.

40. "The Content of the Korea Accord" [editorial], *Washington Post*, October 21, 1994.

41. For example, cf. Jessica Mathews, "A Sound Beginning with North Korea," *Washington Post*, October 21, 1994; also see her "A Good Deal with North Korea," *Washington Post*, October 30, 1994, for an articulate rebuttal to criticisms of the Geneva accord.

42. U.S. Department of State, "U.S.-DPRK Talks: Press Themes," October 18, 1994, p. 1.

43. "Remarks by Dr. James T. Laney," address before the Asia Society, Washington, DC, USIA, May 3, 1995.

44. K. A. Namkung, "The MacNeil-Lehrer NewsHour," Public Broadcasting Service [via Nexis], July 11, 1994.

45. "Jimmy Carter Interview with CNN," Atlanta, GA, June 22, 1994 [via Nexis].

46. As an excellent example, see Paul Bracken, "The North Korean Nuclear Program as a Problem of State Survival," in Andrew Mack, ed., *Asian Flashpoint: Security and the Korean Peninsula* (Canberra: Allen & Unwin, 1993).

47. As an example of the North's position, cf. Sonya Hepinstall, "S. Korea Should Apologize before Talks Start—North," Reuters, November 2, 1994. She quotes the DPRK ambassador to Thailand: "[Ambassador] Li said inter-Korean talks would have to resume some time because it was stipulated in his country's Geneva pact with the United States..., but he believed South Korea should first show a real change in attitude. 'I think they should apologize for what they did during the mourning period... which angered our people too much.'" Rather than resisting the letter of the Geneva agreement, the North has clarified that a requisite atmosphere is needed to recommence North-South dialogue, which does not yet exist, even after the Geneva accord.

48. Selig S. Harrison, "Beware the Hawks in Seoul," *New York Times*, October 21, 1994.

49. Manwoo Lee, "Pyongyang and Washington: Dynamics of Changing Relations," *Asian Perspective*, Fall-Winter 1995, pp. 147-48.

50. "Restrictions on Relations with North Korea," State Department Information Memorandum from Conrad K. Harper, October 27, 1993, p. 1.

51. Harrison, "Beware the Hawks in Seoul."

52. "Pyongyang Again Rebuffs Seoul Economic Overtures," Reuters, November 12, 1994.

53. See Kevin Sullivan, "S. Korean President Calls North's Leaders Weaker," *Washington Post*, July 29, 1995.

54. The International Financial Institutions Act "requires the U.S. Executive Directors of IFI's (e.g., World Bank) to oppose any loan, extension of financial assistance, or technical assistance to any government the country of which engages in 'a pattern of gross violations of... human rights,' or 'provides refuge to individuals committing acts of international terrorism....'" The Gramm Amendment to the Bretton Woods Agreement Act requires the Secretary of the Treasury to direct the U.S. Executive Director of the IMF "to actively oppose any facility involving use of Fund credit by any Communist dictatorship" unless Treasury certifies to the

relevant congressional committees that certain economic criteria are met. Ibid.

55. Jonathan Thatcher, "North Korea's Debt May Now Be a Smart Investment," Reuters, July 18, 1995.

56. Mel Gurtov, "The New World Order and U.S. Policy toward Korea," unpublished paper, June 1, 1992, p. 24.

Chapter 7

North Korea's Foreign Relations in Transition

Kongdan Oh

T he Democratic People's Republic of Korea (North Korea) faces crises in its diplomatic, economic, and security affairs, as well as in its succession politics. These crises are related to Pyongyang's pattern of foreign relations both as cause and effect. Relations with former communist allies are deteriorating, but have yet to be replaced by relations with the democratic capitalist economies. Relations with South Korea barely exist.

A simple accounting of Pyongyang's foreign relations would make for a relatively brief history, given North Korea's adherence to its state ideology of *Juche* (national self-reliance). But the ruling elite in Pyongyang are beginning to realize that North Korea cannot afford to be a modern-day hermit kingdom. An overview of North Korea's current foreign relations, which is the objective of this chapter, highlights the need for the new Kim Jong Il regime to design and execute a bold foreign policy to strengthen its foreign relations in order to gain greater national security, international recognition, domestic prosperity and regime legitimacy.[1] In the 1990s a new foreign policy is beginning to take shape, but it is too early to tell if the policy will be sufficiently bold to address North Korea's multiple crises.

Kongdan (Katy) Oh is co-principal of OH & HASSIG, Pacific Rim Consulting, specializing in policy research on the two Koreas. She was an international policy analyst at RAND from 1987 to 1995 and has taught at Dominican College and at the University of California, San Diego.

Four Crises

The Diplomatic Crisis

At the end of the cold war, in 1992, North Korea's diplomatic scorecard recorded full diplomatic relations with 19 states in the Asia-Pacific, 20 in the Americas, 33 in Europe, 14 in the Middle East, and 42 in Africa. By comparison, South Korea had diplomatic relations with 31, 34, 45, 19, and 41 states in these respective regions. South Korea "wins" by 170 to 128. North Korea is also a member of 22 international organizations, compared to South Korea's 54 memberships.[2] Since the partition of Korea in 1945, the two Koreas have been locked in a fierce competition for international recognition and legitimacy. Since 1976, when the two governments drew even, with 93 and 96 diplomatic relations (for South and North Korea, respectively), the game has gone increasingly in South Korea's favor.

But numbers do not tell the important part of the story. In the Asia-Pacific North Korea has failed to secure diplomatic recognition from Japan, the Philippines, Thailand, or even Vietnam. In the Americas it has no embassy in Argentina, Brazil, Canada, or the United States. Most members of the European Union do not recognize North Korea. Africa is the only continent where North Korea enjoys more diplomatic recognition than South Korea. In short, North Korea does not enjoy good relations with most of the world's advanced industrial economies, a serious disadvantage in an international community that is becoming increasingly interdependent.

The implications of this lack of relations with major economic powers are numerous. First, North Korea does not have friends or partners in the international community that can provide capital and technology to assist its struggling economy. Worse, the United States has imposed an embargo on North Korea that blocks much international trade. Those countries that do have close relations with North Korea are not able (e.g., China) or willing (e.g., Russia) to extend the kind or amount of economic assistance and cooperation that North Korea needs.

North Korea's diplomatic deficit also deprives its government of the international recognition that it sorely needs, perhaps even for its very survival. North Korean propagandists have worked diligently to persuade their citizens that North Korea is a respected and admired member of the international community, but the more knowledge-able cadres must realize that mutual visits and gift-giving with small

African nations do not confer high status on a government and, moreover, do little to validate the legitimacy of its leadership.

North Korea's diplomacy is in crisis because in the last few years Pyongyang has lost its standing (although not its diplomatic recognition) among old friends while failing to gain new friends. This is not simply a question of competition with South Korea but an issue of economic and political survival. North Korea is neither rich nor powerful enough to survive without relying on the goodwill of other nations. Its loss of support from the former Soviet Union was a serious blow, and Pyongyang seems likely to lose much of China's political support as China changes with the times and as North Korea does not. Unless North Korea can make new friends, the country is doomed. *Juche* is not a viable political philosophy for a modern nation-state.

The Economic Crisis

Pyongyang's diplomatic crisis is a serious matter, but a diplomacy deficit will not destroy North Korean society so long as there are sufficient resources to feed the people. A Korean proverb says, "To a hungry person, even seeing the Diamond Mountain is not as important as eating a meal." Numerous reports from visitors to and defectors from North Korea attest to the dire straits of the North Korean economy. Negative GNP growth and bad harvests have taken their toll. There can be no question that the North Korean economy is in a crisis — the question is how bad the situation is.

The evidence of economic crisis comes in the form of estimated data (and indirect North Korean government admissions) concerning industrial output, agricultural production, and foreign trade. Foreign analysts estimate that North Korean factories were operating at between 30 percent and 50 percent of capacity in the mid-1990s due to lack of energy and raw materials. The economy is entirely dependent on foreign sources for its oil, and after trade relations with the Soviet Union were curtailed, North Korea's oil imports plummeted.

South Korea's Ministry of National Unification (MNU) estimates North Korea's annual grain demand at 6.5 million tons, but in the 1990s harvests produced only 4 million tons. A devastating flood in 1995 may have reduced the harvest to 3.5 million tons. Not even foreign grain donations of some 1.5 million tons in the 1995 season were able to rescue the North Korean people from severe malnutrition and, in an unknown number of cases, starvation.

North Korea's trade has been in deficit every year since the late 1960s. Total trade peaked in 1988 at $4.5 billion, with a trade deficit of $1.2 billion. Through 1995, total trade declined annually, dropping to $2.1 billion in 1995, with a $0.5 billion deficit. By 1994, North Korea's net foreign debt was estimated at over $10 billion, with virtually no repayment having been made since 1985.

While the economic crisis in which North Korea finds itself is a direct result of its changed relations with its fellow socialist econo- mies, the underlying problems of the economy are rooted in its structure and will not be cured without a dramatic change in economic policies.

The Military Crisis

The diplomatic and economic crises are not unrelated to the crisis faced by North Korea's military. The loss of cold war allies means that North Korea must look elsewhere for modern arms and for weapons tech- nology. The North Koreans also need allies to come to their defense in the event of a military conflict. It seems extremely unlikely that military support would be forthcoming if North Korea initiated the conflict, and assistance (presumably from China) is not even assured if North Korea were involved in a conflict of ambiguous cause.

North Korea's military situation can be compared to its diplomatic situation in terms of competition with South Korea, the most likely military threat. North Korea's military spending in the 1990s has been estimated at between 20 percent and 30 percent of the national bud- get (25 percent of GNP). But that high level cannot be sustained given the weakness of North Korea's economy, which has been shrinking in recent years by 4 to 5 percent per year. By contrast, South Korea's defense spending continues at about 3 percent of the national budget in the mid-1990s, but with a GNP over ten times the size of North Korea's, the South outspends the North two-to-one on defense. South Korea also continues to benefit from U.S. military support.

The North Korean military faces a challenge that goes well beyond its inability to acquire modern weapons systems. Continued economic problems have affected military personnel in terms of both training and morale. North Korean pilots are said to receive no more than twenty hours of flight training a year, a stunningly low figure. Soldiers, who have traditionally been an economically privileged class in North Korea, are reportedly suffering from food shortages, especially in the lower ranks.[3] Unrest in the military would have a serious impact on

North Korea's political stability. Kim Jong Il, who was appointed to head the military even before his father's death, has no military experience, and his leadership is said to be widely resented among rank and file. If professional and personal conditions worsen in the army, Kim Jong Il cannot count on military support to keep him in power.

In terms of national security, declining military strength constitutes a clear danger for North Korea, which is surrounded by nations either hostile toward the Kim regime—i.e., South Korea and Japan—or increasingly indifferent to the fate of North Korea as an independent state. By advocating *Juche* and "socialism in our own style," North Korea has distanced itself from China and Russia. The fact is that North Korea is a largely unchanged society trying to survive in a rapidly changing environment. It is increasingly out of step with its neighbors.

Beginning in the late 1980s, Pyongyang apparently tried to compensate for its weakness in conventional military power by developing nuclear weapons. Although the North Koreans consistently denied having the intention or capability to develop nuclear weapons, they were able to use the implied nuclear threat to reach an agreement with the United States. According to the October 1994 "Agreed Framework," the North Koreans promised to stop operating their nuclear facilities in return for the future delivery of two nuclear reactors that would be less useful in generating plutonium for bombs, along with a half-million tons of fuel oil a year while the reactors were being built. This agreement appears to eliminate North Korea's capacity to develop nuclear weapons, although some analysts believe that one or two such weapons might have been manufactured before the nuclear freeze went into effect.

The Political Succession Crisis

Kim Il Sung died on July 8, 1994. Despite twenty years of preparation for political succession, Kim Jong Il was not yet fully prepared to step into his father's shoes. The younger Kim has never even given a public speech. Planning and practice for the succession while his father was alive was one thing, but ruling the country without his father's support is something else. It is hard to say that Kim Il Sung died at an especially bad time for his son's succession, because conditions in North Korea have been worsening every year and perhaps would have presented the younger Kim with an even less propitious inaugural environment in the future.

Father-son succession is an anomaly for a socialist state, and in fact until the North Korean constitution was amended such a succession violated state ideology. While Kim Jong Il has apparently been an adequate administrator, his major claim to succession is his family relationship. To those in North Korea who are hard-headed enough to insist on a greater legitimacy than this, he must prove himself by extricating the country from its multiple crises. Kim Jong Il is no diplomat. Nor is he a military genius. But it is just possible that he may surprise his critics and prove to be something of a reformer by instituting the economic reforms that his father was prevented from adopting by virtue of the senior Kim's total commitment to *Juche* and the socialist model. But apart from suggestive evidence that Kim is receptive to limited reform and that he is willing to take chances, there is little reason to expect that he has the ability to implement the kinds of reforms that North Korea needs. Kim Jong Il is no Gorbachev; nor, given Gorbachev's fate, would he want to be.

Two years after Kim Il Sung's death, the political succession is still incomplete. In 1996 Kim Jong Il has yet to be named either president of the republic or general secretary of the Korean Workers' Party. But these appointments, assuming they come, will be the easy part. The real challenge will be to improve the economy so that a large segment of the North Korean people can enjoy a higher standard of living.

Post-Cold War Foreign Relations

The Four Crises and Foreign Relations

To some degree North Korea's crises are a result of its past foreign relations; it is equally true that future foreign relations will be shaped in part by the attempt to solve present crises. Foreign relations (and the lack of them) have had an impact on all aspects of North Korean society. Although the economy has been in trouble since the 1970s, the weakening of Pyongyang's relations with fellow socialist governments, which resulted in an end to barter trade and "friendship" prices, triggered the acute economic crisis of the 1990s. Pyongyang's lack of relations with the West has deprived the economy of alternative sources of trade and of sources of high technology that were never available from the socialist economies.

Pyongyang's lack of political relations with South Korea, Japan, and the United States has kept the cold war alive on the Korean peninsula and blocked the signing of a peace treaty with the United States (as a representative of United Nations forces), a treaty that would formally end the Korean War. North Korea must maintain a high level of military preparedness in the absence of a secure peace. Weakened relations with its former communist allies have left North Korea relatively exposed in terms of security guarantees, at the same time shutting down the pipeline of Russian military aid.

North Korea's domestic political situation is more insulated from foreign relations than are its economy and military. The government in Pyongyang appears to be stable in the mid-1990s, but North Korea is too weak to survive in the long term without better foreign relations. Lack of ideological support from Russia and China threatens Kim's position, because these are the only major powers that recognize the North Korean government.

North Korea's current crises provide an impetus for Pyongyang to adopt a new direction in its foreign relations in order to escape from international isolation. Kim Il Sung may have clung to his *Juche* ideology as a virtue made necessary by the isolation imposed on his regime by the containment policy of the West. But North Korea can go no farther with *Juche*. North Korea's crises now create the necessity of broadening foreign relations, and the crisis is so severe that one can expect (or at least hope) that necessity will be the mother of invention. Shortly before his death, Kim Il Sung hinted in his New Year's Address of 1994 that North Korea would be willing to establish relations with "the capitalist countries which respect the sovereignty of our country."[4] In June 1994 North Korea sent letters to a number of large American corporations (including IBM, Coca Cola, AT&T, and American Express) inviting their investments in the Najin-Sonbong Free Trade Zone (FTZ) at such time when U.S. trade restrictions would be lifted.[5] In 1995, the North Koreans began to host what amounted to investment seminars in the United States, China, and Europe to drum up business for the FTZ.

Foreign relations with the West will enable North Korea to obtain the economic aid, technology, investment, and markets that were formerly provided by the communist bloc. Better relations with the West will also reduce the level of threat, thereby reducing the need for North Korea to maintain a large defense industry. Restored relations with Russia may open the pipeline for advanced weapons and military technology. And the diplomatic recognition that is the most obvious and immediate manifestation of relations with the West will bolster the Kim

Jong Il regime, and may even provide leverage to strengthen relations with Russia and China.

Relations with Russia

For the states of the former communist bloc, economic imperatives have replaced political imperatives. Capitalism has not yet flowered, but the seeds have been planted, albeit on somewhat rocky ground. North Korea's relations with these former communist states, even those which, like China, still officially espouse socialism in the form of a "socialist market economy," have changed for the worse. Nowhere is this more evident than in the case of Russia, where political relations in the early 1990s hit rock bottom and trade virtually ceased as the Russians abandoned socialism and began to scrabble for money.

When Moscow normalized relations with Seoul in September 1990, North Korea's media characterized the event as political prostitution, or "diplomacy that can be purchased with dollars," referring to South Korea's promise to provide the former Soviet Union with some $3 billion in trade credits.[6] The subsequent demise of the Soviet Union as a functional state, following on the heels of the apostasy of Eastern Europe, presented North Korea with two threats. One was the threat of political contamination from contact with these states. *Glasnost* enabled Russian politicians and media to criticize North Korea. North Korea's failure to institute its own reforms and its intensification of the Kim Il Sung and Kim Jong Il cults became popular targets of Russian criticism. Pyongyang felt compelled to recall thousands of North Korean students studying in Eastern Europe and the Soviet Union. The other threat was that North Korea's economic and political lifeline to the outside world would be severed. Its largest trading partner, the Soviet Union, insisted on conducting trade on a cash basis, including weapons purchases. Moscow's strategic and economic interests became centered on Seoul, and trade with South Korea flourished, rising tenfold, from $150 million in 1987 to $1.5 billion in 1993.

Relations with China

In August 1992, Beijing and Seoul established diplomatic relations, and Pyongyang (which had already lost the friendship of Moscow) could not afford to voice any strong objections, at least in public. Relations between China and North Korea cooled somewhat, but the two governments needed each other in order to uphold communism as a political force. However, it seems clear that for China, North Korea had become a burden while South Korea had become an opportunity.

In the mid-1990s, China continues to support North Korea politically and economically. But in private the Chinese are unhappy with North Korea's political succession process, its continued refusal to undertake serious economic reforms, and the extreme personality cults of Kim Il Sung and Kim Jong Il. In contrast, South Korea, with its brand of Confucian authoritarian capitalism, presents a possible political and economic model for China. The Chinese have been extremely patient with North Korea, and even generous. In 1992 China replaced Russia as North Korea's major trading partner, with two-way trade in 1993 increasing 26 percent over the previous year, to $900 million, before falling to $550 million in 1995. (In 1994, China's trade with South Korea was $16 *billion*.) The Chinese have also reportedly responded favorably to Pyongyang's appeals for donations of oil and grain. It appears that the principal North Korean supporter in China is Deng Xiaoping, a comrade of the late Kim Il Sung. Deng has insisted that China honor the "four cardinal principles" in its dealing with North Korea. These principles include the requirement that there be no disagreements among communist parties, and that socialism continue to be the dominant economic principle.[7] As long as Deng is alive, China is likely to continue its support for North Korea. But Deng is at death's door, and if China becomes less cohesive and more chaotic after his death, North Korea may suffer the same fate it suffered after the breakup of the Soviet Union.

North Korea's leverage over China is limited. As a bankrupt state it can offer China little in the way of economic advantages. But Pyongyang does have a card to play, namely, the threat that if it does not receive support it will implode and the resulting domestic instability will spill over into China, initially in the form of a flood of refugees crossing the border. China has reportedly already taken steps to deal with a large exodus of refugees. Another negative tactic is to threaten war with South Korea, a war that would likely involve China to some extent.

Relations with the United States

With the dissolution of the communist bloc, economic relations with the West are essential for Pyongyang. The North Koreans realize this, and they also realize that they must go through Washington in order to establish relations with other major Western economies. Throughout the cold war, North Korea, along with the rest of the communist bloc, was the target of an allied containment policy. In the early 1990s the most obvious barrier to better relations with Western states was Pyongyang's refusal to accept full-scope inspections of its nuclear facilities. The United States made the resolution of the nuclear issue a prerequisite for considering all other issues involving North Korea. North Korea has also lacked the experience and finesse to conduct a sophisticated foreign policy, committing a terrorist act every few years which alienated much of the international community. The North Korean leaders were also hesitant to establish relations with the West for fear that their people would be exposed to undesirable political and cultural influences.

Beginning in the late 1980s, Pyongyang and Washington began to explore issues in a series of meetings at the counselor level in Beijing. Two high-level meetings were held between the two governments in January 1992 and June 1993. At these meetings the two sides were unable to resolve all their differences about the inspection and future of North Korea's nuclear facilities, and Washington prepared to go to the United Nations to ask for economic sanctions. Former President Jimmy Carter took it upon himself to play peacemaker by visiting North Korea in June 1994. Sanctions were postponed, and another round of talks was held between the North Koreans and the Americans in Geneva, which resulted in the signing of the Agreed Framework in October 1994. Among other things, the agreement sets the stage for the two governments to begin the process of normalizing diplomatic relations. The first step toward normalization is to be the opening of liaison offices, but two years after the Agreed Framework was signed these offices still had not been established.

In the future, the United States-DPRK relationship will continue to be tense. By failing to permit full inspections by the International Atomic Energy Commission until the first nuclear reactor is built, North Korea will continue to be in violation of its Nuclear Non-Proliferation Treaty obligations for several years to come, and given the multiple contingencies that are woven into the Agreed Framework, it is possible that the agreement will unravel somewhere down the road. Whether by then the United States will have created a broader-based relationship with North Korea or whether the nuclear issue will continue to dominate the relationship remains to be seen.

The Agreed Framework is not a formal treaty, and certainly not a peace treaty. Signing a peace treaty to replace the Armistice Agreement that ended Korean War hostilities and phasing out U.S. trade restrictions on North Korea will require public consensus and congressional approval, both of which may be difficult to obtain. Many Korea experts in the academic community have been critical of the U.S. government's narrowly focused approach to North Korea, considering it to be a holdover from the cold war. But conservative forces in the government, media, and policy analysis communities, viewing that nation as an irrational, terrorist state, may not be so willing to compromise with North Korea. These conservatives would prefer to use economic pressure to force the North Koreans to open their society. Between these two opinion groups the general public has wavered, as has the Clinton administration. Washington's policy toward North Korea must take into account the opinions of diverse domestic constituencies as well as the opinions of the South Korean government and people.[8]

Compared to the complicated situation that the Clinton administration faces in dealing with North Korea, Pyongyang policymakers may have it easier. At least while Kim Il Sung was alive he was presumably able to impose his will on both the reformers, who wanted North Korea to give up its nuclear option in exchange for an opening with the West, and the military conservatives, who preferred to continue with the nuclear program and build a siege state. Kim Jong Il may not be as successful in imposing his will on these different opinion groups as his father was.

Relations with Japan

One Japanese expert on Korean affairs has argued that during the 1990s the goal of Japan's foreign policy toward the Korean peninsula has evolved from the "maintenance of peace and stability" on the peninsula to "efforts to aid the peaceful unification of Korea indirectly."[9] Others might question whether such a policy shift has taken place. Whatever Japan's goals in regard to relations with North Korea, little movement toward reconciliation has taken place. When Shin Kanemaru, then Japan's deputy prime minister, co-led a delegation of Liberal Democratic Party (LDP) and Japan Socialist Party (JSP) members to Pyongyang in September 1990, Kim Il Sung indicated a willingness to open diplomatic relations with Japan, and the two sides reached an informal agreement on the matter. Shortly afterward, the United States presented Japan with satellite evidence of North Korea's nuclear reprocessing program and, coincidentally, Kanemaru became involved in domestic political scandals. Momentum for developing relations was lost. Japan and North Korea convened a series of meetings to discuss normalization, but a variety of issues, most importantly nuclear inspection, torpedoed these meetings in November 1992.[10] Japan's political establishment has not only been rocked by repeated scandals, but the fragmentation of the LDP has led to a succession of weak governments unable to cope with difficult foreign policy questions. The Japanese and North Koreans have met on numerous occasions since 1992 to explore ways to resume government-level normalization meetings, but as of September 1996 such meetings have not resumed.

One important relationship continues between Japan and North Korea. Approximately 250,000 Koreans residing in Japan are members of Chosen Soren (also known as *Chongnyon*), a pro-North Korea political organization. Chosen Soren is estimated to contribute as much as a half-billion dollars a year to North Korea in foreign exchange, constituting the single greatest source of foreign exchange for the North Korean government (although most of the money is intended for North Korean private citizens).[11] The Japanese government is constrained from exercising control over this transfer of funds because of the delicate nature of relations between resident Koreans and Japanese, and because Chosen Soren has powerful friends in the government.

Opinion within Japan regarding the best course to take with North Korea is divided, just as it is in the United States. While some advocate taking a hard line and even trying to turn off the pipeline of Chosen Soren funds to Pyongyang, others believe that diplomatic recognition, trade, and aid (including several billion dollars in wartime reparations payments) would be a force for reform in North Korea, thereby improving Japan's security environment.[12]

Relations with South Korea

South Korea is many things to North Korea. First and foremost, it is the other half of a divided nation, and Kim Il Sung's goal from the time he took control of North Korea in 1945 was to reunify the nation. His death prevented him from fulfilling the promise of unification that he had made to the North Korean people.

South Korea is also a military threat. President Syngman Rhee was unwilling to sign the Armistice Agreement ending Korean War hostilities, preferring instead to hold out the option of a northward invasion. Whatever plans Seoul may have developed in later years to stage such an invasion, in Pyongyang, which was obsessed with preparing for a southward invasion, the possibility of aggression from the South might have seemed real. North Korea has repeatedly claimed that joint ROK-United States military maneuvers are practice for a northward invasion. Whether the North Korean elite believe this or are only playing the propaganda game is hard to tell. There is no question, however, that the military forces of South Korea and the United States would constitute a threat to the security of North Korea should an event ever trigger war.

Since the 1960s, when the South's economy began to overtake the North's, South Korea has been an economic threat as well as a potential source of assistance. The economic threat came both from the greater legitimacy and superior foreign relations that Seoul gained from its strong economy (e.g., "buying" recognition from the Soviet Union), and from the danger that if North Korean citizens ever became aware of the South's standard of living, they would question whether their government had indeed made North Korea a "paradise on earth" as the propaganda claims.

Under circumstances controlled by Pyongyang, South Korea's economic success could benefit North Korea. The two halves of the peninsula are complementary in terms of resources. Inter-Korean trade began on a small scale in 1989, gradually increasing until South Korea became the third-largest trading partner of North Korea by 1995, although at $310 million the volume of trade remained small by international standards. North Korea has solicited South Korean investments in the Najin-Sonbong FTZ, and the nuclear reactors that are to be built according to the Agreed Framework will be largely of South Korean construction.

North Korea has struggled to find a realistic foreign policy toward its vastly more successful neighbor to the south. The underlying problem of South-North Korea relations is that, from the viewpoint of the leaders of the two sides, this is a zero-sum game: there is not room for two separate governments on the Korean peninsula. In recent years South Korea's relative success in economic and diplomatic fields, coupled with the global demise of communism, seems to make South Korea the clear winner. The Kim government in the North, realizing the futility of its plans to revolutionize South Korea, has adopted a "separate but equal" unification policy, as set forth in Kim Il Sung's 1980 confederation proposal. What this proposal would do is essentially freeze the zero-sum game to keep South Korea from absorbing the North. South Korea may, in the short term, welcome this approach, fearing that an early reunification would bankrupt the South. But in the long term the South remains a very real absorption threat to North Korea.

While trying to keep South Korea at arm's length, North Korea continues to search for new moves in its competitive game. One possibility is to grow stronger through political and economic relations with other nations and then initiate dialogue with South Korea on more equal terms. While the United States has tried to force Pyongyang to deal with Seoul as a prerequisite for better United States-DPRK relations, this tactic has not been successful in the past. In the meantime, a controlled economic opening to South Korea is all that one can expect from North Korea.

The Future of North Korea's Foreign Relations

The period immediately following Kim Il Sung's death may not be the best time to try to read the foreign policy tea leaves in North Korea's cup. As long as the senior Kim was alive, it was prudent to predict that North Korea's foreign policy would continue to be conservative, following the principles of *Juche*. Under Kim Jong Il, assuming that he is able to firmly grasp the reins of power, there is the prospect of greater change in the near future.

Kim Jong Il faces a number of constraints in formulating policy. First, he must hold the loyalty of conservative cadres. Second, he must uphold the principle of *Juche* that was bequeathed to him by his father, and that Kim Jong Il himself has championed. Yet it is clear that Kim and the rest of the ruling elite in Pyongyang realize the seriousness of the crises their country faces, and they may even believe that the game is virtually lost. Under the direction of Kim Jong Il, North Korea played its nuclear card in return for the Agreed Framework that promised eventual diplomatic recognition from the United States. Whether that diplomatic recognition can be translated into foreign aid, foreign investment, and a reduced military threat remains to be seen. In a sense, North Korea must now trust to less dramatic, more conventional forms of bargaining power in its diplomacy. If North Korea reneges on the Agreed Framework, the United States is unlikely to agree to further negotiations, no matter what nuclear threat North Korea presents.

Before considering what Kim Jong Il's foreign policy choices might be, it would be wise to consider how much power he will have to implement his policy choices. It seems unlikely that he will have the same degree of power as his father, because he lacks his father's stature and many of his political skills. But even if Kim Jong Il is able to take control of the government, it is far from certain that he or his advisers have yet (in the mid-1990s) developed a coherent foreign policy.

The first goal of North Korea's foreign policy must be to establish diplomatic relations with the United States and Japan. Without such recognition, North Korea will be unable to obtain the economic assistance and cooperation that it so desperately needs. Once these two global powers have adopted a two-Korea policy, and once North Korea's economic condition has been strengthened, Pyongyang will be in a position to improve relations with Seoul.

The second goal of North Korea's foreign policy is to alleviate the economic crisis, a task that will lead the regime to adopt a controlled economic opening. China provides a model, but North Korea's opening will likely be much more restricted than China's, as the North Korean elite try to avoid the threat to the political status quo posed by economic opening and reform. It follows that a more restrictive opening will also be less successful, perhaps not successful enough to turn around the North Korean economy, regardless of what aid pours in from the West.[13]

Managing economic relations with the capitalist economies will be challenging. A form of "mosquito net opening" (*bangch'ungmang*) is called for.[14] The trick is not only to keep out unwanted economic and social influences but to control the pace of opening so that North Korean citizens do not hope for too much. The Kim Jong Il regime will be in greatest danger not if the economic situation improves too slowly but if knowledge of the outside world and expectations for an improved standard of living rise too fast. This is what happened in the former East Germany.

North Korea's military crisis may be alleviated by the reduced threat that will accompany better relations with the United States, following the signing of a formal peace agreement that offers stronger negative security guarantees than the United States has yet provided to North Korea. Under the Agreed Framework, North Korea will be able to keep any nuclear weapons it may already have developed, at least several years, and perhaps, if it is able to secure plutonium from the international black market, even operate a hidden nuclear weapons program. This nuclear deterrent would provide some substitute for Pyongyang's relative decline in conventional military power.

The political succession crisis may be solved by Kim Jong Il's diplomatic victories and by hope on the part of the populace for a better future resulting from relations with the West. Since North Korea does not have to submit to intrusive nuclear inspections, the hard-line military contingent should also be satisfied. Assuming Kim Jong Il does assume the top leadership positions in North Korea, the greatest danger to his political position will come in a few years if he proves to be a bad manager, or if his diplomatic victories cannot be translated into the improvement in living standards which the people will expect.

Given North Korea's present isolation, its foreign relations can only improve. A diplomatic and economic opening seems to be at hand. This is good news not only for the North Korean people but for South Korea and all other nations with interests in the region. The question for the future is whether this opening can be controlled in a way that satisfies the demands of the North Korean people and at the same time does not seriously threaten the personal security of Kim Jong Il and the ruling elite.

Notes

1. A good background to North Korea's foreign relations may be found in Jae Kyu Park, et al., eds., *The Foreign Relations of North Korea: New Perspectives* (Boulder: Westview Press, 1987) and (Seoul: Kyungnam University Press, 1987). See, for example, Byung-joon Ahn, "North Korean Foreign Policy: An Overview," pp. 15-38.

2. Diplomatic data from *Topyorobon Pukhan-ui onul* [Today's North Korea seen through statistics] (Seoul: Ministry of Information, October 1993), pp. 54-61.

3. "Special Report: Testimony by Chung-guk Lee, a North Korean Soldier in the Nuclear and Chemical Defense Unit," *Shin Dong-A*, May 1994, pp. 180-81.

4. "New Year Address of President Kim Il Sung," *People's Korea*, no. 1633, January 15, 1994, p. 3.

5. "N.K. Sends Letters to U.S. Companies to Lure Investment in Rajin-Sonbong," *Korea Herald*, August 24, 1994, p. 8.

6. "Ddalla-ro palgosa-nun oegyo" [Diplomacy that can be purchased with dollars], editorial in *Nodong Sinmun*, October 5, 1990.

7. James Cotton, "The Unraveling of 'China' and the China-Korea Relationships," *Korea and World Affairs* 18, 1 (Spring 1994), p. 75.

8. Alan D. Romberg, "North Korea: Considerations in American Policy," in Gerrit Gong, et al., *Korean Peninsula Developments and U.S.-Japan-South Korea Relations*, vol. 1 (Washington: Center for Strategic and International Studies, April 1993), pp. 47-70.

9. Hajime Izumi, "Tokyo's Policy toward North Korea and Korean Reunification," in ibid., p. 31.

10. See Kak-Soo Shin, "North Korea-Japan Normalization Talks: Where They Stand and Will Be Headed," *Korean Journal of International Studies* 24, 4 (Winter 1993), pp. 591-92.

11. Statistics from the head of the Japanese Justice Ministry's Public Security Investigation Agency, as quoted by Kyodo News, Foreign Broadcast Information Service's *Daily Report, East Asia*, no. 94-061 (FBIS-EAS-94-061), p. 3.

12. See Yasuo Suzuki, "Toward Establishing Diplomatic Relations with DPRK: Japanese Willingness and Reservations," *Korean Journal of International Studies* 24, 1 (Spring 1993), p. 67.

13. One South Korean government official has been quoted as characterizing foreign aid in the absence of an opening up and reform of North Korea as a mere "oxygen mask that postpones death." Quoted by Kim Chung-il, "Will the 'Basic Principle of Reunification' Change?" *Kyonghyang Sinmun*, August 20, 1994, p. 3, translated by FBIS-EAS-94-162, August 22, 1994, pp. 45-46.

14. This apt description is from an article by Chon Hyon-jun in *MAL*, no. 89, November 1993, pp. 68-75, translated by FBIS-EAS-94-040, March 1, 1994, pp. 32-38.

SOUTH KOREA

★ National Capital
◉ Provincial Capital
● City
— International Boundary
— Provincial Boundary
— Demarcation Line
▬ Demilitarized Zone
⚓ Primary Ports

0   25   50   75 km
0   25   50 mi

Administrative Notes:
• Kyonggi-do is administered from Seoul.
• Kyongsang-bukdo is administered from Taegu.
• Kyongsang-namdo is administered from Pusan.
• Kwangju is an individual province, and the provincial capital of Cholla-namdo.

Sea of Japan (Eastern Sea)

130°50'

37°30'

Ullung-do
(South Korea)

NORTH KOREA

Kansong
Hwach'on
Inje
Sokch'o
Yonch'on
Yangyang
38°
Munsan
Ch'unch'on
Kyonggi-do
Kangwon-do
Kangnung
Uijongbu
Hongch'on
Kimp'o
Soul-t'ukpyolsi
Samch'ok
Inch'on-Jikhalsi
Yoyang-ni
Inch'on
Yangp'yong
Suwon
Yoju
Wonju
Hwangji-ri
P'yongt'aek
Ansong
Chech'on
Chungju
Tanyang
Ch'onan
Ch'ungch'ong-bukdo
Yongju
Sosan
Yongyang
Ch'ungch'ong-namdo
Ch'ongju
Yech'on
Andong
Kongju
Poun
Sangju
Uisong
Yongdok
Taech'on
Taejon
Yongdong
Kimch'on
P'ohang
Kunsan
Iri
Kyongsang-bukdo
Yongch'on
Chonju
Taegu
Kyongju
Chinan
Cholla-bukdo
Anui
Hyopch'on
Ulsan
Chongup
Onyang
Namwon
Namji-ri
Yangsan
Kyongsang-namdo
Kwangju
Chinhae
Yongsanp'o
Chinju
Masan
Pusan
Sunch'on
Samch'onp'a
Cholla-namdo
Ch'ungmu
Mokp'o
Posong
Yosu
Koje-do
Kangjin
Kohung
Chindo
Wando
Chin-do
Huksan-Chedo

Yellow Sea (Western Sea)

36°

34°

Western Channel

Tsushima
(Japan)

Korea Strait

Eastern Channel

JAPAN

126°
Cheju
Cheju-do
Cheju-do
128°

Han-gang
Bukhan-gang
Namhan-gang
Kum-gang
Naktong-gang
Somjin-gang

©1992 Magellan Geographix℠ Santa Barbara, CA

Chapter 8

Korean Unification:
The Zero-Sum Past and
Precarious Future

Victor D. Cha

For decades following the division of the Korean peninsula in 1945, the literature on national unification remained transfixed on chronologies of the numerous and fruitless rounds of dialogue between the two Koreas. This was largely because the actual prospects of unification were, at best, remote. However, with the end of the cold war, the transpiring of events in Germany, and uncertainties about the continued viability of the North Korean regime, the distant goal of national unification may finally be on the horizon. As Korea progresses toward the end of this long and winding road, a sharper focus on the once abstract notion of unification is appropriate. This chapter offers three perspectives on the topic. First, it analyzes from a historical perspective why unification dialogue between the two Koreas (i.e., North-South talks) has been largely unproductive. Second, it considers some of the potential problems and policy priorities in the future process of unification. And third, it assesses the potential impact of a united Korea on the balance of power in East Asia.

The Zero-Sum Game of Inter-Korean Dialogue

As international relations theorists have argued, interaction between states can be conceptualized in the framework of a game.[1] One of the

Victor Cha is assistant professor in the Department of Government and School of Foreign Service at Georgetown University.

determinants of cooperation is the degree to which states see potential gains from the game in zero-sum or positive-sum terms. Put very simply, in the latter context, cooperative outcomes can be achieved that make both states better off, while in the former, gains to one state necessarily come at the expense of the other. Cooperation is also harder to achieve when states assess the benefits of interaction with others in relative gains terms—that is, when they prefer to cooperate only in those situations that make them better off relative to the other state. On the other hand, states that tend to be absolute-gains motivated will cooperate as long as they enjoy gains, regardless of the other side's gains or losses.

Viewed in these terms, the two Koreas have approached unification dialogue in wholly zero-sum, relative gains terms. For nearly two decades following the Korean War, contact between the two regimes was virtually nonexistent.[2] Neither recognized the legitimacy of the other, and dialogue did not advance beyond mutual recriminations over North Korean provocations.[3] Reflecting acute zero-sum attitudes toward cooperation, both governments considered unification only within the context of the overthrow of one system by the other (*sŏnggong t'ongil*). For the South, this was stated during the Rhee Syngman (1948–1960) and Park Chung Hee (1961–1979) regimes in their aspirations to "march north" for "territorial restoration" (*pukchin t'ongil*). In the former case, unification policy explicitly called for a South Korean military offensive to destroy the communist regime in the north (this was despite the absence of both military capabilities and United States support for such a policy). In Park's case, greater emphasis was placed on South Korean (ROK) economic development; however, this was also within the context of better preparing the ROK for its eventual *sŏnggong t'ongil*. For North Korea, such policies were made obvious by Pyongyang's military attempt to unify the peninsula in 1950. It was also manifested in the strategy adopted in the 1960s by North Korean leader Kim Il Sung of fomenting a revolution among the "anti-imperialist" South Korean masses that would pave the way for an eventual North Korean takeover.[4]

The three periods of unification dialogue that followed these early years exhibited a continuation of these zero-sum mentalities. Contacts during each of these periods indeed brought a temporary reprieve to the general atmosphere of hostility that had pervaded interaction. However, in most cases, mutual antagonism and distrust resulted in the termination of dialogue before substantive progress could be made.

In the early 1970s, the first period of dialogue began with humanitarian talks between North and South Korean Red Cross officials on the reunification of separated families.[5] Concurrent with these much-publicized talks, the two governments undertook a separate channel of secret high-level contacts beginning in early May 1972 between ROK intelligence director Lee Hu Rak and his North Korean counterparts Kim Yong Ju and Vice-premier Park Sung Chul.[6] These visits resulted in the release of the surprise July 4 (1972) North-South joint communiqué.

The July 4 communiqué committed the two governments to various principles and objectives to reduce tensions on the peninsula.[7] Seoul and Pyongyang agreed that unification should be sought through (1) independent efforts of the two Koreas, and without interference from external powers; (2) peaceful means, not by use of force; and (3) the fostering of a "grand national unity" that transcended ideological differences. They agreed that the Red Cross talks on family reunion and visitation rights was an important confidence-building mechanism in the humanitarian sphere that would then enable discussion on more substantive political and security issues. In this vein, the communiqué provided for the establishment of the North-South Coordinating Committee (NSCC) which was to serve as the primary governmental channel for direct dialogue on unification issues.[8] Finally, to further increase transparency and avert miscalculation, the two governments established a direct Seoul-Pyongyang telephone "hotline."

These measures represented the first attempt after the division of the peninsula to seek non-zero-sum bases for North-South dialogue. The July 4 communiqué offered a new vision of unification by discarding the *sônggong t'ongil* notion of attaining unity by force, and committing both Pyongyang and Seoul (at least in rhetoric) to the principle of reconciliation through peaceful means. Moreover, the Red Cross and NSCC talks set the precedent of bilateral conferences and exchange visits of delegations, rather than slander and subversion, as the primary means by which to achieve this objective.[9]

In spite of these ground-breaking events, bilateral dialogue quickly deteriorated into mutual recriminations. While inaugural sessions of the Red Cross talks went smoothly, once negotiations turned to more substantive issues, the delegations could not even agree on an agenda.[10] NSCC meetings were equally ineffective, remaining mired in cold war polemics.[11] By mid-1973, a total of three full-dress NSCC sessions and seven Red Cross sessions (in addition to countless preliminary meetings) remained deadlocked on even the simplest issue, mail exchange between separated families, and both sets of talks were eventually suspended in August 1973.[12] Furthermore, statements by ROK officials during the period revealed the degree to which perceptions and attitudes toward a new approach to inter-Korean issues remained unchanged. After the release of the July 4 communiqué, ROK NSCC chief delegate Lee Hu Rak warned that the North-South talks had only advanced inter-Korean relations from "confrontation without dialogue" to "confrontation with dialogue." Premier Kim Jong Pil echoed these sentiments by belittling the communiqué as nothing more than a "piece of paper" that did not change North Korea's basic aspiration to communize the South.[13] Thus, contrary to the rhetoric of the 1972 communiqué, behavior still reflected an entrenchment in zero-sum *sôngong t'ongil* attitudes toward unification.

The second period of inter-Korean dialogue took place in the mid-1980s. Floods in the South in September 1984 prompted the North Korean Red Cross to offer relief aid to flood victims. This unusual gesture by Pyongyang (as well as Seoul's uncharacteristic acceptance of the offer) set off a spate of contacts in various fields. In October 1984, previously suspended Red Cross talks were resumed, and telephone "hotlines" were reconnected.[14] The following month, the two governments agreed to hold vice-ministerial talks on the promotion of joint venture projects and commodity transactions, and in July 1985, meetings of a newly-created North-South inter-parliamentary conference produced a joint declaration reaffirming the principles of peaceful unification and non-aggression espoused in the July 4 communiqué. During the period, representatives from the two Koreas also held meetings on the possible fielding of united national sports teams for the 1984 Los Angeles Olympics and 1986 Asian Games.[15] In total, from November 1984 to 1985, sixteen exchanges took place, including five economic council meetings, three Red Cross sessions, and two parliamentary sessions.

While these events represented a promising turn in relations, subsequent developments again both reflected and reinforced the prevalence of zero-sum mentalities on the peninsula. Tensions remained high as a result of terrorist acts against the Chun regime by the North (in particular, the October 1983 Rangoon bombing which killed half of the ROK cabinet). As was the case with the NSCC talks, the inter-parliamentary meetings and the economic talks could not reach agreement on even the most picayune of procedural and agenda-setting issues.[16] The sports talks also failed miserably to produce a united

Korean national team. For both sides, locked in confrontational mind-sets, compromise or concession was tantamount to defeat. The one exception to this was the Red Cross meetings, which facilitated a limited number of family reunions and cultural contacts in September 1985. These consisted of a four-day exchange of dance troupe performances and "hometown" (*kohyang*) reunions of approximately 65 separated family members.[17] In spite of this accomplishment, any expectations of additional progress were deflated when Pyongyang unilaterally suspended all channels of dialogue in February 1986 to protest United States-ROK Team Spirit military exercises.

The third and most promising period of inter-Korean dialogue occurred from 1988 to 1992. Following unilateral declarations by the South calling for greater openness toward North Korea,[18] Seoul and Pyongyang resumed Red Cross talks for a second set of family reunions. While these meetings progressed slowly, the atmosphere created by their resumption (after a four-year suspension) paved the way for a more successful set of contacts on sports exchanges, which included a series of inter-Korean exhibition soccer matches in September 1990, the fielding of united Korean teams for the world ping-pong championships in Japan, and the world youth soccer championships in Portugal (1991).[19]

Economic relations also saw improvement, with two-way trade increasing from $22 million in 1989 (the first year of direct trade) to $190 million in 1991 and $213 million in 1992.[20] In January 1989, Hyundai chairman Chung Ju Yung made an unprecedented visit to North Korea, where he proposed a number of joint venture projects including a $700 million tourist complex at Kûmgang-san (Diamond Mountain). In January 1992, Daewoo chairman Kim Woo Chung also signed a tentative agreement with the North for development of a light industry complex at Namp'o. And in another unprecedented act, Pyongyang responded positively to South Korean participation in a multinational project to develop the Tumen River area as a free-trade zone.[21]

Highlighting this growth in inter-Korean contacts were inquiries by both Seoul and Pyongyang in early 1989 for high-level political talks. These led to three exchange visits between ROK Premier Kang Young Hoon and his counterpart, Yon Hyong Muk, in September-December 1990. The Kang-Yon talks broke from past precedent in that both officials were recognized by their prime ministerial titles and were accorded treatment as formal representatives of their respective gov-

⌊ernments. Talks stalled in early 1991,[22] but additional meetings in October and December resulted in the signing of two accords: the "Basic Agreement on Reconciliation, Non-aggression, and Exchanges and Cooperation" (December 13), and the "Joint Declaration on De-nuclearization of the Korean Peninsula" (December 31). Briefly, the latter document prohibited the testing, manufacturing, and deploying of nuclear weapons by the two Koreas.[23] It also banned the develop-ment of plutonium reprocessing and uranium enrichment facilities and called for the establishment of a joint nuclear control commission and inspection regime on the peninsula. The declaration represented the first substantive step by Seoul and Pyongyang toward reducing mili-tary tensions.

The Basic Agreement on Reconciliation had a number of features that distinguished it in both form and substance from the July 4 communiqué. First, the 1991 accord was a bona fide "agreement" (*habûisô*) that followed the format of an international treaty. It required instruments of ratification and the signatures of both premiers in their official capacities. This technically gave the 1991 accord more bind-ing authority than the 1972 "joint communiqué" (*kongdong sông-myôngsô*), which was signed by Lee Hu Rak and Kim Yong Ju with-out official titles, and only referred to them as "upholding the wishes of their superiors."[24]

Second, in the Basic Agreement, the two governments explicated in greater depth and scope the principles contained in the July 4 communiqué. The document acknowledged the legitimacy of each system, thereby ending decades of mutual non-recognition (article 1). It committed both governments to refrain from defamatory propa-ganda, make efforts toward removing the current armistice situation on the peninsula, and negotiate a peace treaty. In addition, while the 1972 communiqué envisioned a "grand national unity" for Korea, the 1991 agreement set out more specifically what tasks this would entail. In the economic sphere, these included joint natural resource devel-opment, commodity transactions, and joint venture projects. In terms of infrastructure, the document called for the linking of severed rail-ways and highways, and the opening of air and sea routes. And in the societal sphere, it advocated the promotion of cross-border travel, family reunions, and postal and communication links (articles 15-20). These were clearly positive steps toward recognizing and ameliorat-ing the zero-sum diplomatic competition that had typified both coun-tries' outlooks.

Third, the Basic Agreement went beyond the provisions of the July 4 communiqué by laying out an institutional "roadmap" for unification. The document provided for the creation, within specified time periods (1-3 months), of a liaison office at P'anmunjôm and joint committees for security affairs and cooperative exchanges. In a break from past precedent, it also discussed specific confidence-building measures to be undertaken by both militaries. These included a hot line between the two military commands; arms reduction talks; prior notification of troop movements and exercises; and exchange of military personnel and information (articles 12–13). In essence, the 1991 accord represented a more sophisticated understanding on the parts of Seoul and Pyongyang of the unification process. The two governments acknowledged that a period of reconciliation was necessary prior to unification, and that the starting point of this reconciliation process was the breaking down of decades of distrust and the acceptance of one another as equal negotiating partners.[25]

Although the Basic Agreement and Denuclearization Declaration constituted the most promising accomplishments in the history of unification dialogue, they were flawed from the outset. First, on technical grounds, although the Basic Agreement carried more authority than the 1972 communiqué, the document still did not legally bind the parties. Despite its embellishments as an international treaty, it was technically a "gentlemen's agreement" that was effective only when the two sides expressed the will and intention to abide by it.[26] While dialogue took place through the political and military subcommittees established in May 1992, these bodies did not produce a single agreement.[27] Second, in spite of commitments to confidence-building measures, neither agreement was capable of resolving conflicts of interest over vital security issues—in particular, the controversy over North Korea's suspected nuclear weapons program.[28] Pyongyang's intransigence on submitting to IAEA inspections, and its clear penchant for seeking a resolution to the dispute that excluded Seoul to the greatest extent possible, resulted in a suspension of North-South nuclear talks, failure of the two governments to set up a bilateral inspection regime, and effective nullification of the de-nuclearization declaration.[29] The zero-sum nature of North-South relations was also evident in attitudes in Seoul and Pyongyang toward implementation of the Agreed Framework, and events subsequent to it. In general, the North has complied with those aspects of the Agreed Framework involving the non-proliferation interests of the United States (i.e., freezing nuclear activities and allowing IAEA monitoring), but has resisted those that involve cooperation with the South (i.e., accepting ROK-design light water reactors and improving North-South dialogue). Pyongyang's resistance ignores the fact that the ROK is the primary financer of the LWR project. Through the lens of zero-sum competition, acknowledging the South's role in underwriting the North's future energy-generating capabilities is tantamount to admitting defeat. In addition, opportunities to improve relations pursuant to the Agreed Framework also became hostage to zero-sum politics. In 1995 and 1996, Seoul framed the North's international plea for food aid as a political rather than a humanitarian issue. The South demanded that the North directly request such aid from Seoul (read "admit defeat"), and that third-country donors refrain from heeding the North's pleas until Pyongyang approached the ROK with hat in hand. Thus, regardless of the agreements reached in 1991, the exchanges in the mid-1980s, and the 1972 communiqué, the zero-sum relative gains nature of inter-Korean relations causes every issue to be framed in competitive terms. Not conceding on any issue is a test of regime legitimacy as each side defines its legitimacy in juxtaposition to the other. The result has been the emasculation of all major initiatives and absence of improvement in low politics issues like family reunions, cultural and sports exchanges, and economic ties. (In March 1993, Seoul ordered a freeze on all economic transactions with the North in protest over the nuclear issue.[30]) Rather than a sweeping agreement, it is incremental cooperation on the latter issues that are most important for building confidence and reducing mistrust between the two sides.

The preceding overview of inter-Korean relations has shown that zero-sum mindsets cause unification dialogue to progress at a slow and often tenuous pace. This, however, does not explain what has caused initiatives to be made in the first place. Surveying history, a number of points in this regard become clear. First, a necessary condition for the initiation of dialogue on the peninsula has been a change in the external security environment. As has often been observed, the Korean peninsula sits at the intersection of the geostrategic interests of the four major powers (China, Japan, the former Soviet Union, and the United States) in Northeast Asia. As the division of Korea was a function of cold war power politics, relations between the two Koreas have been inextricably tied to rivalries between the Western and communist blocs. As a result, it was only with an improvement of relations in the latter arena that changes in the former were forthcoming.

For example, the *sônggong t'ongil* policies embraced by both the North and South throughout the 1950s and 1960s clearly reflected the cold war rivalries of the time. Similarly, the breakthrough in North-South dialogue in 1972 was a function of changes in the external environment. In particular, the emergence of Sino-American rapprochement and superpower detente prompted both Koreas to seek a similar relaxation of tensions on the peninsula. Overtures by the North and South Korean Red Cross in August 1971 were a direct response to Richard Nixon's surprise announcement of his intention to visit China only a few weeks earlier (July 15, 1971).[31] In addition, it was only after the Nixon-Zhou February 1972 summit and the culmination of the Sino-American rapprochement process that Seoul and Pyongyang agreed to hold the meetings between Lee Hu Rak and Kim Yong Ju that led to the July 4 communiqué.[32]

Similar changes in the external environment surrounded the 1991 breakthrough. Sea changes in the international system brought about by the events of 1989 lessened the cold war security concerns that bound Seoul's unification policy, and these changes generally imbued the South with greater confidence to induce an opening to the North. Conversely, the bankruptcy of communism and Seoul's recognition by Beijing and Moscow further isolated Pyongyang, prompting greater receptivity to dialogue initiatives on the peninsula.[33] This argument does not propose that the international environment is the sole causal variable in unification dialogue. Other factors, particularly domestic politics, play an important role. For example, North Korea's entering into talks that led to the 1991 agreement was also motivated by its dire economic situation. Similarly, the 1984–1985 initiatives were prompted on the South Korean side by Chun's desire to legitimize his unpopular regime and ensure a serene domestic political scene prior to the 1988 Olympics. On the North Korean side, these initiatives stemmed from the need for foreign investment as well as Kim Il Sung's desire to make some progress on the unification front before the fortieth anniversary of Korea's liberation from Japanese rule. However, while such domestic issues may have provided the incentive for Seoul and Pyongyang to improve relations, the permissive condition for each to take initiatives based on these incentives has been a thaw in the external security environment.

Second, the inability of the two Koreas to sustain progress after the initiation of dialogue is a function of two factors. In line with the argument above, the first factor is the international environment. As this becomes less accommodating, continued dialogue between the two Koreas is less forthcoming. Such was the case, for example, in the 1972–1974 period, when a deterioration in inter-Korean relations followed the demise of superpower detente and Sino-American rapprochement. Second, even when the international environment is accommodating, an additional obstacle to sustained progress in North-South dialogue is a basic disparity in the strategic objectives of the two sides. Throughout the history of unification dialogue, the South Korean position has been to seek confidence-building measures with the North on less controversial issues as a prerequisite to agreements in more substantive areas:

> The policy of the South was that dialogue, exchanges, and cooperation should begin in such non-political areas as social, culture, sports, and economy where mutual differences would not be substantial, rather than in areas like the military and politics where the two sides would find it hard to reach an accord or cooperation. The idea was that, based on achievements made in non-political areas, mutual dialogue, exchanges and cooperation would lead to the political area, step by step.[34]

By contrast, North Korean objectives with regard to inter-Korean talks have been much more ambitious:

> North Korea demands, under the cloak of the urgency of unification, the resolution of all issues pending between the two sides on a package basis rather than through a phased approach, and through a political and military approach rather than through a functional approach.[35]

This disparity in strategies has been present in virtually all interaction between the two sides. For example, the Chun regime's January 1982 Formula for National Reconciliation and Democratic Unification highlighted twenty inter-Korean pilot projects in economic and cultural areas for building trust. On the other hand, Kim Il Sung's January 1984 counterproposal called for a North-South nonaggression declaration and a United States-North Korea peace treaty. Similarly, at the NSCC talks in 1972, the Kang-Yon prime ministerial talks in 1990–1991, and in countless other unification proposals by the two governments, the South consistently called for economic cooperation and humanitarian projects such as family reunions and cultural exchanges as a spring-board for future political and military agreements. The North rejected these proposals and instead called for the following agenda items: withdrawal of U.S. forces from the South, repeal of anti-communist laws, release of all political prisoners, and an arms reduction agreement.[36] This gap in objectives has made progress beyond the initiation of dialogue difficult. Instead, what has resulted is a plethora of empty unification proposals, and recriminations from both sides, each blaming the other for not cooperating.

The Contradictions of "Hegemonic Unity"

Contributing to Seoul and Pyongyang's inability to maintain productive dialogue is the priority placed by both parties on self-preservation as a prior condition to negotiations. Simply put, the two Koreas genuinely desire unification and see it as inevitable; however, neither is willing to sacrifice its own well-being for this goal. What results is an unviable and oxymoronic conception of "hegemonic unity" evident in both the Northern and Southern visions of unification. The Democratic Confederal Republic of Koryo (DCRK), the embodiment of the North Korean vision, calls for immediate unification of the peninsula under a formula of "one nation, two systems."[37] Two subnational governments would maintain autonomy over daily affairs within their region, but would be guided by an overarching national body (the Supreme National Confederal Assembly). Composed of representatives from the two regions, the Supreme Assembly would coordinate the foreign policies of the two regions, promote uniform economic and cultural development between the regions, and generally ensure that each government's internal policies are consistent with the unity of the nation.[38]

The South Korean plan, most recently formulated as Roh Tae Woo's Korean National Community Formula (KNC) in September 1989 (reiterated by the Kim Young Sam government in May 1993), is a multistage approach that first envisions a period of reconciliation in which the two governments would acknowledge the current status quo and engage in cultural and economic interchange as a means of fostering a common national community and identity (*minjok kongdongch'e*). This would be followed by the establishment of a Korean commonwealth (*Nambuk Yônhap*)—a loose federation of two systems ruling autonomously within their regions but linked through a set of overarching institutions. Executive authority would rest in a Joint Council of Presidents and Council of Ministers, legislative duties would be carried out by a Council of Representatives, and administrative responsibilities would be handled by a joint secretariat in the DMZ "peace zone" and by resident liaison missions ("one people, one government, two systems"). This commonwealth government would then draw up a constitution for the final stage of full integration ("one people, one government, one system").[39]

The DCRK and KNC plans differ in their specifics; however, the underlying point in both plans is the same: the preservation of two separate political systems as the only acceptable format for unification. This is clearly reflected in the North Korean plan, which effectively equates the goal of full integration with two regionally autonomous systems. It is more subtly, but no less clearly reflected in the KNC plan as well. While it advocates eventual unification under one political system, the plan's focus is on the interim commonwealth stage of two autonomous political systems.[40] Moreover, while both plans outwardly offer a vision of the two systems' operating equally under an overarching confederal or commonwealth governing body, each plan implicitly assumes that its system will dominate. This "hegemonic" conceptualization of unification is manifest in the preconditions of the North's DCRK plan, which stipulate the legalization of communist parties and the establishment of a "progressive government" in the South before a confederal system can be implemented.[41] For the South, "hegemonic unity" is reflected in the advocating of a proportional-representation voting system for any bi-national bodies—which given the ROK's two-to-one population advantage over the North, would ensure an ROK-dominated commonwealth.[42] Thus, beneath the rhetoric of Seoul and Pyongyang's plans and proclamations lies the conviction that unification is only possible through dominance. Under such zero-sum mindsets and visions of hegemonic unity, the absence of sustained progress in inter-Korean dialogue is hardly surprising.

Korean Integration: Problems and Priorities

Beyond the history of unification dialogue, several questions arise about the actual process of uniting the two Koreas. What will unification look like? Will it be a relatively smooth transition? If not, what are the potential difficulties? Two scenarios are generally offered for Korean unification: "gradual" and "sudden." The former largely envisions an integration process in which there is a period of reduced military tension, substantial economic reform in the North, and a phased linking of the two systems. At every stage, the process would be controlled by the two Koreas, and a peaceful unification settlement would come about through negotiation.

The latter scenario is premised on a sudden collapse of North Korea. This view focuses on the instability inherent in the North's growing domestic problems. Economic productivity has fallen steadily since 1987, with negative growth rates ranging between -3.7 percent and -5 percent for six consecutive years, beginning in 1990.[43] Industrial facilities are operating at 45 percent of capacity, food shortages are near famine conditions, and energy brownouts are frequent. Pyongyang's trade deficit continues to rise, as does its inability to repay foreign debts. Exacerbating this situation were Moscow's (1991) and Beijing's (1993) decisions to discontinue barter-basis trade with the North. Politically, Kim Il Sung's death raises questions as to whether his son has the capabilities and legitimacy (particularly among the military) to succeed him.[44] Over the past few years, the trickle of North Korean defectors to the South has grown into a steady stream. Augmenting these problems, Pyongyang's intransigence on its suspected nuclear weapons program not only further isolated it from the world community but also raised at one point the possibility of international sanctions which would have further starved the economy. The "sudden" unification scenario therefore envisions some chain of events (i.e., economic collapse, political implosion over a leadership struggle) leading to a Romania-type outcome in the North and unification essentially by default.[45]

It is difficult to assess which of these scenarios is more likely. The preferred outcome for the ROK, the United States, and the major powers in the region is obviously the former, in which policies can dictate events rather than having the rush of events dictate policy. The actual process of unification may fall somewhere between the two extremes. However, regardless of which scenario comes to fruition, it is relatively certain that South Korea will dominate the integration process. In 1972, the two Koreas met as essential equals. Aside from the military stalemate and each side's enjoying the support of its great power patron, the economies of the two Koreas at the time were relatively equal in size, with per capita GNP averaging around $260 to $280. Today, it is clear that the ROK holds the upper hand, with a 1993 GNP ($328 billion) over ten times that of the North, and real growth rates at about 9 percent compared with negative growth (-3.7 percent) for the North. Pyongyang has lost the unconditional backing it once enjoyed from Moscow and Beijing. And South Korean military technology, training, and weaponry, in conjunction with the U.S. forces in the region, offset any Northern quantitative superiority in the military balance.[46]

Another certainty is that a key objective during the unification process will be the integration of the South and North Korean economies. The latter possesses a literate, low-wage, and disciplined work force capable of doing "3-D" labor (dirty, dangerous, and difficult).[47] Combining this labor pool with South Korean capital and technology would open opportunities for co-development of natural resources, lucrative common fishing zones, and joint ventures in manufacturing. The latter would include light industry complexes in port cities such as Namp'o (west coast) and Wônsan (east coast), multi-million dollar tourist resorts at Kûmgang-san on the North-South border and Paekdu-san on the Chinese border, and industrial complexes in the area currently occupied by the DMZ.[48] Low-cost North Korean labor could also be profitably employed by South Korean contractors for construction projects in third countries (particularly the Middle East and Siberian Russia). In addition, the North's relative abundance of natural resources and the South's abundance of manufactured goods offer a natural complement to one another. This is already manifest in the content of indirect and direct commodity trade between the two sides.[49] A successful synthesis of the two economies would not only help offset the initial costs of unification (discussed below), but also would reduce the country's reliance on imports, expand the domestic market, and enhance international competitiveness. Given this, there are a number of policy priorities and potential problems that a united Korean government (presumably under Seoul) will have to grapple with.

Infrastructure and Energy

A prerequisite for the successful marriage of the two economies will be the massive redevelopment of North Korean infrastructure.[50] One priority will be transportation. Despite being some 25 percent larger in area than the South, North Korea has less than a third of its total roadway capacity (23,000 vs. 70,316 kilometers, respectively). While the South boasts 56,389 kilometers of paved roads and 1,800 kilometers of expressways, comparable figures for the North stand at a paltry 1,717 kilometers (paved), and 354 kilometers (highways).[51] Moreover,

North Korean railways are highly inefficient and for the most part have not been modernized since the Japanese occupation. The upgrading and construction of comprehensive road and railway networks reconnecting a united Korea will therefore be of paramount importance. In particular, all of the North's border and coastal areas would require linking up with Seoul. On the west coast of the peninsula, this would mean road and railway corridors up through Pyongyang to the Chinese border. These would connect Seoul to newly industrializing areas in the North such as Namp'o, and at the far northwest of the peninsula, areas such as Sinûiju, now the major embarkation point for railways to China. On the east coast, extensive road and rail networks would be laid from Wônsan to Najin. These would connect Seoul with the three cities designated by Pyongyang as special economic zones (Ch'ôngjin, Unggi [Sonbong], and Najin), as well as providing links to the Tumen River project. This corridor would also facilitate commerce at the northeastern border with Russia and along the entire east coast with Japan. As an indicator of the difficulties that transportation links pose to successful integration, recent visitors to the Najin-Sonbong Free Trade Zone noted that access to the facilities via overland travel was extremely difficult; that there was only one single-lane semi-paved road connecting the two areas (requiring thirty minutes to travel seventeen kilometers); and that roads to China or Russia from the zone are unpaved and would be impassable in less than ideal weather conditions.[52] In the inland areas of the peninsula, the Seoul-Pyongyang corridor will obviously be a priority. Another major area of development in this region will be Kaesông. Located only forty miles north of the DMZ, this North Korean city serves as a potential residential area for commuters to Seoul and Inch'ôn.[53]

A second infrastructural priority will be in the power and energy sector. North Korea's total electric output capacity (30 to 35 billion kwh) is currently less than one-fourth that of Seoul (118 to 131 billion kwh). Although the North has relatively smaller energy needs than the South, estimates show that it experiences a chronic shortage of 10 to15 billion kwh.[54] In addition, power transmission lines are grossly inefficient, and visitors to the North have witnessed frequent brownouts.[55] Supplying power to the North therefore will constitute one of the most important tasks in the unification process. The costs of such a project will be daunting. Although Seoul initially will have to reconnect the two national grids and provide thermal and nuclear energy to make up for the North's shortfall, the ROK's current generating capacity leaves little excess energy to be tapped. As a result, substantial costs will be involved in longer-term projects for expanding the North's thermal and hydroelectric generating capacities, and for constructing new power stations and transmission lines. [56] (The general costs of unification are computed below.)

Employment and Population Transfers

A major policy priority will be border control. When unification comes about, there will be tremendous popular pressure for immediate and unrestricted cross-border travel. For Koreans, a Berlin Wall-type dismantling of the DMZ, coupled with the sight of tearful family reunions, would be the ultimate symbol of unification. However, the problems with such a policy are not minor. Once the North falls, its citizens will become cognizant of the relatively higher living standards and job opportunities in the South, resulting in a transborder flood of northerners in search of a better life. Estimates put this influx in the range of 7 million[57]—nearly one-third of the North Korean population. The South Korean labor and housing markets would be incapable of absorbing these new arrivals, leaving the government with the burden of mass unemployment (discussed below), relocation of the homeless, and astronomical social welfare costs. At the same time, one cannot discount the destabilizing effects of southerners pressing northward based on geneological claims for lands occupied by northerners. As a result, it will be incumbent on a united Korean government to maintain border control during the unification process. The DMZ will have to remain intact in some form, possibly with immigration-type checkpoints for north-south travel. The government could target three groups for approved cross-border travel in the initial stages of unification. The first would be separated family members. The second would be individuals seeking to develop business and commerce in the North. And the third would be a limited number of North Korean laborers (possibly through a lottery-type system) for employment in the South. This undoubtedly would be a politically unpopular policy; however, it may be the only way to circumvent the problems described above.[58]

In addition to preventing an oversupply of labor in the South, a united Korean government will have to deal with potentially severe labor redundancy in the North. In particular, groups hardest hit will be the military and workers in the chemical and steel industries. Regarding the latter two, although Kim Il Sung invested heavily in the development of these sectors, they will not fare well once exposed to free-market forces. North Korean steel, for example, was found to be of such poor quality by Chinese, Soviet, and South Korean importers that it was deemed unusable. Similarly, while technology used by chemical industries in the eastern coastal city of Hamhûng was once among the world's most modern (when first built during the Japanese occupation), by today's standards, it is now extremely outdated. As occurred in eastern Germany, many of these firms will have to shut down, or they may be wholly taken over by private South Korean firms for retooling. In either case, the result will be massive layoffs of workers. The same problem appears likely in the case of the military. North Korea's armed forces currently number in excess of a million men. With unification, some of these forces will be absorbed into the South Korean military (currently 650,000); however, many will become redundant as a united Korean military will have little need for forces in the range of 1.65 million, and most likely will be pared down to a third of that number. This promises to be a difficult problem for the united Korean government. Although the North reports gross enrollment ratios of about 96 percent in primary and secondary education (comparable to the South's ratio of 95 percent), the content and quality of this education is suspect. By comparison, in Germany, where the educational gap between easterners and westerners was relatively smaller, some 80 percent of the former population have had to undergo retraining in order to function competititvely in the economy.[59] In the longer term, worker retraining and relocation programs may be able to funnel some of this excess labor into the South as well as into new sectors in the North (i.e., light industry, construction). However, in the interim period, the government will be saddled with paying unemployment subsidies and checking potential social disorder (such as alcoholism and crime) caused by disillusioned masses who thought unification would bring them more. As Nicholas Eberstadt expects,

> a united Korea will have to deal with a much greater social security problem than the one currently facing Seoul. It will have to determine the nature and financial basis of a peninsula-wide pension system. It will have to decide whether benefits will be standard for all, or whether individual and regional differences are acceptable. No less importantly, it will have to deal with the fact that pension payments would raise the nation's labor costs, thus reducing labor productivity and diminishing Korea's international competitiveness.[60]

Linked to the issues of employment and population flows is monetary union. With unification, the government will most likely unify the two currencies under the South Korean won. The challenge here will be to avoid the problems associated with West Germany's decision to convert East German marks at parity. This produced an artificial rise in East German income without concurrent increases in productivity and gave way to high inflation and a 40 percent unemployment rate in the initial stages of unification.[61] The challenge for a united Korean government will be to unify the two currencies at a rate that accomplishes multiple competing objectives. On the one hand, an exchange rate must be set that circumvents the inflation and unemployment problems experienced in the German case. On the other hand, this rate must be close enough to parity to provide northerners enough wealth that they do not choose to flood south. And on the other hand still, the designated rate must devalue the North Korean won enough to keep northern wages competitively low, which will be necessary to attract foreign investment as well as to reap the benefits of the marriage between South Korean capital and North Korean labor. This will be a hotly debated issue for the united Korean government.[62]

Food

Another policy priority for a united Korean government will be to feed the North. North Korean agriculture has suffered from diminishing returns as a result of over-farming and outdated technology. For example, while annual rice production in the late-1970s averaged 5 million tons, totals for 1990 have decreased to 2.9 million. By contrast, the South produces some 5.3 million tons of rice per year, and output per unit (10 acres) stands at 451 kilograms versus the North's 306 kilograms. The result has been an estimated annual rice shortage of 1.5 million tons in the North.[63] The severity of the problem has been evident in Pyongyang's recent instituting of a program of "two-meals-per-day" and "less rice, more vegetables," and in its international appeals for rice since 1995. Reports circulated in 1991 that six consecutive crop failures in the North have caused near famine conditions, and that riots at rationing centers were not uncommon.[64] The best-fed of the northern population is the military, but even here there are countless stories of impromptu exchanges between South and North Korean soldiers at P'anmunjôm in which the latter boast of meals that would be considered poverty-standard in the South. Moreover, the quality of whatever sparse rice North Korea cultivates is inferior.[65] As a result, in the initial phases of unification, Seoul will have to supply its excess rice stocks (approximately 2.1 million tons) to the northern population. This will be critical not only to alleviate any malnutrition-related diseases, but also to reduce the incentive for northerners to migrate south.

Social-Psychological Costs

The final set of points relates to the social aspects of unification. An understanding of these issues is best presented in the form of questions. First, while most Koreans will welcome the marriage of northern labor and southern capital as beneficial to the united Korean economy as a whole, South Korean labor groups may be less enthusiastic. Since the mid-1980s, these groups have struggled to improve working conditions and raise wage levels (currently around $900/month vs. $80/month in the North).[66] The prospect of an abundant supply of northern labor that puts downward pressure on wages will not be looked upon happily. Questions therefore arise as to how southern labor will react to unification. Will workers resist the influx of low-cost northern labor? Will this be a source of social unrest? Or will southern labor groups try to co-opt the new arrivals from the north before management gets to them?

Second, the North Korean population is currently one of the most isolated in the world. Once unification comes about, this population will undoubtedly face a period of psychological dislocation as decades of indoctrination and brainwashing under the "Great Leader" lose meaning. What new moral authority will replace Kimilsungism for the northerners? Will it be Christianity and Buddhism, resulting from an influx of religious groups from the South?[67] Or will it be a resurgence of the Confucian cultural heritage from the Yi dynasty (1392–1910)?[68]

Finally, to what extent will regionalism divide a united Korea? This problem is already well established in the South as competition between the politically dominant Kyôngsang provinces, in the southeast, and the politically alienated Chôlla provinces, in the southwest. Similar schisms exist in the North, between the western P'yôngan provinces and the eastern Hamgyông provinces, stemming from the former's status as the home province of Kim Il Sung, and the latter's as an industrial center and the home of party cadres. These rivalries will continue in some form in the post-unification era. Another possibility is a divide between the northern and southern provinces as a whole. This is not unprecedented in Korean history. The early Three Kingdoms period (pre-seventh century) was marked by decades of warfare among the Silla, Paekche, and Koguryo states (which correspond roughly to the present-day Kyôngsang, Chôlla, and northern provinces, respectively). The Silla dynasty emerged victorious from these wars in the seventh century and dominated Koguryo and Paekche for some three hundred years before being defeated by the Koguryo state, in 935. The ensuing Koryo dynasty (tenth to fourteenth centuries) was marked by the dominance of the north over Chôlla (Paekche) and Kyôngsang (Silla).[69] It remains to be seen whether such regional rivalries will emerge in the form of larger-scale political divisions in a united Korea. In addition, the problems that have emerged in a social-psychological context in Germany are not beyond the realm of possibility in Korea. In spite of Korea's vibrant nationalism, more affluent and educated southerners may feel superior to their northern brethren. Northerners may see their southern counterparts as materialistic and money-crazed. Much as in the German case, South Koreans, while initially welcoming unity, may increasingly grow resentful at the costs they must bear in the form of taxes and social welfare burdens in assimilating the North. These are extremely complex problems which are unavoidable in either a soft- or hard-landing scenario.

United Korea and the Northeast Asian Balance of Power

The final task in a discussion of unification is to look beyond the problems and priorities in the integration process and briefly consider the effect of a united Korea on the strategic balance in Northeast Asia. One triad that deserves particular attention is that of united Korea, China, and Japan. The interaction between the latter two over Korea has always been historically significant. The Mongol and Hideyoshi invasions of the thirteenth and sixteenth centuries, the Sino-Japanese war at the close of the nineteenth century, and the Japanese occupation of the twentieth century all stemmed in one way or another from competition for a foothold on the peninsula. The strategic importance of Korea for the two Asian powers was also evident during the cold war as the peninsula served as both a forward and rear line of defense for Japan and China. Some predictions about the future relationships among these three powers is therefore appropriate.[70] Such an exercise is important for two reasons. First, if the past is any indicator of the future, Sino-Japanese interaction over Korea will again be a key ingredient in the stability (or instability) of a post-unification, post-cold war Northeast Asia. Second, an understanding of each state's anxieties and opportunities regarding a future united Korea may shed light on its current attitudes toward the unification process.

There are essentially two views on a united Korea's position in East Asia. The first might be called the "conventional" view. Simply put, this states that a united Korean government (presumably dominated by the South) will be a key actor in the region, and will be more independent of U.S. influence. Regarding China, growing economic ties, the recent normalization of Seoul-Beijing relations, historical affinities stemming from the Yi dynasty (1392-1910), and a common Confucian heritage will move Seoul in the direction of cooperative relations with its northern neighbor. On the other hand, historical animosities, economic rivalries, and resurgent nationalism will drive a united Korea toward contentious relations with Japan.[71]

The second is the vision of "armed neutrality." This foresees an independent and united Korea enmeshed in the Northeast Asian regional economy. Investment and trade ties would reinforce the recently normalized relations with China and would ease historical antagonisms with Japan. Militarily, a united Korea would remain neutral in the East Asian balance, along the lines of Austria, or more appropriately Switzerland, where Korea would adopt a declaration of neutrality but would develop an increasingly self-sufficient military that could face down any power that attempted to exert influence against it.[72]

Because both views operate in the realm of prediction, neither can be judged incorrect; however, a third vision may be considered. In common with the other two views, this perspective recognizes that the economic and military capabilities of a united Korea would make it a prominent regional power. Even though alliance ties may continue between Korea and the United States in the post-unification era, the absence of the North Korean threat, and Washington's long-term commitment to decrease its regional security responsibilities, will make Korea (by choice or by necessity) less reliant on the United States. The latter policy was made clear by the Bush administration's closing of Clark and Subic Bay bases in the Philippines and plans for the phased withdrawal of troops from Korea. The key piece of legislation in this regard was the Nunn-Warner plan, later known as the East Asian Strategic Initiative (EASI) which called for the transfer of the United

States-ROK joint command structure to South Korea, and the phased withdrawal of U.S. troops from the peninsula. Although mitigating circumstances since 1992 have caused the United States to suspend indefinitely further reductions in Korea and re-state the importance attached to a stable American presence in the region, Asian governments perceive some form of U.S. withdrawal from the region as inevitable in the post-cold war era.[73] Where this view differs from the conventional wisdom and the "neutrality" arguments is in its assessment of relations with China and Japan. In particular, it foresees a triangular dynamic marked by an increasing isolation of Beijing and an improvement in a united Korea's ties with Tokyo. Three factors lead to this assessment: (1) the geopolitical imperatives inherent in a unification of the peninsula, (2) the exorbitant costs of unification, and (3) as already cited, a less dominant U.S. presence in post-cold war Asia.

China: Geostrategic Realities

In order to understand a united Korea's relations with China, one must begin with the 1992 Seoul-Beijing normalization pact. South Koreans were certainly ecstatic over this agreement. It not only marked the end of decades of hostile relations with a former adversary, but also opened a vast array of economic opportunities for Korean business. However, perhaps more significantly, normalization was welcomed by the South Koreans because it amounted to a diplomatic coup over the North. In conjunction with the normalization pact with Moscow, the ROK succeeded in wooing Pyongyang's two primary supporters into its camp. This marked the ultimate victory in Seoul's zero-sum, relative gains strategic competition on the peninsula. In this sense, the diplomatic isolation of Pyongyang has been a major incentive for Seoul's *Nordpolitik*.[74] While couched in the language of post-cold war engagement and liberal conceptions of security, the northern policy was both motivated by and reaffirmed Seoul's cold war containment objectives on the peninsula.[75] In a unification scenario, however, this containment rationale disappears. Instead, a united Korea would have to contend with sharing a vast, 800-mile land border with a militarily and economically burgeoning China, whose intentions are not transparent. China's current rates of military buildup and economic growth, and its sheer size, make it the one power in the region that other states cannot balance against alone. These factors, coupled with Chinese ambitions in Southeast Asia, make consideration of it as one of the most likely threats in post-cold war Asia unavoidable.[76] Moreover, a united Korea would face this situation without the same U.S. security guarantees enjoyed during the cold war. A united Korea might therefore view China as the new proximate threat and almost certainly would heavily fortify its northern border.

A number of additional factors do not bode well for united Korea-China relations. Optimists point out that the rapid growth in ROK-China economic relations will only multiply when Korea unifies. Virtually nonexistent during the 1970s, bilateral trade increased exponentially from the mid-1980s ($461 million in 1985 to $5.8 billion in 1991 and $9 billion in 1993). In 1991, the two governments negotiated most-favored-nation privileges, investment treaties, and direct commercial flights. China has become the third-largest foreign investment market for the ROK, and the ROK has become Beijing's eighth-largest trading partner.[77] In spite of these trends, it is difficult to see how these would wholly mollify security concerns. In fact, much of the initial euphoria among South Koreans since the normalization accord has worn off, and certain economic realities are setting in. For example, despite investing heavily in the China market, South Korean businesses have been victimized by Beijing's abrupt suspension of joint venture projects on numerous occasions. This all-too-common occurrence has made South Korean investors wary of the economic risks associated with an authoritarian government. In addition, the ROK's trade deficit with China is not insubstantial. It reached $1 billion in 1991 and is already spawning trade friction between Seoul and Beijing. Another concern is that China's low production costs and devalued currency have made its products so competitive that they now challenge South Korean exports for market share in Japan and the United States. From the late 1980s to the early 1990s, for example, Korea's advantage over China in exports to the United States decreased from $11.6 billion to $3.3 billion. Similarly, while South Korean exports to Japan outpaced China's by $1.9 billion in the late 1980s, by the 1990s China had surpassed the ROK by $.4 billion.[78] Rather than consider China an economic partner, Koreans may increasingly see China as an economic threat.[79]

Renewed Korean nationalism arising from unification could also translate into animosities toward China. While much emphasis is placed on negative Korean attitudes toward Japan, these seem equally relevant in the Chinese case. It was China, not Japan, with whom the Koreans most recently fought a war. Or, as one analyst more succinctly observed,

When Koreans get around to nursing grudges, they might consider which neighbor [Japan or China] saddled them with Kim Il
Sung, which gave the go-ahead for the Korean War, and which
prevented non-Communist unification in late 1950 by massive,
undeclared intervention.[80]

Coupled with this nationalism, the political mood of a post-unification Korean society will most likely be strongly anti-communist. In
particular, once North Koreans realize how they were deprived by
decades of Kimilsungism, the resulting indignation will eradicate any
residual affinity for socialism that might be harbored in a united Korea. This would infuse Seoul's attitudes toward the Chinese government as it stands today with a considerable degree of distrust and
suspicion.

Similar anxieties and concerns would exist on the Chinese side.
Throughout the history of Korea's division, it has often been observed
that none of the major powers has an interest in a change in the status
quo on the peninsula. This is especially the case for China. As two
Chinese analysts have argued,

Should an adversary force control the peninsula, China would be
deprived of an indispensable security buffer proximate to both
the nation's capital and to one of its most important industrial
regions.[81]

In order to preserve this North Korean "buffer," Beijing on numerous
occasions has expressed its preference for a confederal-type unification formula of "one system, two governments" on the peninsula. The
absorption of the North into a unified Korea under Seoul would present
Beijing with the prospects of another noncompliant power (à la Vietnam) on its southern flank with a competing ideological and social
system.[82] Moreover, China would not pass lightly over the security
implications of such a situation. For example, it has already begun
expressing concerns about the buildup of South Korean (and Japanese) naval forces.[83] These concerns would be exacerbated in the case
of a united Korea. Finally, nationalist fervor from a united Korea may
raise Beijing's concern about the ethnic Korean communities in southern Manchuria. Highly educated and living autonomously in Jilin Province, this population numbers some two million and constitutes the
largest contingent of overseas Koreans in the world.[84] A potentially

serious situation could arise between Seoul and Beijing if China perceived this ethnic minority as an internal security risk.

Japan: Economic Pragmatism

In contrast to the dim outlook for a united Korea's relations with
Beijing, the prospects for cooperation with Japan appear bright. The
primary factor weighing in favor of this proposition is the cost of
unification. A report by the Korea Development Institute (KDI) in 1991
estimated that in a best case scenario (that is, phased unification preceded by a period of economic reform in the North), the total investment required to bring North Korean productivity levels to 60 percent
of the ROK's capacity would be $774 billion—more than double the
ROK's 1993 GNP, $328 billion. Even spread over ten years, this aver-
ages to an annual outlay far in excess of the ROK's entire national
budget ($45 billion/year). A report by the Economist Intelligence Unit
(EIU) in 1992 revised some of the KDI figures. Factoring in additional
sources of domestic financing such as "unification tax" revenues, peace
dividends resulting from a rationalization of the two militaries, and
North Korean contributions, it still found the cost of unification to be
in the range of $500 to $610 billion over ten years.[85] South Koreans
are also fully aware that any attempt to underwrite unification will be
infinitely more difficult than it was in the German case. ROK per capita
GNP is only 25 percent that of West Germany; moreover, the gap
between the East and West German economies was much smaller than
that between the two Koreas'. While Germany's unification cost (estimated between $500 billion and $1 trillion) occupied only some 10
percent of the national budget, a low-end figure of $500 billion for
Korea's unification is over ten times Seoul's national budget. In addition, while West Germany was geographically larger and four times
more populous than its counterpart, the ROK is 25 percent smaller in
area and only twice as populous as the North. This presages a relatively heavier burden in terms of infrastructure and social welfare costs.[86]

The ROK therefore does not possess the will or the capacity to
finance unification alone. It will need substantial inflows of foreign
aid and investment (such as through government bond sales, international borrowing, grants-in-aid, and so on). The most likely source of
this capital will be Japan. The United States, the European countries,
and international organizations will not be capable of undertaking such
a task. By contrast, Japan has a history of economic success in Korea

and extensive business contacts as a result. This is true not only for Seoul but also for Pyongyang, where the North Korean resident community (*Chosen Soren*) in Japan has negotiated trade between the two countries since the 1970s. More importantly, the Japanese will be motivated by the cheap, literate, and proximate labor pool offered by the northern work force after unification.[87] They will be eager to take part in infrastructural projects such as expansion throughout the peninsula of the current $8 billion Seoul-Pusan high-speed railway. Another major area of Japanese investment will be in tourism—in particular, the development of Kûmgang-san and Paekdu-san as resort areas along the lines of Chung Ju Yung's January 1989 proposal. A third area of interest will be development of the entire eastern coast of the peninsula stretching from Wônsan to Najin for trade and manufacturing purposes. In short, just as Japan filled South Korea's foreign capital needs in the early stages of economic development in the 1960s and 1970s, it will do so again during the unification process. Koreans will no doubt oppose a major role for Japan in yet another watershed in Korea's history. Indeed, historical-emotional resentment of the Japanese runs so deep that it is often indistinguishable from Korean patriotism. However, it will be incumbent on Koreans to disentangle these two notions. Nationalism as "anti-Japanism" in the past will have to be transcended by nationalism as "pro-Koreanism" in the future. Koreans should be capable of doing this; besides, if an orderly and financially feasible unification is the central objective, there may be little choice in the matter.

Would Japan cooperate with a united Korea? There have been two basic arguments (advanced largely by Koreans) that Japan would oppose unification. One states that a united Korea would possess the military capabilities and the motive (i.e., revenge) to pose a threat to Japan. The other argues that a united Korea would challenge Japan economically. Both of these are overstated. First, the economic argument is only partially valid. As was the case with the South Korean economy, the infusion of Japanese capital and technology into a united Korea will end up posing challenges to Japanese businesses in certain sectors (the "boomerang" effect). However, a united Korean economy would not threaten to overtake Japan. The combined population of the two Koreas would still be only half that of Japan. Moreover, the South Korean economy, despite its success, is currently only one-fourteenth the size of Japan's. The addition of North Korean industry and mineral resources would marginally close this gap at best.

Second, while Koreans, both North and South, harbor deep resentment toward the Japanese, there is no historical precedent that this would translate into a united Korean military threat directed at Japan. The Korean peninsula has often been referred to as a "dagger" pointed at the heart of Japan; however, aggression against Japan has historically come *through* Korea by the Chinese (for example, the thirteenth-century Mongol invasions), not *by* Koreans per se. As alluded to above, a united Korea would also be preoccupied with threats on its northern border, leaving it little luxury to indulge in fantasies about retribution against the Japanese.[88] Third, arguments that Japan would be threatened by a joint North-South Korean military have little basis. Based on current levels, the two Korean militaries total around 1.65 million, with combined defense expenditures on the order of $14 billion (25 percent of GNP for the South and 30 percent for the North).[89] This would indeed be intimidating to Japan. However, in a unification scenario, a rationalization of the two militaries would almost certainly take place. Using the traditional ratio of military forces at one percent of population, force levels for a united Korea would more likely number around 500,000 to 650,000, which is lower than current ROK levels. Finally, the same concerns that figure in Tokyo's geostrategic thinking in the post-cold war era would be relevant in a unification scenario. Japan would face uncertain relationships with Russia and China, and would have to contend with pressure from the United States to burden-share in the region. Both of these factors would make Japan more receptive to cooperative ties with Korea.[90]

In sum, the regional balance in a post-unification, post-cold war Northeast Asia will be characterized by a growing alignment between Korea and Japan on the one hand, and growing tensions between Korea and China on the other.[91] The latter will be the result of geostrategic imperatives. History has shown that the potential is high for insecurity spirals among states with contiguous land borders. In this regard, a united Korea will face a military and economic behemoth on its northern border. It will not have the autonomous capabilities to balance against this power; in addition, in the post-cold war era, it will not have the luxury of certain U.S. security guarantees. While a united Korea will certainly experience its share of animosities and trade frictions with Japan, these will be dampened by the more proximate Chinese threat and by the need for Japanese financial support during the unification process. Furthermore, this relationship (presumably between Tokyo and a united Korean government under Seoul) will still be grounded in the decades of Japan-South Korean normalized relations since 1965 and in the experience of common security ties with the United States for the entire postwar and cold war eras. While these relations do not constitute "institutions" in the formal sense of a European NATO or EC, they do breed a familiarity between Japan and Korea that is not present in dealings between Seoul and Beijing leaders.[92] By contrast, the reservoir of experiences that a united Seoul government and Beijing could draw on would not extend further back than 1992. Compelled to balance against the more proximate threat and more unfamiliar threat, Korea will look to Japan with greater fondness.

Trends in this direction are already noticeable. For example, during a 1993 trip to China, ROK Foreign Minister Han Sung Joo explicitly told Beijing authorities that while Japan once administered Korea as a colony, it was no longer seen as threatening.[93] ROK Defense Ministry White Papers for 1993 stated that given the fluidity of the security environment in a post-cold war East Asia, expanding cooperation with Japan was an important ingredient for the peaceful reunification of the peninsula.[94] In addition, in 1994 summit meetings between Premier Hosokawa and President Kim Young Sam, the two leaders called for a new relationship "to discard past prejudices and look to the future with open hearts and minds." Kim further stated that a united Korea would pose no threat to Japan, and that the two states would be "trustworthy" partners.[95] Finally, in conjunction with the North Korean nuclear dispute, scenarios predicated on a sudden collapse of the North have already been a topic of discussion in tripartite talks at the assistant foreign minister level among Tokyo, Seoul, and Washington.[96] While this is all admittedly very preliminary evidence, it does suggest some support of the above propositions.

Conclusion

Since the division of the peninsula in 1945, Korea's road to unification has been beset by many obstacles. However, in the 1990s, a wave of change has swept across both the peninsula and the international system. The demise of communism now renders meaningless the cold war prism through which inter-Korean relations have been refracted. As a result of their entry to the United Nations in September 1991, the two Koreas have now attained long-sought acceptance as sovereign members of the international community. In spite of the problems with the 1991 Basic Agreement, it is through this document that the two have tacitly accepted the norm of peaceful coexistence and recognition of one another as equal negotiating partners. Cross-recognition of the Koreas among the major powers is also nearly complete. Seoul's successful *Nordpolitik* has gained it the recognition of Beijing and Moscow. Pyongyang has engaged in preliminary normalization talks with Japan. And as a result of the Agreed Framework, the likelihood of the establishment of U.S. and North Korean liaison offices is imminent.

Finally, the election of a former opposition politician to the presidency in the ROK made irrelevant North Korea's refusal to negotiate with military authoritarian regimes in the South. Thus, the gradual removal of what appeared only a few years ago to be insurmountable obstacles has edged Korea firmly forward on the path to unification. Whether the next steps will continue in the same direction will be a function of the nuclear dispute in the immediate future and, in the longer term, the North's economic viability. In spite of these uncertainties, certain undeniable facts remain. Unification of the peninsula is inevitable. Whether this occurs at the end of this decade or after, South Korea will dominate the new Korean entity. It will be faced with a huge task, and the Korean capacity to wade through adversity will be tested as citizens on both sides of the border will have to brace themselves for a period of social and economic sacrifice. Furthermore, in spite of Korea's desire for unification without the involvement of external powers, the financial burden of unification and the interests at stake for all the regional powers on the peninsula will make this an international project that tests the limits of multilateral cooperation in East Asia. While this analysis does not offer the most sanguine portrayal of unification, the fact that the debate has moved beyond a mere recounting of the history of North-South dialogue to a discussion of the integration process and its implications is itself an indicator that the distance left to be travelled on the unification road grows shorter and its end hovers visibly on the horizon.

Notes

1. For two classic works in this vein, see Robert Axelrod, *The Evolution of Cooperation* (New York: Basic Books, 1984); and Kenneth Oye, ed., *Cooperation under Anarchy* (Princeton: Princeton University Press, 1986). For an overview of the neoliberal institution literature in international relations, see David A. Baldwin, ed., *Neorealism and Neoliberalism* (New York: Columbia University Press, 1993).

2. The origins of the two Koreas date back to the close of the second World War. In what was expected to be an interim arrangement to receive the Japanese surrender, the United States and Soviet Union divided the peninsula into two military occupation zones at the 38th parallel. The two primary criteria for the United States in this decision were to locate a boundary of roughly equal occupation zones that would be acceptable to the Soviets, and to keep the capital city of Seoul within the U.S. sphere. Although an independent and united Korea "in due course" was hoped for (first stated at the Cairo Conference in 1943), nascent cold war rivalries soon made it apparent that unification of the two zones under a mutually acceptable government was not possible. On August 15, 1948, United Nations-administered elections in the southern portion of the peninsula established the Republic of Korea. This was followed by elections in the north establishing the communist Democratic People's Republic of Korea (DPRK) on September 9, 1948. Any notion of a reconciliation between the two regimes was rendered obsolete by the outbreak of the Korean War (June 25, 1950). The three-year conflict cemented a permanent division of the peninsula and made Korea a flashpoint of cold war rivalry in East Asia. See Koo Youngnok and Han Sung-joo, "Historical Legacy," in Koo and Han, eds., *The Foreign Policy of the Republic of Korea* (New York: Columbia University Press, 1985), pp. 3-9; Dean Rusk, *As I Saw It* (New York: Penguin, 1990), pp. 123-24, 167; and Bruce Cumings, *The Origins of the Korean War*, vol.1 (Princeton: Princeton University Press, 1981), pp. 101-31 esp. 117-22.

3. The most serious of these were the January 1968 North Korean commando raids on the ROK presidential compound (Blue House) and seizure of a U.S. intelligence vessel (U.S.S. *Pueblo*); coastal infiltrations by guerilla forces in November 1968; and the shootdown of a U.S. reconnaissance plane (EC-121) in April 1969.

4. After its failure to unify the peninsula in 1953, Pyongyang's rhetoric switched to an emphasis on "peaceful" unification; nevertheless, an underlying assumption was that this would materialize only after a violent overthrow of the capitalist regime in the South. For a good summary of ROK and DPRK unification strategies during the 1950s and 1960s, see Kim Hak-joon, *The Unification Policy of South and North Korea* (Seoul: Seoul National University Press, 1977), chapters 2-7; and B.C. Koh, "Foreign Policy and Inter-Korean Relations" *Korea and World Affairs* 9, 4 (Winter 1985), p. 678.

5. Initial proposals were made by ROK Red Cross President Choi Doo Sun on August 12, 1971. North Korea responded positively, and a series of preliminary talks took place from September 1971 to August 1972. Formal negotiations began in August 1972, and a series of seven full-dress Red Cross sessions were held alternately in Pyongyang and Seoul through July 1973. For a detailed discussion of these meetings, see National Unification Board, *A White Paper on South-North*

Dialogue in Korea (Seoul: National Unification Board, December 31, 1988), pp. 35-54, and 76-104.

6. For a discussion of these meetings, see ibid., pp. 56-62.

7. For the text, see "7-4 Nambuk kongdong sôngmyôngsô" (7-4 South-North joint communiqué), *Taehan Min'guk Woegyo yônp'yo: 1972 bu juyo munhôn* (Major and minor diplomatic documents annual of the Republic of Korea, hereafter Diplomatic Documents Annual) (Seoul: Ministry of Foreign Affairs), pp. 203-6; and *Nambuk Taehwa Paeksô* (Seoul: Kukto t'ongilwon nambuk taehwa samuguk, 1988) (White paper on South-North dialogue), pp. 54-56. For additional analyses, see *Korea Herald*, July 4, 1972; Hakjoon Kim, *Unification Policy of South and North Korea*, pp. 266-70; "Text of Remarks by H.E. Yong Shik Kim, Minister of Foreign Affairs of the Republic of Korea, at the National Press Club, September 29, 1972, Washington DC," *Woegyo yônp'yo: 1972* (Diplomatic Documents Annual), pp. 282-86; and Saito Takashi, "Japan and Korean Unification," *Japan Interpreter* 8, 1 (Winter 1973), pp. 88-98.

8. For a chronology of the NSCC talks, see *White Paper on South-North Dialogue*, pp. 63-75 and 104-108.

9. Later proposals by both Seoul and Pyongyang would reiterate the principles enunciated in the July 4 communiqué. For examples, see *White Paper on South-North Dialogue*, pp. 118-19; B.C. Koh, "Policy toward Reunification," in Koo and Han, *The Foreign Policy of the Republic of Korea*, pp. 94-97; and *Woegyo yônp'yo: 1974* (Diplomatic Documents Annual), pp. 265-79.

10. For a typical example, see "2 Sides Swap No Minutes on Confab Results," *Korea Herald,* March 23, 1973.

11. For example, at the second NSCC meeting in March 1973, ROK delegation chief Lee Hu Rak and North Korean deputy chief Park Sung Chul became embroiled in a heated exchange over which side was responsible for the Korean War. See "South-North Talks Slow to Snail's Pace," *Korea Herald,* April 6, 1973.

12. Pyongyang suspended the dialogue in protest over the KCIA's involvement in the kidnapping of ROK opposition politician Kim Dae Jung from Japan. Both the NSCC and Red Cross talks continued at lower levels until March 1975 (NSCC) and December 1977 (Red Cross) but were effectively dead after 1973. Pyongyang unilaterally cut the "hotline" with Seoul in 1976.

13. For Lee's statements, see *Far Eastern Economic Review* (hereafter, *FEER*), July 8, 1972. For Kim's statements, see Saito, "Japan and Korean Unification," p. 29. For similar statements by ROK Red Cross chief delegate Lee Bum Suk and other high-ranking officials, see *Korea Herald,* March 24, 1973; "US Newsman Told of Danger of NK Provocation," *Korea Herald,* February 12, 1974; and Lee Chong-sik, "The Impact of the Sino-American Detente on Korea," in Gene T. Hsiao, ed., *Sino-American Detente and its Policy Implications* (New York: Praeger, 1974), pp. 190-91.

14. Pyongyang most likely made the flood relief offer for propaganda purposes, not expecting Seoul to accept. The aid consisted of rice, clothing, cement, and various medical supplies. For these events and the resumption of Red Cross talks, see *White Paper on South-North Dialogue*, pp. 187-89, 201-47.

15. For the contents of these three sets of talks, see Aidan Foster-Carter, *Korea's Coming Reunification: Another East Asian Superpower?* Economist Intelligence Unit,

Special Report No. M212 (London: Economist Intelligence Unit, April 1992) (hereafter, EIU, *Special Report*), pp. 51–52; *White Paper on South-North Dialogue*, pp.189–201 (sports), 263–96 (economics), and 296–307 (parliamentary); and Chang Young-jung, "Economic Transactions and Cooperation between North and South Korea," *Korean Journal of International Studies* 24, 1 (September 1993), pp. 20, 25–26.

16. Chang, "Economic Transactions and Cooperation between North and South Korea," p. 25.

17. See *White Paper on South-North Dialogue,* pp. 248-63.

18. The July 1988 declaration called for the promotion of political, economic, and cultural exchanges; the promotion of inter-Korean trade; and pledges to aid Pyongyang in improving relations with the United States and Japan. For the text, see "Special Declaration for National Self-Esteem, Unification, and Prosperity," reprinted in *White Paper on South-North Dialogue,* pp. 461-65.

19. See EIU, *Special Report,* pp. 52-54; and James Cotton, "Conflict and Accommodation in the Two Koreas," in Stuart Harris and James Cotton, eds., *The End of the Cold War in Northeast Asia* (Boulder: Lynne Rienner, 1991), pp. 179-80.

20. This included a deal involving the exchange of South Korean rice for North Korean cement and coal (between the Chonji and Kûmgangsan Trading companies in March 1991); additional South Korean purchases of coal, steel ore, zinc, and scrap iron by Hyundai and Daewoo (previously transacted through third parties); the first extension of letters of credit to North Korean banks by the South; and Pyongyang's direct purchase of $26 million in ROK consumer goods and technology in 1991. See *Korea Newsreview,* June 11, 1994; Koo Bon-hak, "North Korea: Back to Isolationism?" *Korea Observer* 24, 2 (Summer 1993), p. 239; Chang, "Economic Transactions and Cooperation between North and South Korea," pp. 20-21; and Shim Jae-hoon, "The Trade Wedge," *FEER,* August 22, 1991, p. 23.

21. Samsung and Lucky-Goldstar also looked into projects for the manufacturing of apparel and other light-industry products in the North. See Shim Jae-hoon, "The Trade Wedge," p. 24; Mark Clifford, "A Rough Fit," *FEER,* March 26, 1992, p. 57; *Korea Newsreview,* June 11, 1994; and Koo, "North Korea: Back to Isolationism?" p. 239.

22. This was the result of Pyongyang's protests over United States-ROK Team Spirit exercises and Seoul's diplomatic normalization with Moscow.

23. For the text, see Ministry of National Defense, *Defense White Paper: 1992–1993* (Seoul: Ministry of National Defense, 1993), p. 243. This declaration was preceded by the September 1991 U.S. announcement of a reduction in land-based nuclear arsenals deployed abroad (including in Korea), and Roh's November 1991 declaration of the absence of nuclear weapons in South Korea. For a basic chronology of these events, see *Korea Annual: 1993* (Seoul: Yonhap News Agency, 1993), pp. 44-57; and Kihl Young-whan, "The Politics of Inter-Korean Relations: Coexistence or Reunification?," in Kihl, ed., *Korea and the World: Beyond the Cold War* (Boulder: Westview, 1994), pp. 134-35.

24. The two governments exchanged instruments of ratification for the 1991 accord at the sixth North-South premier talks in February 1992. For the text of the 1972 and 1991 agreements, see *Woegyo yônp'yo: 1972* (Diplomatic Documents Annual), pp. 201-202; and *Korea Update* 2, 24 (December 16, 1991), pp. 4-5; for

ratification of the 1991 accord, see *Korea Update* 3, 5 (February 24, 1992), pp.1-2. Also see Hakjoon Kim, *Unification Policy of South and North Korea*, p. 270; and B.C. Koh, "The Inter-Korean Agreements of 1972 and 1992: A Comparative Assessment," *Korea and World Affairs* 16, 3 (Fall 1992), pp. 472, 474.

25. For additional analyses, see Lim Dong-won, "Inter-Korean Relations Oriented toward Reconciliation and Cooperation," *Korea and World Affairs* 16, 2 (Summer 1992), pp. 213-14; Koh, "The Inter-Korean Agreements of 1972 and 1992," pp. 473-75; and Kihl, "The Politics of Inter-Korean Relations," pp. 135-37.

26. Kil Jeong-woo, "Inter-Korean Relations in a Changing Northeast Asian Context," *Korean Journal of International Studies* 24, 1 (Spring 1993), p. 46.

27. For establishment of the various committees at the seventh premier talks, see *Korea Update* 3, 11 (May 18, 1992), pp.1-2. For the contents of the meetings, see Lee Chong-sik and Sohn Hyuk-sang, "South Korea in 1993," *Asian Survey* 34, 1 (January 1994), p. 8; *Korea Update* 5, 5 (March 14, 1994), p. 1; Kil, "Inter-Korean Relations in a Changing Northeast Asian Context," pp. 46-49; Koh, "The Inter-Korean Agreements of 1972 and 1992," pp. 479-80; and Kihl, "The Politics of Inter-Korean Relations," pp. 137-39.

28. A full discussion of this issue is beyond the scope of this work. For a concise discussion of the crisis and the implications for non-proliferation, see Michael Mazarr, "Going Just a Little Nuclear: Nonproliferation Lessons from North Korea," *International Security* 20, 2 (Fall 1995), pp. 92-122. For a discussion of the Agreed Framework, see Victor Cha, "The Geneva Framework Agreement and Korea's Future," EAI Institute Reports, June 1995, East Asian Institute, Columbia University.

29. The North-South nuclear control commission was unable to set up such a regime by the May 1992 deadline stated in the declaration. Pyongyang later suspended nuclear talks in November 1993. For a chronology, see *Defense White Paper: 1992-1993*, pp. 86-92.

30. Chaebol such as Hyundai, Daewoo, Samsung, and Lucky-Goldstar all complied (see *Korea Newsreview*, June 6, 1994).

31. In addition, only three weeks after Nixon's China announcement, Kim Il Sung stated for the first time his willingness to meet with all parties in the ROK, including the ruling Democratic Republican Party (DRP).

32. Seoul and Pyongyang even fashioned their contacts and news of their breakthrough (that is, a surprise announcement) after the secret diplomacy employed by Kissinger and Zhou in negotiating Nixon's visit to Beijing.

33. For concurring arguments on the 1991 and 1972 agreements, see Hakjoon Kim, *Unification Policy of South and North Korea*, pp. 261-71, 273-74; Samuel Kim, "The Two Koreas and World Order," in Kihl, *Korea and the World*, p. 48; Koh, "The Inter-Korean Agreements of 1972 and 1992," pp. 464-65; and Park Kyung-ae and Lee Sung-chull, "Changes and Prospects in Inter-Korean Relations," *Asian Survey* 33, 5 (May 1992), pp. 440-43.

34. National Unification Board (NUB), *A Comparison of Unification Policies of South and North Korea* (Seoul: National Unification Board, 1990), p. 71.

35. Ibid., p. 72.

36. For the respective proposals at the NSCC talks, see *White Paper on South-North Dialogue*, pp. 66-75. For the Kang-Yon talks, see *Korea Annual: 1991*, pp. 63-70,

and B.C. Koh, "A Comparison of Unification Policies," in Kihl, *Korea and the World*, pp. 157-58.

37. The DCRK plan was introduced by Kim Il Sung in 1960 and more fully elucidated at the Sixth Congress of the Korea Workers' Party (October 1980) and in the April 1993 Ten-Point Unification Plan.

38. Rhee Kang-suk, "Korea's Unification: The Applicability of the German Experience," *Asian Survey* 33, 4 (April 1993), pp. 367-68; and NUB, *Comparison of Unification Policies*, pp. 99-108.

39. For the text of the KNC proposal, *South-North Dialogue in Korea*, vol. 48, December 1989 (Seoul: International Cultural Society of Korea, 1989), pp. 20-31. For analyses, see Lee Manwoo, "Domestic Politics and Unification: Seoul's Perspective," in Kihl, *Korea and the World*, p. 174; NUB, *Comparison of Unification Policies*, pp. 122-31; and Rhee, "Korea's Unification: The Applicability of the German Experience," p. 368.

40. For a concurring view on the difficulty of distinguishing whether the KNC plan is a means to an end (i.e., full integration) or an end in itself, see Kihl Young-whan, "The Problem of Forming a Korean Commonwealth," *Korea Observer* 24, 3 (Autumn 1993), pp. 429-49, esp. 443-44.

41. For the notion of "hegemonic" unification, see Koh, "A Comparison of Unification Policies."

42. For an excellent elaboration of some of the above points, see Koh, "A Comparison of Unification Policies," pp. 155-58; and "Foreign Policy and Inter-Korean Relations," pp. 675-76.

43. For example, figures for 1990–1992 were, respectively: -3.7 percent, -5.2 percent, and -5 percent. See John C.H. Oh, "Policy Alternatives for Uniting the Two Koreas," *Korea Observer* 24, 4 (Winter 1993), pp. 477-96, esp. 490; and Shim Jae-hoon, "The Inevitable Burden," *FEER*, August 22, 1991, p. 21.

44. For example, in February 1991 and 1992, unconfirmed defectors' accounts told of executions of Soviet-trained North Korean officers who had plotted against Kim Jong Il. Reports also circulated of clashes between laborers and the military over working conditions and the lack of food at construction sites in preparation for the World Youth Festival in 1989.

45. For a fuller discussion of different unification scenarios, see Young C. Kim, "Prospects for Korean Unification: An Assessment," in Kihl, *Korea and the World*, pp. 253-59; Suh Jae-jean, "Social Changes in North Korea and Prospects for Unification," in Lee Manwoo and Richard Mansbach, eds., *The Changing Order in Northeast Asia and the Korean Peninsula* (Seoul: IFES, Kyungnam University, 1993), p. 245; Rhee, "Korea's Unification: The Applicability of the German Experience," pp. 369-70; Oh, "Policy Alternatives for Uniting the Two Koreas," pp. 482-95; and Chang, "Economic Transactions and Cooperation between North and South Korea," pp. 28-29.

46. For the North-South military balance and an overview of U.S. deployments on the peninsula and in Japan, see *Defense White Paper: 1992–1993*, pp. 43, 74.

47. North Korean monthly wages average $80, while those in the South average around $900. See *FEER*, March 26, 1992, p. 57; and Bradley Martin, "Intruding on the Hermit: Glimpses of North Korea," *East-West Center Special Reports*, no. 1 (July 1993), p. 21.

48. As noted earlier, in January 1992 Daewoo Chairman Kim Woo Chung signed a contract for the construction of light industry facilities consisting of nine factories at Namp'o that would utilize South Korean materials and equipment and North Korean labor for manufacturing textiles, garments, footwear, luggage, toys, and household appliances. Hyundai magnate Chung JuYung in January 1989 proposed a $700 million resort complex for Kûmgang-san. The ROK also proposed a pilot $464 million joint industrial project four miles west of P'anmunjôm in December 1991.

49. For example, the North has traded through third countries steel, zinc, coal, cement, potatoes, peanuts, and fish for South Korean diesel oil, clothing, color televisions, and refrigerators. In March 1991, direct North-South trade of 5,000 tons of rice for 30,000 tons of coal and 11,000 tons of cement took place between the Chonji and Kûmgangsan companies. See Lee, "Economic Factors in Korean Reunification," pp. 201-3.

50. Much of the analysis in the section below draws heavily from EIU, *Special Report*, ch. 8.

51. For ROK figures, see Ministry of Construction and Transportation tables in *Korea Annual: 1996*, p. 301; for DPRK figures, see EIU, *Special Report*, pp. 14, 44-45.

52. Marcus Noland and L. Gordon Flake, "Evaluation of the Najin-Sonbong Free Economic and Trade Zone," Korea Economic Institute of America (September 1996).

53. For many of the above points, see EIU, *Special Report*, pp. 19, 106; Clifford, "A Rough Fit," pp. 58-59; and Lee, "Economic Factors in Korean Unification," pp. 199-200.

54. While the North's hydroelectric generating capacity is respectable (9 billion kwh vs. South Korea's 5 billion kwh per annum), it produces only 21 billion kwh from thermal power stations (comparable figures for the ROK are 70 billion kwh). In addition, the North has no nuclear energy capabilities. All energy output figures are for 1991-1992 (see *Korea Annual: 1993*, p. 301; EIU, *Special Report*, p. 108). Also see Koo, "North Korea: Back to Isolationism?" p. 227; and Clifford, "A Rough Fit," pp. 59, 57.

55. For example, accounts by a Western journalist who visited Pyongyang in 1989 found that stores did not turn on lights during the week and trolleys often stalled due to power failures (see Martin, "Intruding on the Hermit," p. 12).

56. See EIU, *Special Report* , pp. 44, 107-108, for a more detailed exposition of this problem.

57. Ibid., p. 102.

58. In this vein, a January 1993 report by the ROK finance ministry recommended some form of limited cross-border travel in the initial stages of unification (cited in Martin, "Intruding on the Hermit," p. 21). Also see Rhee, "Korea's Unification: The Applicability of the German Experience," pp. 371, 375.

59. Nicholas Eberstadt, *Korea Approaches Reunification* (Armonk, NY: M.E. Sharpe, 1995), pp. 112, 122.

60. Ibid., p. 125.

61. Rhee, "Korea's Unification: The Applicability of the German Experience," p. 371; and Shim Jae-hoon, "German Lessons," *FEER*, August 22, 1991, p. 25.

62. See Mark Clifford, "Expensive Embraces," *FEER*, March 26, 1992, pp. 54-55; and EIU, *Special Report*, p. 102.

63. Figures compiled from *Korea Annual: 1993*, p. 297; and EIU, *Special Report*, pp. 25, 45.

64. On the above points, see Clifford, "A Rough Fit," p. 57; Martin, "Intruding on the Hermit," pp. 6, 12, 16; Shim Jae-hoon, "The Price of Unity," *FEER*, March 26, 1992, p. 55; and Shim, "The Inevitable Burden," p. 21.

65. This became apparent when the North contributed rice stocks as part of its flood relief to the South in 1984.

66. Clifford, "A Rough Fit," p. 57.

67. In this vein, there were reports in 1989 that a Protestant church was constructed in Pyongyang in which none of the clergy were party members. In addition, one of the items discussed by the Reverend Billy Graham during his 1991 visit to Pyongyang was the status of North Korean Christians (see Martin, "Intruding on the Hermit," p. 13; and Michael Shapiro, "Annals of Authoritarianism: Kim's Ransom," *New Yorker*, January 31, 1994, p. 34).

68. See Shim Jae-hoon, "Welcome to Reality," *FEER*, March 26, 1992, pp. 60-61; and EIU, *Special Report*, pp. 111-112, for a fuller discussion of these issues.

69. Kim Han-kyo, "Korean Unification in Historical Perspective," in Kihl, *Korea and the World*, pp. 17-28.

70. The following analysis does not include a united Korea's relations with Russia. Although Russia has played an important role in Korea's past, this analysis assumes that, given its current economic and political difficulties, a proactive role for Russia in a post-unification scenario is, at present, unlikely.

71. Authors who have put forth this view in whole or in part are too numerous to list. For examples of some who have employed the "conventional" view in their analyses, see Thomas McNaugher, "Reforging Northeast Asia's Dagger? US Strategy and Korean Unification," *Brookings Review* 2, 3 (Summer 1993); Aaron Friedberg, "Ripe for Rivalry: Prospects for Peace in a Multipolar Asia," *International Security* 18, 3 (Winter 1993-1994); and Paul Godwin, "China's Asian Policy in the 1990's: Adjusting to the Post-Cold War Environment," in Sheldon Simon, ed., *East Asian Security in the Post-Cold War Era* (New York: M.E. Sharpe, 1993).

72. Representative examples of this view include: EIU, *Special Report*, especially chapter 8, and Hwang In-kwan, "The Two Koreas' Unification Policies and Neutralization of the Korean Peninsula," in Kim Il-pyong, ed., *Korean Challenges and American Policy* (New York: Paragon House, 1991).

73. On EASI, see Lawrence Grinter, "East Asia and the United States into the 21st Century," *CADRE Report*, November 1991, Maxwell Air Force Base, Alabama; and *Pacific Stars and Stripes*, April 6, 1990, and October 23, 1991. On the renewed U.S. commitment to the region, see Joseph Nye, "The Case for Deep Engagement," *Foreign Affairs*, July/August 1995.

74. For a concurring view, see Jia Hao and Zhuang Qubing, "China's Policy toward the Korean Peninsula," *Asian Survey* 32, 12 (December 1992), p. 1145.

75. Victor Cha, "Alliance Termination in Asia: Is the Thrill Gone?" Paper presented at the Annual American Political Science Association Conference, August 29-September 1, 1996, San Francisco, CA.

76. For proponents of this view, see Samuel Huntington, "America's Changing Strategic Interests," *Survival* 33, 1 (January/February 1991); Richard Betts, "Wealth, Power, and Instability: East Asia and the United States after the Cold War," *Inter-*

national Security 18, 3 (Winter 1993/1994); and McNaugher, "Reforging Northeast Asia's Dagger?"

77. See Hao and Zhuang, "China's Policy toward the Korean Peninsula," pp. 1146-48; *Korea Update* 5, 6 (April 4, 1994), p. 3; and Lee Hong-yong, "China and the Two Koreas: New Emerging Triangle," in Kihl, *Korea and the World*, pp. 104-107.

78. For above figures, see Hao and Zhuang, "China's Policy toward the Korean Peninsula," pp. 1144, 1156.

79. This was confirmed by chairmen of several Korean conglomerates in discussions with the author in April and August 1993.

80. Mark Fitzpatrick, "Why Japan and the United States Will Welcome Korean Unification," *Korea and World Affairs* 15, 3 (Fall 1991), p. 430.

81. Hao and Zhuang, "China's Policy toward the Korean Peninsula," p. 1137.

82. For concurring views, see Kil, "Inter-Korean Relations in a Changing Northeast Asian Context," p. 37; Martin, "Intruding on the Hermit," p. 28; and Parris Chang, "Beijing's Policy toward Korea and PRC-ROK Normalization of Relations," in Lee and Mansbach, *The Changing Order in Northeast Asia*, p. 172.

83. See "Chinese Military Wary of Naval Buildup of Japan, Korea," *Korea Herald*, November 10, 1992.

84. EIU, *Special Report*, p. 74; and Fitzpatrick, "Why Japan and the United States Will Welcome Korean Unification," pp. 426-27.

85. See EIU, *Special Report*, pp. 96-102, esp. 99; and Rhee, "Korea's Unification: The Applicability of the German Experience," pp. 372-74. For more recent studies that put the cost of unification in the range of $1-2 trillion, see Hwang Eui-guk, "How Will Unification Affect Korea's Participation in the World Economy?" and Marcus Noland, "Modeling Economic Reform in North Korea," both papers presented at the KIEP-*Korea Herald* Conference on the International Economic Implications of Korean Unification, June 28-29, 1996.

86. For other comparative indicators, see Fitzpatrick, "Why Japan and the United States Will Welcome Korean Unification," pp. 416-18; EIU, *Special Report*, pp. 103-104; and Shim, "German Lessons," pp. 24-25.

87. The main reason Japanese aid and investment shifted from the ROK to Southeast Asia in the 1980s was that, despite the proximity of the former, South Korean labor costs had grown prohibitively high. See Kim Hosup, "The End of the Cold War and Korea-Japan Relations," in Lee and Mansbach, *The Changing Order in Northeast Asia*, pp. 225-26.

88. Fitzpatrick, "Why Japan and the United States Will Welcome Korean Unification," pp. 428-30; and McNaugher, "Reforging Northeast Asia's Dagger?" p. 13.

89. *Defense White Paper: 1992–1993*, p. 74.

90. For arguments against the possibility of a united Korea-China-Russia encirclement of Japan, see Alan Romberg, "The Future of US Alliances with Japan and Korea," *Critical Issues* 1990: 5 (New York: Council on Foreign Relations).

91. It should be noted that "alignment" does not necessarily mean "alliance" in the form of a bilateral defense treaty. The former term connotes a less formal association between states based on perceived common interests and expectations of mutual support. For this distinction, see Glenn Snyder, "Alliance Theory: A Neorealist First Cut." *Journal of International Affairs* 44, 1 (Spring 1990).

92. For a related point on how such institutions engendered a familiarity among Eu-

ropean leaders that mollified anxieties about German reunification, see Friedberg, "Ripe for Rivalry: Prospects for Peace in a Multipolar Asia," p. 13.

93. Frank Ching, "Securing Northeast Asia," *FEER*, November 11, 1993, p. 42.

94. *Defense White Paper: 1992-1993*, pp. 22, 30.

95. *Korea Update* 5, 6 (April 4, 1994), p. 2; and Press Release, Knight-Ridder/Tribune Business News, March 23, 1994.

96. See "Japan Discusses Ways to Counter Sudden NK Collapse With ROK, US," *Korea Times*, March 3, 1993, p. 1.

Chapter 9

Socioeconomic Development in South Korea

Eun Mee Kim

S outh Korea's rapid economic development since the 1960s, based on export-oriented industrialization, has been hailed as one of the third world's most successful such cases. Though South Korea appears to be on the verge of becoming an advanced industrialized nation, there are still important hurdles that must be overcome to attain that status. Unlike Singapore and Hong Kong—two other members of the so-called four mini-dragons or East Asian NICs (Newly Industrializing Countries)—which are now classified as "high-income economies" by the World Bank, South Korea's GNP per capita was $6,330 in 1991.[1] As a late-latecomer, South Korea faces challenges to develop indigenous technology and/or to "create new products and [labor] processes."[2] Having developed its economy with an iron fist, the South Korean state is in the process of renegotiating its relations with the capitalists and labor as the latter gain political influence. As a small nation surrounded by more powerful nations, South Korea must constantly negotiate its geopolitical and economic relations with them—and in particular, with the United States. And finally, as a nation divided, South Korea also faces the daunting task of paying for reunification with North Korea, which, even by a conservative estimate, could easily wipe out its upper middle-income economy.

In order to understand the challenges facing the South Korean economy today, we need to examine the roles played by key actors in the domestic political economy, and the international context of

Eun Mee Kim teaches in the Graduate School of International Studies at Ewha Women's University, Seoul.

geopolitics and the market since the 1960s. This is because South Korea's rapid economic development in the past three decades is a result of concerted efforts of several domestic actors, as well as a convergence of domestic and international political and economic factors. By focusing on key actors and relations between them rather than on achievements per se, we are able to illuminate current problems which are rooted in the successes of the past. Therefore, this essay will examine South Korea's socioeconomic development since the 1960s, locating its experience in the nexus of domestic actors and institutions, and of international security and economic relations. *The state, capitalists*, and *labor* are three key actors in the domestic political economy. The international geopolitical context includes the United States' interest in containing communism in Pacific Asia during the cold war, and its provision of military and economic aid to countries such as South Korea and Japan. The international market condition refers to the state of the international market, either expansionist or recessionary, and the international market's openness to the third world nations' manufactured export products.

The 1960s: The Remaking of the South Korean Economy

Before 1961, South Korea was a poor, agrarian society. Sixty-six percent of the labor force worked in the agricultural sector, and only 9 percent in the industrial sector. The GNP per capita in 1961 was $82.[3] South Korea was barely recovering from the ruins of the Korean War, which had left 45 percent of its factories substantially damaged.[4] Every spring, there was a famine in the countryside, during the period after the rice harvested the previous fall had run out and before barley could be harvested. Families were often further impoverished when, every March (the start of the new school year), in order to send an eldest son to school in Seoul, some would have to sell their only oxen or farmland. Politicians and rich *chaebol* owners did not seem to care, since they were enjoying a comfortable and luxurious life not dissimilar to the lifestyle of the elites in the first world. The cycle of poverty for most people appeared to be unbreakable, since the poor farmers did not have resources and those who had power to change things seemed uninterested.

The seemingly unbreakable cycle of poverty was broken during the 1960s. By 1970, GNP per capita had risen to $266.72, an average annual growth rate of 12.6 percent since 1961. GNP increased nearly fourfold, from $2.33 billion in 1961 to $8.60 billion in 1970. Over 13 percent of the labor force was now working in the industrial sector. Most remarkable was the growth in exports, from $53 million to $1,227 million. Furthermore, the composition of export products changed in that period from primarily agricultural and natural resources (86 percent in 1961) to largely manufactured products (83.6 percent in 1970).[5]

President Park Chung Hee's military regime brought forth the most rigorous and comprehensive developmental state in South Korea's history. Park's commitment to economic development, and the material and human resources his government invested toward this end, are critical elements in our understanding of the South Korean transformation from a rent-seeking, poverty-stricken economy to a rapidly growing industrial economy in less than a decade. The United States' early sanctioning of the Park regime, in spite of its coming to power through a military coup, helped establish this unstable military government. The United States continued to provide military and economic aid during the early to mid-1960s, furnishing vital foreign exchange for Park's new economic development measures. The international economy during the 1960s was in expansion, and the first world nations had not yet erected trade barriers and enacted protectionist measures against countries such as Japan, South Korea, and Taiwan. Thus, the timing was right for the three nations to engage in export-oriented industrialization strategies.

Economic development in the 1960s was clearly led by the state, and the relationship between the state and business was dominated by the state. However, the state did not simply give marching orders to the private sector and the workers. It is equally critical to understand how the latter groups responded to the state's call for economic development. Without the cooperation of private businesses and the workers' willingness to work long hours with little pay, South Korea's economic development would have been impossible.

Birth of a Developmental State

On May 16, 1961, General Park Chung Hee led a military coup to bring an end to a corrupt and inept government, and to achieve economic development. "The Road toward Economic Self-Sufficiency and Prosperity" became the official national goal of the military regime.[6] In light of failures during the Rhee and Chang regimes, the Park government's success in attaining economic development was based partly on three important restructuring efforts in the state. First, economic development was promoted as the top priority of the government. Comprehensive economic development plans were conceived and implemented. Second, reforms were instituted within the government bureaucracy to assist in economic development planning; in particular, the Economic Planning Board (EPB) was created, and its offices expanded and strengthened. Third, vital resources for economic development, including domestic and foreign capital, were put under the state's control.

The last two institutional reforms differentiated the Park regime from the previous regimes. These reforms constitute the establishment of a comprehensive developmental state in South Korea, which largely stayed in place until the early 1980s. The three institutional reforms produced a troika of economic ministries, with EPB at its front and the Ministry of Finance and the Ministry of Trade and Industry forming the two "back horses" supporting the EPB. The relative freedom in decisionmaking provided to these ministries and the centralized control and coordination by EPB were similar to the privileges and power given to the Ministry of International Trade and Technology and the Ministry of Finance in Japan.[7]

The newly formed developmental state performed the following activities: (1) provision of long-term economic goals: comprehensive economic development plans, long-term goals, and projections for the entire economy;[8] (2) provision of capital and technology: capital for investment through domestic and foreign capital loans, capital assistance for research and development, and technology and technical assistance through national and regional research facilities;[9] and (3) provision of indirect assistance: mediation with multinational corporations for foreign direct investment and technology transfers, establishment of trade offices for know-how on exports and imports, provision of tax breaks and tariff exemptions, and easing of regulations.[10]

The EPB, the Ministry of Finance, and the Ministry of Trade and Industry formed the three economic ministries in charge of South Korea's economic development. The EPB was established on July 22, 1961, less than two months after the military coup. EPB became the most important government ministry in the coordination and control of South Korea's economic development. Its objectives were described in the 1961 law as "to establish comprehensive plans for the development of the national economy, and to manage and to regulate the execution of the development plans."[11] Its mission included controlling both domestic and foreign capital (through nationalization of banks and control of the national budget). It remained as the most prestigious ministry within the government bureaucracy throughout the 1960s and 1970s.

The private banks in Seoul were nationalized in October 1961 and were put under the control of the Ministry of Finance.[12] Several specialty banks were established and strengthened by the government, including the Bank of Medium and Small Enterprises and the Korea Development Bank. The nationalized banks were used by the Park regime as a carrot to attract private businesses to conform to the state's directives in the economy, and as a stick to punish those that did not follow by threatening a withdrawal of capital assistance. The so-called policy loans were offered to private businesses at an interest rate substantially lower (by one-half to one-third) than regular bank loans.[13]

Foreign capital was also put under the state's control. The Park regime actively sought to attract foreign capital to finance its economic development plans, since there was very little accumulation of domestic capital. However, great care was taken not to jeopardize the goal of creating a "self-reliant" economy, which meant independence from foreign control of the domestic economy. Thus, the South Korean government sought foreign loan capital, in which the responsibility of distribution and management is in the hands of the borrower. This is in contrast to foreign direct investment (FDI), in which the lender (that is, multinational corporations, MNCs) is in charge of distribution of capital and management. This partly explains the government's lukewarm receptivity toward FDI during the early phase of development.[14]

Various changes in the law and in the organization of government bureaucracy were made in order to attract foreign capital. The Foreign Capital Inducement Law was restructured and expanded in August and December 1961. A new Bureau of Foreign Capital was established within the EPB in 1961. This bureau was later expanded and renamed the Bureau of Economic Cooperation. With an expanded budget and more personnel, the Bureau of Economic Cooperation actively sought foreign capital loans and, to a lesser degree, foreign direct investments. More substantial restructuring of the law and government offices took place between 1964 and 1965, when export was promoted heavily. The EPB and its Bureau of Economic Cooperation played a major role in acquiring and distributing foreign loan capital and foreign direct investment during the early phase of South Korean development.

The Relationship between the State and the Private Sector

In 1961, a very important change in the state-business relationship took place which was critical in the effective implementation of the state's development plans. The institutional reforms within the government ministries and establishment of the finest development plans would not bear the fruit of economic growth unless they had the vehicle of implementation. To this end, the restructuring of the relationship between the state and business was important. Several changes took place after Park came into power: (1) the state formed a tight working partnership with large private enterprises in pursuit of a common goal—economic development; (2) the state was, at least in the beginning, the dominant partner; and (3) the nature of their relationship became formal and institutionalized (compared to a more personal and collusive relationship during the Rhee and Chang regimes). These changes clearly show the different *modus operandi* during the Park regime versus that of the Rhee and Chang regimes.

The state and the businesses formed a close working relationship, yet remained otherwise distant. Closeness was important, since this was an alliance for economic development that required constant consultation and cooperation. The distance resulted from the differing class backgrounds and familial and personal networks of those in government and business and allowed the state to be autonomous as against the interests of the landed and industrial classes. The concept of state autonomy, which is used by development scholars to explain the success of the East Asian NICs, conceals the significance of the close working relationship that evolved between these two actors.[15] A delicate balance in the relationship was achieved, in which each of the two partners was autonomous, yet there was a formalized and close working relationship. This type of partnership helped prevent corruption as it led to economic development. Disposition of charges of illicit accumulation of wealth in 1961 showed how the Park regime took charge of the relationship with the private sector.[16]

Selection of Large Businesses as New Partners for Economic Development

Large private businesses were chosen as Park's partners for rapid economic development. Three other options were considered: establishing state-owned enterprises, attracting multinational corporations to form joint ventures with domestic corporations or to establish subsidiaries, and selecting medium- and small-size businesses. However, these were all seen as going against Park's goal of rapid economic development or as being detrimental to his political survival. First, establishing state-owned enterprises was not a politically sound option. The military officers who led the coup could not risk the chance of appearing to be working as businesspersons, since corruption under Rhee had involved government officials operating businesses in pursuit of their personal interests. Any appearance that the Park regime was running business was seen as politically risky. Second, working with multinational corporations would have been politically suicidal. South Koreans were very sensitive to any hint of foreign domination, whether military or economic. This nationalistic sentiment had been strengthened as a result of thirty-five years of Japanese colonialism (1910–45), which had ended only sixteen years prior to Park's ascendance to power. Park proposed to bring about a self-reliant economy, capitalizing on this nationalist sentiment to justify his coup. Attracting MNCs would have clearly jeopardized this objective. Furthermore, foreign direct investment by MNCs required the latter to see South Korea as a profitable investment site, and South Korea in 1961 was hardly that. Finally, forming a partnership with medium- and small-size businesses would have slowed the pace of economic development. The Park regime recognized that it did not have much time before the public's goodwill ran out.[17] The medium- and small-size businesses simply could not deliver the economies of scale quickly enough for export-oriented manufacturing.

Thus, privately owned large businesses were selected as the partners for rapid economic development. It appears that the Park regime chose to work with large businesses in general, not necessarily with specific *chaebol*. It was only in the late 1960s and early 1970s that the Park regime formed a tighter alliance with a few *chaebol*.

Once the large private businesses had been chosen, they were provided with generous loans. On January 12, 1962, the Supreme Council for National Reconstruction announced that those charged with illicit wealth accumulation could build factories necessary for national reconstruction and donate them to the state instead of paying fines; and on May 9, 1962, the Ministry of Trade and Industry approved ten companies that were to be donated to the state in lieu of payment of fines. In addition, foreign capital had to be approved by the Supreme Council for National Reconstruction, and it was the state that took the initiative in finding the loans for the *chaebol* to build these factories.[18]

The Growth of the *Chaebol*

The story of South Korea's remarkable economic achievement is not simply that the state summarily reformed itself and gave marching orders to the private sector, and that the private sector complied. The success was in part due to the private sector, which went above and beyond the state's mandate and actively took advantage of the favorable economic environment created by the state.

The cases of Hyundai and Samsung illustrate how individual concerns responded somewhat differently to the favorable investment environment created by the state. They also indicate that their growth was not entirely a result of state intervention. Hyundai, which was not even on the top-ten list during the 1950s and 1960s, had emerged as the third-largest South Korean business group by 1974. Hyundai is a good example of a business that took advantage of the supportive environment provided by the state but went beyond the state's directive. The Hyundai Engineering and Construction Company was founded in 1947 by Chong Ju Yong. Hyundai's remarkable success in the 1960s resulted from government projects and low-interest loans provided by the government, and from its vigorous overseas construction projects. Hyundai received many key government contracts during the 1950s and 1960s, including the First Han River Bridge in 1957, the Kimpo International Airport project in 1967, and the first major freeway in South Korea (linking Seoul and Pusan) in 1968. However, Hyundai did not stop with these lucrative government construction contracts. It was the first South Korean construction company to go abroad, first to Southeast Asia (Vietnam and Thailand) in 1966, and then to the Middle East. Hyundai's success in becoming the largest *chaebol* by the end of the 1970s was largely a result of the lucrative construction boom in the Middle East. Clearly, these overseas construction projects were not a direct result of the South Korean government's preferential treatment. Hyundai's success story is a reminder that *chaebol* are not mere puppets of the state, but are private corporations that make their own decisions.

The story of Samsung is somewhat different from that of Hyundai. Samsung, which was the largest *chaebol* during the 1950s and 1960s, had a different trajectory of growth. Instead of taking full advantage of governmental support, Samsung tried to maintain a healthy distance from the state after being embroiled in a scandal involving a member company, Hanguk Fertilizer Company (established in 1964). In September 1966, Samsung was accused of illegally smuggling an ingredient for saccharin, which was banned at that time, to use in fertilizer manufacture. This escalated into a major scandal and caused the public to become weary of the Park regime's commitment to eradicating corruption. Responding to the public outcry, the Park regime arrested I Chang Hui, the son of Samsung Chairman I Pyong Chol, and requested that Hanguk Fertilizer Company be donated to the government in lieu of its paying a fine. On April 20, 1967, the company was presented to the government, and I Pyong Chol resigned from his post as chair of the Samsung *chaebol*.[19]

The stories of the Hyundai and Samsung *chaebol* attest to the varying responses of the private sector to the developmental state's development planning and policies. State-centered studies too quickly dismiss the role of the private sector, especially that of the *chaebol*, in seeking to understand South Korean development. Although the large businesses and *chaebol* may have started out as junior partners in the state-business alliance, that will change with time. The fact that the establishment and growth of many large *chaebol* is directly tied to the state's preferential treatment does not mean that these same *chaebol* will not later demand reduction of state intervention.

The 1970s: Heavy and Chemical Industrialization, and the Growth of the State and *Chaebol*

The 1970s witnessed a deepening of the industrialization process, with the development of the heavy and chemical industries dominating economic growth in that decade. This development was clearly initiated by the government, and more specifically by President Park's staff at the Blue House, without much consultation with economic ministries. It was pushed vigorously, despite the objections of domestic and international capitalists. The heavy and chemical industrialization drive was prompted by the changing geopolitical concerns surrounding the Pacific and by domestic political uncertainties. The policy was instituted to help create a self-reliant military and defense industry and to foster a closer alliance with a few large *chaebol*, which could potentially finance the political regime.

The drive for heavy and chemical industrialization does not fully support the state-centered studies that argue that the state has always been in charge of the economic development process, and that the private sector merely follows orders. In the 1970s, the relationship between the state and the largest *chaebol* became more interdependent. The leverage of the *chaebol* had increased because they had grown so successfully in the 1960s and because they were the only entrepreneurs who could afford to invest in the heavy and chemical industries, which were capital- and technology-intensive. Furthermore, the cooperation and support of the largest *chaebol* were important for political purposes. After Park won a narrow victory in the 1971 presidential election, there was a growing need to forge a conservative coalition with the large *chaebol.*

During the 1970s, South Korea's industrialization continued at a rate much faster than that of most other countries. Despite the two oil shocks in 1973 and 1979, South Korea's average annual growth rate of real GNP was 7.9 percent. GNP per capita rose from $285 in 1971 to $1,589 in 1980.[20] In 1971, 13.3 percent of the labor force were employed in the manufacturing sector; that number had increased to 21.7 percent by the end of the decade. The number working in agriculture, fishing, and mining decreased from 49.3 to 34.9 percent.[21] Exports continued to grow, rising from just over $1 billion to more than $17 billion.[22] South Korea's average annual growth rate of exports was one of the highest in the world. Exports as a share of GNP continued to rise, reaching 34.7 percent in 1980.[23] By 1980, over 92 percent of all export products were manufactured goods, and 20.3 percent of all export goods were machinery and transport equipment (up from 8.1 percent in 1971). All these illustrate that the South Korean economy made the successful transition from being dominated by light industries to having a growing share of heavy industries. The question that needs to be answered is not what percentage of the growth was due to the state's actions, but rather how state intervention in the development of the heavy and chemical industries changed the society and its members.

The entire economy grew at an average rate of 7.9 percent during this decade, but the ten largest *chaebol* grew at least 1.5 to 7 times faster. The stories of the growth of the largest *chaebol* indicate that none relied solely on state subsidies for their tremendous business success during the 1970s, although most benefited from them (some more than others). Those that conformed to the state's initiative for the development of heavy and chemical industries grew most rapidly and displaced some of the older and larger *chaebol.* Others investing in sectors that were not highly subsidized by the state also did quite well, and some successfully attracted multinational corporations to help with the needed capital and technology. The variations in the success stories of the *chaebol* indicate that an analysis of South Korean industrialization from either a neoclassical economics or a state-centered approach cannot help us to understand the complex and interactive process of development. The success of the *chaebol* indicates that they relied both on state support and intervention and on the shrewd entrepreneurship of the *chaebol* owners and managers.

The State and Its Drive for Heavy and Chemical Industrialization

The Park government announced that the goal of the Third Five-Year Economic Development Plan (1972–76) was a "balanced economy": a balance was to be achieved between the light and heavy industries, and between the urban and rural areas.[24] The stated rationale was that economic growth during the 1960s had brought growth to light industries and urban areas only. The drive for heavy and chemical industrialization was pushed much more vigorously than the development of rural areas, and it received much more in the way of resources. This industrialization received the strongest possible endorsement from the government, with President Park making the Pronouncement for the Development of the Heavy and Chemical Industry during his State of the Nation Message on January 13, 1973.[25]

Aside from the stated economic reasons, international geopolitical issues and domestic political issues also prompted Park to push for heavy and chemical industrialization. According to various market signals, this drive was premature for an economy with only a decade of growth focused on light industries and with few natural resources. The International Monetary Fund and the Federation of Korean Industries (FKI) opposed the drive for heavy and chemical industrialization when the policy was first announced.[26]

On the other hand, geopolitics and domestic politics provided justification for this policy. International geopolitics surrounding South Korea changed with an announcement by President Richard Nixon during his visit to Guam in 1969.[27] Nixon announced that the defense of the Pacific must lie in the hands of the people of the Pacific, and he declared that United States troops would gradually be withdrawn from various bases in Asia, including South Korea. Between 1970 and 1971, there was a partial withdrawal of American military personnel from South Korea. This was perceived by South Koreans as a grave threat to their defense against North Korea, and President Park therefore promoted the ideas of a self-reliant military and of the development of defense industries. The drive for greater heavy and chemical industrialization—particularly in such key industries as iron and steel, heavy machinery, and transport equipment—was deemed critical.

Domestic political issues also affected the decision to promote heavy and chemical industries. President Park won a narrow victory against a leading opposition party leader, Kim Dae Jung, in the 1971 presidential election, garnering 53.2 percent of the votes against Kim's 45.3 percent. This precarious victory, amid rumors of extensive vote-buying, caused Park to announce the Yushin Reformation in October 1972, changing the constitution to allow himself a life-term presidency.[28] To earn public support and appease the public prior to the announcement of the draconian Yushin Reformation, Park announced the economic goals to be achieved by 1981 as "GNP per capita of $1,000, and $10 billion in exports." This was another attempt to earn public support and political legitimacy with economic delivery, as in the aftermath of the 1961 military coup.[29]

Unlike most other industrial policies, in whose design the EPB played a central role in consultation with other economic ministries, the heavy and chemical industrialization program was initially designed under tremendous secrecy by the Blue House staff. Park's commitment to this industrial policy was reflected in his use of the authority and power of the Blue House, which stood above the reach of economic ministries.[30] This policy was further fueled by Park's strong anti-communist ideology and his ambition to build a self-reliant military.

Economic ministries underwent institutional reforms to help assist the development of the heavy and chemical industries. Within the EPB, the Department for Foreign Capital Management and the Department for Promoting Investment were both formed in 1973 to assist in attracting foreign capital (that is, public and commercial loans and foreign direct investment). Similar departments within the Ministry of Finance were also expanded. In the Ministry of Construction, the Department of Industrial Plants was created in 1973.

The Ministry of Trade and Industry underwent the most changes. The Department for Industrial Development and the Department for Management of Industrial Plants were expanded and promoted to higher status within the ministry. Many defense-related departments and heavy- and chemical-industry related departments were created, and old ones were expanded to give them more prominence within the ministry.

A new Bureau of Science and Technology was established in 1973 to consolidate and expand the research and development efforts for the heavy and chemical industries. In January 1974, the Development Association for Marine Resources was expanded and renamed the Development Association for Industrial Parks. Its new responsibility was to oversee the establishment and development of industrial parks for heavy and chemical industries.

Various economic ministries provided support through financial assistance, loans, tax cuts, technology, manpower, and infrastructure. An annual average of 14.5 percent of total development finances was used for the development of heavy and chemical industry between 1971 and 1981.[31] A law giving tax cuts to these industries was passed in 1974, and 40.1 percent of tax cuts were subsequently given to such firms. Other protective measures, such as removing tariff barriers and banning imports of certain heavy industrial and chemical products, were also provided. Heavy and chemical firms also received preferential treatment for foreign direct investment. Before other manufacturing firms were allowed to receive 100 percent FDI, many heavy and chemical firms were permitted by law to do so. Metal, machinery, and electronics firms were allowed to accept 100 percent by 1974, and by 1978 all six target industries were allowed to acquire 100 percent FDI.

Specific plans for the development of the heavy and chemical industries called for selecting a few target industries and providing them with generous government support. They were chosen based on the following factors:
1. Forward and backward linkages
2. Contribution to the whole country's economic development
3. Possibility of foreign capital earnings through exports and foreign capital savings through import substitution
4. Usage of natural resources of South Korea
5. Inducement effect of foreign capital

The six target industries were iron and steel, nonferrous metals, machinery, shipbuilding, electrical appliances and electronics, and petrochemicals. These industries received preferential treatment in acquiring foreign capital loans, loans from the newly formed National Funds, and tax reductions and exemptions. Of the six industries, electrical appliances and electronics received the least financial assistance from the government, since the state claimed that the industry had reached a satisfactory level of international competitiveness. This industry was thus opened for FDI before other industries.

Several state-owned enterprises were established following the heavy and chemical industrialization. The Pohang Iron and Steel Company was formed and began production in 1973. In March 1973, the Korea Chemical Company was founded.

Although most domestic capitalists were initially opposed to the heavy and chemical industrialization drive, some of the largest *chaebol* did conform when the government announced various subsidies, including low-interest rate loans and tax breaks. The EPB and the Ministry of Trade and Industry specifically sought the support and cooperation of the large *chaebol.* These *chaebol* were capable of financing—at least partially—the capital- and technology-intensive industries, and they had a proven track record of growth during the 1960s.

Concentration of Wealth in the *Chaebol*

Many large enterprises grew and became *chaebol* during the 1970s. Existing *chaebol* grew in terms of the number of firms and diversification of business to new sectors, some of which were unrelated to their existing businesses. The ten largest *chaebol* expanded very rapidly during the 1970s, at a rate five to nine times faster than that of the economy as a whole. The list of the ten largest *chaebol* changed significantly after Park came to power and promoted rapid economic development in the early 1960s. By the end of the 1960s, a new group of Park-regime *chaebol* had appeared, and this list has remained fairly stable ever since (see table 1).

The *chaebol* that invested heavily in state-target heavy and chemical industries grew at a phenomenal rate during the 1970s, thanks in part to the low-interest loans and other protective measures provided by the state. Other *chaebol* that invested only modestly in heavy and chemical industries sought other sources of capital, especially from MNCs. The variations in the trajectory of growth of the largest *chaebol* in the 1970s indicate that we need to seriously examine the role played by the *chaebol,* apart from the state's economic development plans and industrial policies.

The ten largest *chaebol* not only grew much faster than the economy as a whole, but concentration of wealth has been greatest among the largest five.[32] Samsung, which had been the largest *chaebol* since the Rhee regime, had lost its position to Hyundai by the late 1970s. Hyundai, which had not been a *chaebol* when Park came to

Table 1
Ten Largest *Chaebol*, 1950s-1990s

Rank	Late 1950s	Mid-1960s	1974	1983	1988	1991
1.	Samsung	Samsung	Samsung	Hyundai	Daewoo	Samsung
2.	Samho	Samho	Lucky-Gold Star	Samsung	Samsung	Hyundai
3.	Gaipoong	Lucky-Gold Star	Hyundai	Daewoo	Hyundai	Lucky-Gold Star
4.	Tai Han	Tai Han	Han Jin	Lucky-Gold Star	Lucky-Gold Star	Daewoo
5.	Lucky-Gold Star	Gaipoong	Ssangyong	Ssangyong	Ssangyong	Lotte
6.	Dongyang	Samyang	Sun Kyong	Sun Kyong	Hanjin	Sun Kyong
7.	Keukdong	Ssangyong	Korea Explosives	Korea Explosives	Korea Explosives	Han Jin
8.	Hankook Glass	Hwashin	Dainong	Han Jin	Sun Kyong	Ssangyong
9.	Donglip	Panbon	Dong Ah Construction	Kukje	Dong Ah Construction	Korea Explosives
10.	Tai Chang	Dongyang	Hanil Syn. Textiles	Dae Lim	Kia	Kia

Rank order of the chaebol for 1983, 1988 and 1991 is based on total assets. The basis of rank order for other years was not specified in original sources.

Sources: Bankers Trust Securities Research, *Zaebols in Korea* (Seoul: Korea Investors Service, Inc., 1989); Maeil Kyongje Shinmun, *Maekyong: Annual Corporation Report 1984* (Seoul: Maeil Kyongje Shinmun, 1984); Pyong Yun Pak, "Chaebol of Korea: Its Nature, Financial Connections, and Personal Connections" [in Korean], *Shindonga* 12 (1975); Pak, *Chaebol and Politics* [in Korean] (Seoul: Hanguk Yangseo, 1982); Management Efficiency Research Institute, *Analysis of Financial Statements—Fifty Major Business Groups in Korea* (Seoul: Management Efficiency Research Institute, 1992).

power, became the largest one, with extensive investments in heavy industries and in overseas construction. Daewoo, youngest of the ten largest *chaebol*, was initially established as a textile and garment producer and exporter. However, it quickly transformed itself to become one of the most formidable *chaebol* in heavy industry by the mid-1970s, with an astonishing average annual growth rate of 53.7 percent in terms of total assets between 1971 and 1980. One major characteristic shared by Hyundai and Daewoo was high concentration in heavy manufacturing. In 1970, Hyundai had 85 percent of its total assets in heavy manufacturing, while Daewoo had none. By 1980, 51 percent of Hyundai's total assets and 38 percent of Daewoo's were in heavy manufacturing. Although Lucky-Gold Star had 85 percent of its total assets in heavy manufacturing in 1980, it did not grow as much. Unlike Hyundai and Daewoo, Lucky-Gold Star concentrated on electrical appliances and electronics, which received less financial assistance from the government compared to other target industries.

Those *chaebol* that did not invest heavily in the state-target industries also grew quite rapidly, but as not as fast as those that conformed to the state's heavy and chemical industrialization drive. For example, Samsung grew at an average annual growth rate of 18.4 percent during the 1970s. Although this is a rate twice that of the entire economy, it is modest compared to the growth of Hyundai and Daewoo. And by the end of the 1970s, Samsung had lost its position as South Korea's largest *chaebol* to Hyundai. Samsung's relatively modest growth is partly due to the fact that Samsung was already much larger than other *chaebol* in the beginning of the 1970s—over ten times larger than Hyundai—which thus resulted in a lower growth rate. On the other hand, Samsung had a tremendous advantage over other large businesses or *chaebol* when rapid economic development began in the 1960s, and it is remarkable that it was unable to hold onto its position as the largest *chaebol*. An important reason for Samsung's setback in the 1970s has to do with the fact that it remained largely a light manufacturing *chaebol*, with 29 percent of its total assets in this sector even in 1980, and with investment even in the heavy industries concentrated in electrical appliances and electronics, which were not heavily subsidized by the state. Samsung's reluctance to invest in the state-target industries is due in part to the souring of its relationship with the Park regime following the bitter Hanguk Fertilizer incident in 1967.

Lucky-Gold Star also showed a slightly slower growth than Daewoo's or Hyundai's, with an average annual growth rate of 17.2 percent. Like Samsung, Lucky-Gold Star invested heavily in electronics and electrical appliances. A more extreme case of a *chaebol* that did not grow as fast as those conforming to the drive for heavy and chemical industrialization is that of Kukje. Unlike Samsung, which eventually decreased its share in light manufacturing, Kukje moved in the opposite direction, from heavy to light manufacturing. Kukje was a shoe manufacturing firm for over two decades and could not be defined as a *chaebol* until the mid-1970s, when it rapidly expanded its business. Its share in light manufacturing increased sharply, from nothing in 1975 to 11 percent in 1980. This expansion contributed to its high debt rate and finally to its bankruptcy, in 1985.

Although the *chaebol* that invested in the state-target sectors grew more rapidly, such investment does not account entirely for the tremendous success of these companies. Construction, which was not heavily promoted by the state, appears to have played an important role in many cases. In fact, along with heavy manufacturing, construction experienced the most rapid growth during the 1970s, compared to light manufacturing, financial services, trade, and other services. Construction companies in South Korea played an essential role not only in meeting the increased demand in the domestic market due to rapid economic growth, but also in providing an important source of foreign capital. Construction was beneficial to the development of other heavy industries since it could provide backward linkages with heavy machinery firms, construction material firms, and engineering companies, among others.

Hyundai was the first South Korean construction company to go to the Middle East. Building on its tremendous success there, by 1978 Hyundai had become the largest *chaebol* in South Korea. Samsung, which had been the largest *chaebol* for over two decades, fell to second place. Hyundai's success led the other large *chaebol* to quickly establish construction companies and also send them to the Middle East. By 1980, all ten *chaebol* had construction companies. However, because of the saturation of the Middle East construction market, increased unrest in that region, and the limited experience of some construction companies, *chaebol* that went into construction in the late 1970s with the specific goal of entering the Middle East market left with little profit and in some cases went bankrupt.

The *chaebol* have diversified greatly into services, including construction, financial services, and trade. By 1980, all ten *chaebol* were investing in construction, with nine also investing in financial institutions and eight in trading. The increase in services, especially in construction and financial institutions, did not result from any changes in the state's five-year economic development plans or from any other industrial policies. This further illustrates that *chaebol* are capable of making independent decisions regarding their investment, with regards to the state's directives. In particular, the investment of the *chaebol* in financial institutions was their attempt to be less dependent on state-owned banks. Thus, with increased investment in financial institutions, the *chaebol* were increasing their leverage against the state.

Those *chaebol* that did not rely on the state for capital sought foreign direct investment from MNCs as an alternative source of capital and technology. Although many industrial sectors were not allowed 100 percent FDI, electrical appliances and electronics was relatively open for FDI. Interestingly, those *chaebol* that did not invest in the state-target industries have invested heavily in this area. The cases of Samsung and Lucky-Gold Star show that FDI and technology transfers from MNCs were critical for their growth, showing an alternative means of growth for *chaebol* and going against the state-centered theories, which argue that *chaebol* growth is solely a result of state subsidies and protection.

The trend in MNC involvement among the *chaebol* shows that those that had good relationships with the state and were into heavy manufacturing did not have much FDI or many technology transfers. On the other hand, those *chaebol* that were not heavily involved in the state's direct-support industries were more inclined to receive FDI and technology transfers from MNCs. Samsung began as a light manufacturing *chaebol* and Lucky-Gold Star as an electrical appliances and electronics *chaebol*. What is interesting is that they did not shift over to heavy manufacturing industries but instead retained their initial business orientations. These two *chaebol* were more dependent on MNCs for capital and technology than they were on the state. Although their growth rates were somewhat slower (Samsung had 18.4 and Lucky-Gold Star had 17.2 percent average annual growth rate in total assets) than those of Hyundai or Daewoo, their growth rates were much higher than that of the economy as a whole.

The 1980s: The South Korean Economy and Society at the Crossroads

The 1980s were a time of great social, economic, and political upheaval in South Korea, with both large capitalists and labor becoming important voices of change. The basic formula for economic growth—a strong, comprehensive developmental state, and a tight alliance between the state and the *chaebol*—had worked well during the 1960s and 1970s but now came under fire as the *chaebol* and labor grew. The *chaebol* wanted to stand alone and questioned the viability of a comprehensive developmental state, since the South Korean economy was no longer in its infancy. They demanded that the state become more protectionist, essentially curtailing its intervention and control of the economy and allowing the market to be run by the "business elites." The irony, of course, is that the *chaebol* would never have achieved their status without state support and protection.

As the state and *chaebol* dominated the domestic economy toward the end of the 1980s, labor exploded with discontent. In 1987, after years of repressive labor policies and relatively inactive labor organizations, the number of labor strikes reached a record high (more than 3,600 cases). Despite having one of the most repressive regimes with regard to labor, South Korea now developed one of the most militant labor movements in Asia's history. Workers demanded that the state (1) stop supporting the *chaebol* at the expense of labor, (2) work toward providing a more equitable distribution of income, and (3) provide better welfare services for all citizens.

The comprehensive developmental state was faced not only with mounting social pressure from the *chaebol* and labor, but also with growing internal contradictions and then increasing pressure from the United States to internationalize. In response to these various pressures, the developmental state transformed itself from a comprehensive to a limited state. This transition, however, was seriously challenged when the authoritarian state went through political restructuring with democratic consolidation.

During this decade, South Korea also experienced great political change. In the spring of 1987, thousands of angry demonstrators filled the streets of Seoul and other major cities. Scenes of political unrest were broadcast daily around the world, just as South Korea was preparing to host the 1988 Summer Olympics. On June 29, 1987, Roh Tae Woo announced his Declaration for Democracy, ending nearly three decades of dictatorial military rule. In December of that year, the country held a direct presidential election for the first time in almost two decades. The political restructuring that was done to consolidate the new, fragile democracy made it more difficult for the state to choose between *chaebol* demands for a protectionist state and labor's demands for a welfare state.

Despite the major changes in the nation, the South Korean economy continued to outperform its counterparts in the developing world. The average annual growth rate of GNP per capita was 13.8 percent during the 1980s, with the figure rising from $1,734 to $5,569 by the end of the decade. For the GDP, the average annual growth rate during this decade was 9.7 percent, making the economy's rate of growth the second-fastest in the world. South Korea's remarkable economic recovery after negative growth in 1980 (-5.2 percent), following the domestic social and political unrest of the 1979 assassination of President Park and the second oil crisis in the same year, belied the image of a developing nation that could attain only short-term growth.

The economic structure continued to mature. The percentage of workers employed in agriculture, forestry, fishing, and mining decreased from 35.1 percent in 1981 to 18.3 percent in 1990, while the percentage in manufacturing rose from 20.4 percent to 26.9 percent, and those in services from 44.5 percent to 54.4 percent.[33] Exports remained vital for development and grew rapidly during the 1980s. Throughout the 1980s, exports accounted for more than 35 percent of South Korea's GNP, with an average annual growth rate of 12.8 percent; in 1990, South Korea was the tenth-largest exporter in the world, with an export figure of $65 billion.[34] South Korea-made products were no longer found only in huge piles of reduced-price goods at discount stores. While the country's export products had once been primarily stuffed toys, wigs, sneakers, and cheap clothing, they now included electrical and electronic appliances, computers, and automobiles. Many existing products moved out of the market's low end into the middle and upper ranges.

The Transition of the Developmental State

After nearly two decades of phenomenal economic development, the South Korean state, which had been largely responsible for that development, loosened its tight control of the economy. Several domestic and international conditions converged in prompting the state to undertake restructuring programs. Domestically, various changes in society and in the political arena warranted a serious reevaluation of the comprehensive developmental state. The two most powerful groups to emerge in the economy after two decades of rapid growth were the *chaebol* and labor. Both demanded significant changes in the state structure and its goals, although their demands were diametrically opposed. The state was obligated to listen to the demands of both groups, since the political environment was now democratic and not congenial to autocracy. The capitalists wanted the state to become a *protectionist government*: one that continued to provide protection to but ceased the heavy-handed control of the private sector. Selective control, especially control of the labor movement and of wages, continues to be favored by the large capitalists, as they lament that the rise of labor since the mid-1980s has caused decreased production. On the other hand, labor pressed the state to become a *welfare state:* one that would protect the rights of workers and provide social services to its citizens.

The pressure to liberalize the economy came from within the state as well. When Chun Doo Hwan came to power in May 1980 without a popular democratic election, he adopted an economic policy distinct from the growth-oriented strategies of the past in an effort to earn public support and to demonstrate his distinctiveness. In this venture, he studiously followed the advice of key economic advisers such as Kim Jae Ik and Kang Kyung Shik, who promoted free market ideas.[35] The free market team also blamed the previous regime and its heavy-handed economic policy for the negative economic growth in 1980. Although the negative growth was largely a result of the second oil crisis, which affected the entire world economy, the free market advocates criticized the previous regime for overinvesting in the heavy and chemical industries during the 1970s.

The push to restructure the economy also came from abroad. The growing trade deficit between the United States and several East Asian nations, including Japan, South Korea, and Taiwan, became an important impetus for change. The Reagan administration pressured these nations to open their markets to American goods and financial institutions to redress the trade deficit. Although the pressure was greatest on Japan, which had the largest trade surplus with the United States among the East Asian nations, South Korea was also visited by Trade Representative Carla Hills, who demanded that the country implement a series of economic liberalization and internationalization measures.

As a result of these various pressures from within and outside of South Korea, President Chun forcefully promoted "Economic Stabilization and Economic Liberalization" as his main economic policy. This new policy involved reprioritizing of industrial policies, economic liberalization, and internationalization, which indicated a significant transition in the developmental state, from comprehensive to limited. First, the range of active state interventions that were developmental decreased to a limited number of industrial sectors. Second, policies that were regulatory rather than developmental became prominent. And, finally, important policy tools (domestic banks, policy loans, industrial licensing, and industrial targeting) were removed from the government. These processes irreversibly altered the way the state could intervene in the economy. Since the state dispensed with most of its effective tools of enforcement, it would now be extremely difficult to return to a more extensive and comprehensive state intervention.

Reprioritizing of industrial policies was carried out in the 1980s to find new institutional goals of the state, since economic development could no longer be the sole primary policy objective. Welfare and foreign policy were introduced as new objectives.

Provision of welfare services became a focal point in the 1980s, and the economic development plan was renamed to add "social" to its title, becoming the Fifth Five-Year Economic and Social Development Plan (1982–86). The promotion of national welfare and the equitable distribution of income became the heart of the social development programs. Specific goals included increasing employment opportunities, increasing opportunities for education, providing health care and improving living conditions for the low-income class, implementing a national pension system, extending national medical insurance, and enhancing cooperative labor-management relations.[36] As a result, the proportion of the population covered by medical insurance increased dramatically, from a mere 0.06 percent in 1970 (18,713 of 32.24 million people), to 92 percent in 1989 (39,887,770 of 42.38 million).[37] Government expenditures on social and welfare services rose steadily, while defense spending decreased. Social and welfare services accounted for almost 40 percent of government expenditures in 1990, up from about a quarter in 1976.

However, by the end of the 1980s, the *chaebol* began to urge the state to return to growth-oriented policies and to abandon welfare services. Between 1989 and 1990, President Roh Tae Woo announced revisions in the Sixth Five-Year Economic and Social Development Plan, including slowing down of the provision of welfare services, and appointed economic ministers identified as supporters of growth-oriented policies.

Foreign policy was given a great deal of attention, especially by President Roh Tae Woo (1988–93). The formalization of diplomatic relations with previously communist eastern European nations has become an important goal, and the Roh regime was successful in this endeavor. South Korea, along with North Korea, finally became a member of the United Nations on September 17, 1991. The drive for reunification with North Korea became an important topic in the 1980s, although the government and student activists and dissidents diverged widely in their views of the appropriate scope and speed of the reunification process. On December 27, 1990, Roh promoted the National Unification Board's minister to become one of the two ex-officio deputy prime ministers along with the minister of the EPB.

Economic liberalization included the restructuring of industrial policies to become more limited in scope and more developmental than regulatory. Each of the three economic ministries took steps toward this end, but not without problems. The EPB significantly reduced policy loans to the private sector, which had been used as effective tools of state intervention: that is, loans with substantially lowered interest rates had been provided as inducement for private enterprises to invest in strategic industries, and loans had been withheld to punish private enterprises that did not comply with government's policies. Policy loans were abundant, accounting for 63 percent of total bank loans in 1979.[38] Between 1977 and 1979, 80 percent of total investment in manufacturing went to heavy industry in the form of policy loans.[39] The *chaebol* are strongly represented in heavy industry and so were the largest beneficiaries. However, these loans were gradually abandoned with the drive for economic liberalization and the fiscal tightening of the 1980s.[40]

The policies of the EPB also became more regulatory than developmental. Instead of using policy loans to actively encourage private enterprises to enter certain industries (i.e., developmental policy), the government announced the Monopoly Regulation and Fair Trade Law on December 31, 1980, which became effective on April 1 of the following year. This is a prime case of a regulatory policy that received much attention from the government.[41] Under this law, the Fair Trade Commission and the Office of Fair Trade were established within the EPB in 1981.[42] As a result of the restructuring, the EPB lost much of the luster gained in the 1960s and 1970s, when it was the mastermind of the five-year economic development plans. One important role it retained through the restructuring process was the compiling of the national budget.

In 1981, the Ministry of Finance began to privatize domestic banks that had been owned by the government for the past two decades. This process was completed by 1983.[43] The Bank of Korea, the central bank, still remains under the control of the Ministry of Finance. A tug of war is going on between the Ministry of Finance and the Bank of Korea, as each tries to control the role of the central bank.

The Ministry of Trade and Industry, which had been on the front line in dealing with individual private enterprises, underwent the most drastic changes in the 1980s. First, by the mid-1980s, industrial targeting had changed from the selection of sectors that promised the most growth in the future to the selection of sectors in greatest need of the state's financial assistance and protection, including a select number of both infant and declining industries. The amount and scope of subsidies were also cut during this restructuring. Second, targeting was given a limit of three years, so that private enterprises could no longer depend on government subsidies indefinitely. Lastly, licensing was simplified, and in most cases it no longer required advance government approval. As a result, the hallways of the ministry were no longer flooded with managers from private enterprises trying to obtain industrial licensing and other subsidies.

Internationalization included decreases in regulations covering foreign direct investment and imports and featured the opening up of the financial system. The pressure from the Reagan administration was important in this process, along with the rising contradictions in the institutions within South Korea. The mounting trade deficit between the United States and South Korea in the early to mid-1980s prompted the United States to urge South Korea to open its domestic market to foreign goods and foreign investors.

In 1987 the Foreign Investment Law was changed to remove most of the restrictions regarding which sectors would be closed to foreign direct investment, as well as the amount of investment to be allowed. As a result, the share of manufacturing industries open to foreign direct investment increased to 92.5 percent.[44] During the Fifth Five-Year Economic and Social Development Plan (1982-86), import liberalization and the reduction of tariff rates were instituted.[45] Foreign banks' share in the lending market increased from 4.0 percent in 1975 to 12.9 percent in 1984, after the South Korean government promulgated a policy to gradually open its capital market to foreigners in 1981.[46]

Continued Growth of the *Chaebol*

Chaebol economic and political influence grew significantly during the 1980s. Thanks in part to two decades of extensive state support and protection, the *chaebol* became some of the world's leading industrialists. Even after the reduction of direct state subsidies, they continued to grow at a rate much faster than that of the economy as a whole (which was 10.6 percent).[47] The export boom during the mid-decade "Three-Low Period" (discussed below) was critical for *chaebol* expansion during the 1980s.

The Three-Low Period, roughly from 1986 through 1988, provided tremendous opportunities for the *chaebol*. The price of crude oil was relatively low, the value of the U.S. dollar had fallen relative to the Japanese yen,[48] and interest rates were low. The rising value of the yen made Japanese products very expensive for consumers overseas. Many turned to South Korea for cheaper—albeit somewhat lower-quality—goods. From 1986 to 1987, South Korean exports grew by 36.2 percent, rising from $34.7 billion to $47.3 billion. In 1988, the figure rose to $60.7 billion.[49] This unexpected export boom boosted the economy tremendously; the average annual growth rates of GNP per capita for the three years in question were 12.9 percent, 13.0 percent, and 12.4 percent, respectively.

The *chaebol* benefited most during this boom, since they were the largest exporters (a situation different from that in Japan or Taiwan, where medium- and small-size enterprises produce the lion's share of exports). During this critical period, state subsidies were withdrawn. The *chaebol* not only survived but in fact became even more prosperous. It is not clear how they would have fared without the benefit of the favorable international economy of this period.

The ten largest *chaebol* continued to grow during the 1980s. The fastest-growing were Kia, with a 30.5 percent average annual growth rate, and Samsung, with 25.0 percent. Kia's tremendous growth was the result of its being allowed to reenter the passenger automobile business in 1987.[50] Among the four largest *chaebol* (each of which had total assets of more than 11 trillion won, or $16 billion), Samsung and Lucky-Gold Star grew most rapidly. This was different from the 1970s, when the two in that position had been Hyundai and Daewoo. The 1970s had been marked by state policies that provided for exclusive support to a few target industries and *chaebol*. The rapid growth of Samsung and Lucky-Gold Star, on the other hand, had to do with their ability to take advantage of the export boom of the mid-1980s. The brand-name electrical and electronic appliances manufactured by these two *chaebol* have become familiar to consumers worldwide. More than 21 percent of Samsung's total assets and more than 30 percent of Lucky-Gold Star's were in electronics.

In all of the four largest *chaebol*, trading was one of the largest contributors to total sales. In 1987, sales from trading comprised a large share of the total sales—54.3 percent for Daewoo, 44.6 percent for Samsung, 35.2 percent for Hyundai, and 20.9 percent for Lucky-Gold Star.

The distribution of total assets in 1988 shows a marked growth in assets in the financial services. In Daewoo's case, it jumped from 7 percent of total assets in 1980 to 38.7 percent in 1988. Even Samsung, which already had a large share of total assets in this sector in 1980, more than doubled its share, from 21 percent to 44.9 percent in 1988. This growth is largely due to *chaebol* investment in nonbanking financial institutions. The privatization of the banks, which began in the early 1980s, prohibited the *chaebol* from owning more than 8 percent of any one bank's stocks. Nonbanking financial institutions were not only very lucrative businesses, but were also critical for the *chaebol* in their efforts to become less dependent on the banks and the state. Such growth was contrary to the state's directive prohibiting ownership of private banks, intended to keep the *chaebol* from becoming too powerful (in the same way that the *zaibatsu* had moved prior to the end of World War II).

The rapid growth of the large business groups also led them to provide some of the services previously furnished by the state—such as research and development, financial institutions, and marketing know-how—much sooner in South Korea than in countries such as Taiwan. Both several large *chaebol* and the FKI established their own research facilities.[51] By the mid-1980s, eight of the ten largest *chaebol* owned at least one nonbanking financial institution—insurance, securities, and short-term finance companies.[52] These institutions, developed specifically to get around the nationalized banking system, allow the *chaebol* flexibility with day-to-day cash-flow problems and with lending within the *chaebol*. The *chaebol* are clearly able and willing to invest in services previously provided by the developmental state. If the comprehensive developmental state is to sustain itself, it needs to be seriously reevaluated, and reforms must be carried out.

As the *chaebol* gained prominence in the economy, they began to vie for more political influence. At first, there were rumors of deals made behind closed doors between the state and *chaebol*. Later, as it became evident that many policies simply could not be implemented without cooperation from the *chaebol*, leading *chaebol* owners were invited to provide input on important policies. Despite these gestures from the state, several of the largest *chaebol* openly defied state policies. Furthermore, instead of assuming a reactive position relative to the state's policies, the *chaebol* as a group began to proactively demand important policy changes and reforms from the developmental state. Although we are still constantly reminded of the state's power (as aptly demonstrated by the 1985 bankruptcy of the Kukje *chaebol*), it is clear that the state now exerts much less influence over the economy than it formerly did, and that the political influence of the *chaebol* has grown.

During the 1980s, the *chaebol* became more outspoken about their position in the economy and about what they expected from the state. They became an important voice in demanding the reduction of state intervention in the economy, despite the fact that they owed much of their prosperity and wealth to the state. The 1981 annual report of the Federation of Korean Industries included "Recommendations on the Basic Directions of Management and Control of the Economy in the 1980s," which contained a succinct statement of the FKI's position on state intervention, as follows:

> [1] The Establishment of Civilian-led Management and Control of the Economy
> We must quickly establish a civilian-led economic management and control system which will enable us to utilize the rules of the market economy most efficiently.... We must actively seek and adopt the opinions and expertise coming from various corners of our society, and in particular from the *business elites*.... Thus, we will be able to improve the total efficiency of our economic and social activities.[53]

It is clear that the large capitalists want to be in charge of their individual businesses as well as of the whole economy. They are opposed to a state-led economy, with long-term goals and development plans supplied by the state.

The *chaebol* owners I spoke with in interviews in 1992 said that state support and control had become a hindrance to business activities. One owner said that his *chaebol* would have done even better without the state's leadership, protection, and support. Chong Mong Jun, a son of Hyundai's founder, Chong Ju Yong, was the chairperson of the Hyundai Heavy Industries Co., Ltd. from 1987 to 1990 and is currently the company's adviser. When I met with him in April 1992, he had just been reelected to the National Assembly. About state intervention in the economy, he said, "I think the [South] Korean government should not interfere in the market. The private sector is much more capable of taking care of the economy than the government. In fact, if the government did not intervene so much in the market, we [Hyundai] would have done far better than where we are today."

It is hard to believe that the *chaebol* would have been able to prosper had there been no leadership and support from the state during their infancy. What is clear, however, is that extensive state intervention is no longer seen by the *chaebol* as a critical element for their growth. The 1980s proved to them that they could prosper without direct state support and control.

Several *chaebol* owners and high-ranking managers have run for National Assembly seats. Most prominent of these is the second-term member of the National Assembly, Chong Mong Jun. Family members of Hanjin's Cho Chung Hun have also run for National Assembly seats. Chong Ju Yong, founder of Hyundai *chaebol*, established a new political party in early 1992. His party, Tongil Kugmin Tang (Reunification People's Party), won 25 percent of the National Assembly seats in the March 1992 election. This remarkable achievement came only a few months after the founding of the party. Chong ran unsuccessfully for the presidency in 1992.

The Growth of Labor and Labor Movements

Along with repressive policies toward labor unions and their activities, the state kept wages low to keep South Korean products competitive in the world market.[54] Despite rising productivity, real wages did not increase and in fact actually decreased during the 1960s. In the 1970s, real wages rose, but often at a pace behind the growth rates of productivity.[55] Jang Jip Choi argues that the combination of large business groups and a government policy to control the rise of consumer prices resulted in wages being kept at an artificially low rate, with profits going to the big businesses rather than to wages.[56] South Korea's real wages became more comparable to those in the other NICs in Asia by the 1980s; and in 1990, South Korea's real wage in manufacturing was higher than Hong Kong's for the first time. However, South Korean workers still had the longest work weeks of any nation—49.8 hours. They put in nine hours more per week than their counterparts in America, and almost six hours more than those in Hong Kong.

Responding to years of low wages, poor working conditions, and repressive labor laws, the labor movement took off dramatically in the mid-1980s. The number of strikes and lock-outs skyrocketed, going from 276 cases in 1986 to 3,617 cases in 1987—an increase of more than 1,200 percent in just one year. Nearly 7 million work-days were lost in 1987, compared to 72,000 in the previous year. This eruption of labor activity had serious implications for industrial productivity.

The number of labor disputes has been decreasing since its peak in 1987, but it remains considerably higher than the numbers for the 1960s, 1970s, and early 1980s (see table 2). Figures for the 1990s show that the number of labor disputes has decreased. However, the work-

Table 2
Strikes and Lock-outs in South Korea, 1960–90

	1960	1970	1980	1981	1982	1983	1984
D/C	256	4	206	186	88	98	114
W/T	64.3	0.5	49.0	34.6	9.0	11.1	16.4
D/J	—	—	61.3	31.0	11.5	8.7	19.9

	1985	1986	1987	1988	1989	1990
D/C	265	276	3,617	1,873	1,616	322
W/T	28.7	46.9	934.9	293.6	409.1	133.9
D/J	64.3	72.0	6,946.9	5,400.8	6,351.4	1,836.3

Notes: D/C Number of strikes and lock-outs.
W/T Workers involved (thousands).
D/J Work-days not worked (thousands).

Sources: *Yearbook of Labour Statistics 1970, 1980, 1990, 1991* (Geneva: International Labour Office 1970, 1980, 1990, 1991).

days lost are still much higher than those prior to 1987 and indicate that each dispute is lasting much longer. South Korea's strike and lock-out figures are still among the highest in the world.

Several factors contributed to the rapid growth of the labor movement in the 1970s and 1980s. First, the state's drive for heavy and chemical industrialization in the 1970s produced companies that were much larger in size relative to those of the 1960s, when light manufacturing had been promoted. The heavy and chemical industrialization also required a more highly educated labor force. As a result, for example, among the skilled and semi-skilled workers in the machinery sector, the share of those having high-school education and above rose from 17.6 percent in 1967 to 59.3 percent in 1984.[57] A better-educated labor force in a large factory setting produced fertile conditions for labor unions to grow and to organize labor movements. Thus, growth in union membership was highest in companies with more than 1,000 employees; it grew from 48.2 percent of employees in 1973 to 58.7 percent in 1979.[58]

Second, the role of students and church organizations has been critical. Several church-based groups, such as the Urban Industrial Mission and the Young Catholic Workers, played key roles in organizing labor unions and labor movements after the late 1960s.[59] More student activists were arrested, sentenced to jail terms, and expelled from colleges and universities during the eight years under Chun Doo Hwan (1980–88) than in the previous eighteen years of the Park regime (1961–79). Many of these students disguised themselves to become factory workers. An unofficial estimate shows that over 3,000 students became blue-collar workers in the 1980s, concealing their college education so that they could be hired in jobs that specifically required less than a high school education.[60] They played a critical role in organizing unions and in generating militant labor movements, utilizing organizational skills they acquired from student movements. Between 1985 and 1986 alone, the police reported that 671 such "agitators" were arrested.[61]

Labor had been building strength and becoming more militant during the 1970s and 1980s; as soon as political space permitted, the labor movement exploded in full force, like a pressure-cooker that had been building up steam for two decades. The labor movement in South Korea is the most militant of those among the Gang of Four in East Asia.[62] Labor volatility is a critical outcome of South Korean development, and the labor movement grew *in spite of* repressive labor policies and lack of artisan culture.[63]

Labor wanted the state to become a welfare state, which would guarantee the rights of labor and provide basic welfare services. Workers wanted the state to stop suppressing wages below the minimum standard of living; enforcing repressive labor policies regarding freedom of association, collective bargaining, and collective action; and providing exclusive support for big businesses that tended to be hostile toward labor unions, and that exacerbated the skewed distribution of wealth.[64]

A welfare state, however, is not analogous to a protectionist government. Far from it, the welfare state that labor demanded was one that could punish the large capitalists who were much to blame for suppression of wages and for poor labor conditions. A welfare state also requires a strong state apparatus that is capable of generating resources and of providing welfare services.

Conclusion

The analysis of South Korea's socioeconomic development since the 1960s, which is based on the roles played by the state, large capitalists (*chaebol*), and labor in the context of changing domestic and international political economy, helps illuminate the challenges facing South Korea today.

Domestically, South Korea is in the midst of democratic transition and economic restructuring. The developmental state in South Korea was a powerful agent of social change. Unparalleled in its influence in society, the state carried out bold economic development plans that produced one of the most successful cases of development near the end of the twentieth century. However, the policies and plans that produced rapid growth also planted the seeds for the decline of the developmental state. Two important policies appeared to have hastened the state's reduction of influence in the South Korean economy: industrial policies supporting the growth of big businesses and repressive labor policies. These policies resulted in the shaping of the two powerful groups that would make the strongest demands for reduction in the state's degree and method of economic intervention. The state, in response, undertook various economic reform measures throughout the 1980s. The most pressing issues that still need to be negotiated between various actors in the economy are (1) the role of the interventionist developmental state in the economy; (2) the (unchecked) growth of the large *chaebol*, which continue to threaten the small- and medium-size enterprises; (3) the rights of labor; and (4) finding a new niche for South Korean businesses in the world market via technological innovation or innovation in the production process.

Politically, South Korea has been engaged in democratization since the mid-1980s. As Rueschemeyer, Stephens and Stephens have noted, economic development brings about pressure for democratization through changes in class configuration and in class relations.[65] In South Korea, the growth of the urban middle class and the mobilization of the working class were critical in forcing the breakdown of an authoritarian regime, which had existed from the 1960s to the mid-1980s. The workers, aided initially by student and church groups, formulated their class interests as against both the capitalists and the authoritarian state. Thus, their participation in the democracy movement was vital and enabled the democracy movement of the mid-1980s to be a broad-based coalition, including students (and intellectuals), religious leaders, workers, and the urban middle class. Democratic transition, which began in the mid-1980s, is continuing with a newly elected civilian president, Kim Young Sam. Under Kim's leadership, South Korea has enacted various measures to more firmly establish democratization. This means that South Korea is likely to continue with major social and political changes in the near future, where contested groups may challenge specific measures along the way.

Internationally, South Korea faces challenges based on its tremendous economic success. Its economic prowess as a major exporter along with its East Asian neighbors, has prompted first world nations to erect trade barriers. At the same time, there is growing pressure, in particular from the United States, to open the South Korean economy for foreign financial institutions, products, and services. It is an irony that the United States and other first world nations are enacting protectionist measures and at the same time pressuring East Asian nations to open their markets and reduce protectionist measures. Nations such as South Korea are also facing pressure from the so-called "second-tier NICs" of the third world, including the People's Republic of China, Malaysia, Thailand, and Indonesia. These nations have successfully penetrated the international market with their cheap manufactured products, squeezing out countries like South Korea from the bottom rung of the market. Thus, the NICs face double challenges: pressure to liberalize from the first world nations, and pressure to upgrade their products from the second-tier NICs.

In terms of geopolitics, South Korea faces an even greater challenge. With the cold war all but over, the United States must determine whether to continue its military presence in South Korea. Reunification with North Korea appears, at different times, a distant or an imminent possibility. However, reunification is increasingly seen by South Koreans as coming with a huge economic price tag. Germany's costly reunification process has prompted the South Koreans to become wary of an abrupt German-type reunification. However, regardless of the potentially great cost, reunification remains a deep yearning in the hearts of many Koreans. Thus, many South Koreans see reunification as inevitable, with only the timing and the process remaining to be negotiated, in themselves daunting tasks.

Notes

Portions of this essay are excerpted from the author's forthcoming book, *Big Business, Strong State: Collusion and Conflict in South Korean Development, 1960–1990,* to be published by the University of California Press.

Romanization of Korean words and names is based on the guidelines of the Ministry of Education of the Republic of Korea. Exceptions include well-known names and places, such as Rhee Syngman, Park Chung Hee, and Seoul.

1. World Bank, *World Development Report* (New York: Oxford University Press, 1993). In 1991, Hong Kong's GNP per capita was $13,430 and Singapore's was $14,210.
2. Alice Amsden, *Asia's Next Giant: South Korea and Late Industrialization* (London: Oxford University Press, 1989), p. 328.
3. Bank of Korea, *Economic Statistics Yearbook* (Seoul: Bank of Korea, 1984).
4. Leroy P. Jones and Il Sakong, *Government, Business, and Entrepreneurship in Economic Development* (Cambridge: Harvard University Press, 1980).
5. Economic Planning Board, *Korea Statistical Yearbook* (Seoul: Economic Planning Board, 1978), and International Monetary Fund, *International Financial Statistics* (Washington: International Monetary Fund, 1979).
6. Park Chung Hee, *The Road toward Economic Self-Sufficiency and Prosperity* (Seoul: Ministry of Public Information, 1965).
7. Chalmers Johnson, *MITI and the Japanese Miracle* (Stanford: Stanford University Press, 1982).
8. Chalmers Johnson, "Political Institutions and Economic Performance: The Government-Business Relationship in Japan, South Korea, and Taiwan," in Frederic C. Deyo, ed., *Political Economy of the New Asian Industrialism* (Ithaca: Cornell University Press, 1987) pp. 136-64; Hyun-Chin Lim, *Dependent Development in Korea, 1963-1979* (Seoul: Seoul National University Press, 1987); and Edward S. Mason, Mahn Je Kim, Dwight H. Persons, Kwang Suk Kim, and David C. Cole, eds., *The Economic and Social Modernization of the Republic of Korea* (Cambridge: Harvard University Press, 1980).
9. Jones and Sakong, *Government, Business, and Entrepreneurship*; Anne O. Krueger, *The Developmental Role of Foreign Sector and Aid* (Cambridge, MA: Harvard University Press, 1979); Lim, *Dependent Development*; Mason, et al., *Economic and Social Modernization*.
10. Jones and Sakong, *Government, Business, and Entrepreneurship*, and Krueger, *Developmental Role of Foreign Sector.*
11. Economic Planning Board, *Economic Policies of the Development Era: The Twenty-Year History of the Economic Planning Board* [in Korean] (Seoul: Economic Planning Board, 1982) p. 407.
12. Man Yol I, *A Chronological Table of Korea's History* [in Korean] (Seoul: Yokminsa, 1985), p. 318.
13. Seok Ki Kim, "Business Concentration and Government Policy: A Study of the

Phenomenon of Business Groups in Korea, 1945-1985," unpublished Ph.D. dissertation, Harvard University, 1987.

14. The Foreign Capital Inducement Law does not appear to discriminate FDI from other types of foreign capital. However, in practice, there are many overt and covert obstacles for FDI, including laws on which industries are allowed for FDI. See, for example, Sang Kun Pyon, "The Closing Accounts of the 18 Years of Gulf" [in Korean], *Shindonga* 10 (1980), for details on why Gulf left Korea after eighteen years.

15. Peter B. Evans, "Class, State, and Dependence in East Asia: Lessons for Latin Americanists," in Deyo, *Political Economy*, pp. 203-26; Peter B. Evans, Dietrich Rueschemeyer, and Theda Skocpol, eds., *Bringing the State Back In* (Cambridge: Cambridge University Press, 1985); and Hagen Koo, "The Interplay of State, Social Class, and World System in East Asian Development: The Cases of South Korea and Taiwan," in Deyo, *Political Economy*, pp. 165-81.

16. For details, see Eun Mee Kim, "From Dominance to Symbiosis: State and Chaebol in Korea," *Pacific Focus* 3, 2, pp. 105-21. Park argued that South Korea's stagnant economy under Rhee and Chang had resulted from a lack of political leadership and from corruption on the part of both politicians and businesses. On May 28, 1961—just twelve days after the military coup—the Supreme Council for National Reconstruction (headed by Park) announced the formation of a committee for the investigation and execution of charges of "illicit accumulation of wealth." On the same day, presidents of major *chaebol* were arrested and jailed. These charges served important political and economic objectives of the Park regime. First, by prosecuting the corrupt government officials of the Rhee and Chang regimes, the Park government was able to gain some political support from the public. The Park regime could claim a kind of moral purity over the corrupt Rhee regime. And, perhaps more importantly, the Park regime demonstrated a sense of superiority over a democratically elected and legitimate regime. A military government which took power by force, Park wanted to show, was better than a legitimately elected government which was corrupt. Secondly, the Park regime demonstrated that it would utilize the authoritarian state to interact with the private sector. By punishing the *chaebol* owners with jail sentences, it showed that it would use discipline and punishment to deal with the *chaebol*. The state was clearly in charge.

17. Hagen Koo and Eun Mee Kim, "The Developmental State and Capital Accumulation in South Korea," in Richard P. Appelbaum and Jeffrey Henderson, eds., *States and Development in the Asian Pacific Rim* (Newbury Park: Sage, 1992), pp. 121-49.

18. *Korea Yearbook 1962* [in Korean] (Seoul: Hanguk Yongamsa, 1962); ibid., 1963.

19. *Korea Yearbook 1967.*

20. Economic Planning Board, *Major Statistics of the Korean Economy* (Seoul: Economic Planning Board, 1986).

21. Ibid.

22. Ibid.

23. Ibid., 1990.

24. Ibid., 1972; Federation of Korean Industries, *Korea's Economic Policies (1945-1985)* (Seoul: Federation of Korean Industries, 1987).

25. The State of the Nation Message is similar to the State of the Union Message given

by the President of the United States. Most industrial policies are announced by relevant ministries, not by the president during the State of the Nation Message. That Park would use the occasion to make this pronouncement demonstrates his strong conviction that this policy should be forcefully promoted. It was also a way of dispelling any criticism that could have come from economic ministries by putting the president's stamp of approval on the plan. See Kwan Yong Chong, "Emergence of Bureaucratic Authoritarianism and Policies on Heavy and Chemical Industry" [in Korean], in Sang Chin Han, et al., eds. *Studies on the Changes in the Korean Society and the Role of the State* (Seoul: Hyondae Sahoe Yonguso, 1985).

26. Federation of Korean Industries, *The Forty-Year History of the Korean Economy* [in Korean] (Seoul: Federation of Korean Industries, 1986).
27. This later became known as the Nixon Doctrine.
28. See Hyug Baeg Im, "The Rise of Bureaucratic Authoritarianism in South Korea, " *World Politics* 39, 2, pp. 231-57; and Chong, "Emergence of Bureaucratic Authoritarianism."
29. Koo and Kim, "Developmental State and Capital Accumulation in South Korea."
30. Chong, "Emergence of Bureaucratic Authoritarianism."
31. Ibid.
32. Jones and Sakong, *Government, Business, and Entrepreneurship*; Kyu Ok I and Chae Hyong I, *Business Groups and Economic Concentration* [in Korean] (Seoul: Korea Development Institute, 1990).
33. National Statistical Office, *Major Statistics of Korean Economy* [in Korean] (Seoul: National Statistical Office, 1991).
34. World Bank, *World Development Report* (New York: Oxford University Press, 1992).
35. Amsden, *Asia's Next Giant*; Chung-in Moon, "The Demise of a Developmentalist State? Neoconservative Reforms and Political Consequences in South Korea," *Journal of Developing Societies* 4, pp. 67-84.
36. Economic Planning Board, *Revised Plans for the Fifth Five-Year Economic and Social Development Plan* (Seoul: Economic Planning Board, 1983); Economic Planning Board, *The Sixth Five-Year Economic and Social Development Plan* (Seoul: Economic Planning Board, 1986).
37. Economic Planning Board, *Major Statistics of the Korean Economy*, 1990.
38. Seok Ki Kim, "Business Concentration and Government Policy," p. 181.
39. Moon, "Demise of a Developmentalist State?," p. 69.
40. Ibid.
41. Economic Planning Board, *Economic Policies of the Development Era: The Twenty-Year History of the Economic Planning Board* [in Korean] (Seoul: Economic Planning Board, 1982).
42. Economic Planning Board, *Monopoly Regulation and Fair Trade in Korea* (Seoul: Economic Planning Board, 1989).
43. Federation of Korean Industries, *Korea's Economic Policies*.
44. Economic Planning Board, *White Book on Foreign Capital Loan* (Seoul: Economic Planning Board, 1986).
45. Economic Planning Board, *Revised Plans for the Fifth Five-Year Economic and Social Development Plan*.
46. Federation of Korean Industries, *Korea's Economic Policies*.

47. National Statistical Office, *Major Statistics of Korean Economy*, 1991.

48. In September 1985, the United States and Japan agreed to increase the value of the Japanese yen sharply against the U.S. dollar and other currencies in the world. This was popularly known as the Plaza Accord, since the meeting was held at the Plaza Hotel in New York City. The purpose of the accord was to redress the trade deficit between the United States and several nations by reducing imports into the United States through raising the price of foreign goods, and promoting exports of American-made goods by cutting their prices.

49. National Statistical Office, *Major Statistics of Korean Economy*, 1991.

50. In August 1980, Kia was prohibited from producing passenger automobiles until 1987, when the plans for the reorganization of the heavy and chemical industries were announced. Kia specialized in buses and other transportation equipment during this period. Unlike a few larger *chaebol*, which could defy state orders, Kia had to comply with this policy.

51. The Federation of Korean Industries is an association of owners, chief executive officers, and high-ranking managers of *chaebol* and large enterprises. It regularly lobbies government offices and the National Assembly. Its opinions and advisory reports to the government are published as a collection in *Annual Report: The Federation of Korean Industries*.

52. Management Efficiency Research Institute, *Analysis of Financial Statements—Fifty Major Business Groups in Korea* (Seoul: Management Efficiency Research Institute, 1988).

53. Federation of Korean Industries, *1981 Annual Report: The Federation of Korean Industries* (Seoul: Federation of Korean Industries, 1981).

54. Frederic C. Deyo, "State and Labor: Modes of Political Exclusion in East Asian Development," in Deyo, ed., *Political Economy*, pp. 182-202; Sookon Kim, "Labor-Management Relationship: Past and Present," unpublished manuscript, East-West Center, Honolulu, 1989; Walden Bello and Stephanie Rosenfeld, *Dragons in Distress: Asia's Miracle Economies in Crisis* (San Francisco: Institute for Food and Development Policy, 1990).

55. Jang Jip Choi, *Labor and the Authoritarian State: Labor Unions in South Korean Manufacturing Industries, 1961-1980* (Seoul: Korea University Press, 1989).

56. Ibid., pp. 299-300.

57. Bello and Rosenfeld, *Dragons in Distress*, p. 41.

58. Choi, *Labor and the Authoritarian State*, p. 37.

59. Bello and Rosenfeld, *Dragons in Distress*, pp. 36-37.

60. George E. Ogle, *South Korea: Dissent within the Economic Miracle* (London: Zed Books, 1990), p. 99.

61. Ibid.

62. Deyo, *Political Economy*, p. 67.

63. Hagen Koo, "From Farm to Factory: Proletarianization in Korea," *American Sociological Review* 55, 5, pp. 669-81.

64. Bello and Rosenfeld, *Dragons in Distress*; Choi, *Labor and the Authoritarian State*; Frederic C. Deyo, *Beneath the Miracle: Labor Subordination in the New Asian Industrialism* (Berkeley: University of California Press, 1989); Sookon Kim, "Labor-Management Relationship"; Ogle, *South Korea: Dissent within the Economic Miracle*.

65. Dietrich Rueschemeyer, Evelyne Huber Stephens, and John D. Stephens, *Capitalist Development and Democracy* (Chicago: University of Chicago Press, 1992).

Chapter 10

Politicization of the Korean Mass Public through Value Change

Aie-Rie Lee

Through various forms of government intervention and changes in expectations about the future, Korea has finally overcome Larry E. Wesphal's characterization of the late 1950s, that the country was a "basket case" and was expected to remain that way for the foreseeable future.[1] During this period, Korean policymakers also behaved in manners that were consistent with Wesphal's view and helped to reinforce it. The culmination of pessimistic feelings among the populace, coupled with political corruption and hunger throughout the country, led to student demonstrations and eventually a military coup d'etat in 1961. Under the leadership of President Park Chung Hee, the view that guided government action was that the only way to negate Korea's dependent status and the vicious cycle was by fundamentally changing the economy's trajectory, away from industrialization focused on the domestic market and toward major economic policy reforms. Through austere economic policies, together with the suppression of political freedom, expression, and participation, Korea achieved what no other nation was able to accomplish in modern times—that is, a "miracle" in its economic development within three decades. This achievement is truly a miracle, in the sense that, with an uneducated labor force, no natural resources, and an infrastructure and industrial base devastated by the Korean War, Korea was able to change its status from that of a less-developed nation to its recent

Aie-Rie Lee is associate professor of political science at Texas Tech University, Lubbock.

position as a newly industrialized state, transforming its traditional agrarian economy to an export-led economy, and becoming widely recognized as one of the most successful cases of economic development in modern history.

This rapid economic development brought about drastic changes in Korea's socioeconomic structure. As shown in table 1, for example, between 1945 and 1990 the proportion of the population living in cities with populations over 50,000 increased from 14 percent to 72 percent. The proportion of people engaged in the primary sector (e.g., fishery and agriculture) dropped from 75 percent in 1945 to 18 percent in 1990. In the same period, the proportion of the relevant age cohort enrolled in secondary education increased from 20 percent to 92 percent, while GNP per capita rose by a factor of 50 between 1965 and 1990.

Moreover, the rapid growth of the Korean economy also produced a rapid spread of access to the communications media, which fostered a rise in the resources, skill, and cognitive sophistication of the general public and enhanced their political competence. This, in turn, created growing societal pressures for democratization. The daily newspaper circulation rates in 1990, for instance, were about ten times higher than the rates in 1955. The telephone subscription rates also increased 60 times between 1965 and 1990. Now, every household enjoys watching TV. It is certain that rapid industrialization caused basic structural changes that produced a solid core of middle class citizens.[2] This change is reflected by the proportion of people who felt that they belonged to the middle class—58 percent in 1985, increasing to 60 percent in 1987, and again to 61 percent in 1989, indicating a steady growth in middle-class consciousness (*Joong-ang Daily News*, 1985, 1987, 1989). These middle class citizens were becoming increasingly restive concerning the norms of Confucian paternalism and responsive to the effect of democracy elsewhere in the world. Some of these middle class individuals sided with the student demand for democracy.[3]

Aside from bringing social changes, economic growth also increased the pressure for democratization and facilitated that process. Koreans no longer condoned the continuation of authoritarian rule, in part because the predominant values and norms in society altered over time to reduce tolerance for repression and concentration of power and to stimulate demands for freedom. Beginning in the late 1980s, democracy finally arrived in Korea, at the end of what Samuel Huntington calls, the "third wave" of democratization.[4] By 1992, Korea had open elections, legal opposition parties, and electoral proce-

Table 1
Factor Loadings and Value Scores
of Authoritarian/Libertarian Items, 1982

	Loading on First Unrotated Factor	A-L Score Korea	A-L Score Germany
Deference-Autonomy Items:			
Parents should have their own lives	.633	-34	-18
A job where one can use initiative is important	.621	-22	+28
[Inglehart items coded in Libertarian form[a]]	487	-24	+ 8
I have control over my own life	.470	-24	+46
A child should be taught to be independent	.308	-10	+ 2
A child should be taught good manners	-.322	-38	+18
There is never any justification for fighting police	-.513	-10	-42
Mean		-23	+6
Conformity-Openness Items:			
There is never any justification for:			
Prostitution	.761	-68	-14
Extramarital affairs	.707	-48	-18
Sex when people are legally underage	.701	-62	-20
Divorce	.665	-42	-24
Taking drugs	.649	-50	-64
Homosexuality	.633	-64	-12
Abortion	.616	-14	-10
Euthanasia	.506	+ 1	- 6
To be fulfilled women need to have children	.327	-48	+28
Children are important to a successful marriage	.303	-86	-28
Mean		-48	-17

[a] I gave a weight of -2, -1 for the respondent's choice of "maintaining order in the nation" as his/her respective top and second choices and treated them as authoritarian; a weight of 2, 1 for the respondent's "more say in government decisions" and "freedom of speech" categories as one's first and second choices, respectively, and considered them as libertarian.

dures that allowed the winners of elections to assume control of the government. For instance, the 1992 presidential election, considered a turning point in Korean political history, was peaceful and fair, unlike past presidential elections, which were marred by fraud and vote tampering.

This is by no means to argue that Koreans now enjoy a harmonious and all-agreeable set of social values and norms. Indeed, as a consequence of the rapid social changes in the past thirty years, there are still many conflicting social values among groups in Korea. For instance, the young have been socialized to articulate their demands and interests through the Western-oriented educational system and the mass media. The younger generation, less exposed to traditional norms, thus feel less hesitant about being active in politics. Further, younger cohorts are more likely to receive a secondary or university education. Partly because they have higher educational levels than the older generation, the younger groups have higher political skill levels. Consequently, they have the potential to participate in politics in more active and issue-specific ways than has generally been true in the past.

Conversely, the former political system enjoyed by "traditional authoritarian" minded folks maintained, to a great extent, non-democratic modes of government. In view of this lack of fit or congruence between the developing democratic political culture among the younger and more educated elements of the society and the existing modes of government, it is natural to expect a high level of cynicism or alienation that is conducive to protest activity and a decline in system support. Thus, I wish to argue that social values provide an important clue to understanding the nature of political conflict and its resolution in Korea.

The object of this paper, then, is first to investigate the changing patterns, if any, of basic social values and, second, to analyze the relationship between these social values and their effects on mass political orientations in Korea between 1982 and 1990. In doing so, I will first review the literature on the value change process, particularly Flanagan's Authoritarian-Libertarian value change thesis. Then, via the 1982 and 1990 Korean nationwide surveys that were part of the World Value Survey studies, I will identify and analyze systematically to what extent these social values persist and/or are changing and their influence upon Koreans' political action. The last section is conclusions.

Authoritarian-Libertarian Value Change

In a series of writings, Scott Flanagan has introduced one of the most systematic value change models explaining political attitudes and behavior. Flanagan's[5] and, later, Flanagan and Aie-Rie Lee's[6] basic conceptualization of the authoritarian-to-libertarian value change is that the overarching concept integrating the notion of libertarian values is self-actualization. To achieve the goal of self-actualization, the individual requires freedom in three separate but interrelated domains: a social domain to provide freedom from the tyranny of authority, a psychological domain to free the individual from rigidly held traditional beliefs and customs, and a physical domain to afford freedom from material limitations. The drive for self-actualization and its expression in the social, psychological, and physical domains, then, defines the scope of the A-L value change, which occurs in three distinct subdimensions: Deference to Autonomy (D-A), Conformity to Openness (C-O), Austerity to Self-Betterment. What follows are brief explanations of and distinctions among these three dimensions of the A-L cleavage.[7]

According to Flanagan and his associates, a shift from deference to autonomy refers to growing emphasis on equality rather than hierarchy, on self-assertive individualism and independence rather than passive compliance or submissive resignation, and a general orientation towards seeking more self-determination and control over one's own life.[8] This dimension captures the general decline modern societies are experiencing in the respect, loyalty, dependency, and obedience that all outside authorities and institutions can command, from parental authority, to the community, to the church, to one's boss, to the political authorities. What lies behind this shift is growing equality in incomes, education, information, and lifestyles as a result of industrialization and economic development, which in turn has diminished the scope and magnitude of authority that one individual can exercise over another. With these changes in life condition has come a decline in the primacy of the values of respect for authority, obedience, loyalty, and passive resignation and a rise in emphasis on autonomy, individual rights, self-assertiveness, and personal and political freedom.

The second dimension of the authoritarian-to-libertarian value change, change in the psychological domain, represents movement from an emphasis on conformity to an attitude of openness—that is, seeking a freer environment to facilitate self-actualization by throwing off the constraints of traditional customs and religious beliefs, opening oneself to new ideas, adopting more-accepting attitudes towards new lifestyles and a broader range of moral behavior, and exercising more tolerance of and empathy with people or groups that are different from oneself, including religious and ethnic minorities.

One factor that is undermining conformity to traditional belief is the advance of scientific knowledge and education. The diffusion of knowledge and scientific advances has undermined traditional moral codes and religious beliefs and practices and has increased mankind's ability to understand and control their environment. Further, the diffusion has induced a change from pietism and strict moral codes to more permissive values that are tolerant of a broader range of behavior.

The third dimension, a reaction to change in the physical domain, is a shift from preoccupation with the values necessary for physical survival in conditions of scarcity to the search for personal happiness and fulfillment through improving one's living environment and general quality of life, through a stronger emphasis on self-understanding, self-improvement, and the expansion of one's knowledge, skills, and capacities, and through a greater willingness to relax austere codes that inhibit the pursuit of personal pleasures and self-indulgence. Authoritarian values in this dimension are thus values that stress the importance of hard work, diligence, self-discipline, and other work-centered values, and a frugal and austere lifestyle. Libertarian values are those that put greater emphasis on self-fulfillment, self-indulgence, and the pursuit of personal pleasures and leisure activities.

In short, libertarian values facilitate self-actualization by assigning a higher priority to autonomy, openness, and self-betterment. Authoritarian orientations and modes of behavior are values that inhibit self-actualization.

Data and Measures

The empirical portion of my analysis is addressed by analyzing two sets of the World Value Survey studies, conducted in Korea in 1982 and 1990, the former with the sample of N=970 and the latter with N=1,251.[9]

The World Value Survey studies are particularly valuable because many of the same questions have been used in both years, permitting an analysis of change over an eight-year period. Since the 1990 survey replicates many key items from the 1982 survey, I am fortunate to be able to analyze common indicators of political orientations, including the "Authoritarian-Libertarian" (A-L) value items, along with questions regarding psychological involvement (PI). Those A-L and PI items, together with system trust, protest potential, age, and education, permit an examination of the changing or continuous relationship of the

Table 2
Factor Loadings and Value Scores
of Authoritarian/Libertarian Items, 1989

	Loading on First Unrotated Factor	A-L Score
Deference-Autonomy Items:		
Children should take care of their aged parents	.682	-21
Sons and daughters should have equal inheritance rights	.665	+16
It is important to have a son	.637	+13
Husband and wife have equal rights to control property	.582	-27
People may decide whether to have children or not	.338	-30
People should follow the instructions of their superiors	.328	- 2
Mean		- 9
Conformity-Openness Items:		
It is necessary to predict marital harmony before marriage	.705	+12
A person's destiny may be read in his face or horoscope	.646	+22
Women should not have premarital sex	.518	-52
People should follow traditional customs and practices	.487	- 5
It is all right to have premarital sex if both partners are in love	.440	- 2
Women's smoking is a moral issue	.402	-52
It is best to have big weddings and funerals	.372	+66
Mean		- 2

psychological resources and basic value orientations necessary to Koreans' politicization.

This study utilizes only the D-A and C-O dimensions of the A-L value cleavage. These two dimensions have been identified as constituting the central defining core of the A-L dimension and have been tested in other cultural settings, especially in Japan and Taiwan.

The selection of items to be included in the A-L value dimensions used two steps. I first chose items based on the face validity of their relevance to the hypothesized value dimensions. Then I used factor analysis to choose items further among those having face validity. When the selected items were factor analyzed, the study found two distinct conceptual value dimensions: Deference-Autonomy, and Conformity-Openness.[10]

Table 2 shows results of the final factor analyses for each of the two subdimensions. Seven items from each data set were identified as tapping the Deference-Autonomy dimension that focuses on the conflict between adherents of the two opposing values which

Flanagan[11] and Flanagan and Lee[12] characterize as social order ideology and social change ideology. Libertarians here stress autonomy, self-assertiveness, equality, participation, free speech, and independence, while authoritarians emphasize order, good behavior, loyalty, dutifulness, and respecting the authority of superiors.

As reported in table 2, all seven of the items load heavily on the first unrotated factor. The only exception appears to be item six ("A child should be taught good manners") in 1990. The very weak loading found in that case would seem to be attributable to the fact that by 1990 there was very little variance on this item, with 93 percent selecting the authoritarian responses: teaching a child good manners is important.

The second dimension represents the Conformity-Openness dimension. Supporters and opponents of conformity to the traditional customs and morals are considered authoritarians and libertarians, respectively. Again, seven items were identified that tap traditional moral beliefs, standards, and customs. A quick scan of these items reveals that the questions primarily address issues revolving around traditional sexual morality, family values, and women's roles.

The pattern of clustering based on factor loadings suggested combining all fourteen items into a single scale of the A-L values. This was done by standardizing, equally weighing, and combining the respective items, and this technique was employed throughout the study.

Also employed as intervening variables are cynicism or political dissatisfaction, labelled system support and psychological involvement in politics. Basically, psychological involvement (PI) refers to the attitudinal orientations of an individual citizen, including his/her political awareness, his/her sense of political outcomes, and his/her interest in political matters. In fact, several political scientists have found that the higher the PI in politics, the greater the likelihood that an individual will have an ideological conceptualization of politics.[13] Thus, many conceptual models of political participation and voting behavior, in particular, view psychological factors as the immediate causal influences on participation. Two items related to psychological involvement were available from both waves of the study.[14]

Several studies also show that distrust of government or political institutions is an incentive for protest.[15] One way to measure the degree of distrust in the political system is to ask people directly about the images of political institutions, government performance, or incumbent office-holders. The surveys provided this analysis with five items, tapping system trust. The system trust scale is then constructed by standardizing, equally weighing, and combining these items.[16] Finally, four items tapping protest potential were available from both waves of the survey.[17]

Authoritarian-Libertarian Value Change and Its Attributes

As mentioned, the Korean population has undergone a dramatic socioeconomic transformation across the postwar period. As the social mobilization proceeded, it stimulated a process of value change which began to delegitimize the authoritarian political order. Given Korea's Confucian authoritarian cultural tradition, I believe that mass attitude change played a very important role in linking socioeconomic development with liberalizing political change.

To what extent have the values of Koreans been changing? In order to answer the question, an item-by-item analysis was conducted in more detail for the A-L dimension, to capture the underlying picture. The last columns of table 2 report the extent of the differences in the overall A-L response distributions for each item.[18] In every case, scores were obtained by subtracting the percentages of respondents who offered authoritarian responses from the percentages giving libertarian types of answers. While scores across all seven items for the D-A value dimension showed negative signs in 1982, indicating a predominance of authoritarian values, by 1990 four out of seven items offered positive signs, signifying a predominance of libertarian values.

Overall, the study found a steady trend towards a lessened endorsement of authoritarian values, with an average of -23 selecting an authoritarian response across the seven items in 1982 and falling to -8 in 1990. Even in the early 1990s, however, Koreans were still more inclined to think that an opportunity to use initiative in a job is less important, that maintaining order is more important in the country for the next ten years, and that children ought to be taught good manners at home. Meanwhile, contemporary Koreans held more libertarian attitudes on four items: parents should have their own lives and should not be asked to sacrifice their own well-being for the sake of their children, a person has free choice and control over his/her own life, teaching children independence is important, fighting with the police may be somewhat justified. Although it is difficult to interpret these complex findings, it is safe to say that Koreans have begun to defy some, if not all, of the principles of traditional Confucianism, such as sacrifice of parents' lives.

One Korean traditional value is the importance of obedience to social customs and morality. While the implications of these customs and moral standards may change with time, the principle of upholding them always remains. In this study, the value dimension of conformity/openness refers to the difference in the relative emphasis on traditional customs and morals. Here, the main purpose is to discover Koreans' dominant thinking or mental traits: whether Koreans have retained their moral beliefs and traditional customs or whether they have adopted more liberal outlooks. The study expects to find the libertarian person as one who can more readily acknowledge the process of social transformation taking place around him/her, such as in marriage, divorce, abortion, homosexuality, extramarital affairs, and traditional practices, and who can more freely accept changed opportunities; and the authoritarian person as one who is likely to offer resistance to all of these changes.

At first glance, table 2 reports a similar but weak pattern in the D-A dimension, a decreasing trend towards authoritarian values, from -40 in 1982 to -38 by 1990. Yet, a closer inspection of the 1990 data reveals marked contrasts in the perception of the C-O values. Perhaps most striking, however, is the fact that the pattern for items 8, 11, 12, and 14 is reversed in 1990: a trend toward a diminishing endorsement of libertarian values. Koreans more readily acknowledge the process of social transformation taking place around them on three items: that either married men or women may have an extramarital affair, and that divorce and abortion may be somewhat justified. They are more traditional on four morals and customs/practices items: prostitution, taking drugs, homosexuality, and the idea that a woman has to have children in order to be fulfilled. It would seem that attitudes are still strikingly traditional on some morals items in Korea. One can argue that no change has taken place on these over the eight-year period examined.

Table 3 provides a more concrete representation of the levels of value change. The combined A-L scale (possible range from -3 to 8) was first recoded into four categories for the 1982 sample. As revealed in table 3, there is a dramatic pattern of change across three out of four categories, with authoritarian categories declining by 27 percentage points and the libertarian and semi-libertarian categories gaining by 1 and 14 percentage points across the entire eight-year period. Put differently, 91 percent of the sample held authoritarian values in 1982, while about 24 percent held libertarian values in 1990.

Table 3
Value Types and Value Change
1982–1989

Value Types	1982 %	1989 %	1982-1989 Change
Authoritarian	43	7	-36
Semi-Authoritarian	45	33	-12
Semi-Libertarian	11	48	+37
Libertarian	1	11	+10
Total Percent	100	99	
N	757	724	

One might also argue that the massive changes that have been taking place in Korea over the last four decades as a consequence of the rapid economic development and social mobilization processes have been impacting across all demographic categories. As attitudes have changed, the aggregate profile of Korea's political culture has shifted as well.

Table 4 shows that age and education across two time points are significantly related to the value scale; that is, the younger generation and the more educated exhibit stronger support for libertarian values. In addition, across all four variables in the table, there are consistent patterns of a decrease in authoritarian values and an increase in libertarian values. Here, the displayed percentages present just the pure libertarian and authoritarian categories shown in table 3, with two "semi" categories omitted.

A closer inspection also shows that the patterns of change across the various categories of these four variables are not completely uniform. For example, people with lower education levels reported exposure to libertarian values at higher frequencies than people with greater educational accomplishments. On the other hand, people at the high school education level display a larger decline in the pure authoritarian category. A similar pattern emerges on the age variable. The younger generation, who began with more libertarian values, exhibit higher percentage-point gains in those values, while the wartime generation, who started with more authoritarian values, display greater declines in authoritarian values. An interesting pattern emerges

Table 4
Socio-Demographic Attributes and Changes in Values Types
1982–1989

	Libertarian Type			Authoritarian Type			Association[a]	
	1982 %	1989 %	1982-1989 Change	1982 %	1989 %	1982-1989 Change	1982	1989
Sex								
Female	1	11	+10	48	7	-41		
Male	2	11	+ 9	38	7	-31	.10	(.02) (Eta)
Generation[b]								
Postwar	2	11	+ 9	27	2	-25		
Wartime	1	6	+ 5	58	14	-44		
Prewar	0	5	+ 5	71	33	-38	-.61	-.51 (Gamma)
Education levels								
Primary school	0	3	+ 3	76	27	-49		
Middle school	1	2	+ 1	55	11	-44		
High school	1	13	+12	46	3	-43		
College/Over	3	16	+13	17	2	-15	.59	.38 (Gamma)
Family income levels								
Low	0	6	+ 6	53	6	-47		
Middle	2	11	+ 9	38	8	-30		
High	6	14	+ 8	21	7	-14	.34	(.10)(Gamma)

[a]For nominal variables the measure of association used was Eta, while for ordinal variables it was Gamma.

[b]The postwar generation for the 1982 survey is operationally defined as those between 18 and 34 years of age; the wartime generation is defined by ages between 35 and 49; and the prewar generation is those 50 and over; for the 1989 data, I defined the range of each generation by adding 7 years to the generation limits defined for the 1982 data.

Note: All measures of association are significant at the .05 level except those in parentheses.

for the family income variable. The family with low income experienced a larger proportion in and a large decline in libertarian and authoritarian categories, respectively, which was insignificant in 1990. Also found is an unusual pattern with the sex variable. In 1982, women, who are more closely identified with the traditional Confucian culture, held more authoritarian values than men. However, by 1990 this pattern had changed, with women exhibiting a higher proportion in the libertarian category than men. As a result, women's shift in both value categories is greater than that of men. Consequently, the association between gender and change in values becomes insignificant by 1990.[19]

Finally, the four variables (sex, age, education, family income) in table 4 are used for multiple regression analysis to determine their relative contributions to the growth of libertarian values. As shown in table 5, age and education, albeit with some fluctuations, are clearly and consistently the two strongest predictors of libertarian values across the two time points. Income, which is modestly associated with libertarian values in 1982, becomes insignificant, and the beta approaches zero by 1990, when education is taken into account. Sex has uniformly low betas, which become insignificant in both periods.

Table 5
The Effects of Socio-Demographic Factors on Libertarian Values 1982–1989

Predictors	1982		1989	
	B	Beta	B	Beta
Age	-.12	-.23	-.01	-.34
Education	.38	.31	.08	.17
Income	.06	.12	-.02	(-.06)
Sex(Female)	-.17	(-.07)	.03	(.03)
(Constant)	2.71		2.62	
Multiple R	.52		.44	
Adjusted R Square	.27		.19	
N	636		696	

Note: All coefficients are significant at the .05 level except those in parentheses.

In short, these findings show that the age and education variables are consistently associated with marked contrasts in the perception of the A-L values. In other words, a greater amount of education seems to have a direct impact on extinguishing authoritarian orientations, inducing greater independence and equality. Education also has a liberalizing effect on certain moral, personal, and social values, relaxing strict traditional moral constraints by increasing one's awareness of, tolerance of, and openness towards non-traditional views, customs, and lifestyles. One also infers that increased age seems to produce progressively stricter authoritarian views on the A-L scale: older people tend to choose more loyalty, obedience, and traditional morals and customs than their younger counterparts. In fact, the "generational hypothesis" holds better in 1990: a gradual rise in libertarian values as the intergenerational population replacement takes place. The findings match other empirical studies that have uncovered the importance of education and age factors in changing values or political culture in Korea.[20]

Interpreting the Associations between A-L Values and Key Political Variables

The shift from authoritarian to libertarian values has important implications for a number of key political attitudes. As one of the two intervening variables employed in this study, psychological involvement in politics may also play an important role in determining the scope and intensity of system support or protest potential.[21] As reported in table 6, those holding libertarian values exhibit higher levels of psychological involvement in politics than those retaining authoritarian values. Yet, the relationship between values and the level of psychological involvement disappears by 1990. The very weak correlation found in that case would seem to be attributable to the fact that by 1990 there was very little difference in the high level of psychological involvement between libertarians and authoritarians. While only 7 percent of authoritarians, compared to 12 percent of libertarians, discussed political matters with friends and were interested in politics in 1982, about equal number of authoritarians (25 percent) and libertarians (26 percent) did so in 1990.

Table 6 also reports that libertarian values are associated with a rise in the levels of cynicism, labelled system support. These higher levels of cynicism, in turn, are reflected in higher levels of disaffected forms of political behavior. Thus rather high correlations between libertarian values and protest potential are observed. Libertarians tended to favor protest activity, while authoritarians were strongly against it.

In trying to account for the particular association between A-L

Table 6
Relationship between Authoritarian-Libertarian Values and Opposition Support and Participation Potential, 1989

	Percentage of "Agree" (Libertarian) Responses		
	Authoritarian	Mixed	Libertarian
Would support reformist party	47	52	62
Would support activities of the *chaeya* group	44	45	47
Perceive progress in democratization	44	42	36
Have attempted to influence public decision at the local or national level	9	10	12

values and protest potential, Flanagan and Lee and Lee argue that there is something inherent in these values that inhibits protest activity.[22] Authoritarians value law and order, are deferential to the traditional symbols and holders of authority, and carefully adhere to rules and regulations. These value predispositions, coupled with their conformity to traditional customs and practices, make it unlikely that they would sanction elite-challenging activities. In contrast, libertarians value individualism and self-actualization, building a better self and society through self-improvement and social change. Their greater self-confidence and lack of deference towards authority figures enhance their willingness to question the actions of leaders and forcefully press for new policies, even in the face of official opposition.

Finally, in order to see the dynamic relationship between values and protest potential, causal relations, as a way of summarizing this study, are shown in figure 1 and table 7.[23] Figure 1 represents the results of a multivariate path analytic mode of protest potential in Korea, including four demographic variables (age, education, income, and sex), three political variables (psychological involvement, system support, and protest potential) and values. It is argued that libertarian values promote protest activity and also directly increase psychological involvement in politics, which, in turn, relates to protest potential. On the other hand, libertarian values also decrease support for political authorities and institutions, which again increases political protest. Thus, a person's attachment to authoritarian values, his/her support for political authorities and institutions, and his/her low level of psychological involvement in politics will decrease his/her possibility of participating in protest action.

Fig. 1. Comparative Analyses of Protest Potential

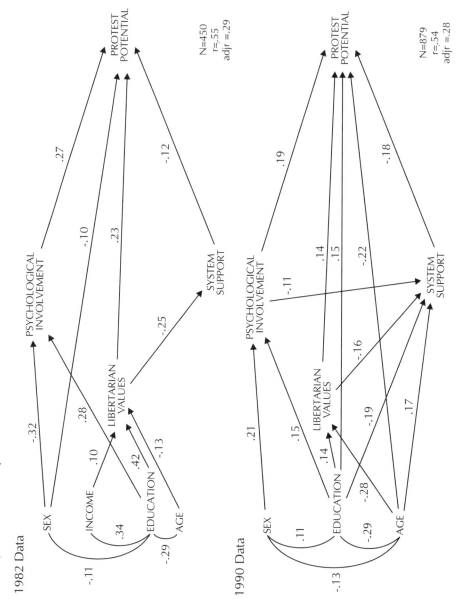

In figure 1 two models are presented that are identical in all respects (except income, which was completely dropped from the 1990 model). First, in both models there are direct paths from values to protest potential, but in the first model the path is substantially higher, more than 50 percent. Values also have indirect effects on enhancing the propensity to engage in protest action through higher levels of psychological involvement and less support for a political system. Second, we note that in the first model, age, education, and income predict values, whereas in the second model only age and education do. Sex has direct effects on protest potential in the first model, and also predicts psychological involvement in both models. Third, education directly stimulates protest potential in the 1990 model, and also indirectly influences protest potential in both models through its association with libertarian values, which lead to higher levels of psychological involvement, in turn directly associated with protest. Fourth, directly in the second model and indirectly in both models, via libertarian values youth are associated with lower levels of system support in 1990 and with higher levels of psychological involvement in 1982, leading directly to protest potential.

Table 7
The Association between Values and Key Political Variables
1982–1989 (Pearson's r)

Political Variables	Authoritarian(-)/Libertarian(+) Values	
	1982	1989
Psychological Involvement	.32	.21
Cynicism	.33	.18
Protest Potential	.47	.24
Left Partisanship	.16	.17

Note: All reported coefficients are significant at the .05 level.

Table 7 summarizes the direct and indirect effects of the variables in each model in predicting protest potential. In the first model, libertarian values rank first in predictive power, with a total effect of 0.30. In the second model, libertarian values rank fifth in importance, with a total effect of 0.17.

An immediate puzzle from the findings is why basic values became less important to Koreans in defining their orientations to politics in the early 1990s than they were eight years earlier. Although it is difficult to prove at this moment, the study underscores one possible explanation: the degree of development of democratic institutions.

One possible explanation for the lessened impact of values on politicization among Korean mass publics is the very nature of my dependent variable. This study did not deal with a so-called conventional type of political participation (e.g., voting, attending political meetings, and campaigning) but with an unconventional type (protest behavior). One could argue that the more developed the democratic or conventional forms of mass political action in a nation, the less crucial the role of value change in providing the individual with the justifying rationale for his/her participation in protest activities. Obviously, the environment of the early 1990s Korea was more democratic than in the early 1980s. In fact, a relatively well institutionalized party system and political opposition were in operation by the late 1980s. Therefore, it is plausible that the institutional devices for democratic participation were on the way in Korea in 1990, and therefore values played a much less dominant role in stimulating protest potential. However, no conclusions can be drawn here.

Conclusions

Evidence from the study indicates that the value change over the last three or four decades played a central role in shifting mass political attitudes, thus enhancing the propensity to engage in political action. This study has defined the Korean value pattern as an authoritarian-libertarian one, though this may not be the only way to conceptualize Korean values. However, in terms of their potential relevance for the exercise of politics in Korea, this conceptual dimension seemed to be an appropriate set to analyze. I found that the A-L values, though diminished in 1990, sharply partition Korean society along the lines of age and education, the former becoming more important in the later period. It was also shown that the differences in the A-L values were found to be strongly related to contrasting protest potential.

Finally, I wish to argue that the A-L shift in social values is closely associated with a change in political values. This change in social values has altered to become less tolerant of authoritarian rule. In this respect, the A-L value change should parallel the movement toward transition to democratization shown in the late 1980s Korea. In fact, the long-term micro-level changes, accompanied by the long-term macro process of change, are believed to contribute as determining factors to the transition process. Since Korea's liberation in 1945 from Japanese colonial rule, Western democracy has been a positive reference point for Koreans in their daily life and value systems. Over the postwar period, the ideology of Western democracy has become a general standard in the fields of education and culture throughout Korean society.

Moreover, because of its export-oriented economic policies after the 1960s, Korea has had to change its political system from a closed system to a more open system in order to survive in the highly competitive international market. Ironically, the authoritarian regimes became victims of their own success, producing high economic growth and rapid social change that generated new interests and coalitions in society demanding democratic change. Although it is impossible to signify a particular threshold level that triggers democratization, at some stage in this process of culture shift, as Flanagan and Shyu succinctly show, the cumulative change in social and political values will reach a point beyond which authoritarian regimes, regardless of how liberalized they have become, are no longer either legitimate or viable.[24] This is exactly what happened to Korea in the transition to democratization in the 1980s. Rapid economic development and social mobilization since the 1960s have produced value change and structural transformation, as people came to believe that the latter could produce a solid core of middle class citizens that could be utilized to pressure the authoritarian regime for democratization.[25]

Notes

1. Larry E. Wesphal, "Industrial Policy in an Export Propelled Economy: Lessons from South Korea's Experience," *Journal of Economic Perspectives* 4 (1990), pp. 41-59.
2. Sung-joo Han, "South Korea: Politics in Transition," in Larry Diamond, Juan J. Linz, and Seymour Martin Lipset, *Democracy in Developing Countries: Asia* (Boulder: Lynne Rienner Publishers, 1989), pp. 293-94.
3. Young Whan Kihl, "Party Politics on the Eve of a Gathering Storm: The Constitutional Revision Politics of 1986," in Ilpyong J. Kim and Young Whan Kihl, *Political Change in South Korea* (New York: Paragon House, 1988), pp. 75-90.

4. Samuel Huntington, *The Third Wave* (Norman and London: University of Oklahoma Press, 1991).

5. Scott C. Flanagan, "Value Change in Industrial Societies," *American Political Science Review* 81 (1987), pp. 1303-19.

6. Scott C. Flanagan and Aie-Rie Lee, "Explaining Value Change and Its Political Implications in Eleven Advanced Industrial Democracies," paper presented at the Fourteenth World Congress of the International Political Science Association, Washington, D.C., 1988; Flanagan and Lee, "The Causes and Socio-Political Implications of Value Change in the Advanced Industrial Democracies," paper presented at the annual meeting of the Midwest Political Science Association, Chicago, 1990.

7. For a detailed discussion, see Flanagan and Lee, "Explaining Value Change," and Flanagan and Lee, "Causes and Socio-Political Implications of Value Change."

8. Scott C. Flanagan, Shinsaku Kohei, Ichiro Miyake, Bradley M. Richardson, and Joji Watanuki, *The Japanese Voter* (New Haven and London: Yale University Press, 1991), pp. 89-91; Flanagan and Lee, "Explaining Value Change" and "Causes and Socio-Political Implications of Value Change"; Scott C. Flanagan and Huo-yan Shyu, "Culture Shift and the Transition to Democracy: The Case of Taiwan," paper presented at the annual meeting of the American Political Science Association, Chicago, September 3-6, 1992.

9. The survey data were provided by the Inter-University Consortium for Political and Social Research of the University of Michigan (ICPSR). The ICPSR bears no responsibility for my analysis and interpretations.

10. A brief description of the steps taken in factor procedures is as follows: I first factored all items thought to pass the face validity test for each subdimension. Loadings on the first unrotated factor were examined to determine inclusion or exclusion. Using this criterion, the number of items selected as the final set to tap a given subdimension were further pared down to include only those with *relatively* high factor loadings. From this second step, fourteen items in 1982 and 1990 were selected. Lastly, I refactored those reselected items.

11. Flanagan, "Value Change."

12. Scott C. Flanagan and Aie-Rie Lee, "Value Change and Political Action in Japan and Korea," paper presented at the tenth annual meeting of the International Society of Political Psychology, San Francisco, July 4-7, 1987; and Flanagan and Lee, "Explaining Value Change."

13. See, for instance, Gabriel Almond and Sidney Verba, *The Civic Culture: Political Attitudes and Democracy in Five Nations* (Princeton: Princeton University Press, 1965); S. Verba, Norman H. Nie, and Jae-On Kim, "The Modes of Democratic Participation: A Cross-National Comparison," *Comparative Politics Series*, No. 01-013, 2 (Beverly Hills: Sage, 1971), pp. 53-63; Paul R. Hagner and John C. Pierce, "Correlative Characteristics of Levels of Conceptualization in the American Public: 1956-1976," *Journal of Politics* 44 (1982), pp. 793-96.

14. The psychological involvement scale is a combination of two items, tapping political interest and political discussion.

15. Lee Sigelman and Stanley Feldman, "Efficacy, Mistrust, and Political Mobilization," *Comparative Political Studies* (1983), pp. 118-43; Susan E. Waltz, "Antidotes for a Social Malaise," *Comparative Politics* (1982), pp. 127-47; James W. White, "Civic

Attitudes, Political Participation, and System Stability in Japan," *Comparative Political Studies* (1981), pp. 371-400; Scott C. Flanagan and Bradley M. Richardson, "Political Disaffection and Political Stability: A Comparison of Japanese and Western Findings," in Richard F. Tomasson, *Comparative Social Research* 3 (Greenwich, CT: JAI Press, 1980), pp. 3-44.

16. Cynicism items are (1) the armed forces, (2) the legal system, (3) the police, (4) the parliament, (5) the civil service.

17. The protest potential scale is derived from four items, tapping the willingness to sign a petition, join in boycotts, attend lawful demonstrations, and occupy buildings.

18. The overall authoritarian-libertarian scores are computed for each item by subtracting the percentage of responses classified as authoritarian from the percentage of those classified as libertarian. Note that my six items (8 to 13) on moral issues are measured by the standard ten-point scale. The problem here is that, in the process of computing the A-L scores, I find a very skewed distribution, with most respondents choosing one of the first three categories and very few picking the last three categories. If I treated the first five categories as authoritarian and the second five as libertarian, the results would tend to show overwhelmingly authoritarian attitudes. The item format employed for this dimension, therefore, does not permit an easy identification of what point on the ten-point scales divides authoritarian from libertarian responses. As one way of overcoming this problem, I computed an average score for each item from the 1982 data, and treated categories below the average as authoritarian and ones above the average as libertarian repsonses. For instance, in the case of prostitution, I first computed the 1982 mean (2.05) and then classified 1 through 2 as authoritarian and 3 through 10 as libertarian response categories. A postiive sign indicates a shift in the libertarian direction and a negative sign a shift in the authoritarian direction.

19. For a further discussion on the relationship between sex and value change, see Aie-Rie Lee, "Consistency of Change in Women's Politicization in South Korea," *Policy Studies Journal* 24, 2 (1996), in press.

20. For instance, see Bae-ho Hahn and Soo-young Auh, *Han'guk Jeongchi Moonwha* (Korean political culture) (Seoul: Pupmun-sa, 1987).

21. Flanagan and Richardson, "Political Disaffection."

22. Flanagan and Lee, "Value Change and Political Action"; Aie-Rie Lee, "Values, Government Performance, and Protest in South Korea," *Asian Affairs* 18, 4 (1992), pp. 240-53, and "Culture Shift and Popular Protests in South Korea," *Comparative Political Studies* 26, 1 (1993), pp. 63-80.

23. Due to missing data problems, the pairwise deletion procedure was employed for the 1982 data. Also, in both models, some paths that were very weak but still statistically significant were dropped from the models. My criterion here was to drop paths with betas of less than 0.10.

24. Flanagan and Shyu, "Culture Shift and the Transition to Democracy: The Case of Taiwan."

25. Doh Chull Shin, "On the Third Wave of Democratization: A Synthesis and Evaluation of Recent Theory and Research," *World Politics* 47, 1 (1994), p. 152.

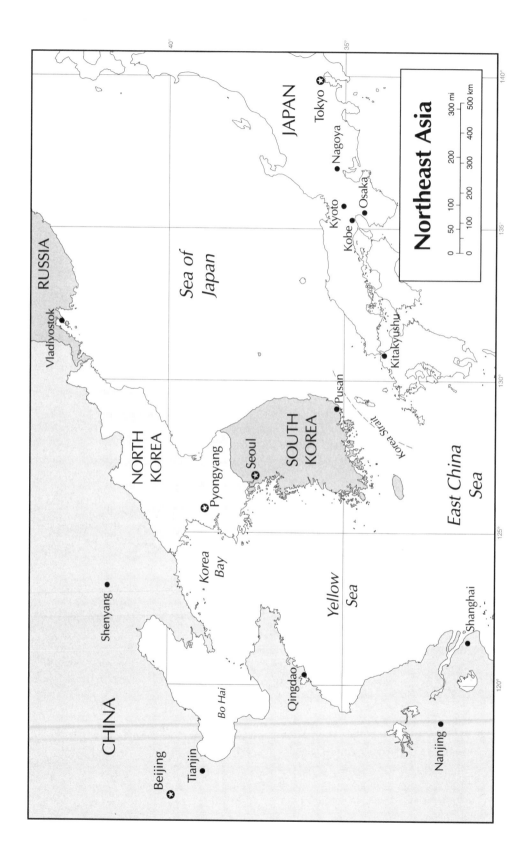

Northeast Asia

RUSSIA

CHINA

Beijing
Tianjin
Shenyang
Nanjing
Qingdao
Shanghai

Bo Hai

Yellow
Sea

Korea
Bay

NORTH
KOREA

Pyongyang

Seoul

SOUTH
KOREA

Vladivostok

Sea of
Japan

Pusan

Korea Strait

East China
Sea

JAPAN

Tokyo
Nagoya
Kyoto
Kobe
Osaka

Kitakyushu

0   50 100   150   200   250   300 mi
0 100 200 300 400 500 km

Chapter 11

Anti-Americanism and Anti-Authoritarian Politics in Korea

John Kie-chiang Oh

M anifestations of anti-Americanism in South Korea were un-
thinkable in the first fifteen years of United States-Korean
relations following World War II. The United States was the
patron, protector, and supporter of the republic. It was the United States
that in fact brought forth the democratic Republic of Korea in 1948,
and when the North Korean military had nearly succeeded in con-
quering the South two years later, it was the United States that res-
cued it from the brink of extinction, at the cost of the lives of some
33,000 American servicemen.

The United States has stationed tens of thousands of troops in South
Korea ever since as the ultimate guarantee of security in the peninsula, which has remained tensely divided. The United States poured
in over $3 billion in strictly economic assistance to South Korea be-
tween 1945 and 1961,[1] and economic and military assistance amounted
to more than $12.5 billion by 1976, according to Richard L. Walker,
former American ambassador to Korea.[2] Not surprisingly, despite frictions and disagreements at contact points between the two countries,
South Korea has been one of the most pro-American nations in the
world until recently.

Public anti-American acts have become increasingly common since
the early 1980s, more specifically since the "coup-like" seizure of power
by Chun Doo Hwan in 1980,[3] a time when the people had expected
a measure of liberalization after the sudden death of Park Chung Hee.

*John Kie-chiang Oh is professor of politics at the Catholic University of America,
Washington.*

Until then, anti-American sentiments had remained largely "private" among members of the Korean elite, those who had direct contact with United States government, military, or business. However, since the 1980s, anti-American phenomena have rapidly spread among the public, beginning with radicalized students.

Anti-Americanism may be defined here as significant manifestations of anger and hostility toward the United States and its policies, practices, institutions, and citizens—either military or civilian. Thus defined, it may be distinguished from mild frustrations and annoyances felt but not publicly expressed by a limited number of people, such as individual Koreans who come into personal contact with Americans. The anti-Americanism as discussed here denotes intense, sustained, and sometimes violent displays of hostility by a sizable number of people toward the United States.

Have there been such significant manifestations of anti-American hostility in South Korea? Certainly, there has been no massive explosion of anti-American violence, and no expressions of hatred similar to that of the Muslim who drove a truck loaded with dynamite into U.S. Marine barracks in Lebanon. Anti-American phenomena in Korea have been comparatively mild, but they have included the burning of American flags and effigies of Uncle Sam at numerous student rallies, the repeated fire-bombing of United States cultural centers in Kwangju since December 1980, in Pusan (March 1982), in Taegu (September 1983), and elsewhere in the 1980s by radical dissidents. There was also a bomb explosion in front of the American cultural center in Taegu just before President Reagan's visit to South Korea in November 1983 and an attack on the American dependents' housing area outside the Yongsan garrison in Seoul by students from Tankuk University in November 1988.

However, a more disturbing incident occurred in May 1989 when Korean farmers and villagers rampaged through the Koon-ni aerial bombing range for over three hours, assaulting American military personnel on station, looting barracks, overturning vehicles, and largely destroying the infrastructure of the American facilities.[4] This and many other anti-American acts prompted President Bush to admit during his short visit to Korea in February 1989, "I think there exists anti-American sentiment in Korea. Korea is not an extraordinary case. Such criticism against the United States is arising in other nations."[5]

This essay will begin with a few highlights of the interaction between the United States and the Republic of Korea, review the key problem of the command authority of the Korean military, the Kwangju Incident, and anti-authoritarian politics as anti-Americanism, and conclude with an assessment of the present climate.

Historical Highlights

It would be useful to consider the historical turning points in United States-Korea relations up to 1980, which clearly was the beginning of visible and violent anti-Americanism.[6] It is important to understand the starkly different perspectives and expectations on the two sides of the Pacific. When the first formal relations between the two countries were established through the 1882 Treaty of Amity and Commerce negotiated by Commodore Robert Schufeldt, the expectations of Korea and the United States had very little in common. The United States evidently had two limited aims: the opening of Korea to possible American trade and the protection of shipwrecked American seamen. However, the Hermit Kingdom, buffeted in the increasingly turbulent sea of changing international politics, naively hoped that the United States would replace the rapidly declining China as its protector.

Article 1 of the treaty stated, in part, "If other powers deal unjustly or oppressively with either Government, the other will exert their [*sic*] good offices to bring about an amicable arrangement, thus showing their friendly feelings." In terms of Western international politics, the article was an innocuous opening to a treaty of amity and commerce—no more, no less. If Korea expected that the Schufeldt treaty was establishing a new form of *sadae* relations, this time with the United States—in which the smaller nation served the interests of the larger, while the larger nation protected the smaller state—Korea was pitifully ignorant of the international *Realpolitik* of the time.[7]

The United States, having recently acquired the Philippines, was more concerned about the security of the new colony than about Korea, which at that time had little value for American commerce. The Taft-Katsura Memorandum of July 1905—an agreement between the United States and Japan that remained secret for twenty years—recognized the "justness" of Japanese suzerainty over Korea as "the logical result" of the Russo-Japanese War, while Japan denied any designs on the Philippines.[8] Japan had become the regional power with its victory in the Russo-Japanese War, exacting a treaty of protectorate from Korea, and the United States was the first power to withdraw its legation from Seoul. Objectively, there were no reasons why the

American legation should be maintained in a country that had lost its sovereignty. However, the United States action is said to have caused a profound sense of betrayal among the Korean elite and also among interested American citizens on the scene.

Korea became a protectorate and then a colony of Japan and remained a virtually unknown land to Americans for over forty years. Then in December 1943, the United States, Britain, and China declared at the Cairo conference that Korea would become a free and independent state "in due course," as part of the settlement that would strip Japan of the fruits of her militarist expansions since the first Sino-Japanese War. In the final days of the Pacific war, when Soviet troops were already pouring into Korea and American soldiers were still hundreds of miles away, the United States hastily proposed the 38th parallel as a temporary demarcation line between the Soviet and United States zones established to accept the surrender of Japanese troops. Unfortunately, that temporary line endured and marked the tragic division of Korea throughout the cold war era. The United States has been blamed for this division by many Koreans, who do not ask a corollary question: What would have happened if the Soviet troops had not stopped at the 38th parallel?

The United States and the Korean Republic

When the Republic of Korea, headed by American-educated President Syngman Rhee, was inaugurated, it was not surprising that Koreans expected a great deal, perhaps too much, from the generous and confident American superpower. For years, the purpose of President Rhee's key foreign and economic policies appeared to be to wring the most aid from the United States. President Rhee was sometimes testy with Washington, because of what he considered to be parsimoniousness in economic assistance to South Korea, but particularly for the American failure to unite Korea during the war by resolutely pushing the million Chinese "people's volunteers" back into Manchuria. Much of Rhee's unhappiness—some Americans now considered him a "cantankerous old man"—and that of his followers, was attributable to these views and other unrealistic expectations of the United States—a rich and powerful benefactor and protector, indeed, but one whose resources and federal budget were certainly not unlimited and were in fact already becoming "overstretched" with myriad global postwar commitments.

But the Koreans could never fault the United States' commitment to the security of South Korea vis-à-vis the communists. This commitment was, of course, part of American global strategic designs. In any case, the maintenance of security was obviously the primary objective of the United States in the East Asian region, followed by the secondary political goal of keeping the nations in the region democratically oriented and friendly toward the United States, and the tertiary goal of promoting capitalist economic development.

South Korea was to be the "beacon light of freedom" in the anticommunist security strategy of the United States in East Asia. However, the Rhee regime, expected to become democratic, had rapidly grown autocratic, particularly since the Korean War. In the face of massive popular protests, including the historic student uprising of April 1960, the regime desperately attempted to cling to power. The United States evidently made a clear choice, and the American government sided with the demonstrating Korean people rather than with a discredited regime that was now not only autocratic but also unable to govern. A South Korean government that could not maintain domestic order was a threat to the American security designs in the region.

After the fall of the Rhee regime, a democratic and pro-American government led by Chang Myon attempted to drastically down-size the Korean military in 1961 and unwittingly contributed to its own demise in the first Korean military coup d'etat, led by then-Major General Park Chung Hee. At the birth of the Chang Myon government, the United States was contributing about a fourth of the defense budget of Korea, and the American opposition to shrinking the size of the Korean military was persuasive. If a drastic down-sizing of the Korean military had occurred in the last years of the Rhee government and early months of the short-lived Chang regime, the Park coup might never have taken place. Park had been given some nine increasingly trifling assignments in the five years preceding the coup. Had the Korean military been reduced, it is probable that Park would have become an unemployed civilian.

The highest-ranking American officials in Korea, namely, the United Nations commander, General Carter B. Magruder, and the chargé d'affaires of the embassy, Marshall Green, made some public but ineffectual moves to reverse the military coup and reinstate the constitutional government of Chang Myon in pursuance of United States security and political objectives in Korea. The timing of the Magruder-Green statements and actions clearly indicate that they were acting promptly, immediately after the military coup, in accordance with standing policy of Washington to support a democratic government in Seoul. However, Park's military takeover quickly became a fait accompli, and he was soon a guest of the Kennedy administration in Washington. The United States was evidently resuming the security-first policy. Thus, Park appeared to receive a stamp of approval by the American government, and with it an aura of legitimacy, just as Korean kings of yore had been inaugurated with a stamp of approval by the Chinese court in the old *sadae* relations with China.

With the successful military coup by Park Chung Hee came the emergence of virulent anti-American sentiments, though still largely inaudible, among Korean elites. The coup leaders, who naturally learned of the abortive American attempts to crush them, replaced the pro-American elements in the military. Furthermore, when the coup group became the military government, anti-American sentiments became palpable in the ruling junta. In his private utterances regarding the United States, Park's favorite comment was "Miguk nomduli muol aro?" ["What do the American bastards know?"].[9] These words succinctly captured the basic attitude of the coup leader, and it quickly spread among his followers.

The Problems of Command Authority

Since the Korean military now came under the control of a regime that was sharply different from the former pro-American and "democratic" governments, thorny problems arose between the American command and related authorities, and the Korean military. Until the first coup, the Korean military had been under the authority of governments headed by Western-educated scions of "aristocratic" Korean families who knew some traditional as well as Western codes of conduct. Rhee traced his ancestry to a princely family of the Yi dynasty and had been educated at Harvard and Princeton, among other institutions. Yun Po-son, president of the Second Republic, also descended from an aristocratic family and was Edinburgh-educated. Chang Myon, premier of the Second Republic, was also from a genteel upper-class background and had studied at Manhattan College in New York, among other places.

With Park's coup, the Korean government came under the control of a prickly and ambitious soldier from a completely different, peasant background. He had been an officer in the Japanese army toward the end of the Pacific war. For Park, survival, security, and the acquisition of naked power were supreme virtues. To execute the coup, General Park mobilized army and marine units without the approval or even the knowledge of the United Nations Command (UNC) in Korea. The American commander who headed the UNC had had "command authority" over the Korean military since July 15, 1950, when President Rhee had transferred "command authority over all [Korean] land, sea, and air forces" to the United Nations commander in the critical early period of the Korean War.[10]

Thus, the American command authority in South Korea had in reality broken down with the coup, though the popular perception of American control persisted, possibly due to the almost total dependence of the Korean military on the United States for its weapons and equipment. The myth of American command survived even the creation of the U.S.-Korean Combined Forces Command (CFC) in 1978, meant to offset the impact of President Carter's initiative to withdraw United States ground troops from South Korea. The mission of defending South Korea against external aggression was now transferred from the UNC to the CFC. According to the "Terms of Reference" for CFC dated July 27, 1978, the Commander in Chief of CFC was to "exercise operational control (OPCON) over all forces assigned or attached to the command in the prosecution of assigned missions," but both the United States and the Republic of Korea retained "the national right of command, including the right to remove units from CFC OPCON upon notification."[11] The CFC commander is always an American officer and the deputy commander a Korean general.

When then-Major General Chun Doo Hwan executed a "coup-like" seizure of power on December 12, 1979, Korean military units, including elements of the Ninth Army Division, commanded by then-Major General Roh Tae Woo, were moved to Seoul without any notification to the CFC.

Naturally, the CFC commander, General John A. Wickham, was incensed with General Chun's actions, and his bitter displeasure was immediately communicated to Chun. With notable dispatch, Washington delivered a "strong warning" to Chun for violating the CFC's operational control. The State Department warning was delivered to him on December 14—less than two full days after Chun's December 12 putsch—by U.S. Ambassador William H. Gleysteen. General Chun—probably muttering, "What do the American bastards know?" as his mentor Park Chung Hee would have done—ruthlessly pushed the

consolidation of his dictatorial power, against the backdrop of increasingly massive and fierce demonstrations by Korean students and opposition political leaders demanding a restoration of "democracy" even
while the country was under partial martial law. Chun appointed himself director of the powerful KCIA on April 14, 1980, and the so-called
"new military" seizure of power was all but complete.

The Kwangju Incident

While General Wickham was in the United States, on May 16 the "new
military" authorities under General Chun quietly notified the CFC of
their intent to remove the Twentieth Division (which had riot-control
training) from CFC OPCON. The CFC deputy commander, Korean four-
star General Baek Sok Chu, acknowledged the release notification.
Full martial law was declared on May 18, and opposition leaders, including Kim Dae Jung, Kim Young Sam, and Kim Jong Pil, were arrested. Colleges and universities were ordered closed and the National
Assembly suspended.

Under these circumstances students and citizens of Kwangju, historically a bastion of protest against oppressive regimes and also the
stronghold of Kim Dae Jung supporters, rose up violently against the
Chun regime. In due time, brigades from the Special Warfare Command, the Thirty-First Division based in Kwangju, and elements of the
Twentieth Division that had been removed from CFC OPCON, completely surrounded Kwangju and overpowered and ruthlessly put
down the rebellion. By the government's count, two hundred people
were killed and thousands wounded or arrested. Most believe that
actual casualties were much higher. The Kwangju Incident was a brutal assault openly perpetrated by the military on Korean students and
other citizens in peacetime Korea. Thus began the Chun regime, the
bloodiest and most oppressive, from many perspectives, in contemporary Korea. Subsequently, the Martial Law Command charged Kim
Dae Jung and twenty-three supporters with conspiracy to violently
overthrow the government. Kim was characterized as a dangerous
revolutionary who was "sympathetic to North Korea" and who had
"engineered the origins of the Kwangju turmoil." A military tribunal
sentenced him to death.

An amazing series of confusing statements by American officials
and Machiavellian manipulations and outright deceptions orchestrated
by the "new military" authorities ensued. In an interview with a Ko-

rean national assemblyman, then-Ambassador William Gleysteen al-
legedly stated that the United States had "approved" the movement of
the Twentieth Division, which had been used in the brutal suppression of the Kwangju rioters. In fact, the Twentieth Division had been
removed from the CFC OPCON through the process of "notification"
just days before the Kwangju Incident, and the other units used in
Kwangju were never under CFC. A U.S. Department of Defense spokes-
man also "misspoke" on May 23, 1980, saying that the United States
had "agreed" to the release from OPCON of the troops sent into
Kwangju. The fact of the matter was that neither the United States nor
CFC had been in a position to approve the use of Korean troops in
Kwangju because they were not under CFC OPCON at the time of the
Kwangju Incident.

Not surprisingly, the government-controlled radio in Kwangju was
broadcasting that the United States had approved the dispatch of the
troops to Kwangju, clearly suggesting that the United States supported
the brutal actions of the Korean troops. That continued to be the gist
of news stories appearing in Korean media for the weeks under martial law. When the United States made a public announcement on May
22 urging "all parties involved to exercise maximum restraint and
undertake a dialogue in search of a peaceful settlement" in Kwangju,
the Korean media did not even report it. Although the Voice of America
broadcast the American statement, the VOA listenership among Koreans is limited, and the Korean public media under martial law remained
mum.[12]

Shortly after the Kwangju Incident, General Chun himself told a
meeting of Korean publishers and editors that the United States had
been informed in advance of his December 12 seizure of power, his
appointment as director of KCIA, and the declaration of full martial
law preceding the Kwangju massacre. The United States Embassy responded that Chun's statement "simply was not true and Chun knew
it."[13] The Associated Press reported the Embassy denial, but it was not
carried in the Korean press. Ambassador Gleysteen's press secretary
then visited with each of the publishers and editors, who met with
Chun to correct the "disinformation," but under martial law Korean
media could not print it.

Instead, the Korean media highlighted remarks attributed to General Wickham by a Korean reporter, to the effect that the Korean people
were like lemmings and needed a strong leader—by implication at
the time, Chun. Wickham in fact detested Chun, as he had completely

bypassed the American CFC commander and had used Korean troops without notifying him. Ambassador Gleysteen was also credited with an inflammatory remark that demonstrating students, presumably including those in Kwangju who had been mowed down by Korean troops, were "spoiled brats."[14] The slogans of demonstrating students now became decidedly anti-American for the first time.[15]

Even the highest-level communication was distorted by the Korean authorities. When President Jimmy Carter wrote to Chun Doo Hwan upon his election as president by a rubber-stamp electoral college on August 27, 1980, Carter reaffirmed United States security commitments to Korea, but added that political liberalization must take place in Korea and democracy should be quickly restored. However, Korean newspaper headlines gave a different picture: "Carter: Personal Message to President Chun Expresses Support for Korea's New Government" (*Dong-A Ilbo*) and "Security Commitment to Korea: the Major U.S. Policy" (*Joong-ang Ilbo*).[16]

To those who were increasingly embittered by what they perceived to be American support for the new regime, whose hands were "dripping with the blood of Kwangju students and citizens," the most disturbing event was President Chun's high-profile visit with newly inaugurated President Ronald Reagan at the White House on February 2, 1981. Chun was President Reagan's second foreign guest.[17] Chun's visit to American cities and invitation to meet with Reagan on the fifth day of his stay in the United States were inflated into a triumphal media event intended to burnish the aura of Chun's legitimacy.

Few in Korea noted at the time the possible connection between Chun's American visit and his ending of martial law on January 24. Chun's commutation of Kim Dae Jung's death sentence came just two days before Chun received the invitation to meet with Reagan.[18] Actually, high-level efforts to save Kim Dae Jung's life were already under way in the summer of 1980, during what turned out to be the last months of the Carter administration. By early fall 1980 it was known that General Chun wished to be invited to Washington "not only to signify full regularization of U.S. Korean relations but to give an aura of legitimacy to his new government."[19] According to two former American ambassadors, as a quid pro quo for Reagan's invitation, Chun promised to commute Kim Dae Jung's death sentence.[20] This trade-off remained discreetly hidden, and ironically Kim Dae Jung's supporters were among the most outspoken critics of Chun's visit, which was publicized in Korea for weeks.

Anti-Authoritarian Politics as Anti-Americanism

The Fifth Republic, headed by Chun, was by most accounts the most nakedly authoritarian regime in contemporary Korean politics. Chun himself was more consistently heavy-handed than his predecessor, Park Chung Hee, who showed some sensitivity to popular mood since he was popularly elected until the so-called Yushin (revitalizing) reform of 1971. Park could justifiably point to the spectacular economic growth in South Korea during his rule, when per capita GNP skyrocketed from $100 (in 1963, when he assumed the presidency) to $1,640 (in 1979, when he was assassinated). While Chun maintained the economic growth rate and kept inflation under control, notoriously authoritarian and politically insensitive measures characteristic of dictatorships became common under his government. For instance, the Press Law adopted on December 26, 1980, by the Legislative Council for National Security, a creature of the "new military," in effect abolished press freedoms, and some two-thirds of news media were suddenly "merged" out of existence, with roughly the same proportion of journalists becoming jobless.[21] Adoption on December 30, 1980, of basic labor laws, including the Labor Union Law and the Labor Dispute Settlement Law, drastically curtailed workers' rights, and when they went on strike demanding their fair share of the prosperous economy, the police broke up their demonstrations. When some female workers took refuge in an opposition party headquarters, the police smashed their way into the building and forcibly detained the workers along with some opposition legislators who happened to be in the building. The government and its coercive forces consistently sided with business interests, particularly those enterprises in which foreigners invested heavily. Americans constituted the second-largest and most visible group of investors, second only to the Japanese, who often hid behind Korean partners.

Anti-government student and worker demonstrations became increasingly anti-capitalist and anti-foreign, thus predictably anti-American. In almost direct proportion to the intensifying autocratic pressures of the Chun regime, the rhetoric of protestors became more and more extreme, radical, anti-foreign, and anti-American. The degree of desperation felt by students and workers in the early and mid-1980s was gruesomely demonstrated by some seventy incidents of self-immolation and suicides who jumped from high buildings.[22]

"Down with the Chun Dictatorship" and "Yankee Go Home!" be-

came the twin battle cries of demonstrators. Clandestine conscious-
ness-raising campaigns were launched on college campuses, now
imbuing activists with a neo-Marxist ideology calling for the complete
restructuring of the domestic society, denouncing the United States
for dividing the Korean peninsula in the first place and for then supporting the dictatorial military government. The radical student movement began to coalesce around the *minjung* ideology, an eclectic
blend of nationalism, Marxism, left-Catholic liberation theology, anti-
dependency economic views, pacifist and anti-nuclear slogans, national reunification demands, and West European-style peace advocacy.

The *minjung* ideology rested on two central tenets. It asserted,
first, that Korea's problems stemmed from the "original sin" of the
division of the country by the United States in 1945, but it never recalled that the United States had liberated Korea from the Japanese or
why the United States had proposed the 38th parallel as a temporary
demarcation line. The ideology held that the division itself had led to
Korea's political, economic, military, and cultural dependence on the
United States. The second tenet was that the successive United States-
backed regimes, which had ruled Korea since the founding of the republic, always opposed the people [*minjung*], the nation [*minjok*],
and democracy [*minju*].[23] Certainly, not all young people and students
believed in these ideas. However, some 62 percent of eligible voters
in Korea were between the ages of 20 and 39, and university students
constituted 2.7 percent of the total population of South Korea (compared with 2.0 percent in the United States and 1.5 percent in Germany), and the *minjung* ideology apparently resonated among a fair
number of students and young people.

While activists demonstrated against military dictatorship in Korea, the radicals in the 1980s made the United States *the* enemy, the
villain behind the illegitimate military regimes and the barrier to democracy and national reunification. Soon these students were forming alliances with alienated workers. Some radical students, disguis-
ing themselves and their educational background, became factory
workers for the purpose of organizing other workers. The spring of
1986 was the peak of the radicalization of student activism and the
rise of virulent anti-Americanism.

The Chun regime had become increasingly apprehensive about
these radical student movements and therefore progressively more
oppressive, introducing a "campus stabilization act." The students responded more desperately and violently. Vicious action-reaction cycles

set in. Violence against American targets escalated. The Chun regime did little to discourage anti-American expressions so long as they served to deflect and dissipate some anti-regime fervor. For anti-American demonstrators, the United States was remote and could not punish them, while the punitive power of the Chun regime was proximate and swift.

In this volatile atmosphere, in January 1987 the death was revealed of a Seoul National University student, Pak Chong-ch'ol, at the hands of the police was revealed. Pak died during interrogation intended to learn the whereabouts of fugitive Pak Chong-un, the reputed mastermind of a 1985 USIS library takeover. Thus, the massive demonstrations of 1987 which followed Pak Chong-ch'ol's death and produced such far-reaching consequences originated in an anti-American act two years earlier. The revelation of police brutality incensed and galvanized students and the citizenry against the Chun regime, as the April 1960 discovery of the body of a high school student, Kim Chu-yol, with a tear-gas shell embedded in one eye, had turned the public against the Syngman Rhee government.

The 1960 incident had ignited the student uprising which toppled the Rhee regime, and the events in the summer of 1987 led to sustained upheavals during which people in numerous urban areas all across South Korea demonstrated against the brutal Chun regime. They demanded democratization and reform of Korean politics and government, partly through sweeping constitutional amendments. Chun Doo Hwan insisted on personally anointing Roh Tae Woo, his closest ally, as his successor through a rubber-stamp electoral college.

In the early summer of 1987, busloads of well-trained riot police battled protesting students, workers, and now middle-class citizens in business suits. Riot police fired volley after volley of tear gas, and residues of the finely ground pepper-gas hung heavily in the air in most urban centers, despite all-out efforts to wash it away. Still the "human waves" of demonstrators kept coming, and by mid-June it was even reported that the police were running out of tear gas. In Seoul, a unit of weary riot policemen who had exhausted their tear gas supply was surrounded by demonstrators, who overpowered the police, disarmed them, set their riot control equipment afire—and then released them, unharmed but humiliated and demoralized.

At this juncture the Chun regime was again on the brink of using military force to crush the demonstrators. Chun had ordered the military to stand by.[24] However, his own lieutenants, including the prime minister, counselled against it, and through a special envoy the United States government sternly warned President Chun against the use of the Korean military for political purposes. Meanwhile, the demonstrations culminated in the "great people's march" of June 10, when all important roads and highways were literally filled with demonstrators.[25]

At this point, Roh Tae Woo disappeared from public view for a few days, and with the help of a handful of assistants, he drafted a conciliatory statement. It was announced on June 29, 1987, as the declaration of "democratization and reforms," which proposed a direct presidential election system under a drastically amended and democratic constitution. For a few years afterward, Chun and Roh attempted to depict the declaration as a courageous move made by Roh alone to avert a political crisis, but it has recently become clear that the June 29 declaration and its dramatic presentation on national television were co-produced by Chun and Roh for maximum political effect.[26]

If it was surprising to some that President Reagan received President Chun very early in his presidency, it was even more noteworthy when President Reagan received presidential candidate Roh at the White House on September 14, 1987. Roh was the ruling party's candidate in the December 1987 presidential election against the two leading civilians who had championed democracy in Korea for decades, Kim Young Sam and Kim Dae Jung. Everyone expected a close contest, and in view of the groundswell of democratizing and reform demands following a quarter-century of military-dominated rule, it was hoped by many that a bona fide civilian candidate, instead of an ex-general, would win. It is debatable how much benefit Roh was able to extract from his visit with Reagan, but Roh ended up winning the presidency by 36.6 percent of the popular vote, while Kim Young Sam garnered 28.1 percent and Kim Dae Jung 27.1 percent. One wonders if the White House knew, as Chun and Roh did, that the two civilian candidates would be unable to agree on a single opposition candidate and would divide the opposition votes.

With the advent of the popularly elected Roh regime, many anti-dictatorship issues faded, but anti-Americanism did not abate and attacks on American targets continued while radical students demonstrated, demanding the arrest of former President Chun. However, a series of events in 1989 began the decline of the radical movement. In an incident that temporarily united the government and the opposition in outrage, seven riot policemen died in a fire set by radical students in Pusan while the policemen were attempting to rescue fellow officers being held hostage. The appearance of a South Korean student radical at the World Youth Games in Pyongyang that summer also offended many South Koreans. Radical student organizations began to fragment. Outrage over the humiliation of the prime minister-designate, Chung Won Shik, at the hands of students also cost radicals much of their remaining support. Students continued to burn American flags, but attacks on American facilities declined.

The birth on February 25, 1993, of a government headed by President Kim Young Sam, an erstwhile opposition leader with no formal military ties, was hailed as an epoch-making victory for democracy and the beginning of a new era in American-Korean relations. President Bill Clinton's extremely cordial visit with President Kim in Korea, July 10-11, 1993, appeared to symbolize a new chapter in the relationship. Anti-Americanism in Korea lost much of its rationale, although anti-Americanism has not always been rational.

Conclusions

Radical movements and anti-American phenomena in South Korea shrank drastically with the inauguration of Kim Young Sam in early 1993—as the first duly elected civilian president in thirty-two years. The sudden shrinkage of anti-Americanism had very little to do with actions of the United States in the 1990s. The perception on the part of many Koreans that the United States was buttressing harshly authoritarian regimes which were brutally oppressing the Korean people now seemed groundless. The basic features of United States-Korean relations had not changed. What was different was the domestic politics of South Korea.

No arrogant authoritarian regime in South Korea now manipulates public opinion on United States-Korean relations. No regime attempts to displace the people's anger onto the United States, or to distort the truth and disinform people about the intent of American cordiality toward their leaders. There is no longer a South Korean government that attempts to characterize the Kwangju Incident as a communist-inspired revolutionary activity designed to overthrow the government. On the contrary, the Kim Young Sam government has formally described the Kwangju demonstrations as a justifiable uprising by the people, comparable to the student uprising of 1960, or the people's demonstrations for democracy in June of 1987.

At the same time, there is increasing realization among Koreans themselves that the anti-American *minjung* ideology is largely a hodge-podge of inconsistent, contradictory, anti-intellectual slogans. *Minjung* was emotionally appealing when desperate students and workers opposing an oppressive regime needed battle cries. But *minjung's* appeal is slight under a duly constituted civilian government, when cooler heads prevail.

The controversies over North Korean nuclear issues are rapidly dissipating the residue of anti-Americanism. There may be a post-cold war world elsewhere, but it has not yet arrived in Korea. The security-first policy of the United States has been resoundingly justified by Kim Il Sung's actions. South Koreans, the elites and the people alike, realize that the United States is still the ultimate protector of South Korea's security, regardless of the long-term validity and enforceability of nuclear nonproliferation policies. The measured and flexible responses of the United States and South Korea thus far appear to represent responsible steps taken after careful consultations, though not always symmetrical or synchronized. Certainly, however, there are no longer South Korean top leaders uttering, "What do the American bastards know?"

It is also clear that the United States is not represented by haughty, careless, and irascible ambassadors, generals, or spokesmen in Korea who would state incorrectly that the United States approved the use of Korean troops in Kwangju, or that Koreans were lemmings that needed strong leaders, or that demonstrating students were "spoiled brats." At the same time, United States and Korean leaders have become more conscious of the need to keep the people of both countries informed, through timely announcements regarding important steps taken, as in the case of the North Korean nuclear problem. This is a different time from 1978, when the CFC arrangements were made and it took more than eleven years before the USIS issued explanations, on June 19, 1989.[27]

At the same time, the South Korean government must become more forthcoming in its public statements regarding trade pressures perceived to be emanating from the United States. Recent events in South Korea surrounding the trade of rice and beef have left the South Korean farmers largely blaming the United States, while President Kim Young Sam and his cabinet members appeared to equivocate on these issues. To avoid another round of anti-Americanism, the South Korean government should clearly explain that some concessions must be made by Korean government representatives in multilateral GATT negotiations and that South Korea cannot enjoy one-way benefits while depending on the world market for the success of its export-oriented economy. South Koreans should bear in mind that South Korea exports some 30 percent of its products to the United States. The United States typically sells about 3.5 percent of its total exports in South Korea. According to a recent survey, over 40 percent of Korean college students understood that they would have to buy more foreign rice to continue to enjoy open markets abroad, certainly including the United States.

Finally, it should be noted that the extent of anti-Americanism even during the worst periods was comparatively mild, and that there remains even among the most shrill nationalists in South Korea today a broad and deep reservoir of good will toward the United States.

Notes

1. Kim Su-kun, "Korean Economic Development and the Role of the United States" [in Korean], in Kim Tuk-chun et al., eds., *Re-illumination of Korean-American Relations* [in Korean] (Seoul: Kyongnam taehakkyo kukdong munjae yonkuso, 1988), pp. 182-83.

2. Kim Jinwung, "Recent Anti-Americanism in South Korea," *Asian Survey* 29, 8 (August 1989), p. 755.

3. The official characterization of the December 12, 1980, events ("12.12 Incident") by the Kim Young Sam government.

4. Julie Bird, "Bomb Range Overrun Again," *Air Force Times*, June 12, 1989, p. 8, and Jim Lea, "Koon-ni Airmen Relive 'Custer's Last Stand,'" *Pacific Stars and Stripes*, June 1, 1989, p. 1, cited by William M. Drennan, Jr., "Student Radicalization and Anti-Americanism in the Republic of Korea," unpublished graduate seminar paper, Catholic University of America, Fall 1993, p. 29.

5. *Korea Herald*, February 28, 1989, cited by Kim Jinwung, "Recent Anti-Americanism."

6. Chang Tal-chung, "A Theoretical Analysis of the Character of Anti-American Movements," *Discourses on International Research* [in Korean], vol. 12 (Seoul: Seoul National University, Kukje munje yonkuso, 1988), p. 1.

7. Jongsuk Chay, *Diplomacy of Asymmetry: Korean American Relations to 1910* (Honolulu: University of Hawaii Press, 1990), chapters 2, 3.

8. Ibid., pp. 143-44.

9. "The Third Republic" [in Korean], a docudrama series produced by MBC Productions of Korea, 1993, passim.

10. James I. Matray, ed., *Historical Dictionary of the Korean War* (New York: Green-

wood Press, 1991), pp. 444-45. This transfer of "command authority" should not be confused with the Taejon Agreement, which dealt mostly with the status and the rights of the United States armed forces in Korea.

11. United States Information Service, "Backgrounder: United States Government Statement on the Events in Kwangju, Republic of Korea, in May 1980," press office, USIS, Seoul, June 19, 1989, p. 5. Much of the agreement dealing with military operations remains classified.

12. Ibid., p. 19.

13. Ibid., p. 24.

14. Donald N. Clark, "Bitter Friendship: Understanding Anti-Americanism in South Korea," in Donald N. Clark, ed., *Korea Briefing, 1991* (Boulder: Westview Press, 1991), pp. 147-67.

15. George E. Ogle, *South Korea: Dissent within the Economic Miracle* (London: Zed Books, 1990), p. 91.

16. Ibid., p. 25.

17. Reagan's first foreign visitor, on January 28, 1981, was Prime Minister Edward Seaga of Jamaica.

18. *New York Times*, February 2, 1981, p. A-8.

19. William H. Gleysteen, Jr., "Korea: A Special Target of American Concern," in David D. Newsom, ed., *The Diplomacy of Human Rights* (Lanham, MD: University Press of America, 1986), p. 98. Gleysteen was American ambassador to Korea from June 1978 to June 1981.

20. Ibid., and James R. Lilley, in an interview with *Wolgan Chosun*, July 1988. Lilley headed the American Embassy in Seoul from November 1986 to January 1989.

21. Kim Tong-son, "Inside the Mergers and Abolition of the Media in 1980" [in Korean], *Shin Dong-A*, September 1987, pp. 576-91.

22. Kim Chong-ch'an, "Those Who Self-Immolated or Jumped to Death in the Eighties" [in Korean], *Shin Dong-A*, November 1987, pp. 385-403.

23. Wonmo Dong, "University Students in South Korean Politics: Patterns of Radicalization in the 1980s," *Journal of International Affairs* 40, 2 (1987), pp. 233-55.

24. Kim Song-ik, *The Spoken Testimonies of Chun Doo Hwan* [in Korean] (Seoul: Choson Ilbo-sa, 1992), p. 429.

25. "The Sixth Anniversary of the June 10 Struggle" [in Korean], *Hanguk Ilbo*, June 10, 1993, p. 4.

26. Kim Song-ik, *Spoken Testimonies*, pp. 423-27.

27. United States Information Service, "Backgrounder."

Chapter 12

The Post-Cold War Environment, Democratization, and National Security in South Korea

Chung-in Moon and Won K. Paik

National security issues in South Korea have traditionally been characterized by the primacy of military security. Military threats from the North have been real and acute, ranging from overt military provocations to covert operations. After the Korean War, which swept the entire country, minor conflicts have continued along the border, a constant irritant to South Korean security. Ensuring national survival in a precarious security environment has remained the primary national goal. In order to cope with insecurity, South Korea has attempted to maximize its military power, to mobilize its human and material resources, and to maintain an effective alliance with the United States.[1]

The end of the cold war and the recent democratic transition have, however, created constraints on the realist prescription to national insecurity in South Korea. The dissolution of the cold war system has significantly altered the strategic landscape surrounding the Korean peninsula, and the democratic opening since 1987 has profoundly restructured domestic parameters underlying national security management.[2] On the one hand, diplomatic normalization with the former Soviet Union and the People's Republic of China has forged a security environment favorable to South Korea, reducing the probability of war in the peninsula. On the other hand, democratization and the prolif-

---

Chung-in Moon and Won K. Paik are professors of political Science at Yonsei University (Seoul) and Central Michigan University (Mount Pleasant), respectively.

eration of contending interest groups have begun to redirect national security policy in South Korea. This study is designed to explore impacts of democratization and the changing security environment on the institutional foundation of national security and patterns of resource allocation in South Korea.

Our findings indicate that the institutional foundation of national security policy in South Korea has undergone a profound change since the democratic opening, while the security environment and defense hardware remain very much unchanged. National security ideology has become diluted, the decisionmaking structure has been decentralized, and the primacy of the military over the civilian sector has disappeared. Such institutional changes have led to a shifting emphasis in resource allocation. While defense spending has been gradually cut, social welfare spending has been on the rise. Such changes have been influenced more by domestic transformation involving democratization than by new security alignments resulting from the end of the cold war. All this implies that South Korea's national security management is likely to take a path which is quite different from the past.

Realignment of the Institutional Foundation of National Security

National security involves multiple dimensions and their dynamic interactions. The first dimension is the security environment, which shapes the nature and type of threats and the resultant national security policies. The second dimension is the institutional foundation of national security, which involves ideology, political structure, and the decisionmaking process. It is the institutional foundation through which external threats are perceived and assessed, national security policies are developed, and actions are taken. Finally, national security involves a military hardware dimension composed of strategies, tactics, force structure, weapons choices, and related military, industrial, and technological capabilities and resources. While the security environment and defense hardware are objectively identifiable, the institutional foundation of national security policy requires subjective evaluation.

In the Korean context, the impacts of the democratic opening and the end of the cold war on the areas of security environment and defense hardware appear minimal. Despite the end of the United States-Soviet rivalry and the rise of a congenial regional system, the military standoff between North and South Korea remains. The recent nuclear quagmire has heightened military tension on the peninsula, and both Koreas have entered a high degree of military alert.[3] The precarious security environment has strengthened, not weakened, the previous strategic postures and degree of military mobilization. This situation has been intensified because of North Korea's domestic political uncertainty and unpredictable external behavior following the death of Kim Il Sung. In fact, North Korea under Kim Jong Il has become more hostile and hysterical toward South Korea than it was under his father. Despite the unchanged security environment and hardware, changes have taken place in two areas. One is the institutional foundation, and the other involves resource allocation. Both have been influenced more by domestic political changes than by external security considerations.

The institutional foundation of national security in South Korea has undergone a profound change. Edward Azar and Chung-in Moon define the institutional foundation as "the software of security management," denoting the political context and policy capacity through which national values are defined, threats and vulnerabilities are perceived and assessed, resources are allocated, and policies are screened, selected, and implemented.[4] The software component goes beyond traditionally defined national will and form of government. It comprises ideology, institutional setting, policymaking machinery, and domestic political structure. The overall security environment and the resulting threat structure are input variables which are to be filtered through the software of security management. Ideology, legal and institutional setting, decisionmaking machinery, and domestic political structure are factors which affect the detection and interpretation of threats and the translation of judgment into actions and policies. The dynamic interplay of these internal variables determines policy and capacity, and these constitute the core of software.[5]

Policy capacity is defined as the ability to plan, formulate, and implement national security policies. The assessment of threat, the making of decisions, the articulation and enforcement of policies, and the mobilization and allocation of resources all belong to the realm of policy capacity. Policy capacity varies among nation-states. Obviously, countries which are endowed with flexible security ideology, optimally centralized decisionmaking authority, and corporatist political structure are likely to show a high degree of policy capacity and a strong security performance. On the other hand, diffused ideological contestation, fragmented decisionmaking authority, and entropic domestic political structure lead to low policy capacity and a weak security performance. Policy capacity also changes over time. Major internal and external events can trigger realignments of domestic political structure, ideological orientation, and decisionmaking authority, eventually altering the quality of policy capacity.

Traditionally, South Korea has been one of the most rigid and regimented security states in the world. Having undergone traumatic insecurity in the 1950s and 1960s, it has been preoccupied with national security, especially military security. The primacy of national security has been justified through a peculiar form of national security ideology, which emerged in the early 1970s with the advent of the authoritarian Yushin regime of Park Chung Hee, under an ideology of "total security" (*chongryuk anbo*), which emphasized nationalism (i.e., supremacy of the nation-state over individuals), anticommunism, military self-help, and economic growth.[6] The ideology justified the sacrifice of social, economic, and political values; for the sake of the military buildup, growth was emphasized over equality. In the name of domestic stability and unity, civil liberties were structurally repressed.[7] At the same time, civil society was reorganized, indoctrinated, and mobilized for national security through legal constructs such as the Anti-Communist Law and the National Security Law. These often superseded the constitution.[8]

Along with the ideological dimension, national security decisionmaking was overly centralized. Executive dominance prevailed, and power and authority were heavily concentrated in a few political elites, such as the president and his staff, the Ministry of National Defense, and the Agency for National Security Planning (formerly the KCIA). The centralization of decisionmaking power placed national security issues in a privileged position by insulating them from contending social and political pressures. Strategic doctrines were formulated and implemented without any social or political resistance. Weapons choices, resource mobilization, and articulation of defense and foreign policies were subject to neither legislative check and balance nor public screening. Defense spending was exempted from ordinary budgetary processes. Overall civilian participation was fundamentally restricted. The National Assembly was nothing but a rubber stamp, and dissenting opinions were not tolerated. Using the legal and institutional shield of the National Security Law, the Anti-Communist Law, and the Military Secrecy Act, the government tightly controlled and manipulated the flow of information on national security affairs. The production and dissemination of national security information belonged exclusively to four organizations: the Agency for National Security Planning (ANSP), the Defense Security Command (DSC), the Defense Intelligence Agency (DIA) under the Ministry of National Defense, and the Defense Intelligence Command (DIC).[9] National security affairs were considered a "sacred domain."

This decisionmaking structure was by and large a reflection of the underlying political structure. The military in South Korea had traditionally regarded control over the national security machinery as its prerogative and often intervened in civil politics for security reasons. The military coups in 1961 and 1979 both exemplified this behavior. Military supremacy in national security matters is clearly visible when the pattern of personnel recruitment in national security is examined. National security-related positions have been virtually all filled by active or retired military officers. After the military coup in 1961, no civilian ever held the position of defense minister. Civilians in national security agencies have been either discriminated against or excluded from every aspect of personnel recruitment and promotion, and even decisionmaking processes. This was possible because of the military dominance in Korean politics, which was authoritarian.[10]

Despite its authoritarian character and the resulting backlash, the old pattern of the software of national security management in South Korea has proved to be effective. While the executive dominance facilitated speedy and effective formulation and implementation of security policies, ideological penetration and the centralized decisionmaking structure allowed neither conflicting views on the ends and means of national security nor artificial bureaucratic compartmentalization. Domestic resources were extracted and mobilized for security purposes without any significant social opposition. There was no need for muddling through a web of contending social and political interests and pressures. As a result, comprehensive security policies were easily formulated and effectively implemented.

The democratic opening in 1987, however, began to alter the overall landscape of national security management in South Korea. In the wake of democratization, the Korean people, particularly the youth, no longer accept national security as *deus ex machina*. For some, the ideology behind it is nothing but an instrument used to justify domination by the military, technocrats, and the capitalist class. They strongly call for change in the ideology of national security, and favor individual liberty over repression in the name of total security, equality over growth, welfare over defense, and ideological tolerance over rigid anticommunism. This popular dissent resonates in growing demands for the abolition of the National Security Law and the Anti-Communist Law, which have served as the legal and institutional backbone of the national security ideology. The dissent is a response to the changing security environment of the post-cold war era but also to the past use of the national security issue as a rationale for oppression designed in reality to ensure regime security and survival.[11] For the past three decades, Korean political leaders have utilized national security as a tool for indoctrinating the masses, controlling civil society, and ultimately consolidating and maintaining political power.

The democratic transition has also begun to reshape the top-down, monolithic structure of the national security machinery. National security policies no longer enjoy political insulation as in the past. The National Assembly's oversight has substantially increased with the revival of a "legislative audit" system. More civilian participation in the security decisionmaking is being strongly advocated. Popular pressures have been on the rise for amendment of the Military Secrecy Law, the dissolution of the Agency for National Security Planning, and a fundamental restructuring of the Defense Security Command, all of which are accused of having distorted national security information and being instrumental in repressing civil society. The government has shown a more receptive attitude toward these demands. The Agency for National Security Planning has gone through extensive reorganization in its functions and mission. The agency is no longer allowed to engage in "security audits" through which it was previously able to control and coordinate other government agencies and civil society. Its budget has also been considerably curtailed. Limited amendment of the Military Secrecy Law is being considered. The Defense Security Command has been substantially reduced in size and its functions restructured. Furthermore, the Ministry of National Defense recently published a white paper on national defense for the first time and allowed journalists to have more access to national security information.

All these developments imply that democratization has created a major realignment of the domestic political structure in South Korea, in which the military's role in civilian politics has diminished. Analytically speaking, the Park and Chun regimes cannot be regarded as "military regimes" like those commonly found in Latin America since the military as an institution or a collective entity in South Korea did not intervene in politics.[12] Yet, these regimes made extensive use of the military for political purposes, and in return insulated the institution of national security from political and social pressures. The military was embedded in the state structure through organic networks, elevating its position to one of prominence. The democratic opening and consolidation have fundamentally changed this, and the military has been forced to become professionalized and civilianized. There is more civilian control of the national security machinery. In fact, after Kim Young Sam was inaugurated in 1993 as the first civilian president in more than three decades, the South Korean military underwent immense internal changes: the removal of the Hanahoi as the dominant military faction, the initiation of an extensive anti-corruption campaign targeted at the military, and the beginning of firm civilian control of the military.[13] These changes reflect the civilian control of the military as well as civilian influence over the other features of national security machinery.[14]

The democratic transition has opened new venues for overhauling the foundation of the software of national security management. These have important implications for the conceptualization and conduct of national security.[15] The dominance of national security ideology has become decolored, while executive leadership in national security management has been increasingly undermined by bureaucratic politics and the interventions of political and civil society. Public interest groups and the National Assembly, along with mass media, have emerged as significant actors influencing outcomes of national security policy. The mass media has become the most influential factor in shaping the nature and direction of national security policy. The limited insulation of national security machinery from social and political pressures reflects the changing institutional landscape followed by democratization. South Korea's recent handling of the North Korean nuclear problem epitomizes the changed climate of national security policymaking par excellence. Ideological polarization, weak executive leadership commitment, bureaucratic infighting, interest group politics, and mass media interference, all of which were bred by democratic governance, literally crippled coherent, consistent, and effective national security policymaking.

It seems, however, premature and even misleading to equate the democratic transition with immediate and automatic reform in the software of national security management. There are several factors impeding such reforms. Lack of consensus on the security environment, the perception of threat, and the end and means of national security itself could make the process of reform more difficult and extended. The structure of deterrence in the region and recurring memories of the Korean War also prevent South Koreans from accommodating the new security environment at its face value. More importantly, a conservative ideology is still dominant and well entrenched in the national security decisionmaking process. The initial triumph of progressive ideology immediately following democratization did not last long. Facing social chaos, South Korean society swung back to favor the old conservative camp, reviving and even accelerating the old processes. The recent confrontation with the North over nuclear weapons has further consolidated the conservative resurgence, which blocks changes in national security policy. One of the most ironical changes is the ideological transformation of the mass media. Such leading daily newspapers as *Chosen* and *Dong-A*, which used to be the champions of liberal perspectives, took the ultraconservative position, significantly altering public opinion and policy outcomes in favor of conservative stances.

Despite the recent civilian triumph over the military, civilian control of the military and of the national security machinery remains uncertain. Efforts to decentralize the national security machinery have so far been slow. Imprudence in the transition of power in the domain of national security could easily invite the opposition of the military, undermining not only civilian control of national security decisionmaking but also the very process of democratization. Democracy has not yet been able to dislodge the powerful vested interests associated with military security and economic growth. In addition to the military, the ruling regime, the military-industrial complex, and other conservative elements favor the status quo.[16] Because of this, major realignments of the software of national security may not be easy. The domain of national security is likely to be further politicized and bureaucratized, weakening its effectiveness, comprehensiveness, and flexibility, while enhancing accountability and consensus-building.

New institutional features of national security machinery in South Korea bear directly on resource allocation. As discussed below, the military sector had always in the past enjoyed a privileged position in the government's resource allocation. While the cold war security environment, tense military confrontations with North Korea, and defense burden-sharing with the United States offered an external rationale for the criticality of defense budgets, the authoritarian mode of governance did not allow any public debate on their efficiency, appropriateness, or accountability, facilitating greater allocation of resources to the military sector without any social or political opposition. Most budgetary demands of the Ministry of Defense were accommodated by the Economic Planning Board. Defense budgets used to be the single largest budgetary item, creating significant substitution effects with social welfare items. However, democratic changes and the subsequent realignment of national security institutions have exposed the defense sector to rigorous public screening, depriving the military of its privileged position in resource allocation.

Shifting Resource Allocation

Resource allocation for the defense sector has long been subject to political and academic debate. Central to the debate is the trade-off relationship between defense and social welfare.[17] Over the years, the substitution of defense for social welfare has also been an important feature of resource allocation in South Korea.[18] Compared with other countries, however, the guns-versus-butter debate was less salient. Social welfare spending has been fundamentally constrained by an obsession with national defense, stemming from actual and perceived national insecurity. Only since the democratic opening in 1987 has resource sharing between the two sectors begun to be balanced.

The regime of Park Chung Hee gave its highest priority to national security and economic development. Especially from 1971 to 1979, the defense expenditure was sacrosanct, and the distribution of resources in society was sacrificed. During the Park regime, the average annual increase in defense expenditures was about 35 percent, whereas the overall average increase since 1961 had been about 21 percent. Under Park, the expansion of defense expenditure was conjoined with heightened military tensions with North Korea, a sharp reduction in United States military aid (which had funded more than half of the total amount of South Korean defense expenditures during the 1960s), and a reduction of American forces in South Korea in the 1970s. Subsequently, guns overshadowed butter, and the share of the total budget allocated to social welfare was relatively small, averaging only about 20 percent of the South Korean budget during the Park era.

With regard to defense spending, Chun Doo Hwan faced two conflicting policy constraints, from internal and external sources. Internally, Chun was forced to curtail defense spending as a part of macroeconomic stabilization and tight fiscal policy. Furthermore, in order to cope with negative consequences of the blind developmentalism pursued under the Park regime, Chun had to divert policy attention to the social welfare sector in areas such as housing, education, social security, and medical insurance. Both measures were essential for Chun's legitimacy. Externally, Chun was under heavy pressure from the United States to increase the defense budget within the framework of defense burden-sharing. The United States was pressing the South Korean government to increase its defense spending to a level comparable to 6 percent of Gross National Product. Increased defense spending was also essential for coping with heightened military tensions with North Korea. During the early period of his regime, Chun tilted toward high defense spending, with an average annual increase of about 28 percent. After 1983, however, the Chun government began to downsize defense spending by realigning it along with the macroeconomic stabilization plans, and the average annual increase was reduced to only about 9 percent. For Chun, regime legitimacy and stability appeared to be more pressing policy goals than responding to American pressure and the precarious security environment.

Although the Roh Tae Woo regime had more legitimacy, its status was fragile and questionable since Roh was the hand-picked successor of the former president. The Roh government made democratization its primary goal. A side-effect of this policy was intensive and extensive bureaucratic politics among the government agencies. In intensified bureaucratic atmosphere, the defense expenditure, which had made up nearly 30 percent of the budget, became the target of other ministries and as a result has been rapidly decreasing as a percentage of GNP. In addition, under the Roh government, the level of privatization declined sharply because of the intensive pursuit of social welfare policy—especially government funding for medical costs.

South Korean defense and social welfare spending between 1961 and 1993 are summarized in table 1, where defense and social welfare spending are broken down into three different time periods: the period of Park and Chun (1961–1987), that of Roh (1988–1992), and that of the beginning of the Kim government (1993). On average, there was a gradual decline in defense spending by all three measures (e.g., percent of GNP, percent of the fiscal budget, and rate of growth). Social welfare spending displays a gradual increase. Notably, through these time periods, defense spending as a percentage of GNP dropped almost one percent, and concurrently social welfare spending expanded

Table 1
South Korean Defense and Social Welfare Spending

Period	Defense			Social Welfare		
	%GNP	%Budget	Rate*	%GNP	%Budget	Rate*
Park/Chun regimes (1961-87)	4.7	29.8	22.4	3.6	22.4	20.1
Roh regime (1988-92)	4.0	27.1	12.7	4.3	28.7	14.4
Kim regime (1993)	3.8	25.2	11.0	4.3	28.6	10.8
Overall (1961-93)	4.6	29.2	20.6	3.8	23.5	18.9

*Rate of Growth

by almost one percent of GNP. Overall, however, defense spending is still greater than social welfare spending, reflecting the heavier defense burden of the 1960s and 1970s coupled with the sacrifice of social welfare spending as a tradeoff.

The annual trends in defense and social welfare spending are displayed in figures 1 and 2.

As shown in figure 1, South Korean defense spending has been averaging about 5 percent of GNP, social welfare spending about 4 percent. Both types of spending have had relatively high variations over the years. The highest defense spending occurred in 1980, at 6.3 percent of GNP, but it has been declining steadily since then. Social welfare reached its highest spending level in 1982, 4.8 percent of GNP, and spending had been steady at about 4 to 5 percent of GNP throughout the 1980s and 1990s. Social welfare spending surpassed defense spending in 1989 for the first time and has maintained its edge since then.

Figure 2 shows a trend similar to that in figure 1. Over the years, South Korean defense spending has averaged about 30 percent of the budget, and social welfare spending has trailed at about 24 percent. The largest share of the budget spent for defense occurred in 1978 with 37 percent, and for social welfare in 1990 with 29 percent. Once again, in 1989 the South Korean government began to spend more on social welfare than on defense, and the difference in spending has been fairly constant since then.

In assessing changes in defense and social welfare spending in South Korea, we can see a profound shift in the spending patterns from the early to the later periods. The averages and trends clearly

Fig. 1. Spending as a Proportion of GNP

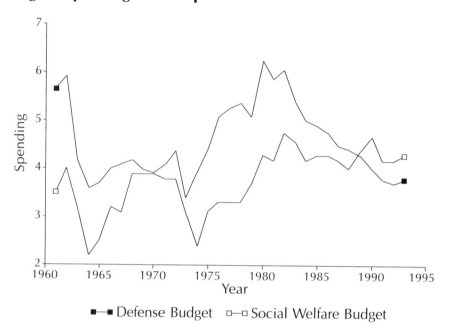

Fig. 2. Spending as a Proportion of Budget

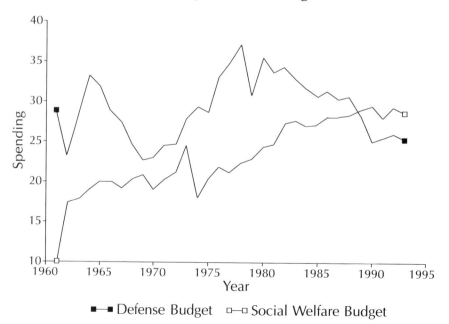

indicate that during the early period, defense spending was sacrosanct and guns took precedence over butter. However, during the second and third time periods, the spending patterns changed and butter outstripped guns. The democratization process initiated in the late 1980s, coupled with the end of the cold war, greatly altered resource allocation in South Korea. Especially in the 1990s, the Roh and Kim governments substituted social welfare spending for defense spending.

Although the absolute amount of defense spending has increased over time, its ratio to Gross National Product declined from 6.3 percent in 1980 to 3.8 percent in 1993. The proportion of defense outlays in the government also sharply declined, from a 33 percent level in the early 1980s to 25.2 percent in 1993. At the same time, social welfare spending increased, and was 4.3 percent of GNP and 28.6 percent of the budget in 1993. A remarkable development in this turnaround is that the Ministry of National Defense is on the defensive end. Breaking a long-held political taboo, several civilian and government organizations, such as the Korean Development Institute and the Federation of Korean Industries, have proposed cuts in the defense budget since 1991. They argue that the defense budget has been the primary cause of fiscal rigidity and has undermined the productivity of fiscal investment and the expansion of the social overhead sector. Backed by these organizations and overall public opinion, the Economic Planning Board (EPB) has demanded a sharp reduction in the defense budget. Especially in 1991, the EPB demanded a cut in budget items for force improvements. This item had been untouchable in the past.[19] Political as well as bureaucratic pressures are likely to increase further in years to come, not only because of changing security environment but because of the overall democratization and the decentralization of the decisionmaking structure in national security affairs.

Likewise, democratic transition has entailed a significant realignment in the patterns of resource allocation in South Korea. It is, however, difficult to imagine South Korea continuing to reduce its defense spending. Several factors are likely to reverse or slow the trend. The first is the sustained military tension with North Korea. The military threat from the North remains real and acute. The North Korean nuclear quagmire has provided the South Korean military with new momentum in pushing for increased defense spending and stalling or even reversing changes in national security management. The nuclear threat provides reactionary elements of the South Korean military with a perfect tool to halt and reverse the progress to civilian rule. Generals can point to the risk of war and demand increasing influence in national security policy councils.[20] The second factor relates to overall security uncertainty in Northeast Asia. Japanese remilitarization, Chinese military adventurism and regional hegemonic ambition, and the uncertain Russian factor all complicate South Korea's security environment. Aware of this precarious structure of finite deterrence in Northeast Asia, military planners in South Korea are strongly calling for increased military spending in order to prepare for national unification and the resulting new threat environment.[21] Finally, conservative forces in South Korea are strong and well entrenched. They are likely to provide political support for the military's struggle to win more funds for the defense sector. Thus, the progress toward reform faces strong resistance from the still dominant and deeply ingrained conservative elements, including the military, the ruling regime, and the military-industrial complex, which favor the status quo. In view of these factors, the guns-versus-butter debate is likely to dominate the public policy agenda in the years to come. South Korea is now facing a difficult choice, between accepting the hard-line military resurgence and pursuing the continued progress of civilian control over national security machinery. For these reasons, major realignments of the software of national security may not be an easy task; any reforms are likely to involve complex processes as the old institutional inertia encounters the new national security thinking. Our cautious anticipation is that the progress of national security reform is likely to be slow and gradual at best.

Conclusion

This essay examines two questions related to the national security of South Korea: How democratic transitions and the end of the cold war have influenced, first, the institutional foundation of national security and, second, the pattern of resource allocation.

For South Korea, the internal and external developments of democratic opening and the demise of the cold war system have had a minimal impact on the national security environment and defense hardware. Nonetheless, the democratic opening in 1987 began to alter the overall institutional foundation by changing the software of security management. In addition, democratic transition has begun to transform the top-down national security decisionmaking structure, which no longer enjoys the political insulation of the past.

Does resource allocation reflect the realignment of the institutional foundation of national security in South Korea? Changes in the defense and social welfare spending of South Korea are quite dramatic. The spending trends clearly indicate that the Park and Chun regimes regarded national security and defense spending as most important. In the late 1980s, however, propelled by democratization and the post-cold war security environment, defense spending became the target of other ministries, especially the Economic Planning Board, and has been rapidly reduced relative to social welfare spending. There is a strong trend toward butter over guns as a result of the substitution effects between defense and social welfare spending.

The institutional changes and shifting resource allocation in South Korea bear several important comparative implications for the study of national security issues. First, contrary to conventional wisdom, the South Korea case shows that internal rather than external factors are more responsible for institutional changes of the national security machinery and reshuffling of resource allocation. Democratic opening and the subsequent political realignment in the form of enhanced civilian control over the military, rather than the ending of the cold war, appears to have played a more critical role in fostering changes in national security institutions and resource allocation. The fact that the South Korean government has constantly reduced the share of defense spending despite an unchanged military threat from North Korea supports these findings. Second, examination of the case of South Korea also reveals an interesting pattern of policy swing from growth and security to distribution and welfare. The conservative resurgence notwithstanding, South Korea is likely to continue to downsize defense spending in such a way as to balance welfare spending. Such efforts will intensify public debate on guns and butter. Finally, democratic opening and systemic transformation involving the end of the cold war have yielded positive dividends to South Korea with regard to national security management, including popular control of the national security machinery, increasing accountability of security management, and optimal use of national resources. This reveals a sharp departure from the past, facilitating the development of a new research agenda regarding national security in South Korea.

Notes

1. There have been both formal and informal multilateral channels of interaction between the United States and South Korea. Formal channels include summit meetings and annual Security Consultative Meetings (SCMs), and military interaction is maintained by the joint military exercise, Team Spirit. However, recent rapprochement between Pyongyang and Washington might pose a new constraint on United States-South Korea relations, undermining their bilateral alliance system.

2. At his inauguration, President Roh Tae Woo declared the end of authoritarian politics and the beginning of true democracy. Also, under the Roh government, South Korea pursued *Nordpolitik*, which was successful in establishing diplomatic relations with socialist countries and creating favorable conditions for peaceful coexistence between the two Koreas.

3. The United States and North Korea aborted the nuclear crisis by reaching a compromise in Geneva. In return for diplomatic recognition and economic assistance to build an alternative nuclear reactor, North Korea agreed to comply with inspections by the International Atomic Energy Agency and to halt further nuclear development. The nuclear fiasco, however, has severely undermined inter-Korean confidence-building. For an overview of the issue, see William J. Taylor and Michael J. Mazarr, "North Korea and the Nuclear Issue: US Perspectives," *Journal of East Asian Affairs* 7, 2 (1993), pp. 345–46.

4. Edward Azar and Chung-in Moon, *National Security in the Third World* (London: Edward Elgar, 1988).

5. See Davis Bobrow and Steve Chan, "Assets, Liabilities and Strategic Conduct: Status Management by Japan, Taiwan, and South Korea," *Pacific Focus* 1, 1 (1986), pp. 23–56, and Azar and Moon, *National Security*, pp. 91–95.

6. See Byung-Chun Min, *Thesis on Korean Security* [in Korean] (Seoul: Daewangsa, 1978), pp. 353–72.

7. Hakkyu Sohn, *Authoritarianism and Opposition in South Korea* (London: Routledge, 1989).

8. Dae-kyu Yoon, *Law and Political Authority in South Korea* (Boulder, CO: Westview Press, 1990).

9. Chung-in Moon, "Democratization, National Security and Civil-Military Relations: Some Theoretical Issues and the South Korean Case," *Pacific Focus* 5, 1 (1989), pp. 5–22.

10. Ibid.

11. Ho-Jin Kim, *Thesis on the Korean Political System* [in Korean] (Seoul: Pakyoungsa, 1990).

12. Chung-in Moon and Mun-gu Kang, "Democratic Opening and Military Intervention in South Korea: Comparative Assessments and Implications," in James Cotton, ed., *Korean Politics in Transition* (Sydney: Longman, 1994).

13. "Hanahoi" refers to the dominant faction in the Korean military during the Chun Doo Hwan and Roh Tae Woo regimes. Its members had been recruited mostly from graduates of the Korean Military Academy with specific regional origins (e.g., North and South Kyungsang provinces). In return for their loyalty to Chun and Roh, Hanahoi members enjoyed privileged positions in assignment and pro-

motion, demoralizing non-Hanahoi members of the military. As Hanahoi became a political issue, President Kim Young Sam undertook an extensive military reform in order to dissolve the faction. In an effort to place the military under his control, Kim has replaced and retired all nine full generals, 73 percent of lieutenant generals, and 63 percent of major generals. See *Joong-Ang Daily*, February 23, 1994.

14. Yong Won Han, *Military Politics in South Korea* [in Korean] (Seoul: Daewangsa, 1993), and Moon and Kang, "Democratic Opening and Military Intervention."

15. For an extensive discussion of security environment, software, and hardware, see Chung-in Moon and Seok-Soo Lee, "The Post-Cold War Security Agenda of South Korea: Inertia, New Thinking, and Assessments," *Pacific Review* 8, 1 (January 1995). The section on institutional (or software) changes in the present article draws heavily on Moon and Lee. Also see Chung-in Moon and Ronald McLaurin, *Arms Control on the Korean Peninsula: Domestic Perception, Regional Dynamics, and International Penetrations* (Washington: United States Institute of Peace, forthcoming), chapter 5.

16. Chung-in Moon, "The Political Economy of Defense Industrialization in South Korea: Constraints, Opportunities, and Prospects," *Journal of East Asian Affairs* 5, 2 (1991).

17. Academic studies on resource allocation for defense spending are abundant and diverse in their scope and methods. We limit our focus on the guns-versus-butter debate in order to illuminate the changes in domestic resource allocation. See Richard Eichenberg, William Domke, and Catherine Kelleher, "Patterns of Western Resource Allocation: Security and Welfare," *Publication Series of the International Institute for Comparative Social Research* (Berlin: Science Center, 1980); Bruce Russett, "Defense Expenditures and National Well-Being," *American Political Science Review* 76, 4 (1982); D. Caputo, "New Perspectives on the Public Policy Economy: A Comparative Analysis," *American Political Science Review* 72, 4 (1975); Steve Chan, "Defense Burden and Economic Growth: Unraveling the Taiwanese Enigma," *American Political Science Review* 83, 3 (1988); and Alex Mintz, "Guns and Butter: A Desegregated Analysis," *American Political Science Review* 83, 4 (1989).

18. Of course, other factors, including external ones, are viewed as intervening variables in shaping the South Korean defense spending pattern. For example, Moon and Hyun emphasize the importance of the alliance factor to illustrate South Korean defense expenditures. The study shows that the 6 percent of the GNP defense spending formula, sustained by South Korea from 1979 to the mid-1980s resulted from American pressure and was set up by the Park-Carter summit meeting in 1979. See Chung-in Moon and In-Taek Hyun, "Muddling through Security, Growth and Welfare: The Political Economy of Defense Spending in South Korea," in Steve Chan and Alex Mintz, eds., *Defense, Welfare and Growth* (New York: Routledge, 1992).

19. The EPB actively advocated the changes in national security policies and defense budgetary allocation for the post-cold war period as South Korea entered into diplomatic relations with Russia and the People's Republic of China. See *Joong-Ang Daily*, August 28, 1992.

20. Taylor and Mazarr, "North Korea and the Nuclear Issue," p. 354.

21. Moon and McLaurin, *Arms Control on the Korean Peninsula.*

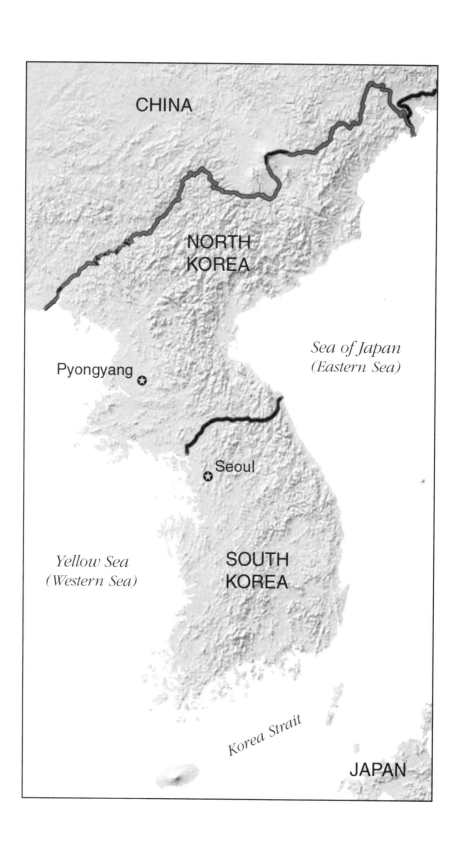

CHINA

NORTH
KOREA

Sea of Japan
(Eastern Sea)

Pyongyang ✪

Seoul ✪

Yellow Sea
(Western Sea)

SOUTH
KOREA

Korea Strait

JAPAN

Chapter 13

South Korea's Nuclear, Conventional Weapons, and Alliance Strategies

Woosang Kim

T he end of the cold war has encouraged the former Soviet Union
and the People's Republic of China, among others, to emphasize economic reform as their national priorities. Naturally, their
foreign policies toward the Korean peninsula have changed considerably. Russia and China, both former allies of North Korea, have now
normalized relations with South Korea. While South Korea is expanding its political and economic relationships with the People's Republic of China and Russia, North Korea is losing a great deal of political,
military, and economic support from both former allies.

Russia is busy with its own domestic, economic, and political problems. President Boris Yeltsin needs strong support from the United
States and other members of the international community, such as the
G-7 nations, to stabilize not only his country's economy but also his
own political power. Yeltsin cannot afford to lose the support of leading countries by backing North Korea's nuclear weapons program. He
would not want anything to cause instability in Northeast Asia, since
both the stability of Northeast Asia and political and economic support of the G-7 countries are essential for the success of Russian political and economic reform.

The People's Republic of China also has big stakes in the issue of
North Korea's nuclear weapons program. China will not allow eco-

*Woosang Kim is associate professor of political science at Sookmyung Women's
University, Seoul.*

nomic and trade relationships with South Korea, Japan, and the United States to deteriorate by supporting North Korea's position on nuclear weapons, which could become one of the most destabilizing factors on the Korean peninsula. China needs strong economic and trade relationships with South Korea, Japan, and other members of the international community.

North Korea's nuclear weapons program may also indirectly threaten China's security. North Korea's newest missile, the 600-mile-range Nodong I, has been tested, and the Japanese worry about the capability of North Korean nuclear warheads to reach one of their biggest cities, Osaka.[1] Some Japanese see this as a good reason for Japan to consider rearming, including with nuclear weapons. Of course, Japanese rearmament, and especially development of nuclear weapons, is not in China's best interest. This is another reason why China will not support North Korea's nuclear program.[2]

These changes in the international environment, which isolate North Korea further from the international community, are bound to influence North Korea's foreign policy decisionmaking. Kim Jong-Il and his followers, who will have to demonstrate their leadership to the people, must cope with the changes in the political environment of Northeast Asia. Kim Jong-il desperately needs to legitimize his succession, and he especially needs strong support from the military. One reason that Kim has pushed the nuclear weapons program so hard is probably to demonstrate to the North Korean military his toughness, and to let them know that one of his priorities is military modernization. By convincing the military that he is not a weak, or even moderate, leader, he hopes to gain their support and endorsement of his "hereditary succession."

In this essay, I will examine South Korea's security and alliance strategies for the year 2000 in conjunction with North Korea's current nuclear weapons program. No matter what the real purpose of North Korea's nuclear program, a great deal has been invested in it, and inducements seem to be necessary for change to take place. First of all, introduction of the "limited no-first-use" policy in the Korean peninsula might not only induce North Korea to give up her nuclear weapons program but would also enhance the possibility of establishing the limited no-first-use regime in Northeast Asia or in the Asia-Pacific region as a whole in the near future. This regime would represent an important security strategy for Korea in the twenty-first century. Finally, I will suggest conventional weapons and alliance strategies that may go along with the limited no-first-use policy.

Limited No-First-Use Policy As Inducement

Elsewhere I have argued that to induce Kim Jong Il and his elite technocrats to accept nuclear inspections and, further, to implement open-door policies, the international community, led by South Korea and the United States, should take the "middle position."[3] The middle position means that South Korea and other members of the international community would show willingness to cooperate with North Korea when it accepts nuclear inspections but would demonstrate strong willingness to punish North Korea's determination to maintain its nuclear weapons program.

To summarize briefly inducement policies, first of all South Korea should maintain good political and economic relationships with both China and Russia and induce them to put diplomatic pressure on North Korea to abandon its nuclear weapons program. Second, South Korea must discontinue its current trade relationship with North Korea but declare that trade will be resumed when North Korea agrees to give up its nuclear weapons program. Trade volume between the two sides is not high, but South Korea's decision on its economic relationship with North Korea may set the standard for other members of the international community, including the United Sates and Japan.

The Korean government, with help from the United States, may also have to push Japan to show willingness to pay for reparations if North Korea actually abandons its nuclear weapons program. For that matter, the Korean government should also encourage both the United States and Japan to resume high-level normalization talks with North Korea in conjunction with North Korea's acceptance of the special nuclear inspections. This will give North Korea not only the economic incentives but the political incentives as well. The cancellation of the U.S.-South Korean joint military exercise, Team Spirit, should also be considered in conjunction with North Korea's acceptance of nuclear inspections.[4]

However, the most important factor will be the United States' nuclear defense strategy toward the Korean peninsula. One of North Korea's excuses for withdrawal from the Nuclear Nonproliferation Treaty (NPT) was the nuclear threat from the United States. Even if not completely sincere, the claim deserves careful treatment. In addition to the inducements already mentioned, the Korean government might want to investigate the plausibility of requesting the United States to change her nuclear defense strategy in Northeast Asia from "flexible response" to the policy of "limited no-first-use."

Flexible response has been the most important concept of United States strategic defense since the beginning of the cold war. The doctrine holds that in case of attack on the United States or its allies' territories, whether nuclear weapons are used or not, the United States will decide whether to employ nuclear weapons against the aggressor based on the circumstances.[5]

For North Korean leaders, flexible response policy has meant that in any kind of conflict between the South and the North, the United States could justify using nuclear weapons against the North. In other words, North Korean leaders may argue that the simple removal of United States nuclear weapons from South Korean soil does not guarantee North Korean protection from the United States nuclear threat. North Korea may use this argument to delay inspection by the International Atomic Energy Agency (IAEA), continuing interminable discussions on the issues while its nuclear program progresses.

One way of coping with North Korea's claim is for the United States to declare a "limited no-first-use" strategic defense policy in Northeast Asia, meaning that the nuclear-capable state agrees not to use nuclear weapons against a state which does not possess nuclear weapons. The nuclear-capable state would agree not to use nuclear weapons even if the non-nuclear state attacked its territory or that of an ally. Under this kind of policy, the United States could continue to use flexible response in the event of attack by an enemy with nuclear capability, but in the case of a non-nuclear aggressor, the United States would agree not to use the nuclear weapons.

The United States should not easily give "assurances that it would not reintroduce nuclear weapons into the Korean peninsula" in return for North Korea's suspension of its withdrawal from the NPT treaty.[6] In withdrawing, North Korea simply went back to the starting point in the nuclear inspection game. Instead, the United States and South Korean governments should carefully examine the plausibility of declaring a limited no-first-use policy, under which North Korea would be unable to use the United States nuclear threat as justification for nuclear weapons development. Since this policy would make it clear that North Korea would be safer from United States nuclear weapons by not building any of its own, the United States' unilateral declaration of limited no-first-use could, in fact, be an inducement for North Korea to abandon its nuclear weapons program.[7] The United States should then expand this idea of limited no-first-use in the Korean peninsula to the Asia-Pacific region. Establishment of a multilateral agreement on limited no-first-use in the region among Russia, China, Japan, and other nuclear-capable major powers should be a priority goal for the United States.[8]

Limited No-First-Use As Korea's Nuclear Strategy

The Korean peninsula is surrounded by great powers such as Russia, the People's Republic of China, and Japan. In the twenty-first century Korea will still be surrounded by them.[9] Both China and Russia have nuclear capabilities. China has more than 400 nuclear warheads, and in the next century she may have more. Russia currently has more than 10,000 nuclear warheads. Based on the announcement of the Follow-on Treaty to Strategic Arms Reduction Talks (START) between Presidents George Bush and Boris Yeltsin during the Washington summit on June 1992, Russia will reduce its stock of nuclear warheads, but will still possess more than 3,000 nuclear weapons. Although Japan does not have nuclear weapons at the moment, there is enough high-quality plutonium in the country to make thousands of nuclear weapons.[10] By the early part of the twenty-first century, Japan could become a nuclear-capable nation.

How can Korea protect itself from potential nuclear threats? There are two possible answers. One is for Korea to maintain its strong ties with the United States, so as to remain under the United States nuclear umbrella. During the cold war period, United States extended deterrence policy was very successful in protecting its allies from enemy nuclear attack. As long as the United States demonstrates determination to retaliate against any nuclear attack on the United States or the territory of its allies, United States extended deterrence will be successful.[11] If Korea can maintain a strong military tie with the United States, it will be safe from nuclear attack.

The second possibility is for Korea to build its own nuclear capability for defensive purposes. However, to successfully deter an enemy from using nuclear weapons to attack or threaten the Korean peninsula, Korea must have a second-strike capability. Since deterrence strategy depends on the ability to inflict unacceptable damage on the opponent, a second-strike capability is required that enables Korea to withstand an initial strike and subsequently retaliate with a devastating blow.

In order to protect its second-strike capability against an enemy with more than 400 nuclear warheads, for example, Korea would have to spend billions of dollars to develop and procure advanced nuclear weapons and would have to produce not only a considerable number of nuclear warheads but also a large number of delivery vehicles so that some would survive an attack. Alternatively, Korea could find ways to disperse delivery vehicles widely to multiply the number of targets, making it difficult for any one attacking warhead to wipe out more than one delivery system. Mobile delivery vehicles, including submarines, is another possibility, or Korea could build underground missile storage silos to withstand the blast of a near miss, although improved missile accuracy makes direct hits possible. Antiballistic missile and air defense systems are another option.[12] Implementation of all of these options to protect its nuclear retaliatory capability would be too costly for Korea. In other words, Korea, with only a handful of nuclear warheads, will never be able to deter an attack from China, Russia, or nuclear-capable Japan.[13]

Developing even a small number of nuclear weapons and a delivery system is expensive and cannot deter a nuclear giant's potential attack. Becoming nuclear-capable might in fact provide a good excuse for potential enemies to preempt Korea with their nuclear weapons. Then, is relying on the United States nuclear umbrella the only option for Korea? What if the United States is not willing to provide extended deterrence to Korea twenty years from now? To prepare for a future loss of alliance relationship with the United States, I suggest the limited no-first-use as a regional nuclear defense principle—that is, that the limited no-first-use regime should be introduced throughout Northeast Asia or the Asia-Pacific region.

The United States has never agreed to no-first-use of nuclear weapons, except on the occasion when President Carter and Soviet Foreign Minister Andrei Gromyko promised each other that their respective states would not be the first to use nuclear weapons in any kind of conflict.[14] Most decisionmakers in the United States, especially military leaders, do not want to give up the nuclear attack option in the event of conflict. The limited no-first-use principle, however, would not require the United States to give up its option of using nuclear weapons against a nuclear-capable adversary. For example, the United

States could use the flexible response option in the event of attack by an enemy which has nuclear capability. The United States would be required not to use nuclear weapons first only if the enemy were a non-nuclear state.

If all nuclear-capable states agreed to establish the limited no-first-use regime in Northeast Asia or in the Asia-Pacific region by the year 2005 or 2015, non-nuclear Korea could protect itself from potential nuclear threats. Even without the United States nuclear umbrella, Korea could be safe from nuclear warfare. If a state were determined to use nuclear weapons against Korea, a non-nuclear power, and were willing to accept the consequences of facing other nuclear powers, then, regardless of Korea's nuclear capability, deterrence might not be successful. However, if the enemy considered nuclear attack to be an option, the limited no-first-use regime in the region would impose a huge additional cost on the potential use of these weapons, and the possibility of nuclear attack could be greatly reduced.

South and North Korea jointly declared the denuclearization of the Korean peninsula on December 31, 1991. If the Korean government later cancels the denuclearization of the peninsula and begins to develop nuclear weapons, the chances of successfully making a handful of nuclear warheads might be very slim. Even if Korea made them, its nuclear program would be politically costly and might invite a preemptive nuclear strike by a potential adversary.

Building its own nuclear weapons is not a good strategy for Korea to protect itself from potential nuclear aggression. Instead, Korea should seek protection under the United States nuclear umbrella. As long as that is possible, the limited no-first-use regime will not be necessary. However, this regime would become important if ever the United States became unwilling to provide a nuclear umbrella for Korea. Then a limited no-first-use regime in the region would greatly reduce the possibility of nuclear attack.

Conventional Weapons and Alliance Strategies

For the limited no-first-use regime to be acceptable, Korea must have a conventional capability which is strong enough to defend against conventional attack. Standing against China's, Russia's, or even Japan's conventional capabilities, Korea may never be capable of protecting itself. Here again, Korea needs the United States' assurance of extended conventional deterrence. As a sovereign nation, however, Korea should not totally rely on the United States but should develop its own military strength.

The former Soviet Union has been spending more than 10 percent of GNP for military purposes. Though Russia has now begun to cut military expenditures, its military spending as an absolute amount is still at least thirty times that of South Korea. China is increasing its military spending. According to Chinese Finance Minister Liu, the defense expenditure in 1992 doubled the 1988 figure, rising to $7.4 billion in 1992. China is also building or obtaining MiG-31 fighter planes, S-300 surface-to-air missiles, Kilo-class submarines, destroyers, frigates, tanks, radar equipment, and bombers from Russia and other countries, and also plans to acquire an aircraft carrier.[15] This buildup seems good evidence of China's determination to become a military power.

Japan spends only one percent of GNP for defense. However, according to *World Military Expenditures and Arms Transfers*, the actual dollar amount for Japan's 1989 spending, for instance, is higher than that of China.[16] Japan is continuously purchasing high-technology military weapons. The new Patriot SAM system was purchased to replace Nike-J, and an escort ship with the AEGIS system was also purchased from the United States.[17] Also, the new prime minister of the coalition government, Morihiro Hosokawa, his foreign minister, Tsutomo Hata, and Ichiro Ozawa, the master strategist of Hata's Renewal Party, have been proponents of an active Japanese involvement in international security.[18] No one can guarantee that Japan will not increase military spending.

North Korea has been spending about 20 percent of its GNP to build up military capability. With its shaky economy, there is no room for North Korea to increase defense spending further. However, South Korea, which currently spends about 4.5 percent of GNP on defense, could increase up to 5 or 6 percent to catch up with its neighbors. South Korea can certainly maintain its current level of military spending. Countries that feel threatened frequently spend more. For example, Israel, surrounded by hostile Arab countries, has spent almost 13 percent of GNP on the military. Taiwan spends more than 5 percent.

As long as others increase or maintain high levels of defense spending, South Korea must likewise increase or maintain military expenditures to prepare for the future. However, if all the actors in the region would agree to stop increasing military expenditures, South Korea should follow suit. If South Korea stopped increasing defense spending or cut back, while China or other major actors in the region increased expenditures, South Korea would be most vulnerable.[19] The recent willingness of great powers to participate in arms negotiations suggests that, sooner or later, there will be arms control talks in Northeast Asia. For Korea to have a strong conventional force, the South Korean government must start now to modernize its army, to strengthen the navy and air force, and to build an air defense system.[20]

Korea should also prepare for theater ballistic missile defense. To accomplish that goal, South Korea must participate in the development of the necessary technology. Based on the new defensive concept, Global Protection Against Limited Strikes (GPALS),[21] the United States is developing the Theater High Altitude Area Defense (THAAD) missile, slated for deployment starting from 1996, and short-range defense missiles, among them an improved version of the Army's Patriot missile. The United States is also modifying the Navy's AEGIS anti-aircraft system to intercept missiles.[22] South Korea's near-term goal should be to support the United States in improving existing systems and to obtain the improved systems from the United States. Its long-term goal should include developing and purchasing missile interceptors and long-range surveillance radars, and establishing strategic command, control, communications, and intelligence (C^3I) systems to ensure the availability of timely attack warning.

Alliance strategy is also very important for Korea to survive in an anarchical system. First of all, Korea must form an alliance with a country distant from the Korean peninsula whose national interests are at stake in the region and which is militarily strong enough to mobilize troops in case of conflict. The best ally for Korea that satisfies the above criteria is obviously the United States.

History suggests that, whenever a system of multiple sovereignty exists, alliance formation is an inevitable result of interaction among sovereign political units. Perhaps the most common purpose of alliance is to increase a nation's power or defend against aggression. Such alliances are common among more or less equal-power states and do not last long. However, in an asymmetric alliance, in which one side is strong and the other relatively weak, the purpose of alliance among members may be different. The weaker side may gain protection and security from the stronger side, whereas the stronger side may gain autonomy from the weaker side.

Since South Korea signed the mutual defense treaty with the United States in 1953, this agreement has provided security to South Korea and some autonomy to the United States. The American provision of extended deterrence in Northeast Asia has been very successful. Over the near future Korea, with a relatively small resource base, should maintain this bilateral alliance relationship with the United States. The best way for a relatively weak Korea to protect itself from the potential aggression of neighboring nations—China, Russia, or Japan—is to commit itself to a military alliance relationship not with any of the contiguous countries but with a distant country such as the United States.

Because the United States is far from the Korean peninsula, the two countries are less likely to become involved in any kind of territorial conflict between them. However, the United States has national interests at stake in Northeast Asia and a strong capability for military mobilization, and can be expected to come to Korea's aid. The Korean peninsula may be one of the best strategic areas to check and balance China's, Russia's, and Japan's potential expansionism and regional hegemony. Like China in ancient times, following the alliance strategy of Suntzu, the famous Chinese military strategist, Korea must maintain a military alliance with a far-away power, in this case the United States.

Another alliance strategy to be examined here involves the role of pivotal power. In any coalition formation, "the greater the necessity to include a player in a coalition to make it a winning one, the greater that player's pivotal power."[23] Despite the pivotal player's relatively small resource base, that player is as valuable a member of a coalition as any great-power members and can rationally demand a payoff as big as any major-power members might demand. Korea may be able to play the role of pivotal power in Northeast Asia. Although it has limited resources compared to its neighbors, Korea can still exert a disproportionate influence on the process of alliance politics in Northeast Asia because the Korean peninsula is geopolitically and strategically very important for all of the neighboring states. None of them would be willing to allow another power to take control of the peninsula, and Korea would not want to be controlled by any of them. However, Korea should not simply be a buffer state for China, Russia, and Japan.

Korea should actively participate in international and regional politics and aim to play the role of pivotal power in the region, never taking a passive position or assuming neutrality. To do so would mean giving up the chance to play the role of pivotal power. For Korea to commit itself to one side in the region would not be a good idea either. In order to play the role of pivotal power successfully, Korea must remain open to any possible combination of relationships. In accordance with balance of power theory and history of warfare, most alliances cannot be expected to last long. In a world of self-help, today's friend can be tomorrow's enemy. Korea will be better off not signing a bilateral military agreement with any of her neighbors—China, Japan, or Russia.[24] On the other hand, as suggested above, Korea must work hard to maintain its bilateral alliance relationship with the United States.

The idea of Korea as a pivotal power is strengthened when the importance of interdependence among nation-states is introduced. The rapid growth of international economic transactions during the 1970s and 1980s raised the question of whether military force was the only means of exerting influence in international politics and challenged the cogency of the state-centric perspective of *Realpolitik*. Complex interdependence among nation-states has made greater attention to transnational collaboration imperative. Although the idea of complex interdependence, supported by neoliberal institutionalism, does not negate the importance of the state-centric system and such issues of "high politics" as peace and security, it emphasizes international economic transactions and gives more attention to the ways certain international regimes or international institutions promote international cooperation.[25]

The stronger Korea's economy, the higher its volume of trade, and the more Korea is involved in economic cooperation with its neighbors, the more important the "low politics" of economic collaboration becomes in Northeast Asia and the less likely it will be that military force will be used to resolve conflicts of interest. Therefore, to play the role of pivotal power effectively Korea should be economically as strong as possible and must maintain good economic relationships with all of its neighbors. Korea should also support the convening of regional conferences to promote regional economic and security cooperation. Such meetings would help China, Russia, and other nations understand that stability in the region is a prerequisite for coexistence and that economic cooperation will promote prosperity.

Conclusion

I have suggested several security strategies for Korea (either South Korea or unified Korea). First of all, Korea must maintain its strong military alliance with the United States, whose nuclear umbrella will effectively deter potential nuclear or conventional attack. To prepare for a situation in which the United States no longer provides extended deterrence, Korea should advocate the limited no-first-use regime in the region. The introduction of limited no-first-use will not only induce North Korea to abandon its nuclear weapons program but also reduce the possibility of any major power's nuclear attack on the Korean peninsula in the twenty-first century.

For this policy to be plausible in the present context of Northeast Asia, South Korea should prepare its own strong conventional army, navy, and air force; and the proposed transfer of the United States global defense strategy to the regional defense strategy must be accomplished.[26] The military assistance of the United States is needed to enhance Korea's rapid deployment capability and to strengthen tactical and theater conventional weapons, including air power, to improve the ground assault capability in case of war on the Korean peninsula. The United States' commitment to her regional allies' security must be reaffirmed.[27] In other words, at the conventional level, South Korea and the United States should be able to demonstrate overwhelming superiority in order to deter North Korea's potential conventional aggression, while declaring the limited no-first-use policy in the region.

Although the idea of limited no-first-use of nuclear weapons in Northeast Asia or in the Asia-Pacific is different from a "nuclear free zone" in the region, persuading major actors to accept the limited no-first-use regime may not be easy. However, there is room for negotiation. Three major powers, the United States, Russia, and China, at one time or another, have announced an intention not to use nuclear weapons first. As mentioned above, in 1978 the United States and the Soviet Union agreed not to use nuclear weapons in any conflict. Recently, Les Aspin (then the chairman of the House Armed Services Committee) also suggested that the United States should "formally pledge not to be the first country in any conflict to use nuclear weapons."[28] In 1964 and 1978, China declared that it would not be the first to use nuclear weapons and would not use or threaten to use nuclear weapons against non-nuclear states.[29] No nation in Northeast Asia welcomes North Korea's nuclear capability. Both China and Russia want stability in the Korean peninsula to allow for their economic reforms, and North Korea's nuclear weapons program also threatens Japan's security. The United States, for its part, wants to discourage nuclear proliferation.

South Korea has a unique opportunity to promote establishment of the limited no-first-use regime. If South Korea could use the proposal of limited no-first-use in Northeast Asia as an inducement to North Korea's abandonment of its nuclear weapons program, major powers in the region might support the idea. If Japan is serious about not building its own nuclear weapons in the future, Japan would support the limited no-first-use regime as a means of protecting itself from potential nuclear threats. The United States has an incentive to support the regime as a means of preventing nuclear proliferation and promoting regional stability.

Finally, South Korea should actively participate in regional and international politics and aspire to play the role of pivotal power in the region. To do so, South Korea must strengthen its economy, actively participate in joint ventures, and increase its trade volume with great-power neighbors. South Korea's strong economic power and leading role in regional economic collaboration will help the divided Koreas unite and provide a better environment, in which Korea in the near future can play the pivotal role.

Notes

1. *New York Times*, June 13, 1993.
2. In the UN Security Council's decision on the issue of the economic sanctions against North Korea, however, China is likely to abstain. One reason must be its "non-interference" policy, one of the "five principles of peaceful coexistence."
3. Woosang Kim, "Inducement Measures for the Opening of North Korea," *Korea Observer* 24, 4, pp. 497-527.
4. For more details about these inducement policies see ibid.
5. For more details about the flexible response, see Richard Smoke, *National Security and the Nuclear Dilemma* (New York: McGraw-Hill, 1993), pp. 86-89.
6. *New York Times*, June 12 and July 20, 1993.
7. Dr. Jeremy J. Stone, president of the Federation of American Scientists, also makes similar arguments. See Hearings before the Subcommittee on East Asian and Pacific Affairs of the Committee on Foreign Relations, United States Senate, 102nd Congress, 1st and 2nd sessions, "Threat of North Korean Nuclear Proliferation," U.S. Government Printing Office, Washington, D.C., November 25, 1991; January 14 and February 6, 1992, p. 10.
8. For a similar argument by Selig Harrison, see Congressional Hearings, "Threat of North Korean Nuclear Proliferation," p. 88.
9. Some expect that the Korean peninsula will be unified in the early part of the new century. My use of "Korea" means a unified Korea in the twenty-first century.
10. Congressional Hearings, "Threat of North Korean Nuclear Proliferation," p. 41.
11. However, United States nuclear extended deterrence during the post-cold war era might not be as successful against dictatorial regimes of minor powers such as North Korea, Iraq, Iran, or Libya. One reason is that often United States nuclear attack is not considered a viable option against a regime such as North Korea. For successful deterrence during the post-cold war era, the United States might have to develop new conventional weapons technologies that could be used as effective deterrents against a minor power's use of nuclear weapons. For similar arguments and for United States nuclear limitations, see Seth Cropsey, "The Only Credible Deterrent," *Foreign Affairs* 73, 2, pp. 14-20.
12. Bruce Russett and Harvey Starr, *World Politics, the Menu for Choice*, 3d ed. (New York: Freeman, 1993), pp. 368-69.
13. Based on the assumption that Japan builds more than 500 nuclear warheads with existing plutonium. For Japan's potential, see Congressional Hearing, "Threat of North Korean Nuclear Proliferation," p. 41.
14. See Charles W. Kegley and Eugene R. Wittkopf, *World Politics: Trend and Transformation*, 4th ed. (New York: St. Martin's Press, 1993), pp. 487-90.
15. See *Korea Times*, June 21, 1992, and *New York Times*, February 3 and March 17, 1993. According to *World Military Expenditures and Arms Transfers*, published by U.S. Arms Control and Disarmament Agency, China's 1989 military expenditure was $22.3 billion, while that of the Soviet Union was $311 billion.
16. Japan's military spending in 1989 was $28.4 billion.
17. Hideshi Takesada, "Japan's Defense Role: A Change in Defense Policy?" in Man-woo Lee and Richard W. Mansbach, eds., *The Changing Order in Northeast Asia*

and the Korean Peninsula (Seoul: Institute for Far Eastern Studies, 1993), p. 176.

18. For example, the Ozawa Report, presented in May 1992, insists on expanding Japan's role in international security matters. See *New York Times*, June 22 and 24, 1993, and Takesada, "Japan's Defense Role."

19. South Korea would end up in the upper right-hand cell in the 2 by 2 prisoner's dilemma (PD) game. In a one-shot game of the prisoner's dilemma, the Nash equilibrium is the one in which both players choose "arms buildup" strategy. In reality, this kind of arms race game is played repeatedly. So there is room for both players to improve their situations by cooperating, i.e., by choosing a "no buildup" strategy.

20. For a detailed comparison of Korea's army, navy, and air force with those of others, see Woosang Kim, "Security Strategies of Unified Korea," presented at the Third World Conference on Korean Political Studies, Seoul, July 20-22, 1993.

21. For details about GPALS, see Richard Cheney, *Annual Report to the President and the Congress: Report of the Secretary of Defense to the President and the Congress* (Washington: U.S. Government Printing Office, February 1992).

22. *Congressional Quarterly*, April 3, 1993, pp. 843-50.

23. For more details about these concepts, see William Riker, *The Theory of Political Coalitions* (New Haven: Yale University Press, 1962).

24. For that matter, it may not be a good idea for Korea to be involved in the collective security system in Northeast Asia. A loose type of multilateral economic and security cooperation would be preferable.

25. For example, see Robert Keohane and Joseph Nye, *Power and Interdependence* (Boston: Little, Brown, 1977), or the 2d ed., published in 1989.

26. Cheney, *Annual Report*.

27. For the recent announcement of the Clinton administration's "win-win" strategy for two simultaneous non-nuclear regional conflicts and its long-range plans for defense spending demonstrating the United States commitment to the Korean peninsula, see *New York Times*, September 2, 1993.

28. *Congressional Quarterly*, January 9, 1993, pp. 82-83.

29. Hee-Kwon Park, *Nuclear-Free Zone in the Korean Peninsula* [in Korean] (Seoul: Kyung Se Won, 1992), pp. 200-1.